Stephan Kanfer's books include *The Eighth Sin*, *A Summer World*, *The Last Empire*, *Serious Business*, *Groucho*, *Ball of Fire: The Tumultuous Life and Comic Art of Lucille Ball* and *Stardust Lost*. He was a writer and editor at *Time* for more than twenty years and was their first bylined film critic, a post he held from 1967 until 1972. A Literary Lion of the New York Public Library  g awards, Kanfer is currently in th t Southampton College, Long Isla e between New York and Cape Cod

Further praise for *Somebody*:

' . . . takes the reader through the screen icon's troubled childhood to his arrival in New York in the 1940s and his Broadway career. Each of his films are examined, providing an in-depth analysis of the actor's craft. His personal tragedies and ambivalent feelings towards his career are also brought into focus.' *Sight & Sound*

'Measured and authoritative . . . [Kanfer] is studiously meticulous in chronicling what he terms this "reckless life and remarkable career". The book gives a clarity and substance to the tall tales and newspaper headlines that have seeped, as if by osmosis, into public consciousness . . . Kanfer brings a cool perspective and clear-sighted context.' Alan Gilsenan, *Irish Times*

'A fine and sustained examination of Brando's tumultuous life and art.' Paul Dale, *The List*

SOMEBODY

The Reckless Life and Remarkable Career of

MARLON BRANDO

Stefan Kanfer

faber and faber

First published in the United States in 2008
by Alfred A. Knopf, a division of Random House, Inc.,
New York

First published in the UK in 2008
by Faber and Faber Limited
Bloomsbury House
74–77 Great Russell Street
London WC1B 3DA
This paperback edition first published in 2011

Printed in England by CPI Bookmarque, Croydon

A CIP record for this book
is available from the British Library

ISBN 978-0-571-24413-3

10 9 8 7 6 5 4 3 2 1

FOR LEA PAGE CASTLE AND ALYSSA TRUE CASTLE

Contents

Introduction

To the end of his life, Marlon Brando insisted that he had done nothing special. In his view acting was a trade like plumbing or baking. The only difference was that he played characters instead of unclogging drains or kneading loaves of bread. This was not false modesty; he believed what he said. But what he believed was untrue.

There was screen acting before Brando and after Brando, just as there was painting before Picasso and after Picasso and writing before Hemingway and after Hemingway and popular singing before Sinatra and after Sinatra, and even the casual observer can tell the difference. As film historian Molly Haskell pointed out, the film star's legend "is written in one word. BRANDO. Like Garbo. Or Fido. An animal, a force of nature, an element; not a human being who must, as a member of society, distinguish himself from other members with a Christian name and an initial as well as a surname. There is only one Brando."

The eminent screen stars of the 1930s and 1940s—Fredric March, Paul Muni, John Barrymore, Humphrey Bogart, Laurence Olivier, Spencer Tracy—were careful to protect themselves even as they convinced audiences that they were taking risks. But from his debut film, *The Men,* in 1950, Brando worked without a mask. The inner wounds were manifest, and the risks he took—doing anything, no matter how outlandish or unflattering, to make the character credible—had never been attempted by a Hollywood star. His predecessors drew a line between their private lives and their movie roles. No such boundary existed between Brando the actor and Brando the man. They were one and the same: complicated, dangerous, vulnerable. That, too, was different.

From today's vantage point it's difficult to gauge the impact of certain film personalities on their time. In 1940 Howard Hawks made full use of overlapping dialogue for *His Girl Friday;* his style has been co-opted so often it has lost its power to electrify an audience. In 1960, ticket buyers were jarred and dislocated when Alfred Hitchcock killed off his star, Janet Leigh, halfway through *Psycho;* his device has since become commonplace. Similarly, when Brando first appeared, he shook up screen acting in a way that had not been seen since performers were given voices in 1927. His work has been sedulously imitated by performers for more than half a century. Those actors have unwittingly obscured the contributions of the man who started it all.

Anthony Quinn once described the cinema of the early 1950s: "Everything was proper. Robert Taylor, Tyrone Power, Van Johnson, and along comes Brando." Marlon was the first to show a profound vulnerability beneath the male exterior, as well as a willingness to depart from the script not out of perversity or an inability to remember lines, but because he was going for the truth of the character *at that moment.* Along comes Brando, and an art form is transfigured.

Many factors contributed to Marlon's achievement. He appeared on the scene at just the right time, he was launched by one of the twentieth century's central stage dramas, and he was trained by one of the most influential acting teachers of all time, the Yiddish-theater veteran Stella Adler. Some of the attraction he held for her—and later for the world—was a physical presence that echoed the animal magnetism and raw intellect of her father, Jacob, a Second Avenue luminary. This was combined with a quality displayed by Boris Thomashefsky, Jacob's greatest competitor. In a memoir, Adler's granddaughter noted that Boris's "overwhelming masculinity was balanced by a softness even more dangerous. His well-known susceptibility crossed the footlights with fatal impact. He was, in fact, a personality impossible to resist." She could have been writing about Marlon Brando when he entered stage left two generations later.

Brando's genius, like that of so many other groundbreaking artists, was mixed with immense character flaws that stained his personal and professional relationships. So disorderly was his private life that an entire book, *Brando Unzipped,* is scurrilously devoted to his numerous affairs, liaisons, and marriages. Many other biographies are little more than clothbound gossip columns, or tell-all narratives by onetime associates hoping to cash in on an old professional or social connection.

These salacious accounts make lively reading. But they have little to do with Marlon Brando's artistic achievement. Indeed, they tend to reduce his reputation by portraying him as a strutting phallus who happened to make a few good movies when he was not otherwise engaged. Part of this can be directly traced to the actor's contemptuous self-appraisals. In *Conversations with Brando,* Lawrence Grobel records the following exchange:

GROBEL: What about acting as an art form?
BRANDO: In your heart of hearts you know perfectly well that movie
    stars aren't artists. . . .
GROBEL: Are any people in your profession artists?
BRANDO: No.
GROBEL: None at all?
BRANDO: Not one.

On other occasions Marlon added to those remarks. Advice to himself: "Never confuse the size of your paycheck with the size of your talent." To his fellow performers: "Acting is an illusion, a form of histrionic sleight of hand . . . it's a bum's life. The principal benefit acting has afforded me is the money to pay for my psychoanalysis." That response was not as blithe as it sounded. Brando's early years disfigured the rest of his life. He never fully emerged from the shadows of a cold and brutal father and a longing, desperately unhappy mother who squandered the best hours of her best years in an alcoholic haze. From the actor's childhood through adolescence, Marlon Brando, Sr., repeatedly told his only son he would amount to nothing. Although Marlon junior proved his father wrong over and over again, the damage had been done. No material success, no critical praise, no financial reward ever served to assuage the wounds Marlon suffered before he could defend himself. Ironically, they were also what gave him such persuasive strength as a performer.

Few of Brando's contemporaries bought his line of self-denigration. "Marlon's work was so beautiful and so pure," said Julie Harris, his costar in *Reflections in a Golden Eye.* "There was no explaining where it came from. He didn't respect acting, but his gift was so great he couldn't defile it. He could put on pounds, he could say it was all shit, but he still couldn't destroy it."

Director Harold Clurman, the husband of Brando's acting coach and mentor, Stella Adler, believed that the disrespect was not a pose. He noted, "[There is] something in Marlon that *resents* acting, yet he cannot help but be an actor. He thinks acting 'sickly.' He'd rather do something for 'the world.' "

Clurman underlined another irony in Brando's career. Because Marlon could so completely lose himself in a role, he was convinced that he could feel the wounds of a disenfranchised black, an oppressed Native American, a vagrant, a bewildered homosexual, a palooka. But the off-screen efforts he made on their behalf had no lasting effect. Acting, much as Marlon resisted it, was the one place where he could give voice to the powerless.

The trouble was, Brando's gift came with a price tag. He was like some cursed figure from folklore who might have anything he wanted—fame, riches, beautiful women, power—provided that he couldn't enjoy it. Immensely attractive to both sexes, he seemed in charge of any and all affairs. But he abandoned all three wives and numerous lovers, often in fear that they would abandon him first. He loved his eleven children, but never knew how to relate to them once they entered adolescence—a shortcoming that would have fatal consequences. At the top of the heap in Hollywood, he called the whole thing a sham and became difficult (and sometimes impossible) for directors and writers to deal with. When this misbehavior was forgiven or overlooked, he deliberately slid downhill to a pile of trash, movies that lost money and nearly wrecked him as an actor. The more beguiling his appearance, the less comfortable he was with it, finally distancing himself from his admirers by putting on weight until he grew morbidly obese. This nearly wrecked him as a man.

"The young Brando," observes psychiatrist Gary Lefer, "saw brutality in his father and self-abuse in his mother. It was constant, but always kept within the walls of the house. Children of such parents live two lives: the false, well-kempt one presented to the world at large, and the real and messy one that they know at home. They think they've put one over on their classmates, and thus know themselves to be phony. They grow up thinking that everything is bogus. Especially their own achievements."

The torment that underlay Brando's art is the subject of this book, as well as the way it played out in his three careers: phenomenal early success, a series of tarnished failures, and then an astonishing renaissance before the fade-out. The man's internal anguish was what drove him on to the heights of his vocation. But it was also the cause of his many public and private mistakes, as well as the reason he could never stop trying to do something for "the world" and its suffering people. For those efforts he was unfairly derided. As we will see, they were born out of the shame and humiliation he never shook off during a life of ludicrous excess, outlandish triumphs, and appalling sorrows.

Somebody

In Disgrace with Fortune

1

I t was typical of Marlon to enter the world upside down. The breech birth took place shortly after 11 p.m., April 3, 1924, in the Omaha Maternity Hospital.

His earliest home was right out of the imaginings of Hollywood at a time when the film industry, dominated by Jewish immigrants, was beginning to reinvent its host country. If status was denied to these rough, uneducated Eastern Europeans, observed historian Neal Gabler, the movies offered an ingenious option. The first moguls "would fabricate their empire in the image of America. They would create its values and myths, its traditions and archetypes. It would be an America where fathers were strong, families stable, people attractive, resilient, resourceful, and decent." This is the superficially idyllic America into which Marlon was born.

Yet even in the peaceful Midwest, ideal turf of the Dream Factory, there were dark spots no one could ignore. In the year of Marlon's birth, for example, two adolescents, Richard Loeb and Nathan Leopold, kidnapped and murdered fourteen-year-old Bobby Franks in a Chicago suburb. That was in May. Detectives closed in shortly afterward, the culprits were arraigned in June, and by August they were on trial for their lives. The defense, headed by star lawyer Clarence Darrow, enlisted mind doctors, "alienists," in the parlance of the day, to establish irresponsibility by reason of insanity. Sigmund Freud was asked to aid the cause, but he was in fragile health and declined the invitation. After being called "cowardly perverts," "atheists," and "mad dogs," Leopold and Loeb were sentenced to life imprisonment. But the debate about capital punishment continued unchecked, touching the plains and cities of Nebraska. At virtually the same time, Chicago crime raged on, fueled by Prohibition. The outlawing of alcohol had become official in 1920; since then the racketeers and illegal importers were thriving, peddling booze to the country's flourishing speakeasies. Turf wars began: Al Capone's brother Frank was gunned down by police when he led some two hundred armed men into Cicero, Illinois, in support of Mafia-backed politicians. And North Side gang leader Dion O'Banion was shot and killed by three men who had entered his flower shop after hours. The murder began a five-year war with the Capone gang that was to culminate in the notorious St. Valentine's Day massacre.

Closer to home, Omaha wrestled with its own Prohibition troubles and with a more intractable problem. Since the end of the Great War, the city's African American population had more than doubled. With the influx came resentments and racial taunts. The *Omaha Bee* was particularly inflammatory. The paper's favorite topic concerned rumored assaults and rapes of white women by black men. The accused were hauled before judges and juries. When they failed to convict, another newspaper, the *Mediator,* warned of vigilantism in Omaha if the "respectable colored population could not purge those from the Negro community who were assaulting white girls." A few months later a volatile combination of labor unrest and racial suspicion erupted. Before it ended, a black man was lynched, two other blacks died of wounds suffered during a street fight, the county courthouse lay in ruins, and the city came under federal military control.

All these provoked conversation at the Brando dinner table through the 1920s and early 1930s, marking an odd contrast to the rustic atmosphere at 1026 South Street. Outwardly all was lyrical. Three children—two pretty sisters and their robust younger brother—played in the large front yard; the backdrop was a capacious wood-shingled house redolent of fresh-cut hay, wild flowers, and smoke from a wood-burning stove. In the next decade Andy Hardy movies would take place in just such an environment.

But there was a secondary aroma, and it revealed what no passerby could sense. "When my mother drank," recalled Marlon, "her breath had a sweetness to it I lack the vocabulary to describe." A furtive alcoholic, she took frequent hits from a bottle she called her "change-of-life" medicine. Dodie—Dorothy Pennebaker Brando—began to spend longer and longer periods with that vessel until, Marlon noted in his memoir, "the anguish that her drinking produced was that she preferred getting drunk to caring for us."

"Us" referred to Marlon senior and his children, Frances (known to the family as Frannie), Jocelyn (Tiddy), and Marlon junior (Bud). Dodie had reasons for allowing her husband to fend for himself. Wrote his namesake, "It was an era when a traveling salesman slipped five dollars to a bellboy, who would return with a pint of whisky and a hooker. My pop was such a man."

The condition of such families as the Brandos, and such cities as Omaha, was well known to Sinclair Lewis. He had portrayed them in his 1922 bestseller *Babbitt,* with its hypocritical real-estate-salesman protagonist and his unhappy wife, and the superficially respectable city in which they lived. "At that moment in Zenith, a cocaine-runner and a prostitute were drinking cocktails in Healy Hanson's saloon on Front Street. Since national prohibition was now in force, and since Zenith was notoriously law-abiding, they were compelled to keep the cocktails innocent by drinking them out of tea-cups. The lady threw her cup at the cocaine-runner's head. He worked his revolver out of the pocket in his sleeve, and casually murdered her."

For Marlon senior, as for George F. Babbitt, money was not a problem; a peddler of products for contractors and architects, the paterfamilias earned more than enough to maintain his family in solid middle-class comfort. Affection, however, was in short supply. He would return home to shower Dodie with gifts, then journey back to a life of one-night stands. There were presents for the kids as well, but precious little concern. Marlon senior continually denigrated his namesake; he mocked the boy's behavior, his way of speaking, his posture. Hugs were only dispensed on birthdays or at Christmastime; Junior couldn't recall a single compliment from his father from kindergarten through adolescence. As a result the child sought attention elsewhere—mainly at school, where he made a habit of flouting authority, and getting punished for it.

Senior's ominous moods and black silences were harder for his daughters to deal with. "I don't remember forgiveness," Frannie Brando wrote many years later. "No forgiveness! In our home, there was blame, shame, and punishment that very often had no relationship to the 'crime,' and I think the sense of burning injustice it left with all of us marked us deeply."

That behavior had profound and twisted sources. Although a number of biographies have suggested that the name Brando was originally spelled Brandeau and was of French origin, the family's founding rela-

tive was Johann Wilhelm Brandau, a German immigrant who settled in
New York State in the early 1700s. Neighbors who remembered Marlon senior from his school days said there was something "Teutonic and
closed" about the youth, but this may have been the perception of
hindsight. In any case, he had reason to be withdrawn; his mother ran
off without a backward glance when the boy was four. Thereafter, the
abandoned father varied between dark and uncommunicative periods
and loud, unpredictable demands. In adolescence, Marlon senior was
shunted from one spinster aunt to another. He grew up rude and
misogynistic, given to binge drinking and bullying. Bud came to see his
father in cinematic terms as a British officer in the Bengal Lancers,
"perhaps a Victor McLaglen with more refinement."

Dorothy Pennebaker came from a background of mavericks, gold
prospectors, and Christian Scientists. She married at twenty-one but
continued to attract whistles and social attention as a vivacious flapper
with artistic yearnings. Early on, Dodie made a small name for herself
by cultivating members of Omaha's little bohemian colony, and beating
out the competition for roles at the Omaha Community Playhouse.
From walk-ons and juvenile leads she progressed to starring parts in
Pygmalion and *Anna Christie*. It occurred to Dodie that she might
take a trip to New York and try a stab at Broadway—especially after she
won rave reviews for her appearance in *Beyond the Horizon* opposite
a twenty-one-year-old Omahan named Henry Fonda. All too soon,
though, Marlon senior's rages, as well as his open and continual adul-
teries, eroded her confidence on- and offstage. She consumed more
liquor, took her own lovers, and narrowed her creative impulses.

Like many homes of the period, the Brando house had a piano in the
parlor. Radio was still in its infancy, and recordings were still only a pale
echo of true musical sound. Dodie had received lessons as a child, and
she still got more pleasure out of playing than she did out of listening.
Solos at the keyboard supplanted group work at the theater. Surrounded by her children—in one of the very few family activities—she
played folk airs and popular numbers, from Irving Berlin's inventive
tunes to a list of lesser numbers, including "I'm Looking Over a Four-
Leaf Clover" and "Am I Blue?" To please her, Marlon learned them
all. He could never summon up the digits of his Social Security I.D.,
and there were times when he couldn't recall his own telephone number. But the music and lyrics from those days around the keyboard
never left him. When, at the age of sixty-five, he wrote his autobiogra-

phy, scores of titles were suggested by friends and publishers, but in the end he settled on *Songs My Mother Taught Me*.

2

When Bud was six, the Calcium Carbonate Corporation offered his father a new job as sales manager. Employment opportunities were few in 1930, the first full year of the Depression. Marlon senior seized the day, even though it meant relocation to Evanston, Illinois. His wife was not so happy with the decision; she still clung to the fading illusion of herself as a stage star, and Evanston had no playhouse and few non-conformists.

Dodie struggled to get her bearings in the new neighborhood. Melancholia settled in like an old acquaintance who had come for a weekend visit and refused to go away. Every day the *Chicago Tribune* brought bad news, and every week *Time* magazine summed them up. Breadlines across the country, new bankruptcies. And lynchings; God, those poor people. She sometimes read the stories aloud to the kids, unsure of whether the reports went over their heads or burrowed into their psyches. "All night two hundred men and boys searched for Davie Harris, found him at dawn, cringing in an empty barn. They lugged him up to the levee, mocked his yammerings for mercy. 'De Lord save me,' cried Harris as guns cracked about him, shots riddled his body. Deputy Sheriff Dayu arrived 'too late' to make arrests. Deputy Sheriff Courtney expected no investigation 'until next fall.' "

In the back of the publications Dodie read news of live performances in the East. They opened old wounds. Like the rest of the country, Broadway was suffering from financial woes. The year before there had been 233 productions; this year there would be 187, and fewer were scheduled for next year. Vaudeville was reeling; five years before there were fifteen hundred theaters in the circuits. One fifth remained. And yet the Fabulous Invalid went on, as it always did, as it always would. Eva Le Gallienne's Civic Repertory staged *Allison's House*, based on the life of Emily Dickinson; it was said to be a shoo-in for the Pulitzer. Maxwell Anderson's *Elizabeth the Queen* starred Alfred Lunt and Lynn Fontanne at the Guild Theatre. Eugene O'Neill's *Marco Millions* was successfully revived at the Liberty. The

Gershwins had a new show, *Girl Crazy.* "I Got Rhythm" was on the radio every night; you couldn't get away from it. The columnists said that Ethel Merman could hold a note longer than the Chase National Bank. And Harold Arlen had written the score for Earl Carroll's *Vanities.* I should have gone east, Dodie would muse aloud. It's not too late even now.

Then again, that might not be the best move. Three quarters of the New York actors were supposed to be heading for Hollywood. And why not? The studios dominated show business now that sound had come in. Powerful men ran them: Goldwyn, Mayer, the Warners, Zanuck. These dream merchants could read the public like a map. *All Quiet on the Western Front* and *Hell's Angels* were playing everywhere. Who knew that this would be the year to look back at the Great War? *They* did. Who knew that you could make money with a gangster picture like *The Widow from Chicago*? Who knew you could make a star of Edward G. Robinson, a little Jewish man with fat lips? *They* did. Maybe I should have gone west, not middle west, Dodie grumbled. Meantime, the neighbors whispered that Mrs. Brando was the kind of woman who saw the glass as half full. That was because she had drunk the other half.

The rumors were cruel, and they were accurate. Too many afternoons Dodie disappeared into an alcohol-saturated haze, unreachable by her children. Frannie and Tiddy were on the cusp of adolescence and found new friends at the tony Lincoln School. Bud attended the same institution, but retreated into his own fantasies. The most obsessive of these concerned the family housekeeper, a young woman of Danish and Indonesian descent called Ermi. During the day he played card games with her; at night the two often slept in the same bed. She was nude, he remembered—though this might have been a boy's wishful dream—and a sound sleeper. On his part the attachment was all-consuming; to her it was of no importance whatever. In fact, she never bothered to tell him that she was about to be married. The housekeeper merely informed him one day that she was leaving on a trip and would return soon.

It took several weeks for Bud to realize that Ermi was not coming back. The night he realized she was gone forever, he experienced a foretaste of death. "I felt abandoned," he said almost five decades later. "My mother had long ago deserted me for her bottle; now Ermi was gone, too." To Bud this was one of the informing incidents of his childhood. Looking back he decided that Ermi's defection kept repeating itself in his life. He would seek out a woman who would encourage him up to a point—and then abruptly and permanently exit. According to Marlon, the day Ermi went away "I became estranged from this world." That summary contained everything a self-dramatizing figure could desire: bittersweet melodrama, unrequited romance, and Freudian insight. It might even have been true.

In her study *Adult Children of Alcoholics*, Dr. Janet Geringer Woititz lists the characteristics of her subjects when young. They tend to:

Guess what normal behavior is.

Lie when it would be just as easy to tell the truth.

Judge themselves without mercy.

Constantly seek approval and affirmation.

Be impulsive. Such behavior would lead to confusion, self-loathing and loss of control.

All these attributes were part of Bud's emerging temperament. At home, as he saw it, "there was a constant, grinding, unseen miasma of anger." Infected by the rage around him, he continued to act out his hostilities, burning insects, slashing tires, tiptoeing close to birds—and then plugging them with the BB gun his father had given him as a birthday present. Bud was no happier in the classroom than he was in the house. One morning he took a can of lighter fluid, squirted the word *shit* on a blackboard and ignited the letters. The incident helped to burnish his bad-boy reputation; he seemed to thrive on that. All the same, after every incident there came a time of remorse and self-reproach.

One day, without warning, neighbors were astonished to see a spontaneous Tom Sawyer turnaround. Bud stopped shooting birds, admonished his friends not to step on ants, ostentatiously helped old people and drunks who had collapsed on the sidewalk. Frances commented on the "new" Marlon junior, scribbling on the back of a photo: "Bud—and he is a grand boy! Sweet and funny, idealistic and oh, so young." When they were all adults, Tiddy summoned up that period in a conversation with her brother: Not only did he try to save wounded animals and birds, he would also "pick the girl who was cross-eyed or the fattest one because nobody paid attention to her and you wanted her to feel good."

Chicago was segregated in the early 1930s. Racially restrictive covenants affected 80 percent of the city and most of the surrounding suburbs. Only two black children attended Lincoln. Perhaps because of what Bud had heard and read, perhaps out of a need to identify with the outsider, he made a point of befriending both of them. He delighted in hanging around the house of Asa Lee, an African American boy whose warm, demonstrative mother seemed to be everything that Dodie was not. One afternoon Bud had trouble with a decision and began counting aloud, "Eeny, meeny, miney, moe. Catch a nigger by the toe. If he hollers, let him go. Eeny, meeny, miney, moe." Asa's mother bent down and said, "Dahlin', we don't use that word in this house." Curious, the visitor asked, "What word?" She told him. "I had no idea what the word meant," he remembered, "but I could tell from Asa's expression that it was significant." The black woman could see the innocence in Bud's eyes. She gave him a gum ball, patted his head, and said, "You're a sweet thing." That incident, he claimed, "was my first experience with a sense of race." There would be a great many more.

Bud's first girlfriend fit Tiddy's description. Eight-year-old Carol Hickock was neither cross-eyed nor overweight, but she suffered from narcolepsy. The blackouts could occur anytime; occasionally she lost consciousness when standing up. One Saturday afternoon the two children went to see a Boris Karloff feature. Sound films had made an enormous impact by 1932, horror movies especially. *Frankenstein* and *Dracula* had preceded *The Mummy*, and Bud hoped that a terrifying scene might drive Carol into his arms. Instead, he was the one overtaken by fear, and fled to the lobby. Later, as they sat on a sofa in her house chatting idly, she suddenly rolled her eyes and fainted. He leaned over and put his mouth on hers—his first kiss.

At about this time Bud acquired a stammer. At first it was just trouble with a few words, but soon he became so tongue-tied that Dodie took him to Northwestern University for speech therapy. He had begun to internalize his wounds, trying somehow to fix the unfixable, to compensate for the misery around him. One of the few people he trusted was the shy, bespectacled Wally Cox, whose mother was also a heavy drinker. The two boys got on; Bud acted as a kind of bodyguard for his smaller friend, though he was not above making Wally a victim when the two were by themselves. One afternoon Bud invented a game in which Wally had to be tied to a tree. Then he wandered off. Several hours later, the Cox family summoned the police, who found

Wally and freed him. The prank did nothing to damage the boys' friendship.

When he could, Bud lost himself in films. In Daniel Boorstin's meditation *The Image: A Guide to Pseudo-Events in America*, the historian makes a provocative assertion. As films took over the center of popular culture, Americans edged ever closer to a "world where fantasy [was] more real than reality." If conditions persisted, they would be "the first people in history to have been able to make their illusions so vivid, so persuasive, so 'realistic' that they could live in them." And in *Life: The Movie*, film scholar Neal Gabler posits that on the ramp leading up to World War II, "old values and the social order that sustained them were being challenged. In their place had come a feeling, fed by democratic wellsprings and encouraged by these brisk social changes, that one could do anything, be anything, dream anything—including what one saw onscreen." For adolescents this was a particularly crucial phenomenon. Going to the movies was not merely a method of escape, but a way of defining their lives. In Marlon's view, for example, the sea adventure *Mutiny on the Bounty* provided a melodrama of tyrant versus righteous rebels—and a glimpse of South Sea romance as different from his own life as a toucan's from a sparrow's. Victor McLaglen, the leathery, valiant sergeant of *The Lost Patrol*, became an idealized portrait of the father he resented and feared. *Manhattan Melodrama* showed him New York City as a breeding ground of gangsters—and also as a place where a tough young man might go to find himself.

At night, in the skull cinema, he acted and directed his own drama, in which no one else was permitted a role—not even a cameo. "I had the fantasy," he said, "that the important people in my life were all dead and were only pretending to be alive. I lay in bed for hours, sweating and looking up at the ceiling, convinced that I was the only one in the whole world who was alive." The idea that one day he might act in somebody else's dream didn't enter the picture.

3

In his twelfth year the ceiling changed when Dodie and Marlon senior agreed to separate. She would take the family to live with her mother, Elizabeth "Nana" Myers, in Santa Ana, California. Marlon senior would stay in Chicago. The split was characterized not as a prelude to divorce but as a cooling-off period. Marlon senior could visit as often as he liked, provided that he didn't stay long. Relocation further distanced Dodie from Broadway fare, but she kept up with the new names in 1935: the bright hope of the New York theater, Clifford Odets, with a pair of plays, *Waiting for Lefty* and *Awake and Sing!* God, what she wouldn't give to see them. . . . On the other hand, she was now nearly in Hollywood, where there was so much action you couldn't keep track of it all: *David Copperfield, The Informer, Les Misérables, The 39 Steps, Top Hat.* The new names: Katharine Hepburn, Errol Flynn—and Henry Fonda in his first *three* movies. A break here, a break there, she might have been in that company.

Well, the hell with fantasy. No matter how she looked at it, this was a rotten world to bring kids into. A drought forcing an exodus on the farmlands. President Roosevelt describing this nation as ill fed, ill clothed, and ill housed. If you doubted him you could look around and see the breadlines for yourself. The newsreels recording the human cost, and worse to come. *The March of Time* booming, "The peace of the world daily grows more uncertain." H. G. Wells pretending to look back: "War was manifestly drawing nearer, in Eastern Asia, in Eastern Europe; it loitered, it advanced, it halted, and no one displayed the vigor or capacity needed to avert the intermittent, unhurrying approach."

The Depression would lead to a big conflagration somewhere—that you could count on. They were getting ready in Spain, Franco's troops versus the anti-Fascists and the Communists; in the United States something called the Abraham Lincoln Brigade was signing up volunteers to fight there. In Berlin there were demonstrations against the Jews. Italy was already in the hands of Mussolini; his pilots were killing Africans in Abyssinia, raining bombs down on black children. Thank God Marlon senior was too old to be in the military, and Marlon junior too young.

As for the girls, they seemed all right in Dodie's unfocused eyes. And for the most part she was correct. Frances showed a gift for oil painting and Jocelyn discovered that she had inherited her mother's performing talent. She won leading parts in the productions at Santa Ana High School and announced her intentions to seek an acting career. Bud had no such fortune. The adults were too busy to give him much notice. As a Christian Science counselor, Nana was preoccupied with her ailing patients. Dodie continued to put away the booze every afternoon, save for a couple of times when Hank Fonda came by for a sentimental visit to recollect the old days in Omaha.

So Junior went his own way, acrimoniously reflecting that he was "always on skinny rations when it came to praise. I never received accolades or adulation, not even encouragement. Nobody ever thought I was good for anything except a few kindly teachers." One of those instructors was the shop teacher at Julius C. Lathrop Junior High, who handed Bud a piece of metal and asked him to make something of it. His student shaped the iron on a forge and put the creation in wet sand. Then he melted some aluminum and poured it into the makeshift mold. Result: a homemade screwdriver. The teacher praised him for his accomplishment and, according to Bud, "for the first time in my life I had done something of which I was proud."

But academically he continued to lag, and various members of the faculty implied—or said outright—that he would never amount to anything. The athletic coaches disagreed; the following year Bud won letters in track and football, finished first in the school decathlon, and set a record by doing one thousand straight push-ups. He might have done more, but a teacher, worried that the youth would strain his heart, ordered him to stop. Alternately sullen and boastful, he seemed a lost boy one moment, an ambitious young competitor the next. Biographer Peter Manso, the most avid chronicler of Marlon Brando's early years, notes that during this time Bud assumed a swagger and a pseudo-mature attitude. In the absence of his father he attempted to act as the man of the house, while "Nana doted, Dodie doted, and his sisters tried to stay out of the way." The trouble was that Bud lacked the emotional maturity to lead anyone, least of all himself. As Dodie confessed to a friend, "He is a grand kid but living with him is like climbing a greased pole in war-torn Shanghai. And the worst," she predicted, "won't come for another two or three years."

Those years were not spent in Santa Ana. After a prolonged separation, Dodie and Marlon senior reunited. If living together had been miserable, living apart was unendurable. Back the family went to Illinois, but this time to exurbia—Libertyville, population three thousand. Although the little town was only thirty-five miles northwest of Chicago, it might as well have been in Iowa. Locals considered it farm country, and they regarded the Brandos, fresh from Evanston and Santa Ana, as sophisticates.

The family lived in a large rented farmhouse, kept a cow, and maintained a vegetable garden, but they dressed better than their neighbors and carried themselves with a somewhat superior air. Marlon senior was a well-compensated executive—he earned $15,000 a year when the average annual salary was $1,600. Dodie, who squandered a lot of the household money in bars, joined the local dramatic club. Her daughters went out for parts in the high school plays. And Bud, once again, was all attitude and rebellion. He was either in jeans and a T-shirt or in shirts so brightly hued that his classmates accused him of wearing pajama tops to school—anything to be different. After a few months he discovered a talent for drumming and joined the school band. But he couldn't be bothered with rehearsing. The director's order, "Get in step, Brando!" became an integral part of the rehearsals, much to the amusement of his fellow musicians. On the athletic fields Bud showed the same distracted approach. He liked competing for trophies, but hated working out. He boxed for a while, then gave that up, bored with the endless sparring, went out for football but horsed around too much to learn the signals or conform to the coach's discipline. In the end he forsook competitive sports and spent hours lifting free weights. Bud was approaching his full height of five feet, ten inches, broadening out in the chest and shoulders like his father, and proud of his mesomorphic build. Still, the face did not keep up with the body; Bud was slow to develop a beard, and there were times when his soft eyes and sensuous lips lent him an almost feminine aspect.

By now he had enough physical confidence to take on anyone his age. When he joined the school's drama club on a whim and volunteered to pantomime a young girl preparing to take a bath, nobody dared tease him. He liked the idea of impersonating villains, and once played the gangster John Dillinger in a sketch. Classmates were chilled by his impersonation, greeting it first with awed silence and then with wild applause. For the most part, though, the club did lightweight fare—Kaufman and Hart's *You Can't Take It with You* was a favorite— and Bud had trouble with comic timing. To no one's surprise he took direction badly and, as a consequence, never got cast in any full-length plays. Yet by now he had acquired the itch to perform. Instead of acting, he got hold of some drumsticks and wooden kegs and organized an after-school rhythm band he called Keg Brando and His Kegliners. When the group failed to get any bookings it dissolved. Bud withdrew into himself again, reading books his mother had accumulated over the years: *The Great Gatsby, The Waste Land,* the tragedies, comedies, and history plays of Shakespeare. And like most children his age, he became an addict of network radio.

Albert Einstein, newly arrived from Germany, explained radio to the American public: "You see, wire telegraph is a kind of a very, very long cat. You pull his tail in New York and his head is meowing in Los Angeles. And radio operates in exactly the same way; you send signals here, they receive them there. The only difference is that there is no cat." The absence of cat was what made the medium so miraculous. Broadcasts in the East, Midwest, and South reached all parts of the United States; regionalisms were no longer confined to discrete geographical areas. Now everyone knew the sound of an Atlantan's drawl, a Brooklynite's nasalities, a Bostonian's flat *a*'s.

Somewhere along the way, the carbon microphone had reversed the conditions of show business. Actors didn't need to be comely anymore; they could get by with a flexible voice and a few sound effects. The journalist Alistair Cooke was fond of quoting a seven-year-old who preferred radio to movies because "the pictures were better"—and so they were for most American children.

In his evocative memoir, *Raised on Radio,* Gerald Nachman recalls that old-time radio was "made of words," addicting him to stage plays with their emphasis on speech. "Radio was America, presented in tones of pure red-blooded patriotism." The youths of that era were inspired to see the places they "kept hearing about each night, sparking a wanderlust the way a passing train and paddle-wheeler might have for a boy a century before."

The attitudes and values of old-time radio programs could be more powerful (and on occasion more insidious) than ones conveyed by parents and schoolteachers. On the upside there was the Shakespeare summer of 1937, when NBC presented condensed versions of the canon, starring John Barrymore, while CBS produced *Hollywood Salutes Shakespeare,* featuring Leslie Howard and Tallulah Bankhead. There were H. V. Kaltenborn's coverage of the Spanish Civil War and President Roosevelt's Fireside Chats, which talked the nation out of the Depression and into recovery. There were the comic feud of Fred Allen and Jack Benny and the sophisticated remarks on *Information Please.*

But these episodes aimed for an adult audience, and the young listened to them with half an ear, if at all. They spent the bulk of their attention on fifteen- and thirty-minute melodramas. *Grand Central*

Station provided glimpses of a city as glamorous and mythic as Oz: "Drawn by the magnetic force of the fantastic metropolis, day and night great trains dive with a roar into the two-and-a-half-mile tunnel which burrows between the glitter and swank of Park Avenue and then . . . Grand Central Station! Crossroads of a million private lives! Gigantic stage on which are played a thousand dramas daily!"

The *Lucky Strike Hour* glamorized the employees of the Federal Bureau of Investigation—"G-Men," in radio parlance. An FBI official later explained that "in the Depression, households would give up the refrigerator they bought on time rather than giving up the radio." This fact was duly noted by J. Edgar Hoover, who cooperated with broadcasters willing to flatter the bureau and its chief. Thus indoctrinated, audiences "were much more willing to cooperate fully when a real FBI agent knocked on their door."

The Lone Ranger and *The Green Hornet* dramatized other aspects of crime-fighting America. These vigilantes were just as idealized as movie heroes—Anglo-Saxons whose trusted (but socially inferior) assistants were nonwhites: an Indian in the case of the Ranger, a Japanese (later Filipino) valet for the Hornet. Racial stereotypes ruled the day: Black actors were relegated to comic roles, the males commonly playing buffoons, the females domestics. CBS scriptwriter Norman Corwin recalled the unheard-of use of an African American performer in a central role: "Through the corridors, it was, 'Hey, you heard about the Corwin show? He's got a Negro playing the leading role. Holy smoke!'" The harshest racial ironies were triggered by the *Amos 'n' Andy* show. Its main characters were played by white men doing black southern accents. Mispronunciations and malapropisms were endemic: "Ah denies de allegation, and Ah resents de alligator"; "You has my infernal gratitude." For the most part, audiences loved the show. But there was growing resentment in the black community. A group of lawyers tried to get the program off the air, and *The Pittsburgh Courier,* an important African American newspaper, said *Amos 'n' Andy* was guilty of nothing less than the "exploitation of Negroes for profit." Already sensitized, Marlon spent a lot of time pondering the situation: "I was born only sixty-two years after one human being could still buy another in America," he was to write. "I remember first being amazed by this discovery and wondering how it could be." He sought out accounts of slaves in the library, empathized with their descendants, and tried to imagine himself as a black man in servitude.

Still, there was a virtue even to the racially distorted melodramas and hack comedies of the 1930s: To differentiate among villains and heroes and supporting players, the actors used different inflections and regionalisms. Listening to them, Bud discovered that he had a talent for vocal mimicry. After he had turned the radio off, he played the dialogue in his mind, replicating what he had heard, then rolling the syllables over his tongue. He carried the process over into real life, watching and listening to neighbors, teachers, friends, copying their voices.

He got more opportunities for impersonation when he picked up his mother at the police station. On numerous evenings Bud heard the familiar, dreaded words from a police desk sergeant: "We have a Dorothy Pennebaker Brando here. Could you come down here and get her?" And those were the easy times. All too frequently he and his sisters would look at the clock at 6 p.m. and realize that Dodie was not coming home. They would have to go door-to-door through the bars of Chicago's skid row, examining the women slumped on bar stools until they found her. The girls were mortified; Bud would make mental notes about the way cops and drunks looked, spoke, and walked, filing it all away somewhere, who knew for what.

The hostility he felt on these occasions was directed toward Marlon senior rather than Dodie. As the fourteen-year-old saw it, the alcoholism was his father's fault, a result of deliberate neglect and brutality. Bud's wrath erupted one evening shortly after he had fetched his mother from yet another spree. Marlon senior took over from there, leading his wife to their upstairs bedroom. Bud heard a body hit the floor. Then came the sounds of slapping, followed by wails of distress. Bud took the stairs two at a time and flung open his parents' door. Dodie lay on the bed, facedown, crying, as Marlon senior loomed over her. Like a hero in one of his favorite noir movies, Marlon junior advanced on his father, and said in a low, clear voice, "If you ever hit her again, I'll kill you."

Marlon senior backed off. Bud reasoned that it was because "he was staring at more adrenaline than he had ever seen in his life. My father was afraid of nothing and we probably would have fought to the death had it not been for the fact that perhaps he felt guilty." Whatever the case, Marlon senior walked out of the bedroom, leaving Dodie on the bed. The incident did a great deal to bolster Bud's protective instincts, but it failed to diminish his father's roughness or his mother's dependence on liquor.

And so he continued to misbehave. According to Sigmund Freud, "acting out" occurs when an individual "does not remember anything of what he has repressed," but reproduces it "not as memory, but as action; he repeats it without, of course, knowing that he is repeating it." In Marlon's case, the bad conduct repeatedly took the form of sass, particularly directed toward authority figures. Hired as an usher at a local movie house, for example, he wearied of wearing a traditional uniform, and he substituted a dickey for the starched shirt and awkwardly sewed a pair of cuffs to the jacket to make it appear that he was in full regalia. When the deception was discovered, Bud was summarily canned. He took swift revenge with another comically anarchic act, chopping up rotting broccoli and mixing it with overripe Limburger cheese, then stuffing the mess into the air-conditioning system. An overpowering stench drove the panicked audience to an emergency exit. On other occasions he wrote a French assignment on toilet paper and unrolled it as he spoke, lit firecrackers and threw them out of classroom windows to give the impression of gunfire, hung a dead skunk on a football scoreboard.

The principal wasted hours lecturing Bud on propriety, but an irritated teacher reached into the boy's record to exact a more devastating measure of revenge. Since the beginning of World War I, intelligence tests had been used to determine future performance. The exams measured chronological age against mental age, with 140 and above as "gifted" and 78 and below as "retarded." The U.S. Army had been provided with thousands of draftees, and the exams were used to categorize them as potential officers, enlisted specialists, platoon leaders, and infantrymen. After the war, schools adopted these severely flawed tests for their own purposes. The numbers were supposed to be kept confidential, but teachers knew the results of the tests—and so did a lot of students. A backlash began. Walter Lippmann, the widely syndicated columnist, commented, "One only has to read around in the literature of the subject to see how easily the intelligence test can be turned into an engine of cruelty, how it could turn into a method of stamping a permanent sense of inferiority upon the soul of a child." That engine of cruelty made its mark on Bud when the teacher announced to his class: "Young Brando here has an IQ of ninety; no wonder he's so disruptive and has such trouble keeping up with the rest of you." Thus another stamp of inferiority was affixed, to go alongside those Marlon senior had supplied. By the time Bud reached the age of fifteen, a lifelong pattern was set: No one in a position of power could be trusted, therefore all symbols of control must be resisted. Given his deportment, close-by neighbors could hardly be blamed for giving him a wide berth, warning their children about too close an association.

Matters seemed to worsen by the month. On many mornings Dodie had to shake off a hangover, get herself together, and drop by the principal's office, summoned there to hear the latest litany of Bud's infractions. In time a letter went out to Marlon senior, asking him to come in and discuss his son's pockmarked report card. At that point, the head of the family saw only one solution. The boy would have to be sent to military school. Marlon senior had been a hellion in his own youth; Shattuck Military Academy in Faribault, Minnesota, had straightened him out just fine. It would do the same for his recalcitrant son.

Resistance was useless. Bud was a minor and the law was on his father's side. In September 1941 the seventeen-year-old signed the appropriate papers, picked up his uniform, and checked into Shattuck. Like all military schools of the period, it was oversubscribed. All year long the countdown to conflict had been resounding like a 4/4 beat from a kettle drum. The German and Italian consulates in the United States had been ordered closed. The American people were being prepared for the inevitable by the White House, newspaper editorials, and radio bulletins. Reporters in Paris fled the country; France was under Nazi control. But there was plenty of news coming out of England. On CBS, the crisp uninflected voice of Edward R. Murrow regularly issued from London: "It seems strange to hear the English, who were saying, 'We'll win this one without help from America,' admitting now that this world—or what's left of it—will be largely run either from Berlin or from Washington."

With all this in mind, Marlon senior convinced himself that putting Bud in a military academy was an act of high patriotism. Shattuck had been in operation since the Indian wars of the 1870s, helping to supply the U.S. Army with an officer cadre. Now, with half the world aflame, the academy geared up anew. More than half the class was composed of difficult children from prosperous midwestern families, among them the Mayos of the Mayo Clinic, and the Hormels, owners of the prominent meatpacking company. These folks could easily afford the annual tuition and boarding fee of $1,500. The Brandos had little in common with them—except that their son had also been sent to Shattuck to learn the values of discipline and rectitude.

When he looked back at the school many years later, Marlon junior realized that by then "any hope I had of receiving love or support from my parents was probably moribund." But the youth was in denial, sending home letters in a futile attempt to win their respect and affection. Intimidation was the first rule of Shattuck, something Bud noted from week one. "Dear Folks," he wrote home. "I am settled materially but not spiritually. The staff is tough and the reward is usually a good, sweet, but firm kick in the ass." Calder Willingham, who had attended The Citadel in South Carolina, used a military school as his milieu in *End as a Man*. The novel describes the treatment of a new recruit, Simmons, by vicious upperclassman Jocko De Paris.

"Is it true you once tapped your sister?"

"Sir, have you no respect for the dead?"

De Paris wailed in imitation, "Sir, have you no respect for the dead? . . . Now let's carve some extra bone from your coccyx. Take hold of those ankles."

Simmons bent over and grabbed his shoe tops.

De Paris took the broom, tested it back and forth with his wrists, and poised it. Then his arms swung back in a graceful arc, and his eyes half shut. The broom came down with a loud whacking noise. Dust clouded up from the trousers and Simmons grunted.

De Paris spelled out F-R-E-S-H-M-A-N. One blow for each letter. There was coagulated blood on Simmons' undershorts when he took them off that night.

IN THE CLASSROOMS of this particular academy, the virtues of integrity, leadership, trust are the orders of the day. But the private life of the cadets amounts to antimatter, and dishonesty, betrayal, anal sadism are the orders of the day. Though Willingham later called his book a "wild, reckless nightmare-vision," it was true to its time, and provided a rare portrait of adolescents in the pulverizing environment of a military school in a military time.

There could have been no more inappropriate place for Marlon, and in response to the institute's rigid class system he assumed an attitude of cool belligerence. Over the years, critics sometimes looked back at family albums and professed to see a seedling superstar. Actually, Marlon Brando, Jr., showed little distinction at the time. He had darkening blond hair, an earnest smile, and the intense, hormonal aura common to most boys his age. He and the camera had yet to establish their complicated love-hate relationship. At his maximum height of five feet, ten inches, he weighed less than 150 pounds. A good deal of that avoirdupois was muscle, a result of the weight lifting begun in Libertyville and continued at Shattuck, and this helped him to get along and go along. Like an apprehensive cat that pushes out its fur to seem larger, Bud "walked big," carrying himself like an athlete. The cocky stance had its effect; upperclassmen kept their distance. "I did my best to tear the school apart and not get caught at it," Bud was to state. "I would do anything to avoid being treated like a cipher, which is what they aim for when they put you in a military uniform and demand conformity."

His hostility notwithstanding, Marlon was still Bud, the kid who acted out, then suffered pangs of guilt. One day, startled by a loud slap on the shoulder, he turned around and decked the cadet who did it. Having made his statement, Marlon promptly apologized. It was the old Tom Sawyer back-and-forthing again, going out for football, then slacking off when it came to practice and injuring his knee in the process; joining the school band as a drummer, then dropping out because rehearsals were so boring; making a try for academic excellence only to fall behind in his schoolwork when his attention wandered. Meantime, he kept hoping for the reinforcements that never came. In his letters home he kept appealing to Marlon senior and Dodie: "Which one of you died, and which one of you has broken your right arm?" The questions were ignored; there were no return letters.

Bud's deteriorating performance was accented with a never-ending series of pranks and capers, ranging from putting Limburger in light fixtures to pouring Vitalis, a liquid hair tonic, over the transom of a hated master and igniting it. From the other side of the door, the mischief-maker was pleased to hear the man frantically beating out the eerie blue flames with his jacket.

The news about Pearl Harbor failed to stop Bud's showy defiance. Classes buzzed with stories of the Japanese sneak attack, the fall of

Wake Island, and the declaration of war after President Roosevelt's "Day of Infamy" speech. Most of the students were gung-ho about becoming commissioned officers, leading enlisted men into battle. Bud rankled at the thought. At a meeting to discuss America's entry into the war, the school's chief administrator informed him that he was in the very same chair where Marlon senior had sat in 1918, when it was announced that the United States had entered the Great War. The implication was clear: Pranks were all very well for adolescence, but this was a deadly serious time. Ergo, Marlon junior must buckle down, get passing grades, and go for a commission in the army.

"Occasionally," Bud remembered, "one of the masters would say something like, 'Marlon, if you ever stop being a smart-ass, you might make a good officer.' " At those instances, he was shrewd enough to keep his mouth shut. But during the school week he continued his wiseguy capers, sticking paper clips in classroom door locks so that no one could enter; faking a temperature to get out of class by rubbing a thermometer on his trousers until the friction made the mercury rise to 103; locking instructors in their apartments by tying a rope to the front doorknobs of two opposing apartments. The doors opened in, so neither could get out. ("Since they usually lived on the second floor," Bud noted merrily, "they couldn't get out a window, so they would be prisoners in their own rooms and there would be no class that day.")

Only two activities truly appealed to the youth. Because of poor marks and a general waywardness, he spent an inordinate amount of time in study hall. There he would ostentatiously take out a textbook, notebook, and pencil. To whatever proctor was on hand, he furrowed his brow and bit his lip as if deep in scholarly work—while he quietly added to the list of some 125 song lyrics his mother had taught him. One volume he did pore over. In an English class, the instructor had provided an introduction to Shakespeare. Unlike most of the boys, Bud already knew some of the texts, thanks to his mother's collection back in Libertyville. But during these study hall periods he awoke to the language, mouthing the words silently, learning their rhythms, and memorizing selected passages. His self-dramatizing melancholia fit well with sonnet twenty-nine:

> When, in disgrace with Fortune and men's eyes,
> I all alone beweep my outcast state,
> And trouble deaf heaven with my bootless cries . . .

As it did with Marc Antony's funeral oration:

> This was the most unkindest cut of all;
> For when the noble Caesar saw him stab,
> Ingratitude, more strong than traitors' arms,
> Quite vanquish'd him: then burst his mighty heart . . .

When Bud was in a lighter mood he perused copies of *National Geographic,* kept on the hall shelves. One morning an article about the Society Islands in the South Pacific caught his attention. He was instantly entranced by Tahiti and its people—most of all, he remembered, "by the expressions on their faces. They were happy, *unmanaged* faces. No manicured expressions, just kind, open maps of contentment." To the boy who regarded himself as a captive in an American Devil's Island, Tahiti appeared to Bud as "at least a sanctuary, and at best nirvana."

4

Besides the forced silence of study hall, young Brando found two other places of fulfillment. The first was the movie house in Faribault. The war, mentioned only obliquely before December 7, 1941, in such films as Alfred Hitchcock's *Foreign Correspondent* and Charlie Chaplin's *The Great Dictator,* had become a studio staple. *Bataan, Commandos Strike at Dawn, A Guy Named Joe, Hitler's Children, Sahara, This Is the Army, Watch on the Rhine*—it would be hard for Marlon to keep track of them all. *Mrs. Miniver,* the story of a stiff-upper-lip British housewife struggling through the Blitz, would earn an Academy Award: "This is the war of all the people. It must be fought in factories, fought in the hearts of every man and child who loves freedom. This is the people's war. This is our war." The following year *Casablanca* would offer its own message: "I'm no good at being noble, but it doesn't take much to see that the problems of three little people don't amount to a hill of beans in this crazy world."

During the war years, casting directors had no trouble finding actors to play German malefactors; hundreds of refugees—some of them Jews hounded out of Europe—found jobs playing Nazi officers and bureaucrats. Japanese villainy was another matter. Internment camps had been set up in Washington, Oregon, and California, and Japanese Americans in those states were rounded up and placed behind barbed wire. Using these citizens was of course impermissible. A *Time* article, assuming correctly that most of its readers couldn't tell the difference among Asian peoples, instructed: "Japanese walk stiffly erect, hard-heeled, Chinese, more relaxed, have an easy gait. The Chinese expression is likely to be more kindly, placid, open; the Japanese more positive, dogmatic, arrogant. Japanese are hesitant, nervous in conversation, laugh loudly at the wrong time." The advisory didn't help much. And so it was that the Chinese Richard Loo and Sen Yung and the Korean Philip Ahn found steady work as evildoers from the Land of the Rising Sun.

Even cartoons played their part in the war effort: Popeye starred in *Scrap the Japs,* croaking out his motto: "I never seen a Jap that wasn't yeller." The Donald Duck cartoon *Der Fuehrer's Face* mocked Adolf Hitler with a song: "When der Fuehrer says, 'Ve is der master race,'/ We HEIL! [Honk] HEIL! [Honk] Right in der Fuehrer's face." And in *Coal Black and De Sebben Dwarfs,* a jazzed-up parody of Disney's *Snow White,* an obese black queen hires hitmen to knock off the pretty heroine. The thugs are so lethal, she brags, they "kill Japs for free."

Officially, the U.S. government issued statements that the enemy was not the German or Japanese or Italian people. It was their leadership that Americans should despise and fight. The facts on the ground were different; there, caricature and exaggeration took the place of reason and history. For a majority of young Americans, the combined efforts of the Office of War Information and the filmmakers were persuasive and long-lasting. Yet even at a tender age, Marlon was not so easily manipulated. He lumped the government and his teachers and his father into one large group whose members could not be trusted. On one level he enjoyed the wartime films as entertainment. On another, they made him deeply uncomfortable, although he could not quite determine why. His racial sensitivities were just developing, and the country's patriotic fervor pushed them to the background. They would not remain there for long.

Marlon's other refuge was the living room of Earle Wagner, one of the academy's English masters. A provincial flaneur and posturing intellectual, the fortysomething Wagner liked to be addressed as "Duke," affected an aristocratic mien, and outfitted himself in well-tailored British tweeds. He had a rakish expression and hinted at flirtations and liaisons with local women, but may well have been a tightly closeted homosexual. Wagner encouraged students to come to his apartment, a place he decorated like a fin-de-siècle salon, complete with Oriental rugs and matching leather-bound copies of works by Dickens and Thackeray. The master had a plummy voice and enjoyed reciting soliloquies to his impressionable audience. And every now and again he allowed one of the boys to have a shot at the Bard's speeches and poems. Bud knew several of those by heart, and impressed the master right away. Other boys also struck Wagner as capable, and the best of them he cast in school productions. Bud was given a major role in *A Message from Khafu*, a one-act play based on the story of King Tut. The audience applauded him vigorously, and Wagner was so pleased he wrote the Brandos a letter praising his protégé. In it he suggested a different kind of education for their boy, one that might take place at Shattuck—or might not. If he stayed he would have to take several subjects over again (thanks to the radio, Bud could fake a Gallic accent, for example, but French grammar was beyond his competence). Yet being left back would have its advantages; a new regimen might "strike at the root of the boy's weakness and give him the work he is best qualified for."

As he read and reread the letter, Marlon senior wondered what that work might be. What in the living hell was this teacher getting at? *Acting?* That was no profession for a grown man. Furthermore, if Bud was forced to take subjects over again, he would have to stay at Shattuck another semester or two, at prohibitive cost. No, Wagner's proposal was completely unacceptable. The lad would straighten up and fly right, and he would do so now. Dodie disagreed with every word her husband said, but bided her time. On Thanksgiving weekend, when both parents visited Shattuck, she sought out Wagner and demanded an answer. Did her son really have a gift for the stage, or was the master just trying to make things easier for an obvious misfit? Wagner maintained that Bud had evidenced a real talent for the performing arts, a knack for reproducing other people's attitudes and intonations. The raw youth would need training, of course; he lacked the requisite polish. That appraisal was all Dodie needed to hear.

Soon afterward she and her son took a private walk on the school grounds. While they strolled she made her case. Bud might as well face it: Academics were not for him. A military institution was of course the hardest of all places, but he was unlikely to do well at *any* school except one—acting school. Nothing to be ashamed of; it was probably in the blood. Look at Tiddy: She was in New York seeking a career on Broadway. Frances was there, too, pursuing her interest in art. Dodie asked her son to think about his future, about the possibilities that had to be seized now, before his number came up in the draft.

The trouble was, Dodie didn't feel strong enough to argue the case with her husband, a man disdainful of "culture" in all its forms. In *Anti-intellectualism in American Life*, Richard Hofstadter points out the suspicion in which artists and thinkers were held by middle America in the first half of the twentieth century: They were " 'man-milliners,' deficient in masculinity." And in his study *American Manhood*, historian E. Anthony Rotundo points out an irony that occurred at the time Bud was coming of age. The stigma of homosexuality "gained insidiousness from the modern notion that sexual 'inversion' was not a beastly moral failure or an unnatural visitation, but a natural condition that might be lurking in anyone, regardless of the individual's purity or moral vigilance." This added urgency to a man's desire to distinguish himself from the homosexual. "The more he feared he might be one of the stigmatized group, the more he needed to prove himself a man." Any hint of androgyny in either behavior or occupation was to be squelched at all cost. So it should have come as no surprise when Dodie brought up the subject of acting school, and her husband exploded: "I'm not going to have this professor make a fairy out of my son, not when I'm having to shell out fifteen hundred dollars in tuition money to make a real man out of him. Not someone who sits in front of a mirror applying women's makeup. Not some faggot who shakes his ass in front of an audience every night." The cadet would goddamned well graduate from Shattuck and then go on to a career in business or the military.

Bud sighed like an artist but obeyed like a son. His parents returned to Libertyville in hostile silence. Marlon senior went on the road and Dodie returned to the solace of scotch and bourbon. By the time spring rolled around Bud was as lost as he had ever been. His grades had slipped yet again. He had engaged in fistfights, committed more pranks, violated curfews to spend time with local girls, including two school maids. His demerits had piled up and he was now on the point of expulsion. The only letup came during his performance in the school production of a British drama called *Four on the Heath*. Bud, as the tragic hero who commits suicide in the final scene, spoke his lines with a high-toned English accent, remarkable in one so young and untraveled. Again, radio and movies had been ideal instructors.

During this semester Tiddy married an aspiring actor named Don Hammer. The two of them briefly visited Libertyville—the last stop before Don entered the air force. Tiddy bore good tidings: She had just landed a job as an understudy in a touring company of the Broadway hit *Claudia*. From here on she would be using her real name, Jocelyn Brando. From his Minnesota outpost Bud heard the news and began to fantasize: If Tiddy could do it, why not him? Crucially homesick, and painfully school-sick, he made up his mind to fail once and for all. A regular army colonel had come to Shattuck looking for candidates he could mold into combat-ready officers. He had been told about Bud Brando, a troubled kid who might yet have the makings of a leader. On the colonel's orders, a blue team and a red team were set up, each instructed to outmaneuver the other in a wooded area. Bud was put in charge of the blue team. The officer waited until all the troopers were outfitted with packs and rifles, then posited a battlefield situation. Their battalion leader has been killed. What now?

Bud said that he would ask the company commander.

And if that man had also been killed?

Well, what about the squad leader?

He, too, had been felled by a bullet.

"Sir," replied Bud, "I guess I'd run like hell."

That reply was considered rank insubordination, especially since it had been overheard by all the cadets. Bud was put on probation and confined to quarters. Shattuck used the honor system, and the detainee lost no time in escaping. He was spotted in town, hauled back into school, and informed that this was his last AWOL. Official expulsion followed the next day.

Now that mischief could no longer be made, Bud experienced another sudden and deep remorse. He went from room to room, bidding apologetic farewells to his classmates. Arriving at Duke Wagner's door, he expected a chewing-out, or at least a lecture on dignity and duty. Instead the master offered assurance: "Don't worry, Marlon. Everything will be all right. I know the world is going to hear from you."

Almost fifty years later, the teacher's words still resonated. "My eyes filled with tears," Marlon Brando, Jr., noted. "I put my head on his shoulder and couldn't stop sobbing. It was the only time anyone had ever been so loving and so directly encouraging and concerned about me."

He would not find similar encouragement when he came home in disgrace. Bud was in the process of unpacking when Marlon senior dismissed him as a failure in everything he undertook. Dodie tried to intervene; as usual she was unfocused and sometimes incoherent. Bud had just begun to look for a summer job when a letter arrived from Shattuck. The outcast had turned out to be more popular than he ever imagined. The student body had gone on strike on behalf of Marlon Brando, Jr.—and they had won. "The administration have agreed to let you return to Shattuck and make up the time you lost in summer school."

It was signed by every cadet in the battalion. Dodie cried when she read the letter, but Marlon senior grumbled that it was undeserved, and Bud knew that it was too late. He sent back a letter thanking his classmates and informing them that while he was grateful for their support he had chosen a different path. This was mere bravado. He had no idea where to turn or what to do. It was 1943. He had turned nineteen in April and would soon be subject to the draft. Some 90,000 German troops had surrendered at Stalingrad. Guadalcanal had been taken back from the Japanese. What the hell, Bud figured—I might as well volunteer, like almost all the other guys my age in Libertyville. He went down to his local draft board and tried to sign up. During the routine physical exam, a doctor discovered Bud's trick knee. He said it was all too likely to collapse during basic training, to say nothing of battle conditions. The volunteer was marked 4-F and shown the door.

"Is there anything else you could fail at?" Marlon senior demanded. With a renewed sense of shame and inadequacy Bud took a job digging trenches and laying tiles for thirty-five dollars a week—a humbling assignment, but all that was available to a youth without a high school diploma. In May Marlon senior sat Bud down, reminding him that ten, twenty years from now he might still be doing scut work because he had no training for anything else. Was there something, *anything*, that interested him?

To his father's astonishment Bud did express some ambition after all. He said he wanted to go to New York City and take acting lessons. By now, Marlon senior was ready to make a concession. The men who were in plays and movies couldn't all be fairies. There was the womanizing Errol Flynn, accused of rape by a couple of teenagers and finally acquitted in court—but not before the phrase "in like Flynn" was coined. And what about Charlie Chaplin? There was a heterosexual if ever there was one. This very year he was on trial for violating the Mann Act, taking a woman named Joan Barry across the California state line for "immoral purposes." The revelations of their love life were scrupulously followed by the tabloids, with much attention given to Charlie's remark, made when he was stark naked, "You know, Joan, I look something like Peter Pan, don't you think?"

On the other hand, Senior could hardly place his awkward, ungainly son in the category of ladies' man. At best he would be somebody's blind date, the kind of guy who takes the fat girl to the prom. Ever derisive, Marlon père told Marlon fils, "Take a look in the mirror and tell me if anyone would want to see a yokel like you on the stage." There was no reply to that, only a sullen expression and Dodie's counterargument that at least the boy was motivated. Later she slipped Bud some money. That, together with his savings from the job, was enough for an eastbound ticket.

"As I got out of the cab delivering me from Pennsylvania Station to Frances's apartment in Greenwich Village," Bud remembered, "I was sporting a bright red fedora that I thought was going to knock everyone dead." On the street, nobody gave him a second look. Crushed, he took the stairs two at a time, catching his breath at the top landing while he waited for his sister to answer the door. In a lifetime of traveling, Marlon Brando would never make a longer journey than the one he had just taken from Libertyville to New York.

1943–1946

This Puppy Thing

1

After Adolf Hitler was elected chancellor of Germany in 1933, a group of artists and intellectuals saw that they had no future in Europe. The most prescient, best connected, and luckiest made their way from Europe to America. The majority of these exiles set down roots in New York, arguing in cafés, dominating ateliers, teaching courses in philosophy, economics, art, and theater at whatever institutions granted them a salaried position.

Foremost among the places of higher learning was the New School for Social Research on Twelfth Street, in the heart of Greenwich Village. Funded by the heiress Dorothy Payne Whitney, the institution was established in 1919 and staffed by such prominent American academics as philosopher John Dewey and economist Thorstein Veblen. But by the early 1940s it had become an outpost of refugees—to such a degree that wags referred to it as the Austro-Hungarian Empire. The school represented a broad spectrum of political and economic thought: Hannah Arendt lectured there; so did John Maynard Keynes and Karen Horney, Wilhelm Reich and Leo Strauss. The man who ran its drama department was Erwin Piscator, a radical German director who had collaborated with Bertolt Brecht on "epic theater." Working together, they had broken down the "fourth wall" separating the actors from the audience, exhorting ticket holders to go out into the streets and bring politics into their everyday lives. The two had been well on their way to transforming the European stage when the Nazis took over. Both were resolutely anti-Fascist, but Piscator had an additional reason to flee: His wife, the dancer Maria Ley, was Jewish. They entered the United States in the late 1930s. Brecht headed for California, where he wrote scenarios for B pictures like *Hangmen Also Die!* Piscator disdained Hollywood; Manhattan was his kind of town.

The young Brandos felt the same way. E. B. White's insight pertained to all three of them: The true New York is the "New York of the person who was born somewhere else and came to New York in quest of something . . . the city of final destination, the city that is a goal." Frannie had settled down in Greenwich Village, where she studied painting with local artists. Franz Kline, Willem de Kooning, Barnett Newman, Mark Rothko, and others were just beginning their careers in the downtown bohemia; for a painter it was the place to see and be seen. As critic Lionel Abel put it, the Villagers didn't know whether an artist or thinker was right. They only judged by one thing: "To be interesting was to be right. Certainly to be uninteresting was to be wrong." Frannie made sure she and her work were never less than provocative.

Jocelyn, already embarked on an acting career, lived in the Village, where she made a great show of independence. But she kept an eye on her kid brother, and, through letters and phone calls, assured Marlon senior and Dodie with a straight face that their son was dying to take courses in performance and movement. The school where she had studied, the American Academy of Dramatic Arts, was perhaps too rigid for Bud, but she had heard wonderful things about Erwin Piscator's classes. And the professor was only one of many distinguished teachers. On his New School faculty were Herbert Berghof, a German exile who had worked with the great impresario Max Reinhardt; John Gassner, an anthologist and historian of modern theater; and a second-generation actress named Stella Adler. The place sounded very stimulating and different; just right for Marlon junior. The senior Marlon felt ill at ease about bankrolling one more scholastic failure. At the same time he was impressed by the fact that Jocelyn had already found acting jobs. Finally he gave in. For a while at least, he would foot the bill for Bud's tuition at the New School.

During the delicate negotiations Jocelyn had been unfailingly positive about her brother. She never mentioned his intoxicated condition. Bud was not high on booze; he was drunk on New York. All he had done since his arrival was wander the streets, subwaying up to Harlem at night, then sleeping all morning, either at Frannie's place or on a bench in Washington Square Park. Others complained about wartime shortages; not Marlon. What did he care that cigarettes were in short supply? Or that makers of adult beverages had diverted much of their output to industrial alcohol? Or that you had to wait on long lines to get meat and butter? He had appetites for other things. One of his sharpest cravings was a need to meet people unlike himself, with different vocabularies, different approaches to life, different skins. Back in Illinois, his jazz idols had been the white drummers Gene Krupa and Buddy Rich. But one night he stepped into a ballroom on Broadway. As he remembered it, "I almost lost my mind with excitement when I discovered Afro-Cuban music." Most of the people on the floor were Puerto Ricans, and they moved in a manner he had never seen before. It took his breath away, and he thought about becoming a modern dancer. After hanging out at the club, he changed his mind, bought a set of conga drums, and considered making a living as a percussionist in a Latin band. Then he went up to Harlem. There had been a race riot the year before, but it seemed to have been forgotten by the residents. The streets were filled, and the nightclubs presented musicians with something new to say. It was there that Marlon heard the first strains of bebop played by fresh talents like Charlie "Bird" Parker and Dizzy Gillespie, artists on their way up. Miles Davis was a Juilliard student in 1944; he described the scene: "The way it went down at Minton's was you brought your horn and hoped that Bird and Dizzy would invite you to play with them up on stage. People would watch for clues from Bird and Dizzy, and if they smiled when you finished playing, then that meant your playing was good."

Intrigued by the heady atmosphere, Marlon kept returning to Harlem. On a summer evening he took his conga drums up to a small nightclub on 132nd Street and asked the proprietor if he could sit in with the band. His request was met with stone silence. He sat at a table, ordered a drink, and listened respectfully. He spotted a young black woman leaning against a far wall. What followed was a mix of fresh sexual desire and old yearning. The woman seemed dislocated, unhappy, like one of those sad girls of his childhood—the ones he would date because he felt sorry for them.

But along with these feelings was something entirely new: the wild idea of an interracial romance, unthinkable back in Libertyville. He made a welcoming gesture to the woman. She sidled over to his table and introduced herself as Sugar. Did he want to dance? As Marlon put his arm around her waist he noticed a man staring at them: "a black icebox with eyes like two .45's." The icebox introduced himself as Leroy. Marlon whispered to the girl. He suggested that they go downtown, drop by some places where they could hear bands, maybe dance a little.

She was agreeable. Marlon put some money down and went to the cloakroom. As he put on his coat, he heard a scuffle. A body flew past him horizontally and slammed into a pile of chairs and tables. It was Sugar. He pivoted on his right foot, opened the door, and headed south down Broadway, running hard, dodging autos at intersections, heading for the subway stop in the white neighborhood at 110th Street. He took the stairway down to the platform four steps at a time. After what seemed an eternity he heard a clattering of many footsteps on the same stairway just as he boarded the train. No pursuers got on with him. But what about the other cars?

The terrified nineteen-year-old had a nightmare vision of himself lying in a pool of blood. There was no way to quiet his heart. At Fifty-ninth Street he rushed off the subway and looked around him. Marlon was the only person to exit. He felt chagrined by his out-of-towner's racial fears and misgivings. And he knew he would have to return to Harlem, not once but many, many times. For in these few hours Marlon had become besotted with what fashionable academics called "the Other." These uptown people were of a race not his own. In his mind they were darker, wiser, more open to experience. Unlike whites, particularly whites from Middle America, they seemed in close touch with their bodies and souls; they had a profound, instinctive feeling for the rhythms of life. He had first attributed these romantic notions to Ermi, the Brandos' half-Indonesian housekeeper. Now he distributed them to any and all black folks, young, dark-skinned women most of all. That appeal would last a lifetime.

To visit the jazz clubs, as well as to pay his share of the rent, Marlon needed money. He took odd jobs, running an elevator at Best & Co. and working as a hamburger slinger. Acting lessons were the farthest thing from his mind. He claimed to be smitten with Frannie's neighbor Estrellita Rosa Maria Consuelo Cruz—he remembered her as "olive-skinned, fetching, extremely artistic and a great cook." Then he took up with another neighbor, Celia Webb. He moved into her apartment for a while, but the truth is that he was only in love with freedom. Jocelyn brought her brother back to earth: He could go to school on his dad's money or he could turn into a vagrant with no training and zero future. There were no alternate choices. He got the message and registered at the New School as a full-time student.

Despite the freedom he savored in New York, the need for parental recognition still gnawed at Bud, and he continued to write home with a pathetic mix of schoolboy excitement and anxiety. He described a "crazy" New York in detail, went on about his efforts to find an answer to the meaning of life—and then, to assure his parents that he was still a good, open-faced midwestern kid, he concluded,

> I'm going to miss the fall at home and the apples and leaves and smells and stuff. I've got a lump in my throat now just thinking about it.

Heartfelt, no doubt, but also prompted by the prevailing wind of nostalgia sweeping the country. In this third year of global conflict, films spent an inordinate amount of time looking in the rearview mirror: *Meet Me in St. Louis, National Velvet, Gaslight.* And popular songs earned big royalties by lamenting the wartime situation of men without women and women without men—"Don't Get Around Much Anymore," "Don't Sit Under the Apple Tree (with Anyone Else but Me)," "Long Ago and Far Away," "Sentimental Journey": "Never thought my heart could be so yearny,/ Why did I decide to roam?/ Gotta take that sentimental journey,/ Sentimental journey home."

Whatever wistful feelings Bud felt about home and hearth—and they were few—vanished upon his entry to the building on Twelfth Street. Not exactly a warm, welcoming place, but a serious one. Here, parental demands were replaced by professional ones. Piscator, a martinet with gray hair, cobalt-blue eyes, and a harsh German accent, insisted on an austere, worshipful attitude toward the theater. He hated Broadway pap. In his view, the war was responsible—pining and escapism had become the opiates of the people. The big musicals, for example, were trivia personified. *Lady in the Dark,* boasting Ira Gershwin's first lyrics since the death of his brother George, concerned the psyche of a neurotic female editor; *The Vagabond King* and *The Merry Widow* were operettas celebrating a vanished epoch; *One Touch of Venus,* with a score by Kurt Weill and Ogden Nash, didn't have a thought in its head, nor did a revue, *Artists and Models,* starring Jane Froman and a former standup comedian named Jackie Gleason. Piscator pointed out that when the new team of Richard Rodgers and Oscar Hammerstein II came up with their breakthrough musical, *Oklahoma!,* they made sure to focus on the there and then, not the here and now. Like everyone else, the professor was amused by the lyrics for "Everything's Up to Date in Kansas City," with an awed hick singing about the fabulous mechanical improvements he has just seen with his own eyes. These include gas buggies that seem to go by themselves, a Bell telephone that allows people to communicate for miles around, a bawdy burlesque theater, a skyscraper that towers seven stories high, and best of all, heated privies.

But the smile froze on the professor's face if he caught an acting student going for easy laughs the way they did uptown at the St. James Theatre. Piscator continually reminded his acolytes that their workplace was called the *New* School for a reason. There was nothing like it anywhere in the United States. Acting was treated as an all-encompassing vocation. Classes began at ten in the morning and frequently ran well into the night. There were lectures, workshops, and seminars in movement and dance, fencing, makeup, psychology, and history, as well as lessons in diction and performance. Word had gotten out about the drama department, and applications came from as far away as Oregon and Maine. The management was not interested in schleppers; every student had to show some ability, and Bud's class was an especially gifted one. In the group were Elaine Stritch, Harry Belafonte, Shelley Winters, Rod Steiger, and Kim Stanley.

Predictably, Bud had a difficult time with Piscator's rigid approach. Almost immediately he started to do skillful impressions of the professor behind his back, portraying him as Hitler to an audience of tittering students. Word got back to the lampooned, and the nineteen-year-old might well have washed out in his first few weeks had it not been for the guidance of a teacher more to his liking: Stella Adler. He had never met anyone remotely like her. No one had.

Now in her early forties, Stella could be just as imperious as Piscator, albeit with a different style and manner. Greasepaint was as familiar to her as lipstick. She had been born into the most prominent family in the Yiddish theater and maintained a lofty, aristocratic mien wherever she was. Once, it was said, as she was being shown a frock at Bergdorf Goodman's, the saleslady asked if she was British. "No," Stella replied frostily, "just affected." Her mother, Sara, had been a leading diva, her father, Jacob, the most celebrated leading man on Second Avenue. In 1903 he became the first Jew to play Shylock on the New York stage, appearing in the Second Avenue version of *The Merchant of Venice*. His forceful interpretation electrified the Lower East Side—but then, it was supposed to. What he could not have predicted was the clamor outside the Jewish neighborhood. In a reference to the nineteenth-century actor/impresario, *Theater* magazine dubbed Jacob "The Bowery Garrick," and a Broadway producer was so impressed he brought the star uptown. In this unique production every actor except Jacob spoke Shakespearean English. He gave his interpretation in Yiddish, just as he had done on the Lower East Side. *Merchant* was showered with raves. Adler never appeared again on Broadway, but it didn't matter. He had vaulted the boundaries of the ghetto and shown his children the way to escape its psychological and physical confinements. Celia, a daughter by his second wife, worked onstage and in film. Luther, a son by Sara, Jacob's third (and last) wife, became a major Broadway and Hollywood character actor, and his sister Stella outdid them all, not as a player but as the most influential acting teacher of her time.

In the 1930s Stella joined the powerhouse Group Theatre and eventually married one of its founders, Harold Clurman. But she never felt comfortable with the Group's politics ("I could live in any communist country if I could be its queen" was one of her oft-quoted statements). Her objection to the Old Left was based on aesthetics rather than politics. Historian Richard H. Rovere, very familiar with the party line of the 1930s, was to say later on that the American intellectuals who fell hardest for communism were people "not of aristocratic tastes in art but of tastes at once conventional and execrable. The cultural tone they set was deplorable because it was metallic and strident." In brief, not the sort of people with whom Stella could be comfortable. She felt just as uneasy with the company's worshipful but distant view of Konstantin Stanislavski. In 1934 Stella had sailed to Europe to meet the great Russian acting teacher, found him in Paris, and asked for lessons. He preferred to address theater companies and groups, but made an exception for this American firebrand. She was the last actor to study with him privately, and she let everybody know it.

Upon her return to New York Stella ignited a feud with Lee Strasberg, Stanislavski's primary advocate in America. Strasberg believed that actors should examine their pasts—dredging up wounds, joys, and passions and reproducing them onstage. Stella felt that this was a misreading of the master. Actors had to range beyond their emotional memories (the Strasberg method called for summoning up the loss of a childhood pet, for example, when a character is called upon to cry). She asked her students to find a new kind of realism: "Don't act. Behave." Above all, performers had to pay attention to the text, plumbing its deepest meanings, becoming the playwright's collaborator. In her celebrated textbook *The Art of Acting,* Stella insists that the actor start "with words, but then must go beneath them. Texts must be examined. They have a secret under and around the words. An actor is one who uncovers and incorporates the secrets of words." To her, anything less would be autobiography masking as interpretation.

Stella soon found the Group Theatre's mix of global and office politics unbearable. She quit New York for Hollywood, altering her name to Stella Ardler and shortening her nose to a more photogenic size. Her timing could not have been worse. There were plenty of Jewish actors in 1930s Hollywood—Paulette Goddard (née Marion Levy), Sylvia Sidney (Sophia Kosow), John Garfield (Jacob Garfinkle), Edward G. Robinson (Emmanuel Goldenberg), Melvyn Douglas (Melvyn Hesselberg), and many others. In every case, however, they played against their ethnicity, and their backgrounds were generally unknown to the public. Not so Ms. Ardler, whose Yiddish-theater background was a matter of record, and who in any case was not the leading-lady type. She appeared in two films, *Love on Toast,* playing opposite a newcomer, John Payne, who got all the notices; and *Shadow of the Thin Man,* a vehicle hoisted by the charm of William Powell and Myrna Loy. Again Stella was pushed to the background. She talked herself into an office job at MGM, where she functioned as an assistant producer on B films. After six years she realized that she had made a wrong career move and headed back to New York to perform and direct. But it was when she joined the faculty of the New School as a temporary instructor that she found the role of a lifetime. Here she gave fiery readings of the Stanislavski approach, delivering lectures that turned into showpieces. She invited her students to come backstage in her memory: "My first feeling of self, my first true consciousness, was not in a home, not in a room, but in a dressing room." This was Jacob's true dwelling place. "One almost did not dare to penetrate the loneliness there. The loneliness came from my father, putting on his makeup. There was a special quality in this choosing of his colors and placing them, like a painter, one next to the other, an almost religious sense of something being created.

"I watched this creation. I watched a man change into another man."

The audience of students sat enthralled as she described her childhood, her career, her approach to the art of acting. "She challenged the imagination," recalled Shelley Winters. "Above all else, Stella never wanted us to bore an audience. That would be the greatest of sins."

At first Bud seemed a most unlikely candidate for her discourses. Always trying to set himself apart from the crowd, he noticed that his fellow students dressed with great care. With his usual perversity he came to class in ripped jeans, a dirty T-shirt, and well-worn sneakers.

"Who's the vagabond?" asked Stella on the first day. They circled each other warily for a month but he was soon her favorite. For one thing, whatever the assignment, he performed it with gusto and originality. In a famous instance, everyone in class was ordered to act like a chicken after it has learned its coop is about to be bombed. While the rest of the class clucked frenetically and searched for shelter, Bud calmly crouched in a corner, miming a hen calmly laying eggs. Asked whether he was just being different for the sake of being different, he replied, "No, I'm just doing what a hen would do under the circumstances. What the hell does a chicken know about war?" Stella beamed. Yes, that was exactly how a hen would behave. The bird would do what it had always done, what nature had programmed it to do.

Over the next few weeks Bud did impressions of cats, dogs, people, even inanimate objects like a cash register, bugging his eyes out to represent the numbers and presenting his palms as the drawer, always to the amusement of the class and the pleasure of the instructor. "One afternoon," Elaine Stritch remembered, "Stella told us to come to class with an impersonation. The next time we met, I impersonated Stella— all her mannerisms, her walk, her posture. I got a lot of laughs, Stella loved it, and I thought, No one can top this. Then I heard the scratchy sound of a record. It began to play 'Clang, clang, clang went the trolley,' Judy Garland's song from *Meet Me in St. Louis*. And on came Marlon in drag, boobs, shaved legs, the whole thing. He was gorgeous. And he was hilarious. He was absolutely the best, that day and every day. Marlon's going to class to learn the Method was like sending a tiger to jungle school."

Physically, Marlon was coming into his own just then; his hair had darkened and his brooding and unusual presence seemed to fill up whatever room he entered. Stella was in her early forties, married to Clurman but ever-flirtatious and proud of her appeal to younger men. She began to address Bud familiarly as "my darling," and "Marlon, dear," and it was not long before she invited him to her apartment on West Fifty-fourth Street. There, over time, he met Jacob's widow and the rest of the Adler children, and stepped into a worldly society far beyond anything he had ever experienced. "One day," Stella told the family, "this puppy thing will be America's finest actor." Marlon was Bud no longer. He made some passes at his teacher; she shrugged them off. This provoked him all the more. But he was not in love with her. He was in love with something she represented.

Eastern European Jewish refugees, coupled with landsmen from Germany who had been in the United States for generations, were energetically remaking the city. Mayor Fiorello La Guardia was half Jewish; Herbert Lehman, the grandson of southern peddlers, was governor of the state. The big department stores, Macy's and Gimbels, were owned and operated by Jews. The musical theater was predominantly Jewish, from Richard Rodgers and Oscar Hammerstein II to Jerome Kern to the Gershwins and Irving Berlin. Paul Muni, a stage and film star, had made the leap from the Yiddish theater to Broadway. Uptown at City College, brilliant Jews argued the world, Bolsheviks versus Trotskyites versus New Dealers—while an ocean away Jews were being slaughtered in Nazi death camps, and this, too, was the subject of debate. Last year such subjects were terra incognita to Marlon. Now he was immersed in Jewish culture, in discussions and arguments about politics, art, literature, love, sex, history. For a youth from Omaha and Illinois, this, too, was the Other. As he was taken with black jazzmen and dark-skinned women, he became philo-Semitic in the company of Stella and the members of her circle. Marlon was permanently captivated by their insatiable curiosity and their dazzling conversation. No topic was forbidden to these people; everyone had an opinion and was encouraged to express it.

Heady stuff to a young man still in his second decade of life. Looking back, he felt himself "raised by largely these Jews. I lived in a world of Jews. They were my teachers; they were my employers. They were my friends. They introduced me to a world of books and ideas that I didn't know existed." Once admitted to their circle, he realized the depth of his ignorance about art, politics, philosophy. He listened at first, then began asking questions. The circle who met at the Adler apartment became his college and, in time, his graduate school. The members of that exclusive group "gave me an appetite to learn everything."

His appetite could take some very odd turns. Darwin Porter's *Brando Unzipped* is a derogatory and credulous examination of Marlon's amatory adventures in New York. Porter lists numerous romances with young actresses, some proven, some not, as well as rumored homosexual liaisons. One, Porter writes, was with a Shattuck classmate who visited Brando in Manhattan, the other with playwright Clifford Odets. According to Robert Lewis, a cofounder of the Actors Studio, "Clifford broke down and confessed everything to me about the affair. He'd fallen for Marlon, and he thought Marlon loved him back. But he'd failed to understand Marlon's mercurial personality." The problem was that "Marlon could be there for you one day, giving you the greatest time of your life, and then he'd be gone the next day. It didn't mean that he was mad at you or even that he found you unfulfilling. In those days, and perhaps for the rest of his life, he was always moving on to some new world to conquer. Perhaps he'd decided that Clifford was never going to write that Broadway play for him." Or perhaps he had to seduce and keep seducing to prove, first to himself and then to the world, that he was not the worthless son Dodie had neglected and Marlon senior had derided for eighteen years.

2

In the spring of 1944, Dodie and Marlon senior separated again. Their avowals had come to nothing: He remained a serial adulterer and she kept on drinking. When the accusations and counteraccusations grew intolerable Dodie packed some belongings and the family Great Dane into a car, slammed the doors, and drove to Manhattan.

At that moment, no greater contrast existed than the one between the bulletins from overseas and the local news from New York City. Allied aircraft were pounding the cities of Leipzig and Russian troops were poised to recapture Odessa and Sevastopol. Hitler ordered the invasion of Hungary but it was clear now that he was playing a losing hand. In the Pacific, General Douglas MacArthur was advancing toward the Philippines. German and Japanese supply lines stretched thin, causing the soldiers to fight with desperate ferocity. Casualties mounted. Rumors said they would rise anew as soon as the Allies mounted their invasion of France. According to the papers it could be a matter of weeks.

On the streets of New York, though, war jitters had almost vanished. Children still took the air-raid drills seriously when a school siren wailed on cue. They herded into wardrobes or ducked under desks until the "All Clear" sounded, just as if they were Londoners undergoing the Blitz. But everyone else just went through the motions of civil defense. Emergency shelters, marked with a luminescent *S*, were ignored by pedestrians, "brownouts"—the dimming of lights in the evening—had become a thing of the past, and the flourishing black market in meat, butter, and gasoline went on undisturbed. It would soon be unnecessary; meat rationing was on its way out. The one constant reminder of World War II was the presence of men in uniform. They were everywhere, crowds of them on the midtown streets, sailors in whites, marines in tunics, soldiers in khaki ogling girls, looking for fun in nightclubs, laughing a little too loud sometimes, kids on their way overseas, probably to action, possibly to injury and death. The butt of comedy was the 4-F, the guy turned down by the Selective Service because of flat feet or asthma. In 1944, the biggest comedy hit was *Hail the Conquering Hero.* The central character was a military reject, unable to serve because of hay fever. The part of Woodrow Truesmith was played by Eddie Bracken, a skilled comedian who specialized in portraying losers. Woodrow has sat out the war in a defense plant far from home, sending letters that suggest he's been a soldier just like his father, a veteran of World War I. A group of marines run into Woodrow and persuade him to return to his little town, getting him up in a uniform complete with medals and accompanying battle stories. He receives a hero's welcome and ends up reluctantly running for mayor before the entire fiction unravels.

It was all very amusing onscreen; to be placed in that position in real life was something else entirely. Movie stars like Clark Gable and James Stewart had enlisted and seen action; heavyweight champion Joe Louis and baseball stars Bobby Feller, Ted Williams, and Joe DiMaggio were in uniform, forcing the major leagues to hire the equivalents of Woodrow Truesmith to play ball, including a squad of superannuated pitchers and a one-armed outfielder. Marlon junior put on his customary mask of bravado and indifference and carried on as before. He was uncomfortable, though, and the stares of military personnel . . . what were they thinking, he wondered, when they saw a well-built, healthy young man walking along without a limp, without a bad eye, without any visible disabilities at all? Maybe he should enlist, get it over with. Maybe he should get out of town, get lost somewhere in the heart of the heart of the country.

And then Dodie showed up. Booking herself into a midtown hotel, she changed clothes and went to call on her children. As far as she was concerned, all three were living in squalor. The following week Dodie signed a lease for a sprawling ten-room apartment on West End Avenue in the Seventies and invited the trio to move in with her, gratis. Money was still not an issue; Marlon senior had agreed to foot the bill—anything to be rid of Dodie for a while. Much to her relief and surprise, they agreed. Jocelyn's husband was overseas and she was raising a small child on her own and was only too glad to have a built-in babysitter. Frannie transferred her easel and art supplies; and Marlon moved his few belongings into yet another part of the flat.

The stage was set for Bohemia West. Dodie welcomed the few people she knew in New York. Her daughters invited their colleagues, and her son regarded the place as a branch of the Travelers Aid Society: Acquaintances, lost souls, girlfriends, classmates were all invited to visit and, if they liked, to stay all night. Dodie's place was sparsely and haphazardly furnished, but at least it was neat. A maid, paid for by Marlon senior, tried valiantly to keep the apartment, in her words, "above dust and dog hairs." Many years later, one of Bud's colleagues at the New School, Janice Mars, remembered the solipsism of that period, when unstable egos fed one another, totally ignoring current events, politics, or anything outside their narrow orbit. "Flouting all the conventions, we were like orphans in rebellion against everything. None of us had emotionally secure family backgrounds, but we gravitated to each other and created a family among ourselves. Orphans of the storm clinging together."

One of those orphans was Wally Cox, Bud's childhood pal from Evanston. The two had run into each other quite by accident, when Bud was out shopping with Frannie. He was trying to persuade his sister to get into a shopping cart so that he could give her a ride around the city. She told him to grow up. He raised his voice. They were just about to get into a heated sibling argument when Cox showed up. The men hadn't seen each other in a dozen years, but Bud immediately recognized the wry little figure. Without a second's pause he remarked casually, "Hello, Wally," as if they had never stopped being neighbors. He complained about his sister's refusal to take a free ride and Cox impulsively jumped into the cart. Abandoning Frannie with the groceries, Bud pushed him down the sidewalk and onto Seventh Avenue, weaving through traffic at insane speeds as taxi drivers applied their brakes and let loose with thunderous invective. As they lurched around town Bud learned that his old friend had been living in New York for months—another 4-F. During that time he had become something of an expert silversmith and craftsman of fine jewelry. His large horn-rimmed glasses and slight frame gave Cox the demeanor of a timid woodland creature, a persona that would be useful to him in the coming years. But it was not the real man. Cox was knowledgeable, witty, acerbic—as verbally threatening as his friend was physically imposing. They resumed their friendship, each supplying what the other lacked.

Even with the advice and counsel of this new pal, Bud relied mainly on his own instincts and a kind of animal grace. He knew he was attractive to women, but, as one female friend wrote to him many years later, "You had a perverse need to humiliate, to see just how far a female would go to indulge you. For you, sex had as much significance as eating a Mars bar or taking a pill." A onetime romance observed, "I felt your power as a palpable aura, a magnetism you knew how to use manipulatively but also protectively."

Bud broadcast a general indifference to women's feelings, but, as in the days of his boyhood excesses, he suffered intermittent pangs of guilt. In time they vanished, and back he would go to the routine of pursuit, conquest, rejection, and remorse. Cox introduced him to a world of literature and once, when he read a passage by Alexander Pope, he took the message personally, slamming the book shut after he read the words:

> Vice is a monster of so frightful mien,
> As to be hated needs but to be seen;
> Yet seen too oft, familiar with her face,
> We first endure, then pity, then embrace.

3

As the summer of 1944 approached, a fresh optimism spread across America. The Allies had rung up a string of spectacular victories: The Marshall Islands were recaptured, the troops of D-Day had smashed through the German defenses, and now General Eisenhower's men were racing toward Paris. Shortages of rubber, nylon, meat, and canned goods gradually eased, and War Production Board members spoke openly of "re-conversion" to peacetime products. *Time* magazine eavesdropped on a barbershop conversation and caught the spirit of the country:

> "Yep," said the man in the second chair. "I got a $10 bet that this little show will be over by Labor Day."
>
> "Well, boys," the big man said, "I guess it's all over now but the shouting. I wouldn't be surprised to see those Heinies fold up tomorrow."
>
> In varying forms, this scene was repeated all over the U.S. last week. The signs were not only in the headlines. Whole communities sniffed the new optimism and reasoned that this would be the last summer for at least the European war.
>
> In some ways it seemed almost like a prewar summer. After two and a half years of war the hardest things to get were Kleenex, Camel cigarettes, and shirts from the laundry.

The euphoria was already part of the city zeitgeist. In *Don't You Know There's a War On?*, a luminous history of the home front during World War II, Richard Lingeman observes that "In the eerily blacked-out Broadway district, patrons queued up outside the clubs, waiting for a table; headwaiters would prowl the line, telling strange faces bluntly that there were no tables and beckoning to old patrons to jump the line and come in." Most of the big spenders were G.I.'s out to impress their dates, along with newly prosperous workers. Owners were only too glad to take their money, but many places had to close because there was a shortage of waiters and busboys. They were willing to hire any-one who could carry a tray, regardless of ability, no matter how young or old. As Lingeman writes, one café owner lamented, "It's getting so I don't even know 5 percent of my customers and 25 percent of my wait-ers." At the "21" Club, a sign over the bar warned: BE COURTEOUS TO OUR HELP; CUSTOMERS WE CAN ALWAYS GET.

Drama students at the New School embodied the spirit of the day; in a burst of exhilaration they lobbied for their own summer theater, collected funds for that purpose, and took a lease on an abandoned venue in Sayville, Long Island. Piscator agreed to go along as director and chaperone. He insisted on decorum, every lady and gentleman in his or her bed every night. This was dismaying to the students, especially the males, who had been planning saturnalias between rehearsals. But as Stritch pointed out, the professor was afraid "there'd be affairs and pregnancies and we'd get thrown out of Sayville. The concern was the local reaction, the townspeople. Remember, this was the 1940s."

To Marlon, of course, the rules about propriety were there to be flouted. In this he was not alone. His fellow predator was another draft-board reject—largely because he had already become a substance abuser with a budding heroin habit. Although he billed himself as Frederick Stevens, his real name was Carlo Fiore. The street kid had been hired for the summer as a company novice. Both men fancied themselves as mad, bad, and dangerous to know, and spent many an off-hour in pursuit of female cast members, ever willing to share their quarries—on certain occasions, if Fiore is to be believed, side by side. The adventures came at a price. The company was under-rehearsed for its first major production, *Twelfth Night*. Few actors knew their parts, and hardly anyone remembered the blocking. To aggravate matters, scores of curious visitors had ferried over from Fire Island to see this new company's first production. On opening night a full house of sophisticated playgoers were on hand. They witnessed a bedlam of forgotten lines and mistimed entrances.

Dodie had come from Manhattan to see her son in the part of Sebastian, the romantic Shakespearean lead. She was mortified by his lack of preparation, his amateurish speeches and movements. The next morning she lit into him: "Take acting seriously or go into business with your father." Before he could reply she walked away. Pouting, Marlon complained to Fiore, "This is the first time I've goofed off in a play, the first time, and she cuts out. Just like that."

He resolved to reform, to learn his lines and maintain a professional routine. The other actors were also chastened by their public failure. Two productions followed, both of them disciplined and well received. In one, *Signarelle,* Marlon played the title role of a simple woodcutter. The second made greater demands on his talent. In *Hannele's Way to Heaven,* Gerhart Hauptmann attempted to reconcile naturalism and fantasy. Described by the German playwright as a "dream-poem," this weighty, symbolic tragedy depicts the imaginings of a workhouse girl. Marlon played a dual role. In one part he was a decrepit schoolteacher tending to the abused child after her suicide attempt; in another he was the shimmering young Jesus of her fantasies. Watching him prepare, Stritch saw the Adlerian instruction come to life: *I watched this creation. I watched a man change into another man.* Onstage Marlon was "absolutely breathtaking; you knew you were in the presence of an acting genius." In the audience was at least one person who agreed with her: Maynard Morris, an MCA agent who prided himself on discovering new talent. He made a note to call the promising young actor after Labor Day.

After these two plays the company caught on. While Dodie forgave her son, Piscator was not so charitable. From the beginning he suspected that young Brando was having his way with the women. Left unchecked, this could sully the company's name and endanger the German's lofty reputation. He was correct about Marlon's amatory habits, but when the impresario made his move he convicted an innocent man. As it happened, he was prowling around the premises and on impulse peeked into a barn. There were Marlon and an apprentice, asleep on the upper level. They were hauled into his office and unceremoniously dismissed. Everyone in the company except Piscator knew the irony of the situation. It was like one of those B-movie mysteries in which a criminal, having slain several people, is framed for a murder he didn't commit. Marlon and the young lady had been innocently practicing their lines and had fallen asleep. She stated that she was in fact still a virgin, but Piscator was deaf to her pleas, and to Marlon's protestations. The accused were gone on the night train out of Sayville.

Back in the city Marlon was invited to call on Maynard Morris. With his customary blend of indifference and curiosity, he dropped by in the company of his sister Jocelyn. Morris made his case. He was a hardselling agent. He had the inside track in New York theater. He had no personal life; every waking effort was dedicated to his clients. At a time when so many young leading men were "out of town," as he delicately put it, he could point an actor in the right direction, get him past the cattle-call auditions and into producers' offices. Marlon was silent throughout the pitch, and might well have walked out had it not been for Jocelyn's insistence. "Sign with Morris!" she demanded, and almost as a lark he put his signature on the contract.

Having made this effort, Marlon went off to Cape Cod for a vacation, only to be summoned back to the city two weeks later. Morris had just the role for him. When Marlon learned what his new agent had in mind, he was crushed: a fifteen-year-old called Nels in the Broadway production of *I Remember Mama*? This after the virtuoso performances in *Hannele*? What was MCA thinking? Dodie knew the book from which the play had been adapted. Kathryn Forbes's bestseller, *Mama's Bank Account*, was a collection of sentimental anecdotes about a family of Norwegian immigrants in bygone San Francisco. To her it was just one more scrap of saccharine nostalgia, like the long-running *Life with Father*, designed to keep America's mind preoccupied. With his mother's judgment ringing in his ears, Marlon blithely and contemptuously went off to audition for Richard Rodgers and Oscar Hammerstein II. *Mama* was the songwriting team's first attempt to produce a straight play, and they were casting with great care. Marlon's reading was, in his own judgment, "a disaster," a jumble of falterings and pauses. Rodgers disdainfully looked away and Hammerstein shrugged. Only the playwright, John Van Druten, evidenced any interest. This Brando person was nonchalant, almost indifferent, and yet he radiated a strange power—the young man seemed to fill up the room. Van Druten was not only the playwright but the director, and thus the final arbiter. His colleagues gave way, and Marlon got the job. "I simply stepped off one lily pad onto another," was the way he put it in later years. It all seemed so easy—and so retrograde, playing an adolescent in a piece of commercial fluff. He took the script home and showed it to Dodie. The dialogue confirmed her worst suspicions: Van Druten had written pulp fiction for the stage. But at least one significant person disagreed. Of all people, Stella Adler, worshipper at the temple of Art, was delighted. She predicted that Marlon would be in a long-running, well-paying hit. He would be making $75 a week, a considerable salary in 1944, when a steak dinner cost $1.50 and a used car could be obtained for $500—if you could wheedle enough gas to run it. And besides, Stella argued, *Mama* would provide excellent exposure. An actor needed to showcase his wares, and Broadway was the biggest window in town. He nodded; his teacher was right and his mother wrong. This was a great shock to him. For all the carefree behavior in school and in New York, for all the pent-up resentment he had about Dodie's irresponsible alcoholism, he was vitally dependent on her approval. This was the first time she had been overruled by someone outside the family. By playing Nels, a role he disliked but needed, Marlon edged out from under the long shadow of home.

4

I Remember Mama opened on October 19, 1944, during the final month of Franklin Delano Roosevelt's fourth presidential campaign. By now the Russians had turned back the German divisions, Guam had been retaken, southern Japan bombed. Victory was within reach, and for men of draft age the pressure was easing. Even so, FDR had to work furiously for votes, attempting to dispel the notion that, at the age of sixty-two, he was too old for office. His opponent, the vigorous forty-two-year-old Thomas E. Dewey, governor of New York State, kept stressing the need for new blood; the government was being run by "tired old men." Admiral Halsey was the same age as the President, the GOP candidate pointed out. Admiral King was sixty-six, Generals MacArthur and Marshall sixty-four. The next generation was hammering at the door.

The polls indicated that Dewey's message would not be enough to defeat a failing but illustrious leader. Yet the governor's subtext had an effect; Americans pondered the coming postwar economy, aware that in every field—with the curious exception of politics—there would be a need for different approaches and new faces. Marlon wavered between profound insecurity and a new self-assurance. For too long he had been told that he would amount to nothing; a Broadway stage could show his inadequacies to the world. On the other hand, Stella had brought him along swiftly, showed him how to move and speak, elevated him not only in his own eyes, but in the eyes of her students, her family, her friends. So perhaps he wasn't so flawed after all. Still, even if the puppy had learned a few tricks, how could the part of Nels help him get on? The Norwegian boy was everything Marlon was not: religious, respectful, decorous. Wasn't this a classic example of miscasting? Or maybe they were casting against the part. Impossible to tell. Well, he would mark time, make the best of a bland part. Easy money.

He soon discovered that it was not so easy. Young Marlon was used to novices and students more or less his own age; *Mama* was peopled with veterans like Mady Christians, a hard-edged, experienced stage and film actress who played the title role, and Oskar Homolka, a scene-stealing pro who could upstage a baby. As a wicked old uncle, Homolka would step on other people's lines, take an eon to roll a cigarette, grumble, wink and smile whenever it pleased him, and generally drive his fellow performers to distraction while he beguiled the audience. Along with Van Druten, these stars brought Marlon up short, constantly forcing him to watch and learn anew. As in adolescence, when he was not studying, he was rebelling. One of his first mutinous gestures was the autobiography he submitted to *Playbill*—a calculated put-on. "Born in Calcutta, India," it read, "where his father was engaged in geological research, [Marlon Brando] came to this country when he was six months old."

During rehearsals, he took another tone and became the soul of decorum. By the time the show opened, Marlon had thoroughly and obediently inhabited the character of Nels, suggesting the slightest Scandinavian intonation, growing a little more mature from scene to scene. He was touching when he had to be and got laughs when they were called for. In the play's finale, which called for him simply to look up in astonishment, the eloquence and modesty of his body language was unfailingly greeted with applause as the curtain lowered.

In later years, those who saw the original production read too much into his performance. (Marlene Dietrich, an opening-night attendee, said Marlon was "the most natural boy I ever saw," and Stella topped her. "He stood in perfect contrast to the overacting of Homolka and Christians, who were practically eating up the scenery. Marlon showed what subtlety on stage can accomplish.") The fact is that most reviewers were dazzled by the efforts of Christians, Homolka, and Van Druten, and omitted the Brando name. Only Robert Garland, the *Journal-American* critic, paid attention: "The Nels of Marlon Brando is, if he doesn't mind me saying so, charming."

If Nels was an engaging figure, the man who played him was anything but. Marlon detested Homolka, whom he recalled as "a brusque, unpleasant pompous man, which made him enjoyable to irritate." The irritation consisted of misplacing props, and once, of substituting salt for sugar. Homolka's favorite moment occurred in the first act, when, milking the scene for all it was worth, Uncle Chris slowly sweetened his coffee with spoonful after spoonful after spoonful of sugar, then took more time to savor the drink. On this special evening Homolka shocked the audience by violently spitting out the contents of the doctored cup. Homolka got through the performance, but swore revenge. It took the form of silence; offstage he didn't talk to the young nuisance for three months. Not that Marlon cared. He was bored with the play after a few weeks. To him it was tantamount to a school assignment, reciting by rote every night and twice on Wednesdays and Saturdays. He tried some improvisations, but Van Druten, a pudgy soft-spoken Briton, was a lot tougher than he looked. The playwright/director kept dropping by and pulling all the actors back to their original interpretations—there would be no ad-libbing or ornamentation, thank you very much. When Van Druten proved inflexible Marlon concluded that *I Remember Mama* was not going to be a springboard for anything. The show ran for 713 performances and became a hit film, but other men played Nels after a season. Marlon could deal with uncomfortable situations and annoying people; against ennui he had no weapons. For diversion he took some modern-dance lessons and boxed a little. These activities never compensated for the sense that he was walking in place. It was either fight or flight, and he flew.

It was a good time to be free of constraints. New York in the spring of 1945 was a place of power and euphoria. Headlines blared good news day after day: American troops crossed the bridge in Remagen and poured onto the turf of the Third Reich. More than a thousand bombers attacked Berlin. Tokyo was firebombed. Even the death of President Roosevelt on April 12 could not dampen the city's spirits for long. Two weeks later, the papers ran photographs of Benito Mussolini, Italy's Fascist leader, along with his mistress, both bodies hanging upside down in a town square, riddled with bullets. Berlin fell on May 2; V-E Day followed on May 8, and in midsummer, after the nuclear destruction of Hiroshima and Nagasaki, V-J Day was announced on August 15. The terrible weapons, instead of instilling fear, brought forth predictions about an Atomic Age, when machines would be powered by the harnessed atom and controlled by a new moral force called the United Nations. Veterans had been trickling back home; soon they would all be back in the United States. They would need houses and jobs, and talk of a booming postwar economy was everywhere.

Somehow Marlon failed to savor the moment. Gripped by malaise, he went back to *la dolce vita,* chasing girls or allowing them to chase him, having multiple affairs with Stella's daughter, Ellen, and half a dozen other women. Within the acting community, much was made of this; later Brando would be characterized as a "sexual outlaw" and a "walking *Kama Sutra.*" In fact, of the seven deadly sins Gluttony ran a bad second to Sloth. Marlon was lazy by nature, and that inclination was useful as a defense mechanism. After all, if you didn't compete, how could you lose? And if you were indifferent about your career, about women, about life in general, who could criticize you? Only your folks.

But in 1945 those folks were not in a position to criticize anyone. Throughout her sojourn in New York Dodie continued to drink heavily, while Marlon senior sulked in Evanston. Damned if he would come to postwar New York to haul his wife out of bars. Nor would he take a trip east to see his son in a play—even if the damn thing was on Broadway. That being the case, Marlon junior should have been the most carefree man in town. Instead, the twenty-one-year-old began to feel twinges of guilt about the way he was squandering his gift—if indeed he really had acting talent, and not just a knack for mimicry.

The big news on Broadway was Tennessee Williams, whose play *The Glass Menagerie* was going to win a lot of awards for him, and for his cast. Marlon saw it, was struck by its honesty and poignance, and was saddened because he wasn't in it. The work was unashamedly personal—Williams's mother, Edwina, was a self-deceiving woman, married to a brutal husband, C.C., who disliked her, regarded his mentally disturbed daughter, Rose, as a social catastrophe, and hated the effeminate son, Tom, he referred to as "Miss Nancy." Trapped by the Depression and the town of St. Louis, where C.C. managed a shoe factory, Tom Williams knew that "somewhere deep in my nerves there was imprisoned a young girl, a sort of blushing school maiden." He also knew that somewhere deep in those nerves was an artist. He watched his mother recede into the fantasies of her youth of cotillions and gentleman callers, and his sister be swallowed up by madness. The worst came when Rose underwent a lobotomy to relieve her depression, and became totally incapacitated, a ward of the state. Tom fled the scene, wandering through Los Angeles, New Orleans, Provincetown, New York, always pecking away at a typewriter that Edwina had given him years before. Whatever else went on in his disordered days, he continued to write. Elia Kazan was to remember the work habits of Williams, who now insisted on being addressed by his pen name. Every morning he "would get up, silent and remote from whoever happened to be with him, dress in a bathrobe, mix himself a double dry martini, put a cigarette in his long white holder, sit before his typewriter, grind in a blank sheet of paper, and so become Tennessee Williams."

An early effort, *Battle of Angels*, introduced a theme the playwright was to pursue obsessively for decades: A young drifter comes to town and awakens the latent passion in a love-parched shopkeeper. *Battle* opened in Boston—and closed there. Tennessee pushed on, encouraged by a sympathetic agent and a grant from the Rockefeller Foundation. The Chekhovian *Glass Menagerie* allowed him to give full range to his poetic talent and sensitivity without directly confronting the subject of sexuality. For that sort of freedom he would need three things: a highly charged drama rather than a play of subtlety and suggestion, a new director, and a very different kind of star. The first requirement was his and his alone, and long before the raves and rewards came in he set to work on *Poker Night,* a story that would become a play. In that form it would take on a new title: *A Streetcar Named Desire.*

5

Montgomery Clift had already appeared in five productions, but always as a supporting player. In 1946 he became the star in *Foxhole in the Parlor,* with his name high up on the marquee. His reviews were the stuff of dreams: The *Journal-American* said he was "terrifying in the role of the returned soldier." The *World-Telegram* put the play on its season's-best list, and the *Herald Tribune* called Monty's work "superb sensitivity." To be sure, Clift, like Marlon, had never been in uniform. But he had more than atoned for his lack of service by playing a wrecked veteran. Meantime his fellow Omahan had done nothing except screw around, and playing the part of the satyr in real life had lost its savor. Marlon jealously watched Monty's rise and thought about the old acting classes, the kind of ambition he once possessed. Had Stella's faith been for nothing? He picked himself up and auditioned for a role in Maxwell Anderson's *Truckline Café.* The drama, a genre play that takes place in an eatery, allows disparate people to drop in and out of one another's lives. Among the patrons of this seaside diner is a disturbed war veteran named Sage McRae. Afflicted by the pain of what he has experienced overseas, and by what he has seen upon his return, he changes from a bewildered figure in the first act to a murderer in the third, shooting his unfaithful wife and casting her into the bay.

Marlon read for the part—a comparatively minor one that would keep him onstage a total of six minutes—with enormous sincerity and a total lack of technique. In a way it was like the audition for *Mama.* Just as Rodgers and Hammerstein had found him wanting, two formidable theater men were also turned off by Marlon's initial reading. In the front row, a displeased Elia "Gadge" Kazan shook his head and sighed. The former actor had already shown his versatility by directing Thornton Wilder's difficult modernist play, *The Skin of Our Teeth,* featuring Clift. Summoned to Hollywood, he had turned out the sentimental, top-grossing Hollywood film *A Tree Grows in Brooklyn.* But the theater was his first love, and he had just returned to New York to co-produce *Truckline.* Next to him sat Harold Clurman, Stella Adler's husband. The director was already famous for his presentations of Clifford Odets's incendiary works *Waiting for Lefty, Golden Boy,* and *Awake and Sing!* A few seats away was the playwright, Maxwell Anderson, recently lauded for such powerhouse dramas as *Key Largo* and *Winterset.* The talk around Broadway was that *Truckline* couldn't miss—provided, of course, that the cast was up to the writing.

Kazan disagreed with the prevailing wisdom. His first choice for the part of Sage McRae was Burgess Meredith, but the star had a Hollywood commitment. Clurman was unwilling to wait and grabbed Marlon, settling, in Gadge's opinion, for second best. Maybe third best. And where did MCA get off with such an outrageous salary demand? The company had just assigned a new agent to guide Marlon's career, and Edith Van Cleve asked for $500 a week. Kazan was outraged; Burgess Meredith got that kind of money, but he had all sorts of film and stage credits. Who the hell was this one-shot wonder to get that money? The line was held at $275 and Gadge thought he was being magnanimous.

Throughout rehearsals he remained suspicious of Marlon, convinced that Stella Adler had oversold him to her husband. In the end Kazan went along with his more intellectual, less instinctive partner— all the while anxious to see the thing flop. At the time, and in later years, Gadge complained that Harold was glib, highbrow, and too deferential to the playwright. In his opinion, the script had to be drastically rewritten; in Clurman's view, the flaws could be fixed in rehearsal.

They were not. Yet if Clurman failed to elicit the right words from Anderson, he did manage to badger and provoke Marlon into giving a star turn. The actor, who began by mumbling, was encouraged to shout his lines; then slowly the director ratcheted down the volume until he got an articulate and touching performance. Maxwell Anderson's daughter, Hesper, was a child at the time; she was allowed to hang around backstage, where she watched the character of Sage McRae being built. Brando, she stated, was "so completely the character that it didn't matter if you didn't catch every word he said." The actor "did pushups backstage before his big entrance, and I'd watch, mesmerized, as he brooded, getting in character, and then wearing himself out physically before collapsing onstage."

In Act One, Marlon turned the playwright's faltering attempts at plain speech into a kind of folk lyricism. When the veteran talked to Tory, the wife he hadn't seen in two years, all eyes were on him, as if the café held no one else.

SAGE: It's a beautiful ocean. Boy, oh boy, I can hardly believe I used to be on the other side, looking this way. The moon used to come up over the water and go down over the land. Here it comes up on the land and goes down over the water. And I used to look over this way, across the water, and know you were there.

By the time he learns of Tory's infidelities and kills her, Sage has reverted to a shell-shocked state. Suddenly eager for punishment, he confesses his crime. The couple had returned to the cabin where they had once been happy and dedicated lovers. Sage looked at Tory, then through the window at the wild ocean outside, then at the objects on the wall, still in place after two years. Something was out of joint, and Sage thought he knew what it was. Tory had been unfaithful to him; she had wrecked their future by sleeping with someone else, perhaps with many someones. He remembers confronting her with a ferocity she had never seen in him before. Trapped in the cabin, and by her own shame, she confessed that she was indeed guilty of infidelity: Sage had been away for so long, and she was lonely. But now he had come back to her, and they could return to the old days, the happy times. Sage hardly listened; he seemed to be in another world. He took a pistol from his belt and emptied the bullets into Tory's body. A burst of five shots was followed by another burst of five shots. She could never betray him now, never make him unhappy again. He picked up the limp body and carried it out to the water. Filled with remorse, but unable to undo his crime, he understands why he did what he did, and why he has to be punished for it:

She was guilty—and everything about her that I loved went through me like a knife. And now I have to die because everything reminds me of her and goes through me like a knife.

Anderson had written Sage's exit as a two-dimensional portrait of irony: A guilt-burdened G.I. leaves the killing fields of war only to bring them home with him. That was not the way Marlon played it. He talked Clurman into letting him walk off in a confident dance step, as if he were embracing his next stop: death row. For the first time in his professional career, Marlon made a perverse and risky move—one that could easily have backfired. It did not. Today, standing ovations are given to chorines and walk-ons. That was not the case on the night of February 27, 1946, when Marlon received a thunderous one. From that evening on, for the next six decades, perverse and risky moves became the mainstays of every Brando performance.

He had only twelve more chances to make an impression. *Truckline* received sulfurous reviews from almost every drama critic—the *New York Times* critic said that Anderson must have written the play "with his left hand in the dark of the moon," and his was one of the kinder appraisals. Audiences felt differently, at least about Marlon. A young Pauline Kael, who was to become one of Brando's most vigorous champions and harshest assessors, happened to arrive late one evening. She looked up and saw a man having a seizure onstage. "Embarrassed," she wrote, "I lowered my eyes, and it wasn't until the young man who'd brought me grabbed my arm and said, 'Watch this guy!' that I realized he was *acting*." And Kirk Douglas was to recall, "I went up for a part in *Truckline*. I didn't get it. Bitter, I went to see the play, watched another actor play my role. I loved the first two acts—he was terrible. I congratulated myself on how much better I would have been. Suddenly, in the third act, he erupted, electrifying the audience. I thought, 'My God, he's good!' and looked in the program for his name: Marlon Brando."

Truckline folded on March 9, to Clurman's regret and Kazan's gratification. Although he praised another brilliant new actor, Karl Malden, Gadge was to confess that he was pleased by the failure. He had predicted it all along. Nevertheless, he signed his name to a letter written by Clurman and sent to the *Times*. It complained that reviewers for the dailies were "acquiring powers which, as a group, they are not qualified to exercise, either by their training or their taste." The signers had forgotten the famous adage never to argue with a man who buys ink by the barrel, and got their comeuppance. George Jean Nathan, dean of the New York critics, replied, "There is much truth in what the Messrs Clurman and Kazan say, though they have committed the error of picking the wrong play about which to say it, and so have made what they say nonsensical."

The quick failure of *Truckline Café* allowed Marlon to reinvestigate the Pleasure Principle, secure in the knowledge that the play's abrupt closure was no fault of his own. Indeed, wherever he went he heard praise for what he had done onstage. He had acquired an otherworldly quality, partly because he was just as compelling offstage as on, but also because he affected a total indifference to the world around him. He appeared at parties in shabby clothing, wore sneakers to semiformal occasions, stood silently at cocktail parties when all about him were chattering. The impression was of a star waiting for his big role, an event about to occur. That was exactly the case.

The Broadway fare that season alternated between the serious and the frivolous. Producers had trouble reading an audience still buoyed by victory but anxious about the economy, the sudden presidency of Harry Truman, the threat of a raucous and bellicose Soviet Union. For those who went to the theater to be diverted, there were musicals like Sigmund Romberg's *Up in Central Park,* Harold Arlen's *Bloomer Girl,* and *On the Town,* with a score by newcomers Leonard Bernstein, Betty Comden, and Adolph Green. Still, even the musical theater had its darker themes; Rodgers and Hammerstein's new show, *Carousel,* daringly abandoned the boy-meets-girl formula and followed the life and afterlife of a carnival-barker-turned-robber. The comedies contained less fluff these days; *Harvey,* about a man who hallucinates an enormous rabbit, and *The Late George Apley,* about a Bostonian stuffed shirt, were thinly disguised social commentaries. The serious plays showed a new maturity; *A Bell for Adano* took a sober look back at the war in Italy, and *Anna Lucasta* offered an all-black cast in its drama of a waterfront prostitute and her lovers.

These last works gave Marlon reason to hope that he could move past juvenile roles and short-lived melodramas to make a theatrical statement. Offers came in, and he and his agent considered them all. One stood out above the rest. Guthrie McClintic was not only a producer and director but also the husband of the Broadway diva

Katharine Cornell. McClintic had been impressed by Marlon's Sage McRae—so impressed that he made MCA an unusual offer. He was about to stage a new version of George Bernard Shaw's *Candida*. Marlon could have the part of Eugene Marchbanks, the hopelessly lovesick poet, *without auditioning*. The actor was flattered but uneasy. It was one thing to impersonate a Brit in acting class and quite another to do it before a full house evening after evening. Dodie came out of her fog long enough to express her enthusiasm for the project: a twenty-one-year-old American appearing in a Shavian comedy at the Cort Theatre—alongside such highly placed professionals as Sir Cedric Hardwicke and the First Lady of the American Theater! Opportunities like this came along once in a performer's life, and then only if he was lucky. Bud knew the lines from *Julius Caesar* as well as she did: "There is a tide in the affairs of men,/Which, taken at the flood, leads on to fortune. . . . We must take the current when it comes,/Or lose our ventures." Do it, for God's sake, do it, Dodie urged, and Marlon allowed himself to be persuaded.

As rehearsals began he was respectful of McClintic and his costars, scrupulous about showing up early, memorizing his part, and paying close attention to the blocking. His deferential attitude lasted about a week. That was when Marlon realized that Ms. Cornell was "quite empty-headed" with "the kind of stage presence that made her a star without having to be good." As for Hardwicke, he was "a Johnny One Note actor who had a single expression throughout the play and his career."

Marlon struck back the best way he knew how: onstage. Early on, two of his New School classmates decided to check him out. Carlo Fiore and Elaine Stritch were appalled. Until Marchbanks's entrance, every entrance and exit had occurred metronomically. Marlon stumbled onstage many seconds after his cue, fidgeting and pale. The actors exchanged anxious glances. From the prompter's box came the hissing of Marchbanks's reply to a query about his politics: "Foolish ideas! Oh, you mean Socialism." Moments later, Marlon said the words as if he had suddenly snapped out of a funk.

It took a while for his friends to realize what was going on. Marlon was not paralyzed by stage fright. Almost alone among the cast members, he was paying close attention to Shaw's stage directions: Marchbanks "is miserably irresolute, does not know where to stand or what to do with his hands and feet and would run away into solitude if he dared." Yet he shows a "great nervous force, and his nostrils and mouth show a fiercely petulant willfulness, as to the quality of which his great imaginative eyes and fine brow are reassuring. He is so entirely uncommon as to be unearthly."

Marlon was unkind about Hardwicke and Cornell, but he was not incorrect. They represented the classical declamatory theater, everything timed to a fare-thee-well, nothing left to chance, the words triumphant, the character secondary. Whereas he embodied Stella Adler's dictum: Range so deep into the text you become the playwright's partner. This assault on the past put him in a strange position. His father's hypocrisy and malice had taught Marlon to distrust all authority figures. Military school had reinforced his contempt for those who would seek the position of leader. And yet here he was, leading by example, inventing a fresh style of acting, bringing a whole group of performers along in his slipstream. Much as he denied the fact, he was the coming man, the founder, however unwittingly, of a new, new school.

At the same time, Sir Cedric was not entirely mistaken about Marlon. The tyro's ways were far too risky for this judicious, hypertraditional production. During one performance Hardwicke gazed at Brando from the wings. He shrugged and shook his head. "Must be sex appeal." At the end of the year Brando's nemesis George Jean Nathan weighed in with his own appraisal. Recalling the three-week production of *Candida,* he predicted that the man who played Marchbanks would "in time learn that sensitiveness lies in more than a pale makeup and an occasionally quivering hand, and that a picture of physical weakness is better to be limned than by acting like a puppy ever in fear of a cat." A revolution had occurred during the run of that play, and nobody seemed willing to acknowledge it—least of all the rebel chief. "I was hopelessly miscast in the role," Marlon bitterly concluded, and let it go at that.

Make Them Wonder

1

Edith Van Cleve thought it was well past time to move her client up to the next level—a major Broadway production, a New York–based television show, or best of all, a Hollywood feature. To that end MCA talked Marlon up to theater and film producers, and on cue the offers trickled in. Even at this point in Marlon's nascent career he seemed determined to undermine himself, a determination that got more perverse as his star ascended. He was, for example, sent the script of a Eugene O'Neill play written in 1939 but never presented on Broadway. Marlon fell asleep while reading the first act, and sent it back to MCA accompanied by an appraisal of this "ineptly written and poorly constructed" work. *The Iceman Cometh* went on without him. He read for the leading lights of Broadway, Alfred Lunt and Lynn Fontanne, then casting *O Mistress Mine*. Seated in the orchestra, Lunt asked the young man, "Would you mind saying something?" Brando paused, then gave a deadpan reply. "Hickory, dickory, dock, the mouse ran up the clock. The clock struck one, the mouse ran down, hickory, dickory dumb." He accentuated the word *dumb*. The next day the Lunts cast Dick Van Patten in *Mistress*. It was to run for two years. Noël Coward tendered a part in his new comedy, *Present Laughter.* Marlon considered the work trivial and unworthy of a time when people were starving in Europe and Asia, and said so. The offer was icily withdrawn.

Several important film producers expressed an interest in Marlon; all of them wanted to tie him up with a seven-year contract. He said no thank you to Louis B. Mayer; Hal Wallis, who offered a weekly salary of $3,000; and Joe Schenk, who instructed him to get a nose job.

More out of curiosity than enthusiasm, Marlon agreed to play a boxer in a one-shot TV drama. In 1947 television plays were done live;

videotape was years away from practical use. To indicate the passage of time, actors and technicians had to dash from one set to another without missing a beat. A key scene showed the middleweight fighting; another, seconds later, revealed him immediately after a ring loss, preparing to take a shower. Marlon stood in his shorts, trying not to breathe hard after a twenty-five-yard run, waiting for the warm water to spurt forth. Nothing happened. The prop man had forgotten to turn on the faucet. Marlon reached out, turned the device counterclockwise—and got hit by a stream of ice-cold water. He dropped out of character and shouted, "Jesus Christ!" Afterward the actor was congratulated for his realistic interpretation of a pugilist—particularly in the shower scene. It was his last experience with live television. The work made little impression on anyone, least of all Marlon. Yet some trace memory remained. He had no idea how to use it just then. So he simply stored the image in the back of his mind, in the unlikely event that he was called upon to play a failed prizefighter.

2

The management of MCA expressed some displeasure with Marlon's next move. Out of regard for the Adler family he agreed to appear in the Ben Hecht drama *A Flag Is Born*. The drama would tour the country, raising funds at every stop to be used to transport Jewish refugees to Palestine. Hecht had been at this a long time. Originally, Britain was receptive to the idea of a Jewish national home. The League of Nations empowered the country to administer Palestine until the Jews there were ready for home rule. But in the run-up to World War II, anti-Jewish riots in the Middle East forced 10 Downing Street to change its policies. Fearful that the Arab nations might side with Nazi Germany, British colonialists blocked Jewish refugees from entering Palestine. A new Labour government took office in 1945, and this, coupled with reportage of the death camps, brought a new optimism to Zionists—those who believed the Holy Land was the most appropriate destination for European Jewry. Ernest Bevin, the foreign minister, quickly put a stop to that. "If the Jews, with all their sufferings, want to get too much at the head of the queue," he warned, "you have the danger of another anti-Semitic reaction through it all." The statement put him at odds with Harry Truman, who favored the creation of a land called Israel. Bevin added more fossil fuel to the fire when he declared that the only reason the United States favored admission of survivors was that "they did not want too many Jews in New York."

This crossfire was Hecht's theme music. Throughout the 1930s, he had been the highest-paid scenarist in Hollywood. His career was the stuff of legend. This son of Russian immigrants once wrote about the most significant moment in his Chicago childhood. When he was six, his aunt Chasha took him to a play. The plot concerned a man wrongly accused of theft. When a policeman came to take him away, little Bennie shouted his protests from the balcony. The theater manager collared the boy and demanded an apology. Chasha struck the man forcefully with her umbrella. "Remember what I tell you," she advised the boy. "*That's* the way to apologize."

The lesson took. At the age of sixteen, Hecht talked himself into a job as cub reporter for the *Chicago Daily News*, climbed over staffers to get his own column, insinuated himself into important circles, became a novelist whose work was judged obscene—until Clarence Darrow agreed to become his attorney and H. L. Mencken came on board as a character witness—and later wrote for Broadway and Hollywood. His credits included *Scarface, Twentieth Century, The Front Page,* and *Wuthering Heights.* Yet the monetary and professional rewards never satisfied him as much as the role of fighter for a Jewish homeland. He described himself as an "honest writer who was walking down the street one day when he bumped into history." The history he bumped into was the Holocaust.

In the early 1940s the systematic murder of European Jewry was the worst-kept secret in Nazi Europe. Germans and Eastern Europeans saw their neighbors forced to wear a yellow star, then barred from institutions and professions, and finally rounded up and sent away in trucks and trains. Though exact details of the Final Solution remained obscure, they knew they would never see those Jews again. Yet much of the horror was deliberately hidden from U.S. citizens. Some sixty years after the genocide, Max Frankel, former executive editor of *The New York Times,* acknowledged, "No article about the Jews' plight ever qualified as the *Times*'s leading story of the day, or as a major event of a week or year. The ordinary readers of its pages could hardly be blamed for failing to comprehend the enormity of the Nazis' crime." That newspaper was hardly alone. In *Beyond Belief,* a study of the American press and the coming of the Holocaust, Deborah Lipstadt confirms that as late as 1941 the *Chicago Tribune* placed the news that German Jews were forbidden to use the telephone "even for a doctor" on the very bottom of page ten. The imposition of "rigid anti-Semitic laws" in Norway was reported by the New York *Journal-American* on page thirty-two. The death of 450 Dutch Jews in Mauthausen concentration camp appeared in the Baltimore *Sun* in a thirteen-line article on the bottom of page ten. Papers in smaller markets carried even fewer items about the fate of European Jewry.

When Hecht learned what was happening to European Jews, the rich, self-satisfied celebrity transformed himself into a wild-eyed militant. In 1943 he wrote and produced a stage docudrama about the destruction of European Jewry entitled *We Will Never Die*, with a gripping score by Kurt Weill. The son of a cantor, Weill had firsthand knowledge of the Nazis' malevolence. In 1927, just as his *Threepenny Opera* was becoming the rage of Berlin, the Nazis made their first moves to power, placing his scores in their exhibition of Degenerate Art. Following an anti-Semitic demonstration at the opening of his opera *Der Silbersee (The Silver Lake)*, the composer fled to Paris and then came to America, where he spoke of the horror overtaking the fatherland. He was only too glad to join Hecht at Madison Square Garden, where forty thousand people cheered Weill's music and the playwright's defiant words, spoken by Paul Muni and Stella and Luther Adler: "Though they fill the dark land of Europe with the smoke of their massacre, they shall never die. For they are part of something greater, higher and stronger than the dreams of their executioners."

We Will Never Die proceeded to Hollywood, where Edward G. Robinson and John Garfield contributed their talents, and to Washington, D.C., where it was seen by the first lady, Eleanor Roosevelt, as well as several hundred members of Congress. Deeply moved, the spectators made pledges of money and political aid. But when it came time to collect, feet were dragged and phone calls were not returned. A month later Weill had turned bitter. "What have we really achieved?" he demanded. "All we have done is make a lot of Jews cry, which is not a unique achievement."

Hecht resolved that this empty spectacle would not recur. Next time out he would hit harder and louder; the survivors of Nazi genocide deserved a homeland, and *pace* the British occupiers of Palestine they would get it. To that end, he raised money for an unregistered ship to take Jewish refugees from Europe, and made himself the main unpaid publicist for the dream of Zion. The crystallization of his efforts was *A Flag Is Born*.

Staged at the Alvin Theatre on Fifty-second Street, this melodrama, like its predecessor, featured a stark plot and capital-letter dialogue. The production company, a proto-Zionist group called the American League for a Free Palestine freely admitted that *A Flag Is Born* was not ordinary theater. It was not written to amuse or to beguile. "*Flag* was written," said the press release, "to make money to get Jews to Palestine and to arouse American public opinion to support the fight for freedom and independence now being waged by the resistance in Palestine."

Set in a European graveyard, the one-act play centered on an elderly couple, Tevya and Zelda, whose family has been murdered by the Nazis. They reflect on the recent catastrophe, and then on the whole of Jewish history. Kings and prophets rise up and speak of the Jews' ancient claim to the Holy Land. The dreamers represent the tragic past; the new future is represented by David, played by Marlon with unaccustomed passion, a shaken, bitter young survivor of the Treblinka death camp, who strays into a cemetery and remains there to envy the dead.

Paul Muni starred as Tevya and Celia Adler as Zelda. Luther Adler directed, delivering the playwright's message with hammer-and-anvil effect. But there were differences between Hecht's sorrowing *We Will Never Die* and his belligerent postwar *A Flag Is Born*. Muni was, as always, a standout. Still, he provided no surprises. Audiences, used to his tricks from *Scarface, The Story of Louis Pasteur,* and *The Life of Emile Zola,* knew that he got as much out of silence as others got out of speech, cocking his eye, hesitating before delivery of a line, making much of whatever makeup he wore—particularly when he could stroke a beard or play with his spectacles. Marlon, on the other hand, was an astonishment, making David awaken to the Zionist hymn "Hatikvah," then marching off, resolute and militant, to join the Jewish soldiers of resistance in Palestine.

At the beginning of Act Two Marlon was illuminated by three spotlights—Luther Adler was not a believer in understatement—as he delivered the play's message. "Where were you?" he asked in a recriminatory tone. "Where were you, Jews? Where were you when six million Jews were being burned to death in the ovens of Auschwitz?" The

effect was overpowering. Wails could be heard at almost all performances, and in some Marlon was accused by audience members:
"Where were *you* . . . ?" Muni, not the most generous of performers,
had been critical of Marlon's style in rehearsals: "He has pauses you
could drive a truck through!" But now he experienced a total change of
mind. In awe, he asked his wife, "How the hell can an actor like that
come from Omaha, Nebraska?"

The project was a phenomenal fund-raiser and a critical favorite.
Columnist Walter Winchell, then at the height of his influence, called
Flag a "compelling blend of fact and fantasy, worth seeing, worth hearing and worth remembering. It will wring your heart and eyes
dry . . . bring at least eleven handkerchiefs." *Time* described the show
as "colorful theater and biting propaganda," and *The Hollywood
Reporter* went it one better: "Ben Hecht has written so moving a
pageant that we have been moved to pen not only a congratulatory cri-
tique—but to write a check to the American League for a Free Palestine in its repatriation program." *The New Yorker* was one of the few
publications to disagree with the majority; its reviewer found *Flag* "a
combination of dubious poetry and political oversimplification."

For Hecht, every knock was a boost. By the completion of the show's
out-of-town tour, the ALFP had raised close to a million dollars,
enough to buy a four-hundred-ton former yacht called the S.S. *Abril*.
Renamed the S.S. *Ben Hecht*, it conveyed a six-hundred-passenger
contingent from Eastern Europe to the Middle East. By then U.S.
newspapers had recorded another historic event engendered by *A Flag
Is Born*. Responding to political pressure, operators of a segregated
venue in Baltimore had agreed to an unprecedented bargain. For a
price, the ALFP became the "lessee of the theater." As such, the color-
blind organization would be allowed to put any ticket holder anywhere.
"Negroes were seated indiscriminately," reported a black-owned
weekly, "some holding orchestra and box seats, without untoward
results." On opening night Hecht told the audience, "Breaking down
this vicious and indecent tradition in Maryland is worthy of the high
purpose for which *Flag* was conceived and written." It was one of the
rare occasions where militant Zionism and black civil rights inter-
sected. That connection was not lost on Marlon.

The cast of *A Flag Is Born* had been working for union scale—sixty
dollars a week—and MCA was relieved when the tour ended. It was
time for its client to start earning some real money. Marlon wrote

home, informing his parents that he might be cast opposite the one and only Tallulah Bankhead. The play was Jean Cocteau's *The Eagle Has Two Heads*, a drama of an aging nineteenth-century queen who falls in love with a young man, unaware that he intends to assassinate her. Bankhead's reputation for bizarre behavior was a Broadway legend. The beautiful daughter of prominent Alabamans had been wild since adolescence—"I was raped in our driveway when I was eleven," she told anyone who would listen. "You know, dahling, it was a terrible experience because we had all that gravel." She began acting onstage in her early twenties, got off to a slow start in New York but wowed London, where she starred in twenty-four plays. When she appeared in *The Little Foxes* in 1939 and *The Skin of Our Teeth* in 1942, she had Broadway at her feet. After those triumphs, however, a combination of pills, alcohol, and ego drove her on to all sorts of professional and sexual disasters. By the time she met Marlon she had become something of a caricature, with a husky tobacco-roughened voice and a series of exaggerated mannerisms.

Her Tudor-style estate in Bedford Village, New York, was called "Windows" with good reason: There were seventy-five of them. It was said that as she sashayed around nude, her eastern, western, northern, and southern exposures could be observed from the house's eastern, western, northern, and southern exposures. Marlon was so wary of her reputation that he consulted Actors Studio founder Bobby Lewis, who lived one town away from Tallulah. Lewis warned him that the lady was hard-used and resentful of her middle age, that she drank far too much, that she could be a termagant, and that his contract had better include an escape clause in case she made his life miserable. Then he dropped Marlon at Tallulah's doorstep. She eyed the young man and welcomed him in. After some polite exchanges she handed him a script, he read aloud, and was hired on the spot. "I think," he reflected, "that she was more interested in me for sex than for the part of Stanislas." It didn't take much thought to arrive at that conclusion. Tallulah tried to invade his trousers that very afternoon. Speaking about it later, Marlon told Lewis that he was interested in her actions "from an engineering point of view." She entered at the cuff, and "I wanted to see if it was possible to get all the way up through that route because people usually unzip your fly. But you know, you can."

Rehearsals were a nightmare. Tallulah began to invent excuses for her costar to visit her rooms at the Elysee Hotel. Seduction was the first thing on her mind, and the very last on Marlon's. He found her unattractive and, in a strange way, frightening. For once he resisted the advances of a female. He took to chewing garlic before their staged embraces. When that failed to dampen Tallulah's ardor, he made a show of gargling with mouthwash in the wings after every kiss.

The end of this not-quite relationship was quick and final. Stories vary; a stagehand recollected that Tallulah, angry with Marlon for his remoteness, whacked him with a riding crop during a scene in the first act. Furious, Marlon pursued her up a staircase, and when his costar suddenly found there was no exit, she retreated down the stairs, taking part of the curtain with her. Another account says that Marlon, weary of the star's hogging of the stage, turned his back and urinated onto a potted plant during one of her long speeches. She heard the audience buzz, turned around, finished the play, and sacked him that night. In any case, she told the producers Marlon was all wrong for the part; he was dismissed after six weeks on the road. Luck was still with him. The Austrian actor Helmut Dantine replaced Marlon and *The Eagle Has Two Heads* opened at the Plymouth Theatre on March 19, 1947. It closed twenty-nine performances later.

The play and its stars were not missed; Broadway was enjoying a renaissance of great performances and fresh ideas. Having struck it rich with *I Remember Mama,* Rodgers and Hammerstein stayed in their producers' chairs and found backers for the musical *Annie Get Your Gun.* Jerome Kern had been scheduled to write the score; when he died suddenly of a stroke in 1946, Irving Berlin took his place and wrote one of Broadway's all-time smashes. The show was headed by Ethel Merman, the loudest diva in Broadway history. "I had to write a good lyric," Berlin remarked. "The guy in the last row of the second balcony was going to hear every syllable." Dynamic as she was, Merman was old news. Judy Holliday grabbed everyone's attention; the twenty-five-year-old had become an overnight celebrity as the enlightened "dumb blonde" in *Born Yesterday,* replacing Jean Arthur out of town when the film star got sudden attacks of stage fright. Tigers were at the gates, and among that group were two young, ambitious black actors: Ossie Davis and Ruby Dee debuted in *Jeb.* The play addressed the plight of another army hero, this one returning to a still-segregated nation. Two months later Jackie Robinson would break into the minor leagues, and José Ferrer, then starring in *Cyrano de Bergerac,* would use his own fame to advance the cause of the African American performer. In an article for *Variety* he wrote of playing Iago to Paul Robeson's Othello. Their company toured places where the two stars had to stay at different hotels, and Ferrer took a public vow that he would never appear at any venue that assigned blacks and whites to different sections. He urged colleagues to follow his lead.

A green playwright named Arthur Miller had one Broadway failure behind him. With *All My Sons,* an examination of a wartime profiteer, he reestablished himself—thanks not only to his Ibsenesque dialogue but to the vibrant direction of Elia Kazan. Broadway was pushing the boundaries in 1947, advocating social change, introducing compelling new personalities. Marlon wondered if he had made the wrong choices in life as in art, if the parade had passed him by. It certainly looked that way. In addition, his financial outlook was bleaker than ever. After leaving Tallulah and her awful play, he had fallen asleep on the train ride back from Boston. When he awoke, his wallet was gone—eight hundred dollars, all the money he had earned from the Cocteau play, had been lifted. He was close to insolvency, and five months away from legend.

3

Meager savings kept Marlon going through the late spring and early summer. Feeling an acute need for privacy, he traded his room in Dodie's flat for one in the Park Savoy Hotel on West Fifty-sixth Street. The place served as a way station for actors on the come or on the way down; rooms were twenty dollars per week. There, amid other hopefuls, Marlon set up as a bachelor about town, and welcomed a steady stream of young women. There was no mystery to his physical attraction; his sensuous, feline grace was a magnet for female residents and for young women he met at social gatherings. Along with his appearance Marlon employed a devious psychological approach, an anger distilled from childhood experience. It rarely failed him. "I circle around and around," he explained. "Then, gradually, I come nearer. Then I reach out and touch them—ah, so gently. Then I draw back. Wait a while. Make them wonder. At just the right moment, I move in again. Touch them. Circle. They don't know what's happening. Before they realize it, they're all entangled, involved. I have them. And suddenly, sometimes, I'm all they have." He could sense the emotionally impoverished across a crowded room: Years of watching Dodie had informed him well.

But the game of predator and prey was soon to be interrupted. Like most readers Marlon believed the theatrical reportage in the *Times* and *Herald Tribune* on August 1. They stated that Tennessee Williams's new play, *A Streetcar Named Desire,* formerly titled *Poker Night,* would be directed by Elia Kazan and would star Jessica Tandy and John Garfield. So producer Irene Selznick had informed reporters; however, only two thirds of her story was accurate. Garfield, originally enthusiastic about the script, began to have second thoughts. Advance word on his new film, *Body and Soul,* was terrific; he felt sure it would put him back on top. Flexing his muscles, he demanded a rewrite; the character he was scheduled to play, Stanley Kowalski, was eclipsed by the play's centerpiece, Blanche DuBois. That would never do. Furthermore, the curtain lines would have to be changed to give Stanley greater impact. Williams refused to touch his text. Garfield walked. The next choice, Burt Lancaster, had prior commitments. *Streetcar* was due to go into rehearsal at the beginning of October. As the clock ticked down, Edie Van Cleve seized her opening. She collared Kazan and reminded him of Marlon's phenomenal stage presence: Look what he did in that turkey *Truckline Café.* Gadge protested that Garfield and Lancaster were both in their thirties. Marlon was twenty-three. Yet that night the director reflected that there was no reason why Stella and Stanley Kowalski couldn't be in their early twenties and Blanche in her mid-thirties—if Williams would go along with the idea of a younger cast. He decided to roll the dice. Williams was holed up in Provincetown; Gadge got hold of Marlon, advanced him twenty dollars for the bus ride, supplied the Cape Cod address, and hoped for the best.

Three days later he called Tennessee and asked him what he thought of the actor he had sent. Williams was bewildered; no one had appeared. The next day, as Kazan started to ransack the casting directories, Marlon showed up at Williams's place. He was dressed in his customary outfit of T-shirt and jeans and in the company of a girl he had picked up en route. He had spent Gadge's money in New York, and hitchhiked some three hundred miles to the end of the Cape—hence the delay. The guests in Tennessee's rented Provincetown house included his lover as well as the theatrical director and producer Margo Jones, a Texan who had codirected *The Glass Menagerie.* They were amusing and cultured folk, and not one of them knew a thing about plumbing or electricity. A pity, because the toilet had given up flushing and the fuse had blown. In the evenings they read by candle-light, an experience that palled after a few days. When they needed to relieve themselves they were forced to use an outhouse. That had frayed tempers to the breaking point. Marlon's entrance was welcomed less because he was an actor than because he knew how to handle household crises. He had been taking care of such things since Omaha, when his sisters were preoccupied with school and friends, his father was on the road, and his mother was drunk. He immediately put a penny behind the dead fuse, and the lights snapped on. Then he cleaned out the toilet tank, freeing a blocked pipe. Marlon was a hero before he'd read a line.

A day later Kazan received a call from the playwright in a voice bor-dering on hysteria. Brando's reading of the dialogue "had overwhelmed him." Margo Jones pronounced it "the greatest reading I've ever heard—in or outside of Texas!" By the time Marlon returned to New York, sans the pickup girlfriend, Williams had written his agent, Audrey Wood, "I can't tell you what a relief it is that we found such a God-sent Stanley in the person of Brando. It had not occurred to me before what an excellent value would come through casting a very young actor in this part. It humanizes the character of Stanley in that it becomes the brutality or callousness of youth rather than a vicious older man."

Rehearsals got under way on the morning of October 6, 1947. The New Amsterdam Theatre on West Forty-second Street had once been the glittering venue of the *Ziegfeld Follies,* but by the end of the war it had become an echoing, grungy movie house—emblematic of the play's decaying centerpiece, Blanche DuBois. On the morning of the first day Gadge introduced each member of the assembled group, including stagehands, the stage manager, the producer, and the jittery, chain-smoking author. "This is the company we are going to stay with," the director said firmly. "Anybody gets fired it'll be me." This was custom-ary Kazan bravado, a way of giving assurance to a deeply insecure gath-ering. As they all knew, the director was the only marquee name *Streetcar* had to offer. His first film, *A Tree Grows in Brooklyn,* had been a critical and popular hit, and his most recent stage production, Arthur Miller's *All My Sons,* had burnished his reputation. Williams's *The Glass Menagerie* had been a sensation. But it was the star, Laurette

Taylor, who got the rave notices, not the playwright. Jessica Tandy, who would play Blanche DuBois, had been on the English stage from the age of sixteen, working with the likes of Laurence Olivier and John Gielgud. In the United States, though, work had been difficult to find. For the last several years she had played small and conventional supporting parts—viewers could spot her as a housemaid in the overheated movie *Forever Amber*. Kim Hunter, who would play Stella, Blanche's sister, had also come up empty in Hollywood. She had begun acting in regional productions and that, according to Hunter, was what convinced producer Irene Selznick to select her: "She took my going back on the stage as a sign that I wanted to become a 'serious' actress." Karl Malden, a blunt actor with a face like a closed fist, was cast as Stanley's working-class pal Mitch. He had been in *Truckline Café* and *All My Sons;* Kazan considered him talented and reliable but hardly a box-office draw. Rudy Bond, an Actors Studio veteran, was hired to play Steve, the Kowalskis' upstairs neighbor, because Kazan liked his rough-hewn style. Just how rough Gadge was to learn when the actor palavered with a street musician, took the man's violin in hand to show him how to play a riff—and promptly got hauled into the local police station for panhandling. Allowed one telephone call, Bond dialed Selznick. As he explained the situation he heard the distant voice of Tennessee: "Ah hope he's in for murderin' a critic."

Marlon was the youngest of the team; outside of the theatrical community few had heard of him. And many in that community knew him only by reputation. He was thought to be greatly gifted, but as devious with colleagues as he was with women. Half the time he just acted weird to throw you off; and the other half he really *was* weird, self-involved, murmuring his lines indistinctly, a performer from another planet.

With this as background, the cast began the reading with little spirit or mutual trust. The tragic drama was unlike anything they had ever encountered. It had no hero, no heroine, no "through line" leading to catharsis and redemption. Blanche DuBois visits her married sister, Stella, in the French Quarter of New Orleans. The faded and neurotic beauty is a teacher, thrust on her own after the family's Mississippi plantation is sold out from under her. To recover from the shock of loss—or so she says—she has obtained a leave of absence from the school. Unhappily, more traumas are under way. Stella's husband, Stanley, is the polar opposite of the genteel southern tradition. He represents the new immigrant class, a life force, brutal, sensual, wholly uninterested in the past. The introduction of Blanche upsets the delicate balance of the marriage; she is attracted to Stanley, and he to her. Before the final curtain, Blanche, half teasing, half terrified, is raped by Stanley and revealed as a self-deceiving poseur whose exit from the Deep South was prompted by a history of alcoholism and sexual scandal. The truth proves too much for her; the old gives way to the new, and Blanche is taken off to an asylum, exhaling the line that is to go into theatrical history: "I have always depended on the kindness of strangers."

The cast could recognize the poetic quality of the dialogue, but the drama itself seemed to them jumbled and hard to understand. Yet something uncanny happened after the lunch break, when the cast read Act Two. Williams's lines abruptly caught fire; sentiments rose to the surface, actors got in character, and by the time Tandy spoke her final words the principals were in tears. Their sniffling was suddenly punctuated by the voice of Gee Gee James, the only African American in the cast: "Hallelujah! I think I'm going to pay the rent!" Nervous laughter greeted her shout, along with mumbles of "From your mouth to God's ear."

Later Kazan was to write that the rest of the rehearsals were "a joy." His definition of joy differed from some others', though. Tandy privately considered Marlon "an impossible, psychopathic bastard," especially when he created long, unscripted silences, forcing the actress to lose her timing. Tandy's husband, actor Hume Cronyn, dropped by during a run-through. A ruthlessly honest appraiser, he told Kazan: "Jessie can do better." The director understood: Tandy was giving a performance. In contrast, Marlon was *living* onstage, riding his emotions wherever they took him. His work was "full of surprises and exceeded what Williams and I had expected. A miracle was in the making." Unlike Katharine Cornell, Tandy realized that she had been tied down by her training, and that she could be liberated by this play. Her husband was profoundly right, she recognized; a lot could be learned by working with this psychopathic bastard. Together and apart, Cronyn and Kazan urged her to dare to be exceptional, and as the weeks wore on she strained to give Blanche a heartbeat.

Marlon provided no help at all; he never yielded an inch to her or any of the other players. He was always Stanley, and Stanley was always in the process of happening. As Kim Hunter acknowledged, her colleague could make "terrible choices, but they were always *real*. That's why it was such a challenge." Each day Marlon got closer to the core of his character, trying new and angrier ways to say his lines, becoming increasingly physical, working out with heavy weights at a local gym to gain the muscularity of a manual laborer. In this he was aided by the costumer, who dressed him in well-worn, skintight trousers and a T-shirt carefully ripped to suggest that Stanley might have been tussling violently with Stella.

Kazan watched the results with mounting satisfaction. For the first time, Marlon seemed happy. The mood was infectious, and the entire cast seemed at ease when *Streetcar* opened in New Haven, the first tryout en route to New York. Yale undergraduates heard that something special was going on at the Schubert Theater; they filled the place and led the applause. Irene Selznick invited her father, MGM boss Louis B. Mayer, a man stingy with praise. "You don't have a hit." The voice of the tough old mogul thrummed with authority. "You have a smash." That said, he had a few suggestions for Gadge. Once Blanche was hauled off to the loony bin, Stella and Stanley would live happily ever after, right? Well, Williams would have to rewrite the final scene, clarify the happy ending, send the audiences out on a high. "It never occurred to him that Tennessee's primary sympathy was with Blanche," Kazan wrote. "Nor did I enlighten him." Yet in Mayer's ham-handed way he had recognized a basic flaw. *Streetcar* was now the Marlon Brando Show. The young man was so compelling he had changed the focus of the play. In a rare moment of self-doubt, the director asked the playwright about Stanley's attitude toward Blanche. "What should I do? Sometimes the audience laughs when Brando makes fun of her." Responded Tennessee: "Nothing." He wanted no moral, no point of view, simply a group of lives observed without flinching. Marlon might be a genius but, given time, Jessica would rise to meet him.

Tennessee was correct on all counts. By the time of the Boston tryout Tandy and Brando had reached a modus vivendi, and when the show debuted at the Ethel Barrymore Theatre in New York they were peers. Like the rest of the Broadway critics, Brooks Atkinson rushed from the theater on opening night to make his deadline, even before Blanche had spoken of the kindness of strangers. It didn't matter. The first sentence of his review in the *Times* guaranteed a box-office landslide and, within months, a Pulitzer Prize: "Tennessee Williams has brought us a superb drama." In the *World-Telegram*, William Hawkins singled Marlon out for playing "the blunt and passionate Stanley Kowalski with astonishing authenticity. His stilted speech and swift rages are ingeniously spontaneous, while his deep-rooted simplicity is sustained every second."

The other notices, all raves, were read aloud at a party given at the "21" Club by George Cukor. The Hollywood director had nothing to do with *Streetcar;* he was a front for Irene Selznick, who didn't want to be perceived as a rich Hollywood doyenne slumming in New York. That evening she suspected something was amiss when Marlon showed up with a well-dressed older couple and identified them as his parents. All through rehearsals Marlon had spoken to her about the traces of Dodie in Blanche and the suggestions of Marlon senior in Stanley. Small wonder, then, that the producer refused to believe these sweet, upright folks were the elder Brandos. "If I fell for it," Selznick wrote later, "he'd tease me forever. I greeted them pleasantly but very briefly. Then I rushed off to find out if they were genuine, came back full of apologies, and started over."

Marlon's lover at that moment was Ellen Adler, Stella's daughter, and she remembered the opening night well. "He walked into our apartment at two o'clock in the morning. He was wearing a black turtleneck and jeans, same as always, but I could tell from his stride that his life had changed. But I knew not to mention it to him. You couldn't say, 'You were great tonight, Marlon.' Then you'd be out of the club. It was like a club, or a domain, all the in-people, and he was the president, or the duke, and he made up the rules, like never praising his work or mentioning his fame."

The cast of *Streetcar* settled in for a long run. They grew comfortable in their parts—but never too comfortable to be surprised by the audience reaction. Sitting in the theater one evening, the young actor Walter Matthau amused himself by counting the laughs engendered by Kowalski's speeches. "There were half a dozen leading men in Broadway comedies that season," he remembered, "and Brando got more hoots and chortles than all of them."

He kept evoking laughter and tears along with the rest of the cast. The difference was that privately they grew in stature with the months, whereas Marlon ran downhill with all deliberate speed. Having moved in with Wally Cox, he lived like a welfare client. Dinner frequently consisted of peanut butter eaten directly from the jar. When he was not out on a date, he amused himself by running a Lionel electric train acquired from a downtown toy store. Some twenty years later, Jocelyn looked back at this time. "You were a twenty-three-year-old when all the *Streetcar* stuff hit the fan," she wrote her brother. "Can anyone remember how insecure it is to be twenty-three and be saddled with the kudos and the notoriety you received? It was embarrassing. You couldn't think it was deserved. You couldn't believe you were actually responsible, and Poppa always said you'd never amount to a tinker's damn."

Marlon had been happy shadow-boxing downstairs during rehearsals. Now, in the wake of rave reviews, the contentment vanished. The judgment of the critics should have erased his father's harsh predictions—but they didn't. Subconsciously, and sometimes consciously, he thought that Marlon senior had been right all along. This sudden fame was bogus. The critics had been conned. Marlon's misery grew in reverse proportion to his success, and in an attempt to alleviate the pain, he consulted Gadge. The director referred him to his own therapist. Dr. Bela Mittleman had recently told the director what every egoist wanted to hear—"Your problem is that you're not selfish enough. You're always trying to please other people." Naturally, Kazan thought the world of him. Marlon had no such sentiments. He considered the orthodox Freudian a cold and unresponsive figure. And yet he could never bring himself to leave. During those early years of analysis a murderous anger was unearthed. Marlon grew frightened of his temper on those occasions, but claimed he "had no idea where his rage was coming from." Anyone who knew about his early childhood could have furnished a working hypothesis, but Mittleman was either unable or unwilling to offer much relief. A Hungarian trained in New York, he sometimes seemed more intrigued by fame than by therapy. Marlon and Gadge gave him entrée into the theater world, furnishing tickets and referrals. In general, the doctor got more out of his patients than they got out of him. Kazan ultimately left the psychiatrist and, in his words, "later saw a very good analyst." Marlon, for all his protestations, stayed with Mittleman on and off until the psychiatrist's death a decade later.

All the same, he knew in his bones that the one person who could rescue Marlon Brando was Marlon Brando. That would have been hard enough for a more mature individual, and the emerging star was, as his sister suggested, emotionally retarded. From childhood on, Marlon continued to provide pop-psych speculators with a rich field. But medical experts also had their say, and their observations seem inarguable. Psychologist Sibyl Baran finds that his conduct in early manhood is illustrative of many pages in the *DSM*—the *Diagnostic and Statistical Manual of Mental Disorders.* "For one thing," she says, "he kept replicating his childhood defiance of authority, continually challenging his father in the person of officers, directors—anyone who tried to tell him what to do or how to behave." The manual categorizes this as oppositional defiant disorder. Marlon also displayed many characteristics of narcissistic personality disorder, an affliction, according to the *DSM,* that results from an "impairment of the person's relationship with his parents. . . . The patient typically comes to believe that he has some defect of personality which makes him unvalued and unwanted." In addition, observes Dr. Antoinette Lynn, a psychologist who specializes in artists and their difficulties, "Brando clearly had an oral fixation, common to many neglected children. For him, food was compensation as well as nourishment." The overeating meant little when he was a new and hyperactive performer, interested in bodybuilding and in preserving his image as an attractive man. But with the passage of time, the craving for food would prove to be as destructive as his parents' hankering for alcohol.

If Marlon was bad at counting calories, he was totally inept at saving money; it seemed to evaporate before his eyes. Chagrined, he turned the $550 weekly paychecks over to Marlon senior. The elder Brando paid his son's rent, gave him walking-around money, and invested the rest in a Nebraska farming project. On the other hand, Marlon junior had no trouble attracting and holding on to women. Newly famous, unattached, he radiated an animal magnetism and a carefree attitude that brought gaggles of beautiful girls to his dressing room. When he was in the mood Marlon would choose one candidate from the group. The rejects were welcome to try again, or to date his insecure roommate, Wally. "It was intoxicating," Marlon remembered. "I loved parties, danced, played the congas, and I loved to fuck women, any woman, anybody's wife." He couldn't handle liquor, though, and on the occasions when he had a couple of drinks, he stopped being a grownup and slid backward to adolescence. At one party he faced the assembled guests, announced, "I can't stand you people. I'm sick of this life," stepped out of the open window, and disappeared. They were on the eleventh floor. The gasps were audible. Some of the women began to scream. One of them courageously leaned out and peered at the street below, fully expecting to see a body sprawled on the pavement. That was when she spotted him. Marlon had lowered himself to a six-inch ledge directly below. "Go ahead, drop—see if I care," she shouted. Sheepishly, he climbed back and joined the others.

More juvenile behavior followed. Leila Hadley, who would later marry Henry Luce III, was one of several young socialites who collected literary and theatrical celebrities. At a party she met Marlon and found him "too gorgeous to resist"—or so she thought. At one of her own parties Marlon showed up, admired her collection of antique clocks, and about an hour later excused himself and disappeared into the night. When the guests had gone, Leila noticed that several timepieces were missing. She knew Edie Van Cleve well enough to phone her and suggest that Marlon might know where the clocks had gone. That evening she opened the door of her apartment to find the purloined items laid out in the hallway, all ticking, all in a row. An accompanying note read, "Oops!" It was signed anonymously, "A Thief." All this merely intrigued their owner, who contrived to spend an evening with Marlon. He paid court to her—and then abruptly handed her a chocolate bar. "He suggested places to put it, and I was not about to go there no matter how attractive he was," she remembered. "I told him, 'Look, Marlon, why don't you see my friend Laura? She's a lot more fun than I am.' And off he went, out into the evening in search of her."

4

While these frenzied occasions were playing out offstage, another drama had to be performed onstage six nights a week plus matinees. *Streetcar* had been playing less than two months when Marlon expressed a strong desire to quit. MCA reminded him that the contract was ironbound; he had agreed to stay for a year and a half. Marlon responded as he always did when thwarted. He assumed a subversive attitude. One form of rebellion was to arrive as late as possible, sometimes after curtain time, putting the entire cast on edge. Another was to make Stanley Kowalski an ever-changing character who bore the weight of Marlon's sentiments on that particular afternoon or evening. Tandy shook her head when she thought about those times. "When he was tired, as he often was, he played the role tired. When he was bored, and he was often bored, he played the role bored." But Marlon also played the other parts of his own personality—the conflicted soul, the pained artist, the turned-on satyr, the grownup child, the wiseguy, the misfit. The effect could be dazzling, but it always unbalanced the play. Harold Clurman's early assessment remained true throughout Brando's run. The actor had "high visibility . . . his silences, even more than his speech, were completely arresting." Kowalski's psychic wounds showed beneath the "muscled, lumpish sensuality, and crude energy" and "make us wonder whether he is not actually suffering deeply." All along, Williams intended Blanche to be the focus of his most avid attention and most lyrical writing. It was she who was supposed to wring the heart. Yet, thanks to Marlon, *Streetcar* became "the triumph of Stanley Kowalski with the collusion of the audience, which is no longer on the side of the angels." There was little anyone could do about it. The others received applause; Marlon got ovations. He was the one audiences had come to see. And so the routine went on, Tandy bitter and haughty, returning to her husband every night via chauffeured limousine, Brando grabbing his motorcycle and noisily riding his latest date around the neon city.

What everyone missed, including the psychiatrist, Kazan, actors, Wally Cox, and the innumerable girlfriends, was Marlon's deep-seated ambivalence toward fame, and much more significant, toward acting itself. Was it an art? A craft? Or was it just another ego trip, a part of the big American publicity machine? He was hostile to journalists, ad-libbing a half-true autobiography while they watched and scribbled. He told them his diet consisted of raw eggs, peanut butter, and pomegranates. "My hobbies are bongo drums, tom-toms, and riding motorcycles through the streets of New York. I like to box and swim in the nude. My reading matter consists entirely of Spinoza. My pet peeves are wearing shoes and giving interviews." As to his love life: "I can't talk about something that doesn't exist." When Jocelyn landed the sole female role in *Mister Roberts*, giving journalists two Brandos to consider, *Life* scheduled a feature. Brother and sister sat for the magazine's photographer; she had a short haircut and bangs; Marlon wore a suit with a dress handkerchief in the jacket pocket, but his hair was tousled for the occasion. The reporter described Jocelyn as "quiet and domestic," her brother as "moody and unpredictable. When a lady in *Streetcar*'s audience a few nights ago became too talkative, he walked to the footlights and told her to keep quiet, which she did." During a group shot of all three Brando siblings, Frannie and Jocelyn did the talking. Their descriptions of childhood in Nebraska were full of lyricism and sunshine. Marlon just nodded.

Among all the ironies that were to pursue him throughout his long life, one of the most significant came in April 1949, in the boiler room of the Ethel Barrymore Theatre. Boxing, as Kazan observed, was a source of considerable pleasure in Marlon's life. It gave him a chance to work out his aggressions and allowed him to show off the skills he had learned in the gym. The problem was, those skills were minimal. Pugilism is a game of technique as well as strength; for contemporary champions like Sugar Ray Robinson and Joe Louis, quickness was as important as power. They saw an opening, sometimes no more than a nanosecond long, and pounced. So it was with the young stagehand sparring with Marlon.

That night, Marlon's friend Carlo Fiore was scheduled to have dinner with him. When the visitor arrived he was told to go to St. Luke's Hospital. There, speaking from behind a layer of bandages, Marlon explained what had happened. "All of a sudden he winds up and throws a haymaker from the floor. I saw it coming but I couldn't get out of the way." He slammed into a pile of crates and suffered a copious nosebleed. Somehow he got through the play, but as soon as the curtain lowered he was rushed to the emergency room. Irene Selznick gave Marlon a week off. His rangy, dangerous-looking understudy, Walter "Jack" Palance, took over.

When the bandages were removed, everybody got a look at the terrible job done by the surgeon. Their shock could not be hidden from Marlon, who condemned the doctor as "a sadist and a butcher." Selznick begged him to get his nose broken again and reset. A cosmetic surgeon could repair the damage; she would give him some of the top names in the business. In an instinctive, and very Brandoesque move, Marlon stubbornly refused. "That perfect face," Tennessee Williams sighed, "those classic looks, would never be the same." He was correct, and it was the saving of a career. Upon reflection many years later, Selznick admitted, "Luckily for him, Marlon didn't listen to me. Because I honestly think that broken nose made his fortune. He was too beautiful before."

Marlon sought to get away from Kowalski by dropping in every so often at the new Actors Studio, a group recently cofounded by Kazan. Much has been made of the Brando-Studio connection. Actually, he loathed Lee Strasberg, the man who would become its artistic director. Marlon's appearances there were sporadic and whimsical, and when he sat in on a class he made a point of appearing indifferent, always more attentive to the girl in the next seat than to the lecturer. Moreover, he loudly advertised his disdain for Monty Clift, the one Studio actor whose critical and popular reputation was as high as Marlon's. The two had first met when Marlon, roaring down Madison Avenue on his bike, recognized a young man window-shopping. He pulled up and asked, "Are you Montgomery Clift?" The man graciously replied, "I am. And you're Brando. I recognize you."

"People tell me I remind them of you."

"Oh?"

"I don't think so."

With that, Marlon kicked the motorcycle into gear and sped off.

The rivalry of theatrical stars was nothing new to New Yorkers. In the mid-nineteenth century two Shakespearean actors, the rough-hewn American Edwin Forrest and the elegant Briton William Charles Macready, were the subjects of a violent riot between nativists and aesthetes. The two men were playing in rival productions of *Macbeth* when their fans came to blows in Astor Place. The resulting disturbance involved police, soldiers, and civilians and left some sixty people dead or wounded. Less abrasive confrontations occurred more than half a century later in the Yiddish theater. Marlon knew a lot about this one, because it involved Stella Adler's father, Jacob, and his rivals David Kessler and Boris Thomashefsky. Once and only once, all three were cast in the same production. During a weekend performance Kessler upstaged Thomashefsky, aping the younger man's broad gestures. His partisans egged him on. Boris's partisans got into the act, yelling for their man to take revenge. The play called for him to break a plate; he smashed two. David, who was not supposed to touch the crockery, broke four plates. Jacob, in the role of a mild-mannered rabbi, had his own fans to please. He demolished some china on his own. By the end of the act the stage was covered with shards and the fans continued the fight outside on Second Avenue.

Given these examples, Marlon saw himself as the bearer of a great tradition, and went out of his way to keep the rivalry going. It could hardly have been otherwise. Clift was as introspective in life as he was onstage, stylish, courteous, cool. By contrast, Brando was slovenly, loud, and abrasive. Ellen Adler, Stella's beautiful eighteen-year-old daughter, was Marlon's frequent companion during his first days of celebrity. "They were always running into each other," she said. "In the late 1940s every artist knew every other artist in the city. It was a wide world and yet a small one. The circles of painting, music, theater were concentric. If you knew Marlon you knew Kazan, and if you knew Gadge you knew Jerome Robbins and Leonard Bernstein and Betty Comden and Adolph Green and Judy Holliday and Miles Davis and Willem de Kooning." At one of the many parties they attended, Marlon regarded Montgomery from across the room. "What's the matter with your friend?" he asked actor Kevin McCarthy. "He acts like he's got a Mixmaster up his ass and doesn't want anyone to know it." For his part, Monty told intimates that Marlon was "too clownish and a slob." In her affecting biography of Clift, Patricia Bosworth describes another soirée attended by Brando and Ellen. Clift was already there and pulled the young lady aside and listened to her attentively, offering a light for her cigarette. Marlon watched impatiently, "then came barging over and pulled Ellen away. 'She's my Jew, Monty!' he roared. Monty just grinned and shrugged."

Marlon was not always so uncouth. To show the acting community that he, too, could be elegant, he agreed to appear in a one-shot Studio production 180 degrees removed from *Streetcar*. By now his appearances in *Streetcar*, still electrifying to audiences, were beginning to bore him stiff. Rehearsals for Robert Sherwood's *Reunion in Vienna* came as a relief; he was gratified to lose himself in the part of Archduke Rudolph Maximillian von Habsburg. The images that everyone had in mind were from the twinkling 1933 film starring John Barrymore as the archduke and Diana Wynyard as his former lover, Elena. No one expected Marlon to approach the grace of the Great Profile in this period piece.

The Habsburg clan, driven out by the *anschluss,* have fallen on hard times. Rudoph's tumble has been the most precipitous; he has become a cabbie in Nice. Elena, once Rudoph's favorite lady of the court, has suffered the least damage; she married a psychiatrist and now lives among the haut monde in the Austrian capital. When a reunion of the old aristocrats takes place, she hesitates to attend. But Elena's husband encourages her to go, to confront her former lover, and rid herself of a clinging, adolescent passion. Rudolph has other plans: He intends to seduce his beloved one more time.

"I want a complete transformation, Marlon," ordered the director,

Bobby Lewis. "The works—full uniform, including a sword, moustache and monocle, long cigarette holder, accent, Habsburg lip, and waltz music offstage." Marlon dived into the role. Enlisting an old girlfriend, Joan Chandler, to play Elena, he examined Velázquez's portraits of royalty and rented a hussar's uniform, complete with glittering epaulets and medallions. He tightened his face to accommodate a monocle, and to accent the pendulous lower lip characteristic of the family, penciled in a narrow black mustache. After a series of nervous delays—he forgot the phonograph record of Viennese music, he couldn't hold the monocle in his eye, his uniform didn't fit quite right—Marlon went on in the part. *Reunion* was staged in February 1949 at the Actors Studio on Fifty-ninth Street. That evening Karl Malden rose before the assembled performers and curious guests and asked them to close their eyes for a moment. When the curtain rose they blinked back at a very different Brando. Gone was the simian Stanley. In his place was a peer of the realm, moving with subtle grace and speaking with flawless Austrian intonation. The reaction was palpable, and Marlon sparked to it. He kept getting laughs as he encircled Elena, peering down her bodice. The dialogue, written years before, seemed to have been composed with him in mind. Rudolph speaks of the many women he has known since their breakup: Europeans, Asians, Africans. Elena's curiosity is aroused: Has he "known" twins?

RUDOLPH: No, unfortunately. But I can swear to you, Elena, that all of them were no more than incidents. Whatever enjoyment I've had from them—and I'll be generous and admit that there has been some enjoyment—has been vicarious. Every quivering one of them has been no more than a proxy for you.

Just then, wrote Lewis, "in that predictable way that was to become his trademark, he suddenly slapped her, grabbed her, kissed her passionately and ad-libbed: 'How long has it been since you were kissed like that?' " The line was met with a roar of approval, whereupon Marlon improvised again, pouring Champagne down Elena's *poitrine*. More cheers. Marlon acknowledged them with a stiff bow, in keeping with the character. If this evening pleased the onlookers, it astonished the star. It had never occurred to him that he could do light sophisticated comedy. "He was like a young Barrymore," Lewis remembered. In retrospect, others were not so amused. They saw an attempt at

humiliation within the comedy—a key to so many Brando performances. "Some of us weren't sure what Marlon had done to Joan was
fair," commented Malden. "Were we laughing at the situation in the
play," Malden wondered, "or what Marlon had done to her as an actor?"

Afterward, Marlon did his own wondering. He had just demonstrated an unexpected versatility; he had surprised himself, as well as
everyone else, by being elegant, funny, charming. He had shaken the
curse of Kowalski. So why wasn't he gratified? Why wasn't he filled
with energy, ready to seek new work? Why did success continue to
leave him depressed and anxious? He had no answers, only questions.

5

As the last days of the *Streetcar* contract approached, Marlon was still
at loose ends, the body engaged, the mind treading water. Encouraged
by his politically active sister Jocelyn, he signed a roster of sponsors
endorsing the Cultural and Scientific Conference for World Peace.
This was one of the oddest and most confused assemblies ever to take
place in New York, the agora for political schemers, dupes, and odd-
balls. By March 1949 the Soviet Union had acquired an arsenal of
nuclear weaponry. From Moscow came new threats almost every
week. Communists and fellow travelers sensed that the Cold War had
thoroughly abraded the nerves of Americans. Since Joseph Stalin had
once been an ally, they repackaged him as a leader who only wanted
peace, but who was stymied by the "warmongering" and "fascistic"
U.S. leadership. Held at the Waldorf-Astoria Hotel, the conference
was covertly backed by the U.S.S.R. and featured endorsements by
prominent intellectuals and artists. Some, like the novelist Howard
Fast, were members of the Communist party; some, like Lillian Hellman, were enthusiastic fellow travelers; some, like Norman Mailer,
were naïve and fond of their own sonorities.

The stated purpose of the conference was a modus vivendi between
Bolshevism and democracy, the hidden agenda a promotion of détente
on Stalin's terms. The good will among attendees was palpable; few
were aware that the Russian representative, Dmitry Shostakovich, had
been compelled to come to the United States by Comrade Stalin himself—even though the composer's works had recently been banned in

his own country. Asked about intellectuals who had "disappeared" in the U.S.S.R., he looked uncomfortable and remained silent. A translator stepped in: "That leads away from the question of peace."

Perhaps the most forthright of the speakers was the fully employed screenwriter Clifford Odets, who declared, "I am proud to reach out and shake the hand of any man or woman who has the courage to appear here. If I speak here Sunday, I may be without a job Monday. The country is a little in the state of unholy terror from coast to coast." The Brandos applauded vigorously. Marlon wondered aloud about the cause of peace: Clapping hands on the sidelines was not enough. He needed to make a personal antiwar statement.

The following year, he saw his chance. The Korean conflict was in full sway when a letter arrived from the Selective Service, informing Mr. Marlon Brando that his status had been elevated from 4-F to 1-A. He appeared at the local draft board with fire in his eyes, ready to take on the entire U.S. military-industrial complex. First he filled out a standard autobiographical questionnaire. Under *race* he wrote, "human." Under *color,* "seasonal—oyster white to beige." After he filled out the form, Marlon entered a cubicle to be interviewed by an army physician. The doctor asked him if he knew any reason he should not enter the armed services. Replied Marlon: "Yes. I'm psychoneurotic." He was passed down the line to a uniformed psychiatrist. Marlon went though his history of defiance at Shattuck.

The doctor asked whether he was being treated for those difficulties, and if so, who his psychiatrist was. Marlon told him he was seeing Dr. Bela Mittleman.

"Bela Mittleman! For Chrissake, where is he?"

Marlon gave him the address.

"I'll be goddamned." As it developed, the two doctors had known each other years ago. The army man wrote on Marlon's induction papers, "Not suited for military service." It was the least a colleague could do for an old friend.

6

No matter how sullied Marlon's relationships were with women, parents, or colleagues, he treated one person with solicitude. Wally Cox had turned into more than a crony in New York; he had become Brando's shadow. Wally was now partner with another metalworker named Dick Loving, who would soon marry Marlon's sister Frannie. Since the opening of *Streetcar,* Wally—dubbed "the Walrus" by his sidekick—had acquired a motorcycle and now sported jeans and T-shirt and went unshaven on weekends in sedulous imitation of Marlon. They made an incongruous pair, the mesomorph and his wispy roommate biking around the city, occasioning comment wherever they rode. Their apartment was an extension of two disorganized selves, full of windup toys and dirty laundry, augmented by Marlon's pet raccoon Russell, sent to him by Dodie in a moment of whimsy. To amuse Marlon, Wally would occasionally perform some improvised living-room routines. Unlike his roommate, he had actually served in the army. His tour lasted for four months, after which the military gave him up as a hopeless misfit and issued an honorable discharge. That brief exposure was all Wally needed to develop an impersonation of his lunkheaded sergeant giving instructions to draftees. Another monologue concerned Dufo, a dumb, daredevil kid he remembered from Omaha. Marlon broke up every time he heard these routines and urged Wally to perform them for various drop-ins, male and female. In each case, they came to see the big star but stayed to applaud the little comedian. Word got around: This shy silversmith was actually a gifted standup monologuist; all he needed was a little exposure to become famous. Marlon pressured some well-connected people to get the Walrus a booking at the Village Vanguard, a hip nightclub in Greenwich Village. Without quite realizing it, Wally had joined a new movement. In standup comedy, as in almost every aspect of postwar American life, a new style was assuming command. The days of Bob Hope's USO tours were waning. Hope, Marlon said, "will go to the opening of a gas station in Anaheim providing that they have a camera there and three people. Pathetic . . . a bottomless pit." He wanted the Walrus to get in on the new edgy style, standup comedy without a set shape, commenting on society, childhood, hypocrisy, absurdity, racism, families, venturing where the careful crowd-pleasers would never dare to go. Unfamiliar names were part of this movement: Lenny Bruce, Mort Sahl, Elaine May, Mike Nichols, and other young untried comedians edged toward the center spotlight. Why couldn't Wally be in their company? Marlon knew the Walrus would be nervous on opening night, so he positioned himself down front to make sure that everyone paid close and quiet attention. The engagement was a smash. Others followed, at the Blue Angel and Café Society clubs. The slight, modest figure was on his way out of metalwork and into show business in 1950. He looked upon the change as liberating. In fact it was to become a prison from which there was no escape—one more resemblance between the Walrus and his best friend.

The Illusion Is Complete

1

N ow that Marlon had fulfilled his *Streetcar* contract, he was free to consider movie offers. They issued from an unaccustomed place. Once arrogant and peremptory, Hollywood was currently overloaded with angst. A Supreme Court decision had finally broken the biggest monopoly in the history of show business, and just like that, the movies' Golden Age was over.

For decades, the major studios had owned and operated every phase of the motion-picture business. Scenarists, directors, performers, and even producers were under contract, well-paid wage slaves, but indentured nonetheless. The majors also owned the film-processing laboratories at one end, and the theaters at the other. "Block booking" guaranteed that main features and B movies would be linked, along with newsreels and cartoons—a package put together by a specific studio. Any films made outside the system had no place to be shown, save for a handful of independent art houses of no financial importance.

The U.S. Department of Justice had been trying to break the studios' power since 1938. Each time, powerful lawyers argued for the status quo. For the film industry to operate successfully, they insisted, every aspect of the business had to be controlled by the majors. How else could they turn out products that entertained the entire world, make a profit for the customary "widows and orphans" stockholders, and keep thousands of employees on salary? The legal tactics worked wonders; again and again court decisions got postponed to another day. But in 1948 that day arrived. Writing the majority opinion, Supreme Court Justice William O. Douglas stated, "The policy of the anti-trust laws is not qualified or conditioned by the convenience of those whose conduct is regulated." In a pen stroke, block booking was abolished. The studios sold off their theaters in hopes of cracking a new market:

television. They were late to the game, and as they tried to muscle into a new phase of show business, another crisis shook their already cracked foundations.

It had begun with investigations by the House Un-American Activities Committee. According to its researchers, Hollywood radicals had been placing subversive messages in films. Film-colony liberals, along with some genuine Communist party members, argued that no such activity was possible: The studio heads, all of them Republicans or mainstream Roosevelt Democrats, controlled the end product. Sam Goldwyn had famously expressed their view of politics in the arts: "Pictures are for entertainment, messages should be delivered by Western Union." HUAC members themselves had a great deal of trouble citing examples of left-wing propaganda slipped into mainstream films. The best, and worst, they could mention were films that showed a football coach stating that it was better "to die on your feet than to live on your knees"—a phrase coined by the radical spokeswoman La Pasionaria during the Spanish Civil War; a character whistling the Communist anthem "Internationale" while waiting for an elevator; and the fatuous *Mission to Moscow*, featuring a smiling, avuncular Stalin. *Mission* was a Warner Bros. film, one reason Jack Warner went overboard to prove his Americanism. At a HUAC hearing he stated that the real radicalism was not based in California but in New York. On one visit he had seen Arthur Miller's *All My Sons*, the drama of a manufacturer whose shoddy procedures caused the death of American pilots. Warner loathed it. "They write about twenty-one-cylinder heads that were broken. They can't write about the five hundred thousand good airplane motors produced. That play disgusted me. I almost got into a fistfight in the lobby. It was directed by a chap named Elia Kazan who is now at Twentieth Century–Fox as a director."

Warner leaned forward. "Can I say something off the record?"

The answer was no.

Very well then, he would put his remarks *on* the record. "This fellow is also one of the mob. I know of him. I pass him by but won't talk to him."

During the same period a group of scenarists and directors refused to discuss their political activities in testimony before HUAC; labeled the Hollywood Ten, they were cited for contempt and given one-year jail sentences. They appealed to higher courts, and to their former employers. Not a chance. Those executives had made themselves crystal clear in a meeting at the Waldorf-Astoria, announcing in a press release, "No Communists or other subversives will be employed by Hollywood." As for the courts, they, too, could find no sympathy for the defendants. By 1950 the last legal means were exhausted and prison doors opened wide to admit them.

These conditions were the talk of two towns, Manhattan and Los Angeles, as Marlon mulled over film offers and wondered about himself. Should he be a political activist like Gadge, thumb his nose at the bosses? He loved Kazan's recent comeback: "They always have to have a pet project in Hollywood, something they're going to do next year, when the crap they're doing now is finally finished." He would have to seek out the director, find out what was really going on out there. If it was as bad as it looked, the hell with the movies. He made sure the press knew where he stood. In an interview Marlon haughtily dismissed the American product. "I do not think anybody connected with the films in the United States has ever made a sincere effort to avail himself of their fullest potential the way they do, say, in France." Having said that, he proceeded to act out again, sailing for Europe as soon as his *Streetcar* contract expired. He told his sisters he needed to get away from the tempters in Celluloid City. Besides, he had never been overseas and the Continent seemed to offer the best and most reasonable refuge.

Once the *douaniers* stamped his passport he became a completely different personality: calm, self-possessed, full of charm. The notoriety that had clung to him in New York meant little in Paris, and for Marlon the relief was palpable. He had very little French, and the people he saw on the streets and shops had almost no English. For the first few days no one recognized him, asked for his opinion on anything, or requested an autograph. He stayed at a cheap hotel, dropped in at an actors' cooperative, tried to do a little mime on the streets of the Marais, where amateur clowns and magicians disported. When he smiled at a mademoiselle and she smiled back, it was because of his manner, not his résumé.

A few highly placed Parisians were aware of his accomplishments. Artist/director Jean Cocteau, on the ascent after the films *La Belle et la Bête* and *Les Parents Terribles,* had recently visited friends in New York. There he was taken to see the celebrated Stanley Kowalski at the Ethel Barrymore. Deeply impressed, he exclaimed, "There was a beast onstage!" When someone told him that the beast was in Paris, he arranged a meeting; to his astonishment the American troglodyte turned out to be soft-spoken and deferential. This, he was to observe, "is the only man who can make noise without disturbing anybody." Marlon was invited to a dinner; that led to more parties and social engagements. Some were ill advised. He went backstage to see the French version of *Streetcar,* with Arletty, the great star of *Les Enfants du Paradis,* as Blanche. Marlon arrived at the stage door, only to be met with a withering glance. The actress thought his blue jeans and T-shirt vulgar, unbefitting a performer with his reputation. Marlon later acknowledged that Arletty was a "tough article" and that his casual drop-in was indeed a gaffe. But other meetings went well; he impressed two African American expatriates, James Baldwin and Richard Wright, and hit it off with a group of young achievers, including Christian Marquand, a handsome, ambitious actor who was to become a close friend, and Juliette Gréco, a singer he besieged with flattery and gifts until she succumbed to his blandishments.

From Paris, Marlon pushed on alone to Italy. Here he made an error of omission that would change his life and career for the worse—and yet he had no notion of its severity then, or for many years to come. Because he was intimidated by Rome he bypassed Cinecittà, center of Italian filmmaking, where Vittorio De Sica, Michelangelo Antonioni, Luchino Visconti, Roberto Rossellini, Federico Fellini, and others were beginning to make their marks with *neorealismo* films and larger works of the imagination. Their movies were populated with locals, children as well as untrained adults, rather then professional extras hired for crowd scenes. Some of them, as in De Sica's *Bicycle Thief,* played major roles, giving the narrative an authenticity unknown in American features. The style reached out to Europe and beyond; the Indian director Satyajit Ray was inspired to become a filmmaker after he saw De Sica's movies, and the French New Wave was a direct descendant of films like Rossellini's stark depiction of postwar Rome, *Open City.* Yet for all his swagger, Marlon was intimidated by that city. A historic version of *Streetcar* was playing there, but he declined to buy a ticket, thereby missing Vittorio Gassman as Stanley and Marcello Mastroianni as Mitch.

Marlon pushed on to the south. Here he encountered a land totally unlike anything he had ever known. The Neapolitan girls, or so he asserted, were more intoxicating than the local wines. On the island of Sicily he wandered alone through a field of flowers, lay down, and woke up to a perfect sunset. Upon reflection many years later, he insisted that this was the only moment of pure, unsullied happiness he had ever experienced. That serenity came with a price tag. Preferring slumber to challenge, he had turned his back on Cinecittà, the one place that could have enriched his talent and taken it to a new level of performance and achievement. Much of his indifference could be ascribed to sloth—but not all. The old feelings of ambivalence about celebrity, about money, about the whole enterprise of show business, continued to haunt him. He could not shake the idea that acting was an elaborate charade. It followed, then, that those who practiced it were nothing more than well-paid pretenders.

The following week he returned to Paris and recognized an American walking on a street near his hotel. It was Maynard Morris. The MCA man wondered where the hell his old client had fled. Edie Van Cleve had found Marlon Brando's address and sent wire after wire. None were answered. Had Marlon opened the telegrams? Well, no, he hadn't. He had been in another country. Would he have the goddamned courtesy to read the messages now? He would. The two men shook hands and parted. As promised, Marlon went upstairs to check through a pile of neglected messages and letters from home. One caught his attention, just as Morris thought it would. The large envelope with the seal of the Stanley Kramer Company included a one-picture offer of $40,000 to play the main role in a feature called *Battle Stripe* (soon to be retitled *The Men*) plus a six-page outline of the film, and the offer of a ticket back to the States. Marlon sent back a wire asking MCA how much Montgomery Clift had received for *his* first film, *Red River,* made two years before. "I want a dollar more," he wrote, but the demand was tongue-in-cheek. Forty grand was just fine. Wary of air travel, he bought a one-way ticket on a trans-Atlantic liner and came home to launch his movie career. No wonder he was to look back with such fondness at that Sicilian moment. Already a stage star, he was about to become a product of Hollywood's celebrity machine. Life would never be pure or unsullied again.

2

At thirty-six, with only three films to his credit, Stanley Kramer had given notice that he was the next major film producer. His first independent project, *So This Is New York* (1948), was a Ring Lardner comedy, called "so-so" even by its star, radio personality Henry Morgan. But Kramer's second picture—a grim feature based on another Lardner tale—scored with critics, the public, and the National Society of Film Critics. *Champion,* about the rise and fall of a vicious prize-fighter, earned five Oscar nominations and made a star of Kirk Douglas. Kramer's 1949 film, *Home of the Brave,* took on racism in the armed forces, and established him as the ideal producer for Hollywood's socially conscious postwar period.

The Men was Kramer's answer to *The Best Years of Our Lives,* the blockbuster 1946 film about returning G.I.'s and their rough adjustment to civilian life. One of the main roles in that film had been played by a truly disabled war veteran, Harold Russell, whose missing hands were replaced by prostheses. The hero of *The Men* was intended to be as tragic and noble a figure. Paralyzed below the waist by a sniper's shot, Ken Wilcheck is assigned to a paraplegic rehab center. Surrounded by veterans with similar afflictions, he rages against them, against his physicians, his fiancée, his fate. He remains one of the wheeling wounded until, with the help of friends and a tough but sympathetic therapist, he becomes reconciled to his condition. Marlon was intrigued by the challenge of the role. Acting from the belt up, he would have to redefine manhood by playing a twenty-five-year-old whose sexual life had been taken from him. He could hardly wait to get started. Then the trouble began.

It did not originate with Kramer, or with the director, Fred Zinnemann, or with the scenarist, Carl Foreman. It came from the ethos of the industry itself. The era of the blacklist was in full sway, intensified by Soviet agitation in Europe and Asia. Alger Hiss had just been found guilty of perjury about his Communist past. In London, physicist Klaus Fuchs was imprisoned for conveying British atomic secrets to Russian agents. Seizing the moment, Senator Joseph McCarthy of Wisconsin gave a speech to a women's club in Wheeling, West Virginia. Offering no proof, he claimed to have a list of more than a hundred "known Communists" employed by the State Department. The Korean War heated up, pitting Communist forces against American and South Korean troops. A pamphlet called "Red Channels" was privately and anonymously published; in it were the names of "subversive" film and television actors, musicians, playwrights, and directors. At a meeting of the Screen Directors Guild, Cecil B. DeMille addressed his colleagues. Deliberately mispronouncing the names of Billy Wilder, William Wyler, and Fred Zinnemann, all of whom had accents, he demanded the ouster of Joseph Mankiewicz for his allegedly leftist associations.

As if this political agitation were not enough, a new scandal rattled Hollywood. In the spring of 1950, Senator Edwin C. Johnson of Colorado took to the floor of the Senate to denounce the Swedish-born actress Ingrid Bergman as a "free-love cultist" and a "powerful influence for evil." The actress's crime was an adulterous affair with Roberto Rossellini. After seeing *Open City* she had written a fan letter that described her contempt for the commercial features the studios had compelled her to do. Was there a chance she could appear in one of his films? They met, a romance was ignited, and she left her husband. The press made much of the story, Bergman became the butt of jokes at the Academy Awards ceremonies, and she was no longer welcome in American films.

The swirl of political and sexual scandals missed Marlon, whose devotion to causes was always undercut by ambivalence. But his sister Jocelyn had been much more of an activist, and she was suddenly unable to find work in cinema or television. He was angry about that, but also confused. Would he be painted by the same brush? Should he go back to New York, maybe get into theater again? Everyone knew about the film actor Stanley Prager, who had defied HUAC by refusing to inform on his colleagues. He was immediately struck from the casting lists of movies, radio, and TV, headed to Broadway and began a new career as a musical comedy star. Arthur Miller expressed a particular pride in the theater's immunity from the blacklist: "I have never been told who I can use or not use. I hire solely on the basis of competence. I would use a man who was in complete disagreement with me politically if he were right for the part."

The more Marlon saw of California, the more he felt displaced. Yet he was contractually obligated. New York glittered like Oz—distant, glamorous, unreal. He sought refuge with his maternal aunt Betty and his grandmother "Nana" in Eagle Rock, an unglamorous suburb fifteen miles from downtown Los Angeles. Try as he might, though, he couldn't hide from reporters; they sought him out and asked prying questions. He answered the fools according to their folly. Hollywood was "one big cash register." The only reason he had come west, he went on, was "because I don't yet have the moral strength to turn down the money." A single law operated in the film studios: "The larger the gross, the worse the picture." As usual, his autobiography freely mixed fact and fantasy. Hoping to deflate the paparazzi by being even more ridiculous than the rumors, he told them that his mother was "a drunk" (actually, she had recently joined Alcoholics Anonymous), and that his upbringing was "terrible," not least because he was born in Outer Mongolia, where breakfast consisted of gazelles' eyes.

Lew Wasserman, the head of MCA, tried to placate his new client. He assigned Jay Kanter, a twenty-one-year-old mail-room clerk in the Los Angeles office, to chauffeur Marlon around town, steering him away from the most hostile journalists. Kanter did better than that; he catered to the actor's every wish, buying him everything from sandwiches to shoelaces. By the time Wasserman offered Marlon his pick of top MCA agents, Marlon had made up his mind: "I want the kid who's been driving me around." This impromptu remark was the making of Kanter; he would rise like an express elevator at MCA, becoming the representative of Grace Kelly and Marilyn Monroe along with Marlon and many other major film stars. Eventually he learned to protect actors from themselves, but at this point in his career he had no way of keeping Marlon Brando and Louella Parsons apart.

As Hollywood foundered, Parsons remained a feared and loathed columnist. Few dared to malign her in public. Actress Mamie Van Doren, who privately called her a "power-mad, nasty, destructive, vengeful bitch," waited until the writer's death to strike back. In a memoir, she claimed that Louella ascended to her position because she was aboard William Randolph Hearst's yacht *Oneida* when a series of mysterious events occurred in the fall of 1924. "In celebration of the forty-third birthday of the silent movie director Thomas Ince, Hearst, fifteen guests—including Hearst's live-in girl friend Marion Davies and Charlie Chaplin—and a complete jazz band, embarked on a cruise from Los Angeles to San Diego. Ince, the story goes, was caught paying too much attention to Marion."

According to Van Doren, Hearst went below, got the gun he always kept on board, and fired at Ince, killing him outright. Ince's body was taken off the boat in San Diego and cremated before anyone could mention the word "autopsy." Newspapers in the Hearst chain reported that Ince had been struck with an unnamed illness and died at his home. But, claimed Van Doren, passengers had seen him taken off the boat on a stretcher. "Chaplin's secretary swore that she saw a bullet hole in Ince's head. Everyone on that cruise that day was taken care of. . . . Louella's payoff was the permanent column."

Parsons certainly behaved as if she had lifetime tenure on any paper that carried her maunderings. Marlon was from the East, however, cared nothing for the town's politics, and even less for its gossip queens. He found Louella difficult to look at and repulsive to read, and implied as much when he met her. She expected deference from new-comers; he arrived on a loud motorcycle, proudly wearing ripped jeans and an aggressively soiled undershirt. Helping himself to a chair, he sat in a wide-legged, provocative manner and filled his conversation with ribald phrases. Unnerved, Lolly coiled and struck. In her widely syndi-cated column she described this revolting Brando person. He had "the manners of a chimpanzee, the gall of a Kinsey researcher, and a swelled head the size of a Navy blimp, and just as pointed—as far as I'm concerned he can ride his bike off the Venice pier."

Marlon relished every word. The column gave him a perverse plea-sure, but it was just about the only gratification he was to find during his Hollywood initiation. Everything else seemed to be hard work or bad news. From his aunt came the dispiriting information that Jocelyn and her husband, Don, were at odds and would soon seek to divorce. Marlon senior had wasted a good deal of his son's paychecks on bad investments. Money was draining out of the account at alarming speed. In a funk, Marlon began work on *The Men*.

Kramer had prepared the way by casting real paraplegics, veterans maimed in battle. Although the roles were minor, they were there to lend verisimilitude. But the sense of authentic pain and rue had to come from the film's centerpiece. To understand what these vets were going through, Marlon checked into the Birmingham Veterans Hospi-tal near Los Angeles, a facility catering to the needs of the severely wounded. At the time such procedures were rare. Humorist S. J. Perel-man, who had spent a few years as a screenwriter, once parodied studio attempts at verisimilitude. For the 1945 film *The Lost Weekend*, "Ray Milland will go to the bars on 10th Avenue. Formerly 10th Avenue was brought to Ray Milland."

Over the course of three weeks Marlon learned how to live in a wheelchair, wear heavy leg braces, rely only on his arms for movement. More important, he discovered the sources of mental endurance that allowed paraplegics to deal with the attacks of "Why me?" resentment and depression. Most of the patients had a tough, ironic humor drained of lament and self-pity. He picked that up as well. When the men in the ward realized that Marlon had come to understand, not merely to mimic, they accepted him, shared memories and meals, and asked him to come along—in his wheelchair—when they visited their favorite hangout, a restaurant called the Pump Room.

When Marlon was in *A Flag Is Born*, Paul Muni told him about a trick he had played on a judge. The actor, who had come to the United States as a child, went through the final naturalization ceremony at the age of thirty-five, speaking in a hesitant, heavy middle-European accent, squinting his eyes as if he didn't quite understand each question. During the interrogation his accent slowly diminished. The final answer was delivered in impeccable English. Muni smiled at the astonished official. "Your honor, it's remarkable. Now that you've made me a citizen, I can speak perfectly!" At the Pump Room Marlon had a chance to enjoy a similar put-on, with more spectacular results. As the group sat in their wheelchairs downing their drinks, a wild-eyed woman entered the restaurant and rounded on them. She recognized the young men as veterans, and told them they needed to believe in Jesus. His healing powers would let them walk again.

The men listened with growing unease. They were not there to be given a sermon; they were there to get drunk and have some rare laughs. That was of no concern to the lady. While the others looked away Marlon gave her all his attention, a rapt, exalted look on his face. She concentrated on him alone, urging the paraplegic to get born again.

"You know, ma'am," he responded, "I believe you. I believe in the Lord."

"Well, I *want* you to believe. You should believe it, soldier, because I know that with the Lord's work you can recover."

"I do believe! I do believe!" Marlon gripped the sides of his wheelchair until his knuckles whitened. "I feel the Lord has come right into this room and into my body. The Lord is in my body. I feel it . . ."

As he started to raise himself, the tension was palpable. Busboys moved in, anticipating a hard fall. But Marlon kept rising until he stood erect. Step by ungainly step he made his way to the bar. Then, without warning, he suddenly broke into an improvisatory dance, complete with leaps and jetés. The woman shrieked and fled as laughter filled the Pump Room. The loudest roars came from the wheelchair table.

Marlon missed the workouts and banter the day he started filming.

He was in a crowd again, but it was a crowd of players he didn't know and technicians he didn't trust. Like most films, *The Men* would be shot out of sequence, making it difficult to maintain an emotional truth from scene to scene. Disoriented, he hesitated and mumbled, sometimes inaudibly. Director Fred Zinnemann, an Austrian who paid meticulous attention to the look and sound of things, was beside himself. In desperation he called Kazan in New York and went through a litany of the actor's mannerisms and affectations. "Marlon will be all right," Gadge advised. "Just be patient. He'll come through, I promise you."

Just as Marlon had searched for the soul of Stanley Kowalski, he tried to locate the center of Ken Wilcheck. After several weeks he did feel more comfortable in the part, aided by a group of outstanding performers. Richard Erdman, an underrated character actor, played one of the mordant ward mates along with Jack Webb, shortly to become famous as the deadpan cop on the radio and TV series *Dragnet.* Everett Sloane, Mr. Bernstein in *Citizen Kane,* was the psychiatrist who goads Ken into an acceptance of his condition. But the film was hurt by the miscasting of Teresa Wright. The sweet-faced actress specialized in the support of heroes who were physically afflicted (*The Pride of the Yankees*) or psychologically burdened (*The Best Years of Our Lives*). This time out, though, her costar was unlike Gary Cooper or Dana Andrews—or any other film actor. In a vital scene of sexual failure, for example, Marlon's powerful combination of sensuality and wrath was more than she could handle. It was difficult to believe these two ever had anything in common, even when Ken was whole. As a result, hardly anyone noticed her when the film unreeled. Once again, Marlon was the whole story.

The *New York Times* reviewer Bosley Crowther called *The Men* a "fine and arresting film," and made much of "Mr. Brando as the veteran who endures the most difficult time." As Ken, he "is so vividly real, dynamic and sensitive that his illusion is complete." Marlon's face, his arrhythmic body movements, "and especially the strange timbre of his voice, often broken and plaintive and boyish, are articulate in every way. Out of stiff and frozen silences he can lash into a passionate rage with the fearful and flailing frenzy of a taut cable suddenly cut. Or he can show the poignant tenderness of [a] doctor with a child." *Time* referred to the actor as "Broadway's Marlon Brando," and went on to hail his cinematic debut as "magnificent." Ken's hesitant speech, "glowering silences and expert simulation of paraplegia do not suggest acting; they look chillingly like the real thing." Marlon made the cover of *Cue* magazine and delightedly gave out copies to friends and acquaintances. Sympathetic press coverage rolled on; the chorus of approval was nearly unanimous. The only holdout was the public itself. The United States had sent its first big wave of troops to South Korea shortly before *The Men* opened nationwide. A cinematic look back at maimed veterans, no matter how lofty its aims, elicited too many painful feelings about another war. Grosses slumped off sharply, and after two weeks the movie was judged to be a box-office failure. No one blamed the disappointment on Marlon. He had made his film debut, acting only from the waist up, and he had still wowed them all. As far as the executives at MCA were concerned, he was the next big thing.

3

At first, studio discussions about an adaptation of *Streetcar* went nowhere. All Hollywood was on tiptoe, fearful of making a wrong move. The notion of presenting a drama with a loud vulgarian at its center, plus a rape, plus the suggestions of the homosexuality of Blanche DuBois's husband . . . the project was deemed dicey and distasteful by most production chiefs. But not all. The rights to Tennessee Williams's play had been acquired by the cultivated, smooth-talking superagent Charles Feldman, head of the Famous Artists talent agency. ("Charlie," Kazan was to observe acidly, was "rather handsome in a soft yielding way, the body suited to bed and armchair.") The company's clients included Cary Grant, John Wayne, Gary Cooper, Olivia de Havilland, Ava Gardner, William Holden, and Lauren Bacall. No one failed to return Feldman's calls. He had already sold *A Glass Menagerie* to Paramount. That film was stultified and miscast—Gertrude Lawrence and Jane Wyman had no resonance at all—but the payment had satisfied the playwright, and he agreed to entrust Feldman with his new work.

Slowly and cannily Feldman worked his way around the majors, daring the big names to underwrite this masterpiece and accusing them of cowardice when they didn't. Darryl F. Zanuck, the most outspoken mogul at Twentieth Century–Fox, snapped at Feldman, "You are entirely wrong about my views on *A Streetcar Named Desire*. I had the story bought *before* you bought it. I worked out the deal completely with Kazan in New York and then Spyros [Skouras] came in with his objections. He was so violent on the subject that he even offered to resign the presidency of the corporation if we produced the picture. . . . In the face of this, I withdrew." Others found reasons not to take the leap.

Ultimately Jack Warner agreed to back the film, with certain provisos. The script would have to be presented to Joseph Breen, a conservative Catholic, and censorious head of the Production Code Administration. That was fine with Feldman. After a close reading, Breen decreed that the profanity must go, and that the "gross sex" be reworked and made acceptable to the American public. Any hints of perversion were, of course, to be eliminated. The playwright went along with some of the changes, but insisted that the rape scene would have to stay—it was critical to the entire structure of *Streetcar*. He presented it as a metaphor: "the ravishment of the tender, the sensitive, the delicate, by the savage and brutal forces of modern society." After much haggling Breen bought the interpretation, but would not yield in his demand for a new conclusion: The brute must be punished for his conduct. Williams caved. Just before the fadeout Stella would whisper a new and crucial bit of information in her baby's ear: They were not going to return to Stanley, thereby punishing the transgressor.

Feldman replaced Irene Selznick as producer; otherwise the Broadway nucleus remained intact. Kazan was scheduled to direct. Marlon, guaranteed star billing and a $75,000 salary, would repeat as Kowalski. Karl Malden, Kim Hunter, Rudy Bond would reprise their stage roles as well. According to Warner, though, the movie needed the punch of a proven box-office star. Jessica Tandy was out. Some top actresses came up for consideration, with Olivia de Havilland leading the pack. Her credentials were impeccable. She had already won two Best Actress Academy Awards—for her work in *To Each His Own* in 1946 and three years later for the title role in *The Heiress*. She had been a favorite of filmgoers for over a decade. She was also very pricey. Feldman, who represented De Havilland, demanded $175,000 for her services. Warner Bros. looked elsewhere. The best candidate appeared to be Vivien Leigh. The English actress had first learned to speak like a southern belle for her role as Scarlett O'Hara in *Gone with the Wind*. And this last season she had appeared as Blanche in the West End production of *Streetcar,* directed by her husband Laurence Olivier. Jack Warner had long considered Leigh a woman of class and intelligence. Now she seemed even more appealing; her agent wanted a mere $100,000. That meant Warner Bros. could have Marlon *and* Vivien for the price of Olivia. The studio snapped her up.

Now the hard work began. On the first day of rehearsal Kazan spoke to the company about his intentions. Leigh was unhappy with what she heard. "When Larry and I did the play in London," she began, and went on to trill about the Oliviers' interpretations of the Williams text. Kazan ground his teeth. He could not allow the power to pass from director to actress—especially with the cast looking on. Yet he maintained an air of gentility, pointing out in the simplest terms that Vivien was in Hollywood, not London, and that she was acting opposite Brando, not Olivier. Rather than force an open confrontation, he never varied from his soft, reasonable approach. Two weeks into the filming the star and director got on the same page. Even so, it was too late to rescue the early scenes, marred by her posturing and theatrics. Meantime, Vivien and Marlon had to define their own relationship. Those who expected emotional wrangles were wrong. The two actors shook hands at the first meeting and thereafter maintained a veneer of calm professionalism. It was sheer artifice; Marlon remembered that Leigh was "very much like Tennessee's wounded butterfly. Like Blanche, she slept with almost everybody and was beginning to dissolve mentally and to fray at the ends physically." The "almost everybody" did not include Marlon—or so he wrote in his memoir. Though he informed Wally Cox that he was so anxious to bed his costar that his "teeth ached," Olivier was in Hollywood at the time, and "I liked him too much to invade his chicken coop."

That is not what Leigh told Kazan: "I must say this for Marlon. When it comes to couples, he's an equal-opportunity seducer. On many a night he rose from Larry's bed and joined me in mine." She was a woman of notorious instability, and her testimony is thus unreliable. But David Niven had no such mental difficulties. Of course, he could have been pulling the leg of biographer Darwin Porter, but the account seems credible enough. Newly arrived from London, Niven was Olivier's houseguest. One evening he chanced to be walking in the garden, where he came upon "Brando and Larry swimming naked in the pool. Larry was kissing Brando. Or maybe it was the other way around.

I turned my back on them and went inside to join Vivien. I'm sure she knew what was going on, but she made no mention of it. Nor did I. One must be sophisticated about such matters in life."

By some adroit cutting, and by the use of Leigh's precarious psyche, Kazan corrected the imbalance of the Broadway *Streetcar.* The film was no longer the Marlon Brando Show—nor was it quite as toned down as Breen wanted. But the studio had the final say, and some four minutes were excised from the feature, infuriating Kazan. Other stresses did not sweeten his disposition. Gadge's onetime membership in the Communist party had just been revealed to the public, and he was shortly to be grilled by HUAC congressmen. With his career in jeopardy, Kazan fought long and hard for the director's cut. Against the advice of friends he went public with his dissatisfactions. When the movie opened he sent a letter to *The New York Times* complaining that the studio had excised vital footage from Tennessee Williams's master-work. Gadge toyed with the Solomonic idea of showing two versions of the movie, one before the deletions were made, the other afterward. But he knew the answer would be no; Warner Bros. had no intention of roiling any more waters. It was enough that *Streetcar* could be released without pickets from the Catholic Legion of Decency or some other righteous outfit.

The Warner Bros. strategy worked. *Time* put the film on its Ten Best list, and the *Times* rated it as the best film of 1951. *Streetcar* was one of the five biggest money earners that year; grosses topped out at $4.25 million. It was nominated in eight Academy Award categories. Vivien Leigh won for Best Actress in a Leading Role, Karl Malden and Kim Hunter for Best Supporting Actor and Actress. (For months afterward, wrote film historian Sam Staggs, "friends and strangers would stand in the street and yell up 'Stelllla!' at [Kim's] second-floor apartment on Commerce Street.") Possibly because Kazan's old political affiliations had just come to light, he lost to George Stevens for his direction of *A Place in the Sun,* a forceful adaptation of Theodore Dreiser's *An American Tragedy* starring Elizabeth Taylor and Montgomery Clift. Neither Clift nor Brando could beat the long odds on Humphrey Bogart, the engaging grouch of *The African Queen.*

In now-typical Brando style, Marlon affected Oscar indifference. He failed to show up for the ceremonies at the Pantages Theatre and forsook Hollywood for Manhattan. Reporters were told that performing had no magic for him anymore. He was going back to school. "Another Brando put-on," concluded Wally Cox as soon as he read the interview, and he was correct. Marlon had taken his tone from Ernest Hemingway's aperçu. Papa stated that "a built-in, shock-proof shit detector" was the radar of all great writers. Actors, too, Marlon decided. The man who was always aware of the insincere and the fraudulent in others had spotted symptoms in himself. How long would it be before friends saw them, and then critics, and then the public? From here on, he decided, no awards, politics, or scandal would affect his life in any way. You had to be difficult in this difficult business, with the congressmen at your past and the paparazzi at your door. Screw the press. Screw the politicians. What did it matter what they wrote or did? You kept your eyes on your work, you stepped over the steaming pile, and you moved on.

4

Brando and Kazan were reunited in *Viva Zapata!*, John Steinbeck's biographical story of Emiliano Zapata, a Mexican revolutionary who flourished in the early twentieth century. The story of rebel versus government was not exactly what Hollywood was looking for in 1952. Leo McCarey's *My Son John*, being prepared at the same time, seemed more to the point. The Paramount drama concerned a wily young Communist (Robert Walker) who lies to his sainted mother (Helen Hayes) and reviles his upright father (Dean Jagger). That paterfamilias summarizes the theme when he breaks into a xenophobic World War I song:

> *If you don't like the stars in Old Glory,*
> *If you don't like the Red, White and Blue,*
> *Then don't be like the cur in the story,*
> *Don't bite the hand that's feeding you!*

At the denouement John is shot by Reds and bleeds to death on the steps of the Lincoln Memorial. The reason for his execution is soon made manifest. Realizing that Dad was right all along, he has taped an anti-Communist confessional. Posthumously broadcast at a college commencement, the voice speaks to potential "useful fools" who might turn left after graduation:

"I was flattered when I was immediately recognized as an intellect. I was invited into homes where only superior minds communed. It excited my freshman fancy to hear daring thoughts that I wouldn't have dreamed of when I lived at home—a bold defiance of the only author-ities I knew, my Church and my mother and father. I know that many of you have experienced that stimulation—but stimulation leads to narcotics." Reviled by critics for its crudity, *My Son John* was nonethe-less an indicator of mid-century Hollywood angst. The HUAC and oth-ers on the Right had to be appeased. The last thing the town needed was a politically controversial movie. And yet that was precisely what the scenarist and director had in mind.

Kazan regarded the life of Emiliano Zapata (reconfigured by Stein-beck) as a commentary on 1950s America. The real Zapata came from a family of landowners, and spent his early years amusing himself with a wardrobe of elegant suits and a stable of fine horses. The indulgence was not to last. Moved by the sight of an oppressed peasantry, he joined two other militants, Pancho Villa and Pascual Orozco, and led brigades of rebellious peons against the armies of the dictator Porfirio Díaz. After forcing Díaz into exile, Zapata rose to power only to resign his office and go into hiding: He had become convinced that the new men were as corrupt as the ones they had replaced. His instincts did not play him false. A year later Zapata paid the ultimate price for his honor, slain by conniving officers who lured him into the open. Robert Frost commented on the trouble with revolutions: ". . . it brings the same class up on top / Executives of skillful execution / Will therefore plan to go halfway and stop." The real Zapata would have understood.

Gadge intended to portray himself as a latter-day Zapata, a former Communist who had renounced the party and its mendacious leaders, but who had never compromised his principles by going over to the other side. It was a canny move; Kazan was preparing to furnish the HUAC with the names of cell members back in the 1930s, and he knew he would be pilloried for the act. As he planned out the film, he made ready to portray himself as a man made into a martyr by extremists on both sides. "Whenever the Communists stake a claim to any concept or person the people value," he maintained, "the overanxious Right plays into their hands. . . . If they would treat the Communist claim to peace, to free speech—and to men like Zapata—with the same good sense that greets the Communist claim to the bicycle, it would make life easier for those who value those things."

Because the film had to entertain as well as instruct, *Viva Zapata!* was written and directed on two levels. Producer Darryl Zanuck always regarded the film as a simple, well-made Mexican oater, punctuated by gunfights and peopled with valorous peasants and squinting bad guys. In Gadge's private view, *Zapata* was a metaphor for the power struggle taking place in the United States among three forces: a) the congressional investigators; b) the hard-line Communists; and c) the anti-Communists like himself, wise, experienced observers who took the middle road. It was a bit too much freight for such an elemental story. As Kazan biographer Richard Schickel points out, when, toward the end of the script, Zapata tells his followers, " 'A strong people doesn't need a strong leader. Strong leaders make a weak people,' we don't hear a peasant speaking; we hear well-meaning Yankee ventriloquism. Indeed . . . there is something overripe in Steinbeck's dialogue, something a little too self-conscious—'the people, *sí!*'—in its diction."

Zanuck had lobbied for the handsome "Black Irishman," Tyrone Power, to play Zapata. Kazan knew better. To dissuade his boss, he filmed a screen test with Marlon and an important young Broadway actress, Julie Harris, in full costume, as Emiliano's wife, Josefa. Zanuck viewed the footage in his private screening room and pronounced it unacceptable. These two gringos as Latinos? Ludicrous. Harris was definitely out. The mogul conceded that Marlon had presence, but wired Kazan in New York: I DON'T UNDERSTAND A GODDAMNED THING THE SON OF A BITCH SAYS. CAN'T YOU STOP HIM FROM MUMBLING? Kazan guaranteed that audiences would hear every diphthong, and that Marlon would look as Mexican as Pancho Villa by the time the makeup department got through with him. Grudgingly Zanuck went along. But there was a price attached. Jean Peters would play Josefa. This was a nonnegotiable demand. The actress had recently won a beauty contest, she had a dark exotic look, and Fox had big plans for her. Of somewhat greater significance, she was the current love interest of Howard Hughes. Kazan accepted the terms. Zanuck had a cornball idea of ending the film with Zapata's white horse roaming the hills. Gadge went along with that, too.

While the tone and tempo of the film were being planned, Marlon did his now-customary preparation, journeying down to Sonora, Mexico, in the company of his pet raccoon, Russell, to observe peasant life for himself. Zapata had been gunned down in 1919; there were plenty of folks around who still remembered him. He was said to be a heaven-sent figure who walked like an ordinary man, a born leader, unedu-cated but wise in the ways of the world, an appreciator of female beauty, a fine equestrian. Some swore that Emiliano had never died, that on certain nights he could be heard riding his stallion somewhere in the hills. Marlon found those myths irresistible. He immediately identified with the character and returned to the set in Roma, Texas, in a state of jubilation.

There were additional reasons for his upbeat mood. While in Mex-ico he had become bedazzled by a dark-skinned, exotic woman named Movita Castaneda. She was at least seven years his senior, an experi-enced actress who had appeared in the 1935 film *Mutiny on the Bounty*. Part Indian, part Spanish, Movita had known many men, including the husband she had discarded but not divorced—and, she let it be known, Clark Gable and Errol Flynn. In the ways of love she was extremely sophisticated. In other areas she was a total naïf. Movita believed that inanimate objects had a life of their own; ghosts and angels haunted her world. As superstitious and credulous as a child, she was the one person who believed Marlon's tale of eating gazelles' eyes for breakfast. All this attracted and delighted him. Here was the essence of woman, primitive, earthy, as far from vanilla as he could get. He brought Movita north and wangled a walk-on role for her so that she could legitimately hang around the set. Not that this prevented him from seeking other liaisons. Jean Peters came to the set with a duenna who never seemed to leave her side. "Since nothing energized my libido more than a well-guarded target," Marlon admitted, "I was determined to have her." He also went after another actress who hung around. At the time Marilyn Monroe was seeing Kazan. When Gadge's family paid a visit, Marlon took over the role of lover until the coast was clear.

Once filming began, he stopped showing off and became a consum-mate professional. In *The Men* and *Streetcar* the star had played con-temporary figures in modern dress. *Viva Zapata!* put him in period costume. Some artful work was done on Marlon's face and hands—skin artificially darkened, eyes slanted a bit, nostrils flared, a dark turned-down mustache stuck on to suggest ferocity. A dialogue coach was brought in to help give his words a slight Spanish intonation, and Gadge supplied a few insights: Emiliano is, *au fond,* a politician. He would not understand the word *romance* as Americans think of it. He doesn't love Señora Zapata, for example; he loves his *compadres.* The man "has no need for a special woman. Women are to be used, knocked up, and left." In a word, macho. In two words, typecasting.

Kazan imparted only enough information to get his star under way. Perhaps he thought minimalism was the way to go on this picture, but it seems more likely that he was preoccupied with surviving. Zanuck knew that his director had been a member of the Communist party; Fox had gone ahead with the project anyway. But Gadge knew he was walking a tightrope: "There was no doubt where I stood—with the business boys, with the movie moguls, with the 'gonifs,' [Yiddish for *thieves*] with the old, unfeeling, insensitive, crass vulgar industry barbarians. I trusted them most because I could rely on one thing: If in an open competition I could make an exciting film that people would want to see, they'd go with me. If they thought they could make a bundle, they wouldn't knuckle under to censorship—at least not yet."

In this, he was to acknowledge, he made a grievous error. The admired barbarians turned out to be the kind of men Groucho Marx had in mind when he cracked, "Those are my principles. If you don't like them, I have others." In his memoir, Kazan said he was "to find out that there were many conspiracies a filmmaker in our country had to deal with—that of the right, that of the left, that of the self-appointed moralists of the Catholic Church, and that of the men who tend the springs of gold." Gadge placed his trust in the studio chiefs, only to discover that Jack Warner had given confidential information to the Committee: "Arthur Miller and Elia Kazan worked on Broadway where they practiced some sort of subversion."

Even without the backstairs intrigues, Kazan had reason to feel apprehensive. And so he might have, save for his wife Molly, who had arrived with the children and taken up residence in a nearby hotel. Zanuck, notorious for sending memos on every conceivable subject, had been bombarding Kazan with directives sent by Western Union. At the beginning, wrote Gadge, "they were laudatory and appreciative." But all too soon they were hints that the picture was falling behind schedule, "then more than hints, complaints and bitter ones." Abruptly, the wires stopped. It was a relief not to receive a scolding after long days under the relentless Texas sun. In fact, Zanuck had not ceased his complaints and warnings. They were sent to the hotel, where Molly headed them off and hid them from her husband.

In a way her decision proved unwise; Gadge, who liked to be in control at all times, was unaware of the hostile climate back home. Yet because of his ignorance, he was free to concentrate on the picture, to get the best from his crew and cast—particularly Marlon. Under his guidance the star vanished into the role. He came across as a peasant with a rough, untutored intellect, at once forceful and intimidated by learned people like his wife, who possessed a formal wisdom beyond his reach. One of the film's most telling moments occurs on the Zapatas' wedding night, when the fumbling, uncertain Emilio confides to Josefa that the revolution requires something he cannot give it—knowledge. Once the battle is won, he realizes, "my horse and my rifle won't help me."

Kazan encouraged a friendship between Brando and his costar Anthony Quinn—after all, they had both played Stanley Kowalski on Broadway. But there were enormous gaps between the two. Quinn had been in the movies since the mid-1930s, usually playing swarthy "heavies"—Arabian sheiks, Hawaiian chiefs, Chinese guerrillas, and the like. His career inched forward when he married Cecil B. DeMille's adopted daughter, Katherine, but the marriage didn't last nor did the parts get much better. Not without reason, Anthony believed his career had been held back because of his ethnic appearance. Although he was 50 percent Mexican and 50 percent Irish, the Mexican half was dominant in his physiognomy and personality. He had been raised in a Los Angeles barrio, and was proud of the fact that several of his ancestors fought with Pancho Villa. Mexico and its citizens were well known to him; he rode a horse with a confidence that Marlon never gained, and gave convincing authority to the character of Zapata's brother Eufemio. Marlon, a star with only two pictures under his belt, had to work diligently to present his persona, and was never truly satisfied with his work. Yet in the beginning there was no resentment between the men; onscreen they shared a sense of mission, and at the end of the day's shooting they enjoyed each other's company.

Later in the story, shot more or less in sequence, drink and greed start to erode Eufemio's character. Then the brothers feud, one harsh and accusatory, the other blustering and defensive. At that juncture, Marlon remembered, Quinn was no longer amicable. "I sensed a bitterness toward me, and if I suggested a drink after work, he either turned me down or else was sullen and said little. Only years later did I learn why." Quinn, meanwhile, felt that Marlon was standoffish and deliberately remote. He asked some of the actors who knew Brando back in New York, "Is he queer?"

The reason both men behaved so badly to each other was that the scenes of sibling rivalry needed a white-heat authority: In Gadge's opinion such emotion could not be faked. In order to get it he drove a wedge between the actors, first favoring one, then the other, creating a jealousy where there had been comradeship. When Quinn suggested that peasants would communicate their anger by banging stones together until the entire group filled the air with that harsh sound, Kazan was quick to use it. He praised Anthony openly and quietly whispered in his ear that Brando had been spreading scurrilous rumors about him. When Quinn took a break, Gadge told Marlon that Anthony described him as an overpraised, cosseted performer. In time the actors realized that they were being manipulated, but it would take decades before they felt thoroughly at ease in each other's company. They had learned the hard way that every Elia Kazan picture came with a curse—Elia Kazan.

Most critics focused on the actor rather than the picture; *Zapata* was considered a Brando film rather than a biographical epic. A few reviewers complained about Marlon's tendency to speak indistinctly in the romantic episodes. Bosley Crowther called them "clumsy inter-changes." For the most part, though, the *Times* critic was impressed. "When this dynamic young performer is speaking his anger or his love for a fellow revolutionary, or when he is charging through the land at the head of his rebel-soldiers or walking bravely into the trap of his doom, there is power enough in his portrayal to cause the screen to throb." *Time* and *Newsweek* published raves, and when Oscar time came Marlon received his second Academy Award nomination for Best Actor. He knew he wouldn't get the statuette and, in fact, thought he didn't deserve it. Watching the picture straight through, Marlon expressed a dislike of his accent and concluded that he was "too soft, too sweet" in the role of Zapata. He packed up Russell the raccoon, took Movita in hand, and returned to New York. Of all the past girl-friends in his life, Marlon bothered to look up only one: Ellen Adler. The reason was sad but simple. His distaste for fakery had been with him since the days of childhood, when he and his sisters smiled and hid their hellish, punitive family life from schoolmates. And by his lights he was still a phony, as bogus as a Hollywood set with a mansion in front and two-by-fours in back where no one could see them. "In all the time we remained friends," she was to remember, "I observed one rule. I never, ever mentioned his work. Not a word about his performance in any film, no matter how great. Marlon's unwritten law was that he had other concerns, other things to talk about, and that these were foremost on his mind—mutual friends, politics, racism, history. So we talked of those and *only* of those. Our relationship was unique for that reason. I respected his feelings, and among all the people he knew, outside of his family we remained the closest friends for over fifty years."

While in New York Marlon made sure to see Wally Cox go through his paces at the Century Theatre. There, before a live audience every week, the Walrus played the title role in *Mister Peepers*. The pioneering TV sitcom was built around his bespectacled, bumbling personality. Playing the part of an amiable but bewildered high school science teacher, Wally had grown nearly as popular as his friend. Georgeann Johnson, a member of the Peepers troupe, ran into Marlon during that time. "People always thought those two made an incongruous pair," she said. "Marlon was one of those actors who seemed to have lights on him at all times. In a store, he was what you looked at, not the merchandise. But Wally was so intelligent, so well informed about so many things, that intellectually he was often way ahead of Marlon. And Marlon knew it." Indeed, Brando said that Cox "probably came closer than anyone I've ever known to being a genius. He was absorbed as I was by human foibles, and was one of my greatest teachers. I was untutored and uncertain in my use of language. Almost as if he were leading me by the hand, Wally taught me how to speak and to see in words the melodies of life." At this point, Marlon relished his friend's success more than his own. He had been given $100,000 for an unsatisfactory performance and said he didn't care if he ever acted again. Anywhere. Once again, neither Wally nor any of his other friends believed a word he said.

5

"I can see the thing's body. It's large, large as a bear and it glistens like wet leather! But that face, it . . . it's indescribable! I can hardly force myself to keep looking at it. The eyes are black and gleam like a serpent. The mouth is V-shaped with saliva dripping from its rimless lips that seem to quiver and pulsate!" The terrified voice issued from radio sets on October 30, 1938, throwing a nation into panic. By using a documentary format, the twenty-three-year-old actor/scriptwriter/director Orson Welles convinced his listeners that Martians had landed in New Jersey and were heading their way. In a follow-up newspaper column, journalist Dorothy Thompson discerned a new and dangerous world being born: The producer John Houseman, Welles, and the members of their company "have demonstrated more potently than any argument, demonstrated beyond a question of a doubt, the appalling dangers and enormous effectiveness of popular and theatrical demagoguery."

Impressed by her conclusion, Houseman went on to produce a modern-dress *Julius Caesar,* with the emperor as a leader along the lines of the Italian Fascist Benito Mussolini. Following that he staged a sensational *King Lear* on Broadway in 1950. By then the protean Englishman had shown an unerring instinct for works that caused chatter and/or made a satisfactory profit for their investors. Bigwigs at MGM had already invested in *Kiss Me, Kate,* Cole Porter's rendition of *The Taming of the Shrew;* they thought it was time to do a straight adaptation of Shakespeare to showcase the studio's glossy style. Houseman was the logical choice to produce *Julius Caesar.* The director would be Joseph L. Mankiewicz, a major force in film since his Oscars for writing and directing *A Letter to Three Wives* in 1949 and *All About Eve* the following year. There was no need for this team to pore over casting directories. They had already filled the roles in their minds.

Louis Calhern had proved himself as a Shakespearean actor as well as a movie villain; he would make a pompous, vulnerable Caesar. John Gielgud, with his "lean and hungry look" and elegant diction, was ideal for Cassius. James Mason would be Brutus; Edmund O'Brien, a veteran of the Mercury Theatre, but better known for his tough-guy roles in B movies, was cast in the small but pivotal role of the provocateur Casca. Deborah Kerr would play the blindly loyal Portia, Brutus's mate; Greer Garson was Caesar's anxious wife, Calpurnia. That left one major role to be filled: Marc Antony. The rising young actor Paul Scofield was mentioned for the part and a screen test arranged in London. From Hollywood, Houseman cabled Mankiewicz and asked him to delay things for a few days. "I had just had a mad but brilliant idea," wrote the producer in his memoir, "that we seriously consider Marlon Brando for the role of Antony." The suggestion was met with general disbelief by Houseman's English colleagues. When they heard Marlon's name, they immediately thought of Stanley Kowalski bellowing for Stella and assumed that this was his natural speaking voice. The producer knew better. He remembered a young, articulate Marlon playing opposite Paul Muni in *A Flag Is Born* and convinced Mankiewicz to let the actor audition. Marlon was in no mood to get into costume but he did agree to tape one of the speeches. After all, he argued, it wasn't his looks they were worried about, but his diction. Marlon didn't use the familiar "Friends, Romans, countrymen" speech. Instead he chose Marc Antony's vengeful prediction to the Senate after the assassination:

> *A curse shall light upon the limbs of men;*
> *Domestic fury and fierce civil strife*
> *Shall cumber all the parts of Italy. . . .*
> *And Caesar's spirit, ranging for revenge,*
> *With Ate by his side come hot from hell,*
> *Shall in these confines with a monarch's voice*
> *Cry "Havoc!" and let slip the dogs of war . . .*

Houseman appraised it as a "powerful and flawless recording." It was so good that a false rumor made its way around the industry: Laurence Olivier had made the tape and Houseman had fallen for the substitution. Mankiewicz was not so enthusiastic at first. In his opinion Marlon needed to work on his articulation—the voice was supple enough but self-consciously gentle or, as he put it sardonically, "exactly like June Allyson." Just the same, he could see the virtues of casting a maverick in the role, particularly since Marlon was willing to take a pay cut in order to work with such a distinguished group. When he signed on, no publicity was issued. That led Hedda Hopper to tell her readers, "I don't believe the rumor that Marlon Brando will play Marc Antony in MGM's *Julius Caesar*. His voice just wouldn't blend with the rest of the cast."

In fact it did, for two reasons. He was moved anew by the passages he had pored over in the Shattuck Academy library. And Gielgud went over the speeches with Marlon, line by line, adding fervor and grace to his approach. As they worked together, the Englishman passed on a lifetime of wisdom about playing Shakespeare: how to clarify a subtext, how to recite iambic pentameter in a natural manner, how to sustain interest over the course of a long monologue. Some of the coaching is evident in the finished film but, Houseman insisted, the real credit had to go to Brando himself. In take after take he repeated his speeches without a hitch, never losing his energy or concentration.

Houseman was unaware that the Brando performance had its own subtext. During the filming Marlon learned that Elia Kazan had cooperated with congressional investigators, naming a whole string of "subversives." The director set up an elaborate defense of his films for the HUAC, pointing out that *A Tree Grows in Brooklyn* was strongly pro-American and that *Viva Zapata!* was discernibly anti-Communist. Some of Gadge's onetime friends responded by cursing him in public, or by crossing the street rather than greet him. Arthur Miller topped them all: He wrote a play called *The Crucible*. Set in eighteenth-century Salem, Massachusetts, it reviled those who gave in to hysterical witch hunters.

Marlon hardly knew how to respond. At this point he was a sentimental activist with only a superficial knowledge of American politics, Left or Right. All he had was the scuttlebutt: Fox chief Spyros Skouras warned Gadge that if he wanted to continue his movie career he would have to spill his guts. Yet Gadge's defenders said the Committee already had the names he mentioned: Morris Carnovsky and his wife, Phoebe Brand; J. Edward Bromberg; Art Smith; Clifford Odets. The detractors responded: In that case why wasn't Kazan satisfied with his testimony? Why did he have to follow it with a self-justifying full-page ad in *The New York Times:* "Secrecy serves the Communists. At the other pole, it serves those who are interested in silencing liberal voices. The employment of good liberals is threatened because they have allowed themselves to become associated with or silenced by the Communists. Liberals must speak out."

Looking back, Conrad Bromberg, son of J. Edward, coolly appraised Kazan's situation. Gadge "wasn't about to be destroyed. Business was involved, too. Twentieth Century–Fox had pictures in the can directed by Kazan. In a sense he had leverage. He also had a contract for several hundreds of thousands of dollars. So if he did a number for them they had to do a number for him." Bromberg's take, spoken many years later, was exactly what Marlon believed the day he took a morning break with Mankiewicz. As they walked along one of the studio streets, the director turned to say something and noticed that tears were coursing down the actor's face. In a low voice, Marlon asked, "What do I do when I see him? Do I bust him in the nose, or what?" Mankiewicz knew very well who the "him" was; the story of Kazan's capitulation was in every paper and on everyone's lips. The director knew that he had to calm Marlon down or risk the loss of a pivotal member of the cast. As they ate lunch, Mankiewicz discussed Kazan's career move, using the vocabulary of a Los Angeles self-help guru. "Try to understand his pain," counseled the director. "He's got to have pain." Booming generalities filled the air. As feel-good and fatuous as the advice was, it seemed to take hold. Marlon never again raised the subject of Gadge in Mankiewicz's presence. He swallowed the sadness and rage, and used it to make his performance all the more memorable.

Marlon's autobiography devotes one line to his work on that film: Among all those British professionals, "for me to walk onto a movie set and play Marc Antony was asinine"—yet another example of his persistent self-denigration, and wholly incorrect. Indeed, the actor who played Marc Antony's servant was quick to praise Marlon's self-discipline. "The anti-Brando people would have been astonished at how professional he was," said William Phipps. "They were quick to think of him as being a rogue and sloppy. But he came to the set extremely well-prepared. Yeah, he was a Method actor—Marlon's method." After a screening, John Huston praised Marlon in a different way: "Christ! It was like a furnace door opening—the heat came off the screen. I don't know another actor who could do that." Gielgud offered the young American a full season at Hammersmith, costarring with Scofield. In time he might even get to play *Hamlet*. Marlon politely declined; he said he had no interest in acting in the theater. The reply was both true and disingenuous. *Streetcar* had been instructive; repeating the same lines for months at a time revealed his low threshold of boredom. But something else lay behind the refusal. Gielgud was a workaholic, so committed to his vocation that he scarcely knew anything else. In 1939 a story about him made the rounds. Returning home with a bunch of newspapers, he was asked whether Germany had declared war on Britain. "Oh, I don't know anything about that," he said. "But Gladys Cooper has got the most terrible reviews." He was also an out-of-the-closet homosexual who brought his lover to the set, but who could assume any character in any play, gay or straight. When

Gielgud put Cassius's uniform on for the first time, the entire cast watched in wonderment as he turned from a WASP-ish gentleman into a hard-edged, convincingly masculine Roman soldier. What they saw was more than artifice; it was art, and Marlon could not bring himself to acknowledge that truth. It implied that what he did for a living was an honorable and worthy vocation.

1954–1955

That *Streetcar* Man Has a New Desire!

1

Upon the release of his latest film, Marlon became everything MCA had hoped for, and more. With four edgy and lauded roles behind him, he was the hottest property in Hollywood, the first sexually threatening star since Rudolph Valentino.

Separated by thirty years, Rudolph and Marlon appeared to be as different as Naples and Omaha. In fact, the similarities were uncanny. Pre-Valentino, the silent screen's male ideals were straight arrows like Douglas Fairbanks and William S. Hart; after *The Sheik* opened in 1921—exactly three decades before the debut of *Streetcar*—conditions changed. The hot-eyed Italian electrified the postwar American female. In her biography of Valentino, *Dark Lover,* Emily W. Leider wittily asserts that the actor's image "helped to deflower America." A movie magazine put it in a less extravagant manner: Rudolph "does not look like your husband. He is not in the least like your brother. He does not resemble the man your mother thinks you ought to marry." Men tried to denigrate him as a slinky androgyne, a "pink powder puff." It did no good; the ladies were crazy about him. Soon, young men on the make were being called "sheiks," and sometime afterward a brand of condoms called Sheiks carried a profile of Valentino.

In a valedictory, Charlie Chaplin saluted the great lover of the silent screen, who died young: "He had an air of sadness. He was intelligent, quiet and without vanity, and had great allure for women." H. L. Mencken was more pointed and tragically accurate: "Valentino's agony was the agony of a man of relatively civilized feelings thrown into a situation of intolerable vulgarity, destructive alike to his peace and to his dignity. Here was a young man who was living daily the dreams of millions of other young men. Here was one who was catnip to women.

Here was one who had wealth and fame. And here was one who was very unhappy."

Marlon Brando could relate to those sentiments. Upon his arrival the contemporary *beaux idéals* of the cinema also turned into back numbers. Overnight, Anthony Quinn noticed, "everybody started behaving like Brando." The hesitant, wounded, sexually volatile presence of this new star was irresistible. Like Valentino, Marlon did not look like anyone's brother or husband—he was unfraternal and did not in the least resemble an ideal candidate for the altar. Men tried to dismiss him as androgynous; retouched pictures of Marlon engaged in sex acts with other men circulated in New York and Hollywood. If they served to make him attractive to male homosexuals, female filmgoers were turned on in much larger numbers and with greater intensity. They continued to be iron filings to the Brando magnet. Yet for all the workmen's compensations of money and fame, he, too, exhaled an air of melancholia; he, too, was a surprisingly vulnerable figure surrounded by wretched excess. It was one thing to be a sly ladies' man about town and quite another to be the latest sex symbol. It reduced you from a private seducer to a public joke, a punch line, a satyr with a permanent erection. The only way to deal with the process was to characterize the city as Tinseltown and himself as a wage slave like any other guy. He just had a bigger paycheck; that was the only difference. What was Hollywood? he asked anyone who would listen. Before they could reply he supplied the answer: "Simply a place where people, including me, made money, like a mill town in New England or an oil field in Texas." He could see by their faces that they didn't believe a word he said.

2

"The Fifties," observed John Updike, who came to maturity in that period, "should be understood as, like the Twenties, a post-war decade. The returning veterans had set the tone for the colleges; serious study, leading to the private redoubt of the career, the kids, the collie, and the tract house. As in the Twenties, business interests reasserted control over government."

These conditions were not to last. Although the youth of the 1950s were subsequently labeled as the Silent Generation, a great deal of angst and fury bubbled just below the surface. Americans, particularly American working men, had to deal with mixed messages. On one hand, executives were encouraged to play the game: white shirt and tie, gray flannel suit, and political opinions to match. On the other hand, numerous bestsellers warned about the price of conformity. The titles of two were especially eloquent: *The Lonely Crowd* and *The Crack in the Picture Window.*

Through that crack, intimations of a rebellion could already be seen. A young blues singer attracted the attention of Sun Records, whose founder was looking for "a white man with a Negro sound and the Negro feel." Handled correctly, he "could make a billion dollars" for the two of them, cutting across the race line. "That's All Right" and "Blue Moon of Kentucky" went out on one 78-rpm record, and Elvis Presley caught on. He already had his musical role models, but he needed a look, a pictorial style. He had already seen Marlon's first three movies; he would slowly begin to take on the actor's smoldering, alienated affect.

Signs of change were everywhere. In the field of art, avant-garde ateliers displayed the aggressive "drip" paintings of Jackson Pollock, the violent, disturbing artworks of Willem de Kooning and Robert Motherwell, the abstract dirges of Mark Rothko. In the concert halls the strange aleatory compositions of John Cage were taking hold, and in the far-out jazz clubs Charlie Parker's saxophone played ninths, elevenths, and thirteenths, notes so far removed from the original tune that audiences were at once intrigued and baffled.

Unsurprisingly, movies were the last art form to address these stirrings. Hollywood faced enormous losses if its products failed to please; filmmakers could hardly be expected to lead the way in any social or aesthetic movement. Even so, executives were not numb to what was going on outside the studio gates, and among the canniest of them was Stanley Kramer. The producer sensed that he could tap into the emerging spirit of the age—and make money in the process. To that end, he bought the rights to "The Cyclists' Raid," published in *Harper's* magazine. The article recounted a weekend in Hollister, California. Back on July 4, 1947, a gang of young bikers invaded the small town, terrifying its populace before they were finally subdued and ejected.

To Kramer this was a glimpse into the nation's dark side, a side that had recently been given wide publicity by the FBI. The director, J. Edgar Hoover, reported that "persons under the age of eighteen committed fifty-three percent of all car thefts, forty-nine percent of all burglaries, eighteen percent of all robberies, and sixteen percent of all rapes." Adult authority seemed to be slipping away, and someone or something had to be blamed. The most obvious target was popular culture. Psychiatrist Fredric Wertham accused comic books of glamorizing violence and crime. In his book *The Seduction of the Innocent,* he declared, "Here is the repetition of violence and sexiness which no Freud, Krafft-Ebing or Havelock Ellis ever dreamed could be offered to children, and in such profusion. Here is one man mugging another and graphic pictures of the white man shooting colored natives as though they were animals. 'You sure must have treated these beggars rough in that last trip through here!' And so on." Publishers mocked Wertham at first, but his agitations ended in a regulatory code for comic books. Film and TV producers, already reeling from financial and political pressures, were painfully aware that censorship was an idea whose time had come around again. They regrouped, attempting to clean up their act without losing their audience.

Kramer used a time-honored way to operate in this cautious new atmosphere. His new picture aimed to satisfy the censorious and the prurient at the same time, detailing the criminal activity—and then deploring it. Lázló Benedek, a Hungarian director who had done an admirable, if financially unsuccessful, job with *Death of a Salesman,* signed on. Kramer persuaded Marlon to take the lead role: He would get to ride his motorcycle and act at the same time. The offer proved irresistible. Scenarist Ben Maddow, best known for writing the John Huston film noir *The Asphalt Jungle,* was hired to do the adaptation. In typical Hollywood fashion, several months later Maddow was replaced by another screenwriter, John Paxton, a specialist in thrillers. Things went downhill from there. Harry Cohn, Columbia's imperious production chief, made certain that everyone knew the extent of his power. He had always been like that. When he learned that his first wife was infertile, he selected a minor actress, had her struck from the payroll, then went to her apartment with an offer that rivaled Rumpelstiltskin's: "I would like you to have a child by me. On the day you are certified to be pregnant, I will put $75,000 in a bank under your name. On the day the child is delivered to me, our relationship is over." The proposal was turned down and Cohn never spoke to her again.

Uneducated but proud of his gut feelings, he hired major directors like Frank Capra and George Stevens, and such stars as Fred Astaire, Cary Grant, Irene Dunne, and Claudette Colbert. Because so many of Columbia's films were hits, Cohn was convinced he knew more than anyone—particularly writers. He once bawled out his staff for creating an anachronism in an *Arabian Nights* fantasy. "It's all through the script, goddammit," he complained. "You've got 'em all saying, 'Yes, siree.'" The producer read the offending page. "But, Harry," he explained, "that's 'Yes, sire.'" This was not the sort of man who could allow *The Cyclists' Raid* to go into production unscathed. First he changed the title to *The Wild One,* making Marlon the center of the action. Then he learned that the Breen office had examined the script and found it licentious. He agreed. The central part of Johnny, played by Brando, was far too sympathetic. Worse, the bikers' violent behavior was left unpunished. Cohn ordered a rewrite. Paxton did as he was told. Marlon examined the revisions and threw them across the room. He attempted a version of his own, but it came to nothing. He was locked into his contract, and as one of his friends recalled, "He finally said, 'What the hell, I'll ride my bike and drawl some lines. And it'll be over in a month and then I can quit the business for good.'"

On the set he behaved himself, but let it be known that Paxton's dialogue was difficult to believe and harder to articulate. The indulgent Benedek allowed him to ad-lib a lot of his speeches, throwing off the film's love interest, Kathie Bleeker, played by a snub-nosed, twenty-two-year-old starlet named Mary Murphy. In later years she claimed to have been enthralled by Marlon, swiftly adding that her longings went nowhere because "there was always Movita." Occasional flashes of emotion between Johnny and Kathie were not enough to make their relationship convincing, and Marlon's biking rival, Chino, played by a craggy Lee Marvin, was one of the most superannuated juveniles in movie history. Offscreen the two men rarely spoke, and when they did it was to exchange witless insults. Brando thought Marvin was a ham; Marvin, a decorated combat veteran, was well aware that Brando had been 4-F during the war. During the last days of filming, he told Marlon, "I'm thinking of changing my name. To Marlow Brandy." Replied Marlon: "I think I'll change my name, too. To Lee Moron." The star's assets—his brooding sensitivity and screen presence—were offset by the liability of stilted, pseudo-hip dialogue that aged as it was spoken:

KATHIE: Do you just ride around, or do you go on some sort of picnic or something?

JOHNNY: A picnic? Man, you are *too* square. . . . You just *go*. The idea is to have a ball. Now, if you're gonna stay cool, you got to wail. You got to put somethin' down. You got to make some jive.

The Wild One was further hampered by a confused prologue, tacked on to appease the bluenoses. "This is a shocking story," proclaims an unseen announcer. "It could never take place in most American towns—but it did in this one. It is a public challenge not to let it happen again." This was followed by Marlon's voice-over: "It begins here for me on this road. . . . Mostly, I remember the girl. I—I can't explain it—sad chick like that. But somethin' changed in me. She got to me." Marlon detested the words he was forced to say, and assumed a peculiar and unpersuasive southern accent when he voiced them at a recording studio. Benedek could hardly blame him: He said the actor was secretly communicating to his audience, "This isn't me talking. It's someone else. It was his own way of saying to the Breen office, 'Screw you.'"

The Wild One was marketed in a sordid manner, accentuating its weaknesses. "That *Streetcar* man has a new desire!" proclaimed one of the Columbia studio's ads. Others read, "Marlon Brando! driven too far by his own hot blood!" and "Hot feelings hit terrifying heights in a story that really boils over!" The film opened in New York at the Palace Theatre, then featuring two-a-day live performances in what was to be vaudeville's last gasp. *Time*'s critic was not deceived by Paxton's cosmetic revisions. "The effect of the movie," stated his review, "is not to throw light on a public problem, but to shoot adrenaline through the moviegoer's veins." The *Daily News* said much the same thing: *The Wild One* failed "to place the responsibility where it obviously belongs, with the gangs and their leaders, who are not juvenile delinquents but thrill-crazy adults."

In the *Times*, Bosley Crowther, who had been informed of the Breen office's demands, administered the coup de grâce: Though the feature is "engrossing" when it examines mob psychology, "Mr. Paxton and Director Lazlo Benedek—or somebody—have pulled it down. They begin by bringing the gang leader, Mr. Brando, into contact with a girl—a good, clean, upright, small-town beauty—who apparently fills him with love. And before you know it, this maiden and her father, the cowardly cop, are pleading forgiveness for the mug. Although it is not clearly stated that the obvious ties of love are going to bind, the mug does ride off into the sunrise, a presumably clean and fine young man." The picture "tries to grasp an idea, even though its reach falls short. It is too bad that some mutterings in the industry have seemed to depreciate it, and it should turn up as the passing feature on an eight-act vaudeville bill."

This marked Marlon's first cinematic failure. However, despite the pans and the meager box-office take, his performance changed a turkey into a cult movie, first in America and then throughout the world. Novelist Parménides García Saldaña watched the phenomenon in Mexico City: "The imitators of Marlon Brando look for that equivalent language, that similar mode of speaking, prohibited and subversive, which commits an outrage against *buenas costumbres* [the well dressed.]" Elvis Presley was transfixed by the film. One exchange jumped out from the *The Wild One* and changed the King's affect. Soon the words would become a shibboleth of American youth:

LADY: What are you rebelling against, Johnny?
JOHNNY: Whaddya got?

Just as friends were forbidden to mention any aspect of his burgeoning celebrity, Marlon did not permit himself to reflect on the film's enduring popularity. If anything good had come from this, his fifth movie, it could not have been the result of talent or magnetism; it had to be chance, fortune, coincidence. Reflecting on *The Wild One,* Marlon wrote, "I simply happened to be at the right place at the right time in the right part—and I also had the appropriate state of mind for the role." More amused than gratified, he watched from the sidelines as teenagers imitated Johnny's slouch and sullen attitude, sales of motorcycles boomed, and leather jackets became the adolescent uniform of the day. He said it reminded him of *It Happened One Night,* "when Clark Gable took his shirt off and revealed that he wasn't wearing an undershirt, which created a disaster for the garment industry."

There was more to come. As Updike observes, just about the time Marlon became an icon of American youth, the country's artists and intellectuals, and soon afterward the young, "felt mostly a sardonic estrangement from a government that extolled business and mediocrity." President Eisenhower identified what he called "the great problem of America today." It was "to take that straight road down the middle." But that road was not where teenagers wanted to go. They preferred a different kind of music, a fresh set of heroes, a new kind of expression. In *American Chronicle,* Lois and Alan Gordon list the words that came into use in the 1950s, revealing an earthquake taking place beneath the repressive crust of the decade. Among them: apartheid, H-bomb, integration, miniaturization, cool jazz, ponytail, TelePrompTer, drag strip, countdown, discount house, jet stream, captive audience, windfall profit, fallout, greaser, junk mail, Thorazine, stoned, Third World, cop-out, put-on, headshrinker, shook up, funky, beatnik, sex kitten, sick joke, polymorphous perversity.

Quite by accident, Marlon had become a leader of this seismic activity, and it made him uncomfortable. Leadership was never his strong suit; he preferred to be on the outside, watching, copying gestures, cracking wise. The discomfort got so severe that he signed no new contracts and truly considered retiring to the ranch his father managed in Nebraska. Realism caught up with him when he discovered that the property had lost a lot of money—his money—with no hope of recovery. Marlon was at the point of sailing off to Europe with Movita when he learned that some of his old acting pals, among them Carlo Fiore, Janice Mars, and a new friend, William Redfield, were out of work. He organized a summer-stock company and took Shaw's *Arms and the Man* on a tour of small towns in New England.

To call this venture a catastrophe would be to flatter it. The others took the play seriously. Not Marlon. "I don't want to work," he told Fiore privately. "I want to fuck around. And I want to try comedy for a change. A farce. I want to leer, wear a moustache, make asides to the audience, like Groucho Marx." He regressed to the old school days, when preparation was a snore. His name was enough to pack the houses, and some nights he got ovations just for showing up. Most of the time, however, audiences left dissatisfied. One ticket holder collared Redfield and asked him to convey a message to Marlon. "We'd like you to tell him that we're not a bunch of yokels. Does he think we can't see he's laughing at us while we sit out there? Does he think we're deaf and dumb?" The actor dutifully conveyed his words to their target. Replied Marlon: "Man, don't you get it? This is *summer stock*!" He clowned his way across Connecticut, Rhode Island, and Cape Cod before finishing up in Framingham, Massachusetts, blowing lines, camping it up onstage, throwing off everyone's timing for the sake of a cheap laugh. Until the last stop, most reviewers, impressed by the Brando celebrity, went along with the gag. But Elliot Norton, the most important reviewer outside New York, had no intention of indulging a movie star run amok. In *The Boston Globe* the critic fulminated, "In recent years, no major star, no actor with anything like Brando's reputation has ever given such a completely ridiculous performance. He strides and struts and overdoes it, suggesting not a man of normal vanity—but a ham actor who just doesn't know how to play comedy."

Marlon tried to put a good face on the disaster, clowning around, writing blithe letters home. He fooled no one but himself. The close observer of human behavior, the acute mimic of others, had no self-perception at all. The strategies of survival, operating since childhood, were now being used to block anything that might lead him to confront his shortcomings. Rather than appraise what was happening, he made light of everything—his achievements in drama and his failures in comedy. Nothing mattered to him in the mid-fifties, and he didn't know why that was so. His live-in, Movita, was of no help. Nor was his therapist, Bela Mittleman. Marlon senior's early ridicule still rang in his son's ears, diminishing any sense of real accomplishment; Dodie's lack of communication, a silence that was interpreted as indifference, further diminished any feelings of self-worth. But to confront the buried child was more than Brando could bear at present, and Mittleman was not about to force the hand of so famous a client. When things went bad, he simply allowed his patient to take the knife out of the critics' hands and stab himself before they could get around to it. When things went well, he permitted Marlon to ascribe the occasion to a series of happy accidents. The T-word—*talent*—didn't enter the picture.

3

The plump, influential Austrian filmmaker Sam Spiegel had always been one jump ahead of his pursuers, whether they were Nazis or creditors. It used to be said of him that if he were dropped stark naked without a dime into any capital city, by the next morning he would be dressed in a Savile Row suit and living in a penthouse. Hollywood provided a fertile field for smooth talkers, and in keeping with the old show-business aphorism "Anyone who calls himself a producer *is* a producer," he managed to persuade investors to back several inconsequential movies. Then Spiegel took on the *nom de cinéma* S. P. Eagle and his luck changed. He had to endure the much-repeated gibe of Herman Mankiewicz "How about Darryl Zanuck as Z. A. Nook? Or Ernst Lubitsch as L. U. Bitch?" But Spiegel received compensation in the forms of profit and prestige when his film *The African Queen* won an Academy Award for Best Picture. Fresh from this honor, he set his sights on a very different kind of film.

In 1949, scenarist Budd Schulberg came across Malcolm Johnson's series "Crime on the Waterfront," published in the *New York Sun*. Financed by an independent film company, Schulberg acquired the rights to this Pulitzer Prize–winning work, and started on an adaptation. At roughly the same time Elia Kazan and Arthur Miller began collaborating on their own waterfront drama for Columbia Pictures. Schulberg's company couldn't come up with the financing, and dropped the project. A little while later, Miller and Kazan hit a wall in their relationship and the playwright quit cold. There were two reasons for his walkout.

First came the order from Harry Cohn: The villains of the piece had to be Communists. Miller knew better; the agitation on the Brooklyn waterfront had to do with racketeers, not Reds. Cohn's insistence on making the laborers into a Cold War army was an absurd, corrupt demand. The scenarist wired Columbia that he was withdrawing his script. The next morning Miller received a telegram in reply: IT'S INTERESTING HOW THE MINUTE WE TRY TO MAKE THE SCRIPT PRO-AMERICAN YOU PULL OUT. HARRY COHN.

Second came the business of Gadge, the Committee, and the naming of names. Kazan's ad of April 13, 1952, in *The New York Times* had slammed the door shut on their relationship.

Then, also in 1952, the last men standing got together. Both Kazan and Schulberg had been "friendly" witnesses at the HUAC hearings; both saw a way to dramatize life on the docks—and, not coincidentally, to show that under certain circumstances informing was morally justifiable. Admitted Gadge, "When critics say that I put my story and my feelings on the screen, to justify my informing, they are right." Budd was not so militant, but went along with his partner's stance. They completed the script for *The Hook* in a state of exhilaration and took off for Beverly Hills, convinced that Hollywood producers would line up to buy their work. Zanuck put the scenario down in two sentences: "I don't like a single thing about it. All you've got is a lot of sweaty long-shoremen." Warner Bros. turned them down, then Paramount and MGM. Harry Cohn passed, even though Arthur Miller was no longer attached to the venture.

The Hook was hardly the first landmark film to be rejected by the majors. *Sunset Boulevard* has a winking reference to such errors. When a young reader dismisses a script, the scenarist objects, "You'd have turned down *Gone with the Wind*." An executive sighs: "No, that was me. I said: 'Who wants to see a Civil War picture?' " But holding *The Hook* at arm's length was different. It came with impeccable credentials. Schulberg was the son of B. P. Schulberg, onetime head of Paramount. He was a child of Hollywood, a man who knew the film industry well enough to anatomize it in *What Makes Sammy Run?* The novel's colorful and aggressive central character, Sammy Glick, had been part of the American vocabulary since 1941. Kazan was the most talked-about film and stage director in the country. The project had received its chorus of refusals not because of American history but because of Hollywood history.

It was 1953, a pivotal year for cinema. In the wake of investigation and scandal, controversy of any kind—political, social, sexual—gave production chiefs the creeps. A blacklist of actors and directors was in full sway, and even this failed to satisfy the most rabid Red-hunters, who flyspecked scripts for "subversive" themes and casting lists for activists they might have overlooked. Movie executives had quite enough worries without the threat of picket lines and newspaper editorials. Yet this was not their principal concern. They were far more troubled by the cycloptic box that had grown from amusing baby to voracious monster. In less than three years the makers of *I Love Lucy*, CBS's modest TV sitcom, had risen to become the most powerful couple in show business. By the end of the decade, Lucille Ball and Desi Arnaz would buy RKO, the studio for which she had once labored. Movie attendance was tumbling, the studio system, in place since the 1920s, was all but gone, replaced by broadcasting companies. Louis B. Mayer had already been forced out of MGM, and Sam Goldwyn was scrambling to stay in the game. Harry Cohn was getting tired and ill. Darryl F. Zanuck, the great survivor, was planning to leave Fox for independent film production. In the movie business, this was equivalent to the Cretaceous and Tertiary periods, when the dinosaurs vanished and were replaced by a very different kind of animal. The talk of the town was not about the peccadilloes of film stars but of how to cover the seats with *tochuses*. The buzzwords were Cinerama, 3-D, VistaVision, CinemaScope. Risk takers were an endangered species in the Celluloid City of the mid-fifties, and getting rarer by the day. Schulberg and Kazan were realists. When they received the last refusal they made ready to leave town, Budd to novelize *The Hook,* Gadge to revive his career on Broadway.

At that very moment there came a deus ex machina. Packing up, Kazan and Schulberg heard noises across the hall from their hotel room. A party was under way, hosted by Sam Spiegel, who knew them both by reputation. They stopped by and got his ear. The producer listened to their sad story and asked them to come to his room the next morning. At the stroke of 7 a.m., writer and director knocked on Sam's door. To an inert, yawning figure, Schulberg read the script, acting out all the parts. He described the experience as "talking to a cave of silence," but the cave did not remain soundless for long. Shortly after Budd said, "Fade out," S. P. Eagle pronounced the magic words: "We'll make the picture." Within weeks he arranged private financing and sold the distribution rights to Columbia.

Spiegel had only one choice for longshoreman Terry Malloy, centerpiece of the drama: Marlon Brando. Kazan was not so sure; given the HUAC business, Marlon would probably want no part of him. Sam then encouraged Gadge to consider Frank Sinatra for the starring role. After meeting the singer, now turned serious actor, Kazan convinced himself that "Frank had grown up in Hoboken, where I was going to shoot the film, and spoke perfect Hobokenese. He'd be simple to work with."

He had not reckoned on Spiegel's silver oratory. The next thing Kazan knew, Marlon Brando had signed a $100,000 contract to appear in the film, now called *On the Waterfront*. The famous Spiegel charm had roped him in, and Marlon would work with Gadge after all. Sinatra had already been promised the part, but Kazan made no protest because, he subsequently confessed, "I always preferred Brando to anybody." Stung by the betrayal, Sinatra sued Spiegel for $500,000, charging breach of contract (later settled out of court), refused to talk to Kazan for months, and thereafter referred to Marlon as "Mumbles."

The hard work now began. Spiegel, who posed as a laid-back money guy, was actually an instinctive and severe editor. He knew what was wrong with the script and what was right with it, and insisted on all sorts of fine-tuning. At three-thirty one morning Schulberg's wife, Virginia, awoke to find the bathroom light on in their Bucks County house. Budd was shaving and muttering to himself. "I'm driving to New York," he explained.

"What for?"

"To kill Sam Spiegel."

Instead of murdering Sam, though, Budd and Gadge obeyed him, rejiggering scene after scene. After all, Sam had made the picture possible, when all around them had turned away. But there was an end to gratitude; when Kazan said the words, "Let's shoot!" the editing sessions were over. Rehearsals took place at the Actors Studio in November 1953. It was an appropriate venue; many Studio actors were hired to play featured roles, among them Karl Malden as Father Barry, modeled on an outspoken Hoboken priest, Father John Corridan; Rod Steiger as Charley "the Gent" Malloy, Terry's brother; Rudy Bond as a local goon, Nehemiah Persoff as a cab driver, and Martin Balsam as a crime investigator. Other performers brought New York accents and faces every bit as convincing as Sinatra's New Jersey persona. Among them were Lee J. Cobb (another "friendly" HUAC witness, wryly named Johnny Friendly in the film), Fred Gwynne, and Leif Erickson. Kazan also hired the retired prizefighters Abe Simon, Tony Galento, and Tami Mauriello for more verisimilitude. Schulberg's friend Roger Donoghue, a middleweight who had killed another boxer, George Flores, in the ring and then hung up his gloves, was hired to teach Marlon the moves and postures of an ex-pug. When they were getting to know each other, Budd asked him, "Could you have been a champion?" Roger thought about it. After a pause he said, "I could have been a contender." Budd put that phrase in the script.

The key Studio veteran was Eva Marie Saint, a beautiful twenty-nine-year-old blonde with a modicum of stage experience. Kazan had seen her in Horton Foote's Broadway play *A Trip to Bountiful*, and asked her to read for the part of Edie Doyle, the sole love interest in *Waterfront*. One other actress was under serious consideration for the role, Elizabeth Montgomery, and Karl Malden helped both of them prepare for their reading. Kazan stayed on the fence—until Saint auditioned with Marlon. Kazan put them in a room and told her: "You're a Catholic girl. You have a little sister. Her boyfriend is coming. She's not home. Do not let this man in."

Marlon listened to the instructions and talked his way into the imagined apartment with a combination of charisma and salt-of-the-earth purity of heart. "We laughed and giggled," Saint remembered, "and I ended up laughing and crying at the same time. Gadge could see that sparks were flying, that Marlon had his way and that I was very vulnerable to him." She sensed that what Brando did "was more than improvisation. It was that this young man had the power to see through you—you felt like glass. I stayed off balance for the whole shoot."

Gadge cherished that unstable quality and tried to preserve it throughout the filming. As before, he kept everyone's nervous tension at maximum strength. Some things eluded even his iron control, but Kazan's luck held: The foul weather, for instance, worked in his favor. The winter of 1953 was especially miserable in the East, and on rainy days the chill seemed to get into the actors' bones. The misery on their faces—caused by cold fronts rather than plot points—supplied the scenes with an unexpected pain, and the misty breaths, the stripped trees, and threatening skies gave every exterior scene an austere Italian *neorealismo* tone. "They were miserable-looking human beings," Kazan observed, "and that includes Brando." Indeed, at one point Marlon exhaled a steamy breath and muttered, "You know, it's so fucking cold out here there's no way you can overact."

Although he insisted on leaving the set at 4 p.m. in order to see Dr. Mittleman, Marlon never gave Kazan the hard time everyone expected. When his parents visited the set, he was especially solicitous, introducing them to the cast and crew and making an extra effort to be polite to everyone. His mother was no longer hitting the bottle; she looked slim and chic and well turned out. But the years of alcoholism had done her in; she had lost weight because of liver and kidney trouble. Despite her cheery countenance, she was gravely ill.

Perhaps because Marlon was aware of his mother's precarious health, perhaps because of a self-protective diffidence, the star's relationship with Saint remained strictly professional. She was at the beginning of a long, happy marriage to theatrical producer Jeffrey Hayden, and if she was attracted to Marlon, and he to her, there was no offscreen liaison. "It was as if we were safe *for* each other," she remembered. Kazan used Saint's natural shyness to advantage; she had to play a romantic scene in a slip, and her discomfort before the cameras was noticeable. Kazan approached and whispered one word in her ear: "Jeffrey"—his way of saying, "You're not going to bed with Terry Malloy; you're going to bed with your husband." In a moment the inhibitions were swept away, and she played the moment with a delicate fervor.

With all its metaphors and muckraking postures, *Waterfront* turned out to be, in essence, a film noir, following the stations of Terry Malloy, as the failed middleweight boxer rises from mobbed-up punk to transfigured hero. Terry, whose favorite company is the pigeons he raises on a rooftop, operates in a treacherous and claustrophobic environment. Racketeers run the Hoboken docks and Johnny Friendly, head of the longshoremen's union, is as dirty as the loading platforms. In this little world defiance is a death sentence. Terry's brother Charley is Friendly's trusted henchman; Terry got his undemanding job because of Charley's influence with the boss. When Friendly is challenged by Joey Doyle, a valorous dockworker, Friendly has him rubbed out— with the full knowledge of Charley and the unwitting assistance of Terry.

Outraged, the local priest, Father Barry, delivers an on-the-spot sermon: "Some people think the Crucifixion only took place on Calvary. They better wise up. . . . Every time the mob puts the crusher on a good man, tries to keep him from doing his duty as a citizen, it's a crucifixion!" He exhorts the longshoremen to stop the blind obedience to Friendly, to fight the corruption on the docks by going before the Waterfront Crime Commission. Terry wavers, torn between his loyalty to Charley and his growing affection for a neighborhood beauty, Edie Doyle—sister of the murdered man. Ultimately he decides to give evidence—to name names—at the commission hearing. Afterward he finds his own beloved birds slaughtered in their rooftop cage: This is what happens to stool pigeons. Charley Malloy is literally hung out to dry, a corpse dangling from a meat hook. And worse is still to come. At the finale Terry is attacked by vicious thugs, as the longshoremen stand by, unwilling to help. But Terry will not be silenced. After the beating Father Barry urges him to his feet. Bloody, intrepid, the wounded man inches his way toward the workplace. Thanks to Terry's grit, the longshoremen realize that the savagery was Friendly's curtain call. The committeemen are about to take away his authority, leaving him with nothing but a loud mouth and empty threats. As he bellows, the men defiantly fall in line behind Terry. They have a new leader.

The Christian symbolism of *Waterfront* was so obvious Schulberg felt obliged to speak to Catholic laymen at Fordham University. Even though he was Jewish, he told the rapt audience, "I agreed with so much of the social message of Jesus and I was moved by it, and further moved by the depth and commitment of people like Father Corridan. It wasn't a problem for me." Nor was it a problem to portray Terry as noble. If the scenarist was more objective than the director, their ideas meshed in Terry's speech: "I'm glad what I done—you hear me?—glad what I done."

Yet it was not this calculated speech that audiences remembered, nor was it the scene they cherished most. Nor did they attach much meaning to the story of a good, simple man whose informing was justified. Marlon, as usual, had lost himself completely in the role, had picked up the loping gait and halting, insecure speech of the boxers he'd sparred with years before. ("I can make a hell of a middleweight out of this kid," Donoghue burbled after one session. Schulberg intervened. "Just get us through this movie. Then you can have him back.") In Hoboken, Marlon had watched real longshoremen at work, old sagging bulls of men, and younger guys with hard bodies and closed faces. He made their gestures part of Terry Malloy's persona, and the authenticity of the performance was what hypnotized filmgoers. In many ways, Terry was the flip side of Stanley Kowalski, still inarticulate, but now compassionate and perplexed, searching for affection rather than conquest, wanting to do right in an atmosphere of compromise.

Among the film's many memorable encounters, two stood above the rest. As Terry and Edie first get to know each other, she accidentally drops a glove. Terry picks it up, and, after absentmindedly playing with it, gently tries it on his own hand. What could have been a paperback Freudian moment became one of the film's few tender exchanges. To Terry, who once wore Everlast ten-ounce mitts in a boxing arena, her glove is a delicate and exotic item—like Edie herself. He treats it with unaccustomed care, winning her trust and the audience's heart.

But it was the second scene that journeyed from the screen to the lexicons. With the exception of Clark Gable's "Frankly, my dear, I don't give a damn" from *Gone with the Wind* and Ingrid Bergman's oft-misquoted "Play it, Sam" from *Casablanca,* no lines were to be so repeated, mimicked, satirized, and admired. When Johnny Friendly learns that Terry plans to testify before the committee, he orders a hit. As an extra twist of the knife, Charley Malloy is ordered to do the job.

The brothers take a ride downtown, during which Charley pulls out a pistol and turns it on Terry. The script called for Steiger to give Brando a choice—cancel the testimony or die: "Make up your mind before we get to 437 River Street."

Marlon thought the incident was bogus. The audience, he complained to Kazan, would never believe that Charley, "who's been close to his brother all his life, and who's looked after him for thirty years, would suddenly stick a gun in his ribs and threaten to kill him. I can't do it that way."

Gadge insisted that the exchange was credible and touching.

The two actors gamely performed the scene as written. They did it again. And again. Marlon kept insisting that the result was false to the characters until Gadge sighed, "All right, wing one."

In the improvised exchange, Steiger spoke of his kid brother's all-too-brief boxing career. The brevity had to be blamed on Terry's manager: "He brought you along too fast."

Marlon added to Schulberg's lines, reaching for the words that would put him in the books. "It wasn't *him,* Charley, it was *you.* Remember that night in the Garden you came down to my dressing room and you said, 'Kid, this ain't your night. We're going for the price on Wilson.' You remember that? 'This ain't your night!' *My night!* I coulda taken Wilson apart! So what happens? He gets the title shot outdoors on the ballpark and what do I get? A one-way ticket to Palookaville. You was my brother, Charley, you shoulda looked out for me a little bit. You shoulda taken care of me just a little bit so I wouldn't have to take them dives for the short-end money. . . . I coulda had class. I coulda been a contender. I coulda been *somebody* instead of a bum, which is what I am, let's face it. It was *you,* Charley."

Kazan, quick to claim credit on many occasions, was unusually candid about the Brando monologue. The praise he received for directing that scene belonged to Marlon. "Who else could read 'Oh, Charley!' in the tone of reproach that is so loving and so melancholy and suggests that terrific depth of pain? I didn't direct that; Marlon showed me, as he often did, how the scene should be performed."

Kazan didn't mention Marlon's dark side, evident when it came time for Charley to react to Terry's speech. "Marlon wouldn't give up his appointment with the shrink," said one of the supporting cast members, "and that bent Rod Steiger into a pretzel. He had to do his close-ups with Gadge reading Marlon's lines." Kazan didn't mind; a great film was worth any number of inconveniences and bruised egos. Marlon didn't give it a backward glance. When he saw the dailies, he said the taxi scene was effective because of the subtext, not the performance; almost every viewer believes he could have been a contender, whether in boxing or dry cleaning. The star's refusal to recognize his own worth was a long story with many chapters to go.

4

Waterfront wrapped in January 1954. Two months later, Dorothy Pennebaker Brando hovered between life and death. Marlon, at her bedside along with Jocelyn, heard his mother advise both of them to "try to get along with people." He nodded dutifully and kept the tears back. But when she assured her children, "I'm not scared, and you don't have to be," he broke down. He had never made his peace with Dodie, never found a way to forgive her weaknesses, or to express his gratitude. After the funeral and cremation he seemed even more rudderless than usual. Out of nowhere he felt the need to dump Movita, to be alone again, to find new work or abandon acting entirely. During the filming of *Waterfront* he had signed a two-picture deal with Zanuck, but the first movie was supposed to be *The Egyptian,* a fatuous, pseudo-historical epic of the ancient Middle East—the diametrical opposite of *Waterfront* and its gritty, emotional truth-telling. Nothing seemed to be going right, and Kazan, ever-mindful of Kazan, was worried. Gadge hankered for an Oscar, a demonstration from the town that whatever he had done in the past, the only politics that counted now were studio politics. Damned if he would let anyone spoil things.

When *Waterfront* was edited and Leonard Bernstein's edgy score added, Kazan took a print out to the Coast. For formality's sake he sat at Harry Cohn's side at a private screening room, pretending to take notes for an already edited movie. To his relief, Harry only wanted to know how much the filming had cost. The answer provoked a smile: $900,000, very cheap for a top-of-the-bill feature. Gadge recalled: "He had a girl with him, of course; they always do." The pair had already dined, and probably indulged in some other pleasures, because about a third of the way through the screening, heavy, rhythmic breathing filled the air. Cohn was fast asleep. Kazan let him snore away, fearful that if the mogul woke he would ask to see the film from the beginning.

Kazan knew what he had. A day before the notices were printed, three hundred people stood in line at the Astor Theater. The following morning *Waterfront* was greeted with critical raves. Even so, Columbia had no idea how to market its hit. In a sidelong reference to Bing Crosby's Academy Award–winning role as a benign priest, one early poster read, "A story as warm and inspiring as *Going My Way* . . . but with brass knuckles!" Other ads used money quotes—"Movie making of a rare and high order!" (*New York Times*). The film needed no such promotion; word of mouth did it all. In the end, the strongest evidence that *Waterfront* was a blockbuster came not from the box-office receipts, but from Abe Lastfogel, president of the William Morris Agency, who assured Gadge that he could now make any picture he chose. From Hollywood, Darryl Zanuck sent a note to Kazan, indicating the temperature of the town: "The advent and debut of Cinema-Scope was responsible, more than anything else, for my final decision against the property." His peers fell all over themselves to curry favor; Kazan, filmmaker, was back. But there was still one hurdle to go: the volatile Marlon himself.

To that end, Gadge dispatched Roger Donoghue to keep his eye on the star. Brando was to make no public statements about acting or Hollywood or writers or informers. All he had to do was shut up and make nice and the Oscar was his. The boxing coach conveyed this advice to Marlon, who groused about it but complied. Though he refused to admit the truth to Donoghue—or anyone else, for that matter—he wanted a statuette almost as much as Gadge did. During the run-up to the Oscars, no provocation could make him say anything that might embarrass himself or the film. *Waterfront* received twelve nominations, including Best Picture and Best Actor. Once more Marlon was pitted against Humphrey Bogart, who had starred as Captain Queeg in *The Caine Mutiny*. But this time out the oddsmakers favored Brando three to one—the multiple of his next salary offer.

The bookies were on the money. At the Pantages Theatre on Oscar evening, *On the Waterfront* garnered eight Academy Awards, tying the record for a black-and-white feature set the year before by *From Here to Eternity*. Montgomery Clift had received his third Oscar nomination for Best Actor for his performance in that film; now it was Marlon's turn—and Gadge's—for a stronger affirmation. Kazan was gracious, Marlon shy. In the presence of a thousand attendees, including Marlon Brando, Sr., plus an estimated thirty million viewers, the actor held the gold figure and smiled down on it. With his signature mumble, he allowed that "it was much heavier than I thought," vaguely mentioned those who had been "so directly responsible for my being so very, very glad," called the occasion "a wonderful moment and a rare one," and went offstage to wild applause. Whether the reticence was itself an act, no one could tell.

Euphoria took over. Columnists called the winner America's greatest and most influential actor. Over the next month Brando and Clift found themselves dubbed "The Gold Dust Twins," and read predictions about a renaissance of American filmmaking. Smiles and kudos greeted Marlon wherever he went. Someone was always picking up the check for him and listening to the young man pontificate: "Acting, not prostitution, is the oldest profession in the world. Even apes act. If you want to invite trouble from one, lock your eyes on his and stare. It's enough of an assault to make the animal rise, pound his chest and feign a charge; he is acting, hoping that his gesture will make you avert your eyes." Offers crowded the in-box of his ambitious agent, Jay Kanter. There seemed no limit to what this thirty-year-old star could achieve in the next decade or so. Laurence Olivier was generally acknowledged as the world's greatest actor. But Sir Laurence was a forty-seven-year-old intellectual whose technique was in every sense a world away from Brando's. Besides, he was a Brit. With all his professed diffidence, Marlon was keenly aware that he had only two real rivals: Montgomery Clift and a twenty-four-year-old the columnists were calling "The New Brando." The title did not sit well with the old Brando, and something very much like jealousy began to invigorate him. He had met James Dean at parties and found the youth a little too idolatrous for comfort. He referred to him as "the kid" and was displeased to find him copying every Brando gesture, down to the T-shirt, the motorcycle, the conga drums, and the habit of throwing his jacket on the floor when he entered parties. At one of those soirees Marlon took him aside and dispensed a little advice: "Jimmy, you have to be who you are, not who I am." In later years Marlon remembered that Dean "had an idée fixe about me. Whatever I did, he did. He was always trying to get close to me. I'd listen to him talking to the answering service, asking for me, leaving messages. But I never spoke up. I never called him back."

5

Although he was used to tumult, Hollywood got to be too much for Marlon. In the spring of 1954, having deleted Movita from his life, he traded California for New York. There he settled into an apartment adjoining Carnegie Hall and acquired a new girlfriend, fashion designer Anne Ford. The affair was brief and cleansing; he needed to start over, to find a different path. But choosing the next woman turned out to be a lot easier than selecting the next film. He dreaded *The Egyptian*, a bloated epic that would feature Darryl Zanuck's latest protégée, Bella Darvi, née Bella Wegier, whose screen name had been concocted from the first names of the producer and his wife, Virginia. One meeting with Ms. Darvi was enough for Marlon to see that she was not Zanuck's acting discovery, but Zanuck's inamorata, and that the film would be a colossal waste of time and energy.

Without informing anyone, Marlon vanished. Aware that Zanuck had hired professionals to locate him, he kept changing locations before he could be run to earth. He dressed elegantly, in contrast to his usual T-shirt and jeans, to throw off bounty hunters. Wally Cox and Janice Mars helped with the deception, giving their friend shelter in their apartments when he was not registered at an East Side hotel under the name of his maternal great-grandfather, Myles Gahan. Just when things had quieted down, Marlon made the mistake of returning to his apartment to get some personal items. The place had been staked out, and U.S. marshals nabbed him. Zanuck announced a lawsuit; court papers said that the actor had violated his contract, forcing production for *The Egyptian* to close down while the producers awaited Marlon Brando's replacement, Edmund Purdom. MCA stepped in and worked out a deal. Zanuck would forgive the debt, provided that Marlon appeared in his next production, *Desirée*, the story of Napoleon and his consort, Josephine.

Trapped, Marlon was forced to agree to the producer's terms. His way of fighting back was the same one he used in military school: insurrection. The director of *Desirée* was Henry Koster, né Hermann Kosterlitz, yet another German refugee who had caught on in Hollywood. This particular German was a featherweight, best known for his work on Deanna Durbin musicals and for bringing the comic team of Abbott and Costello to Hollywood. Marlon distrusted the man on sight, and proceeded to follow his own first law of cinema: "Never give a stupid, egotistical, insensitive or inept director an even break." He made a policy of forgetting his lines or reciting them with a nasal pseudo-British intonation and creating havoc between takes, passing around a football, squirting extras with a fire hose, and mocking the Anglo-Indian intonations of his costar Merle Oberon.

More galling than the weakness of Koster, or of the property itself, was the ascent of James Dean. The novice actor was filming *East of Eden* under Kazan's guidance, and word was that the kid had an extraordinary presence, an aura. Marlon went to the set to see what the fuss was about. Jimmy didn't seem all that much when they met at parties, but there was no question that Gadge had an eye for actors on the come. The two men stared at each other. James dropped his eyes. This adulation meant very little to Marlon; as he watched a new star being created he felt uncomfortable and strangely obsolete. With ill-advised, revealing words, he told reporters, "Mr. Dean appears to be wearing my last year's wardrobe and using my last year's talent." Marlon returned to the *Desirée* set surlier than ever, and for a while it appeared that the feature would be a kind of live cartoon, a filmed asylum run by a man pretending to be Napoleon. Discipline was required, and Koster was obviously not the man to supply it. Producer Julian Blaustein took the job. He drew Marlon aside and warned him that the picture would be summarily shut down if there were any more hijinks or showing-up of the director or his fellow performers. End of contract, end of salary, end of story.

Marlon couldn't tell whether Blaustein was making an empty threat or a real one, but he was unwilling to take a chance. From that day forward he stopped capering and tried to remember his lines. If his impersonation of the Corsican was uninspired, the picture finished on time and within its narrow budgetary constraints. En route, he acquired some additional girlfriends. One, Josanne Mariani-Bérenger, a striking nineteen-year-old, had been serving as an au pair for Bela Mittleman's family. She wanted to pursue a career in Hollywood, regarded Marlon as the catch of a lifetime, and expressed the desire to marry him right away. The other was the exotic Puerto Rican actress Rita Moreno, who seemed to desire freedom every bit as much as Marlon did.

As soon as *Desirée* wrapped Marlon took off for Europe on the *Île de France*. The man who played Terry Malloy tried to look the other way as he crossed some picket lines on the docks, but the incident did not escape alert photographers and tabloid editors, who made an item out of it. Josanne had preceded him, and several weeks later the two met at her hometown, Bandol, near the Riviera. Her father was an unworldly French fisherman, but he, like his neighbors, had heard of Marlon Brando and gave interviews to the local paper. To one reporter, he announced the engagement of his daughter and the *acteur américain*. When this made the *International Herald Tribune,* a journalist sought out the ex-girlfriend Movita. Her forecast: "I do not think he will marry her soon. He isn't the type to walk into something unless he's sure." Whether her feelings were prompted by jealousy or realism, Movita had Marlon's number. Seeking to escape the snares of publicity, he had walked into a trap. Paparazzi descended on the village, snapping pictures of the couple walking on the shore, peeking in the windows of the Bérenger home, even lighting up the interior of the local church with flashbulbs as Josanne knelt and prayed. It was all too much for Marlon. Suffocating, he sought to escape the "carrion press." Perhaps, theorized a friend, "he would have felt like a heel, cutting out on Josanne. Then he learned that the year before she had posed in the nude for an artist. The paintings were in several galleries. No harm done, but it was enough to give Marlon a sense of self-righteousness. If she could do that, how pure was she after all? And so he got away without guilty feelings."

In the fall Marlon made the cover of *Time*, scowling out from newsstands as Napoleon Bonaparte. The portrait helped to boost the picture, even though the accompanying headline was not indulgent. It inquired: TOO BIG FOR HIS BLUE JEANS? Inside, an unnamed producer tried to sound eupeptic. "Two more like Brando," he predicted, "and television can crawl back into the tube." This was an exercise in graveyard whistling. Everyone in the business knew the truth: There were some fifty million sets in U.S. homes, and thousands more were being purchased every week. Despite the inducements of wide screens and high-fidelity sound, more people were staying home to watch the little screen instead of going out to see the big one. Brando couldn't save the studios; no one could.

Not that this meant much to Josanne. In France they still watched movies in theaters; television was something you saw in bistros. Eager for reconciliation, she took advantage of the American publicity swirl, flying to New York and appearing on television news programs. She identified herself to everyone as Brando's fiancée. Marlon played along; when he debarked from the liner *United States* he went to her hotel and escorted Josanne to his Carnegie Hall apartment. Reporters had been waiting for days for a glimpse of the actor, and seeing the couple arm-in-arm made them ecstatic. With unaccustomed amity, Marlon and Josanne posed for pictures. It was all a sham. He knew theirs would be a fishbowl marriage, doomed before it began. He picked fights with her; she returned the insults with some of her own. During a dinner with Marlon and Tennessee Williams she suddenly turned on her fiancée and accused him of closet homosexuality. She told Williams that Brando and the actor Christian Marquand had been lovers. The playwright was too drunk to take it all in. Marlon said nothing. He seemed to lack the energy to pull down the curtain. Before the spring of 1955, though, he was spotted in the company of several women, among them Rita Moreno and the Swiss actress Ursula Andress. Josanne angrily left Marlon and took her own apartment. She went out on a number of dates with new escorts, but carried a torch for months, perhaps years, afterward. Occasionally Marlon would phone and chat for a while, and she allowed herself to fantasize about a reunion. Then weeks went by while she waited for the call that never came. One of her dates remembered Josanne imbibing too much wine, reminiscing about Marlon, then going into the bathroom, where she smashed wineglasses against the tub and wailed, "That *fucker*, that son of a beech!" By that time, the son of a beech had thoroughly extricated himself. His mind was on a new project, an adaptation of the Broadway hit *Guys and Dolls*, costarring the runner-up in the Terry Malloy contest, Frank Sinatra.

6

WANT VERY MUCH TO HAVE YOU PLAY MASTERSON, read the telegram from Joseph Mankiewicz. IN ITS OWN WAY ROLE AS I WOULD WRITE IT FOR YOU OFFERS CHALLENGE ALMOST EQUAL OF MARC ANTONY.

Marlon teetered; the director pushed him over. "You have never done a musical; neither have I." And bear in mind: Before *Julius Caesar,* "we never did Shakespeare, either."

Sam Goldwyn had spent the unprecedented sum of $1 million to acquire the hit musical *Guys and Dolls,* and he wanted to ensure that his money would come back tenfold. The secondary comic parts would be played by the Broadway regulars Stubby Kaye, B. S. Pully, and Vivian Blaine. For the male leads, however, no less than superstars would do. Kirk Douglas came up for consideration, as did Robert Mitchum and Burt Lancaster, even though none of them had ever sung a note onscreen. Clark Gable had; he was in the running, along with Bing Crosby. Goldwyn briefly pondered the idea of casting Dean Martin and Jerry Lewis as Sky Masterson and Nathan Detroit before coming to his senses. In the end he decided that Marlon was a box-office draw, and that all fans who bought a Frank Sinatra record would spend good money to see the Chairman of the Board in a big role.

The casting of Brando and Sinatra seemed inspired—one of the great show-business confluences of the twentieth century. Even at this early point both were on their way to the pantheon. No one would come close to the influence they wielded on their fellow actors and singers, and they might end up showing each other a modicum of courtesy and regard. It was not to be. Danger signs were apparent during the earliest days of production. Sinatra told the press he was ecstatic to be playing Nathan Detroit; in reality he much preferred the part of Sky Masterson, the romantic lead. For the second time Brando had been given a role Sinatra coveted, and the word "forgiveness" had never found a place in Frank's lexicon. Moreover, he saw in Marlon a figurehead of youthful rebellion, an avatar of all that threatened his career. The wounded swagger notwithstanding, Sinatra was a deeply insecure man in the mid-fifties. For by then rock 'n' roll, the new favorite of American youth, had reached out from the black ghetto to the white world. The electronic sound, the new young voices, the strong backbeat, pushed most of the established crooners from center stage. Frank condemned it outright as "the most brutal, ugly, desperate, vicious form of expression it has been my misfortune to hear." Elvis Presley, a fan of Marlon's rebel pose, sang the kind of music that was "deplorable, a rancid-smelling aphrodisiac. It fosters almost totally negative and destructive reactions in young people."

Against such a personality Marlon stood no chance. And there were technical problems as well. After all, this was a big-league musical, requiring everyone to dance and sing. Marlon had taken some choreography classes as a newcomer in Manhattan, but had never sung anywhere except in the shower. All that would be taken care of, he was assured. His character would be built up, dance lessons would be furnished: MGM's vocal coach, Leon Ceparo, was the best in the business. True enough, but like the boxing coach Roger Donoghue, Ceparo would be conned by the Brando ability to ape the mannerisms of others. A couple of lessons were enough to convince the coach that Marlon "could make the Met if he studied hard," an event as likely as the Metropolitan Opera tenor Jussi Björling playing Stanley Kowalski.

The tone for the film was set on the first day of rehearsals, when Brando was introduced to Sinatra. "Frank," Marlon confided, sotto voce, "I've never done anything like this before, and I was wondering, maybe I could come to your dressing room and we could just run the dialogue together?"

Sinatra was succinct: "Don't give me any of that Actors Studio shit."

From that point on, the wall between them rose a few more inches every time the actors spoke. The two men were diametrical opposites: Marlon required multiple takes; Frank detested repeating himself. Marlon repeatedly changed the dialogue. Frank, who had committed hundreds of lyrics to memory, rarely blew a line. Marlon tried to find the essence of Sky Masterson. Many of Frank's intimates were gamblers; he had known Nathan Detroits in New York, Atlantic City, and Las Vegas and needed no research. Marlon was in strange territory. Frank had nothing to prove. He had risen from bobby-soxer heartthrob to the most popular self-described "saloon singer" in America, had already made more than twice as many films as Marlon, and, as proof that he was not just a pop icon, had received an Academy Award for Best Supporting Actor in *From Here to Eternity*. Marlon was essentially a loner. Frank's entourage followed him everywhere.

Could this marriage be saved? Mankiewicz did his part. He listened sympathetically to Sinatra's complaints about Marlon's repeated errors and retakes, and then heard Marlon out when he objected to *his* costar's romantic crooning. Detroit was supposed to be a character, for Chrissake, not a disc jockey's dream. Masterson was the love interest here.

Nothing helped. By the time the cameras were ready for the big number, "Luck Be a Lady," Marlon had lost his confidence. He begged

producer Sam Goldwyn to let him lip-synch to the voice of a professional tenor. Goldwyn refused; he knew a film with the legitimate claim
"Marlon Brando Sings!" would be worth millions at the box office.

And he was correct. The picture turned out to be better than anyone
expected, but was still an aesthetic failure. The second bananas did all
the heavy lifting: The Broadway veterans were unfailingly funny, and
the dialogue, based on Damon Runyon's charming tales of an under-
world that never existed, worked well onstage:

SKY: Nathan, figuring weight for age, all dolls are the same.
NATHAN: Oh, yeah?
SKY: Yeah!
NATHAN: Then how come you ain't got a doll? How come you're
going to Havana alone without one?
SKY: I like to travel light, but if I wish to take a doll to Havana there
is a large assortment available.

But onscreen the men Goldwyn and Mankiewicz had considered
"ideal casting" delivered their lines in an arch, humor-killing manner.
Preoccupied with his battles with Sinatra, worried about his singing—
which he privately referred to as "the sound of a yak in heat"—Marlon
had overlooked the female star, Jean Simmons. There was not a hint of
attraction between Sky Masterson and his love interest, Salvation Army
Sergeant Sarah Brown. *Time* found the picture "false to the original in
its feeling." While the Broadway production was "as intimate as a hot-
foot, the Goldwyn movie takes a blowtorch full of Eastman Color and
stereophonic sound to get the same reaction." Both principals were
inadequate: Brando "sings in a faraway tenor that sometimes tends to
be flat," and Sinatra "not only acts as if he can't tell a Greek roll from a
bagel; he sings as though his mouth were full of ravioli instead of gefilte
fish." *The New Yorker* headed its review with a tongue-in-cheek scolding of Goldwyn: "Sam, You Made the Film Too Long." Sinatra, bitter
about the whole experience, went public with his contempt for "Mumbles." Brando replied with a prophecy: "Frank is the kind of guy, when
he dies, he's going to heaven and give God a hard time for making him
bald."

The public bought *Guys and Dolls* anyway. It cost $5.5 million to
make and grossed $13 million, boosted by the publicity tours of
chorines called the Goldwyn Girls, as well as by the personal appear-

ances of Sinatra and Brando. (Goldwyn, a master salesman, had bribed Marlon with a white Thunderbird convertible.) The worst experience was the first—the New York premiere at the Capitol Theatre. The trauma turned Marlon into a lifelong opponent of film flackery. He and Simmons were driven to Times Square in a stretch limo. As they pulled up to the movie house, fans broke through police lines and charged the limousine. One of its windows broke under the pressure of the crowd, and the panicked driver surged ahead, barely missing a group of nearly hysterical adolescents.

Six large policemen closed in, opened the door, grabbed Simmons, lifted her high above the crowd, and carried her into the theater. Then it was Marlon's turn to be conveyed in the same manner. En route, someone got hold of Brando's tie and nearly garroted him. Ultimately, policemen saw what was happening, broke the choker's grip, and took Marlon to the lobby. There he sat on a flight of stairs, ashen "and muttering to myself, 'Jesus Christ, what the hell am I doing here?' " One way or another, he was to keep asking that question for the rest of his life.

1956–1959

A Mess Pretty Much

1

U ntil the era of political correctness, Caucasians were frequently cast as Asians. The personification of the Yellow Peril, Dr. Fu Manchu, was represented by Boris Karloff; Peter Lorre made eight films as the Japanese Mr. Moto; Warner Oland and then Sidney Toler played Charlie Chan from 1931 to 1947. In the twenty-first century such casting would be unthinkable, and perhaps should have been by 1955. But sensitive as he was to the feelings of minorities, Marlon wanted to disappear into another race, another skin, another accent, for his next role. Sakini provided the ideal opportunity.

In 1951, a book about the postwar American occupation of Okinawa made the bestseller list. Two years later, John Patrick adapted *The Teahouse of the August Moon* for the Broadway stage. It became the hit of the season, starring David Wayne as the play's Japanese narrator, Sakini. During his sojourns in New York, Marlon saw *Teahouse* three times. "I laughed so hard," he asserted, "I almost ended up beating the hat of the lady in front of me."

Determined to play Sakini onscreen, he lobbied the powers at MGM as soon as the studio acquired the property, reminding them of his assets. He had recently been named the number one box-office star, ahead of such favorites as John Wayne, James Stewart, and Cary Grant. Every week, some six thousand fan letters to Marlon Brando were received at an official Hollywood address. Edward R. Murrow had featured him on his popular CBS show *Person to Person*. Marlon had cleaned up his act, sold the motorcycle, abandoned the leather jackets as "yesterday's news," released Russell the raccoon in the woods of Libertyville, and remade himself as a businessman/artist establishing his own production company, called Pennebaker in honor of his late mother. Five studios had offered to go into partnership; Marlon chose Paramount.

He did not go into details about Pennebaker—with good reason. He had given his father an office on the Paramount lot, as well as the title of treasurer. It was not a happy arrangement. Carlo Fiore, Marlon's old friend from the Studio days, had recently emerged from a new bout of drug addiction. Marlon invited him to drop in. The two were in mid-reminiscence when Marlon senior appeared in the doorway, igniting a battle between father and son.

Junior had asked Senior for $5,000. The money was to be forwarded to Stella Adler to back her New York stage production of *Johnny Johnson*. Senior informed him that the cash was unavailable. Nothing was liquid; everything was in securities. This was no time to sell bonds or shares. Besides, backing a play was just about the worst investment he could make; the entire $5,000 might be lost overnight.

"I'm not *investing* in a *play*," Junior said through clenched teeth. "I'm *lending* money to a *friend*."

Senior remonstrated; Junior blew up. He ordered his father to make out a check for the whole amount and bring it in for a signature.

Senior blushed and withdrew.

It was not in Marlon to apologize, but for some time after that he spoke softly to his father, listened to complaints of loneliness and depression, sent him to his psychiatrist, and said nothing when Senior began to date a woman who reminded them both of Dodie. Life seemed Freudian enough as it was.

Pennebaker's declared purpose was to develop feature films that contained "social value and would improve the world." This lofty goal received quite a few sneers when it was announced; a television comedienne had Marlon in mind when she came on as a Miss America contestant whose specialties were "baton twirling and world peace." Nevertheless, Marlon meant what he said, and he viewed *Teahouse* as an ideal project for his socially responsible agenda.

In reality, he was pushing on an open door. Of his two main rivals, one was dead and the other in rapid decline. In September 1955 James Dean had perished in a head-on automobile crash in his cherished Porsche. Over the next two years, reported Dean's biographer Donald Spoto, film magazines would present Dean with more than twenty awards as "the best" in one category or another; he had achieved in death an unimaginable prominence. Frank O'Hara wrote a tribute in *Poetry* magazine:

> *Men cry from the grave while they still live*
> *and now I am this dead man's voice*

Marlon could only look on Dean's posthumous fame with wonder and resentment. Nevertheless, Jimmy would make no more films, and the only other comparable American figure, Montgomery Clift, had become a deeply troubled, unapproachable man. At least as complicated as Marlon, he had taken to drugs and alcohol and was in no shape to compete. Thus MGM was prepared to grant Brando just about anything and he was ready to demand just about everything. The head of production, Dore Schary, confided to colleagues, "If he had wanted to play Little Eva, I would have let him."

As soon as Marlon signed the contract he made plans for a tour of the Orient. There he would soak up the exotic atmosphere and learn Asian mannerisms and dialects. The trip never materialized because he suddenly changed his mind and decided to stay close to home. It was the usual reason: A new woman had entered his life. He was smitten, and couldn't bear to leave her.

Her name was Anna Kashfi, she was twenty-two years old, and she had impressed Paramount enough to win a role in *The Mountain*, alongside Spencer Tracy and Robert Wagner. Kashfi's official bio stated that she was an Anglo-Indian, born in Darjeeling and educated in a French convent. She displayed all the Brando requisites: lustrous eyes, olive complexion, and a reticent, almost virginal manner. At the beginning of their relationship, Marlon was as decorous as he had been with Eva Marie Saint on the set of *Waterfront*. His Pennebaker partner, film producer George Englund, actually functioned as chaperone on their first date. In her vindictive memoir, *Brando for Breakfast*, Kashfi writes of their early dalliance: "I went to bed with Marlon mostly out of curiosity. His seduction technique showed all the subtlety of a guillotine." The pair were watching television when Marlon abruptly picked up Anna, Rhett Butler–style, and carried her off to the bedroom. Physically, she noted, Marlon was "not well appointed." He compensated for that deficiency, she said, "by undue devotion to his sex organ. 'My noble tool.'"

She was drawn into his orbit anyway, and he into hers. The overheated affair was interrupted in April 1956, when Marlon was summoned to Japan; filming had begun on *The Teahouse of the August Moon*.

From rehearsals onward Marlon was preoccupied and miserable. His costar was the versatile old pro Glenn Ford, newly popular because of his recent successes in *Gilda, The Big Heat,* and *Blackboard Jungle*. He was conservative by nature, and Marlon, his social conscience freshly aroused, made their differences a battleground. They argued on the set, giving director Daniel Mann fits, and when Marlon was interviewed by Japanese journalists, he made a point of sticking it to U.S. foreign policy: "Of all the countries in the world that suffer from backwardness, America is first." He went around quoting Sakini, the narrator of *Teahouse,* to anyone who would listen—and to many who would not. The narrator's opening lines describe the island's subjugation by English missionaries, then Japanese warlords, and now by American marines. With a wry smile, he concludes: "Okinawa very fortunate. Culture brought to us. Not have to leave home for it."

Ford faced off with Brando. Did he know that the United States contributed more money and aid to Okinawa than any other nation in the world? And anyway, what was a white guy doing playing a Japanese with that bogus accent?

Matters and manners grew so hostile that Mann had to step in and growl: "You're not really doing a scene—you're doing a show about two actors who are trying to fuck each other." The actors shaped up for a little while, then went at it again.

The weather turned foul, the set gloomy. *Teahouse's* comic lead, Louis Calhern, had been an elderly cheerleader, insistent that whatever the differences between the stars, this would be "a marvelous picture." As it developed, he was the most depressed of them all, grieving for a recently failed marriage to a much younger woman, knocking back too much liquor, concerned that his long career was in a tailspin. Marlon had admired Calhern since their *Julius Caesar* days; he listened sympathetically and tried to match him drink for drink. One rainy evening the old man failed to show up. It was announced an hour later that he had suffered a fatal heart attack. The stunned actors cobbled together a funeral service and tried to carry on, with farceur Paul Ford flown in to take Calhern's place. Ford learned his lines quickly and filming resumed. But so did the rain. It went on for a month. With no end to the monsoon in sight, the crew and cast packed up and went home. The rest of the picture was shot in Culver City.

Minutes after he unpacked his luggage, Marlon learned that Anna had been hospitalized with tuberculosis. The shock of the news made him go into reverse gear. Instead of being manipulative, he became solicitous; instead of taking her to his bed, he took himself to her bedside. Shooting resumed within the week, and at the end of each day's work he stopped by the City of Hope hospital, still wearing his Asian makeup and costume and breaking up the nurses with an atrocious Japanese accent: "Herro, herro. I am Doctor Messhugener Moto. Don't raff. I don't ordinariry make house cawrs." The mock physician and his patient spent hours discussing travel, philosophy, and religion—anything but acting. Anna's recovery was painful and slow. By now, Marlon watchers expected the romance to fade. Instead it grew more intense. He presented Anna with Dodie's earrings, her brooch, her favorite pillow. Reflecting on his mother's last days, he grew solemn. Pain makes man think, he told Anna reflectively, and thinking makes him wise. She learned later that the lines came from *The Teahouse of the August Moon*.

Just before Anna was discharged from the hospital in the fall of 1956, Marlon slipped his mother's engagement ring on her finger and proposed. By now he had acquired a house on Laurel Drive, but issued no invitation to share quarters with his fiancée. With his encouragement and financial help, she rented an apartment in the same building where Marlon senior was living. In this way Marlon junior could keep her at the proper distance—not too far, but not too close, either. The couple spent the Thanksgiving holiday at the California home of Jocelyn and her second husband, the writer Eliot Asinof. Talk of marriage was spirited but kept *en famille*. There were two reasons: Marlon was wary of the publicity that would surely attend the announcement. And emotionally he had never let go of Movita.

2

At an earlier time, Marlon would have turned down the part of Major Lloyd Gruver in *Sayonara*. He disliked the scenario of a doomed inter-

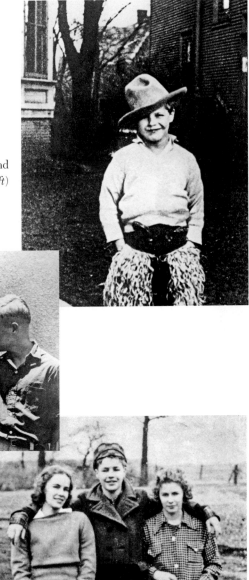

TOP: Eight-year-old Marlon struts in his first Western costume, c. 1932.

CENTER: Horsing around with his sisters, Frances (*left*) and Jocelyn, 1937.

BOTTOM: Several years—and inches—later, with Jocelyn (*left*) and Frances.

The role that changed the world: Marlon as Stanley Kowalski and
Jessica Tandy as Blanche DuBois in the Broadway production of
A Streetcar Named Desire, 1947.

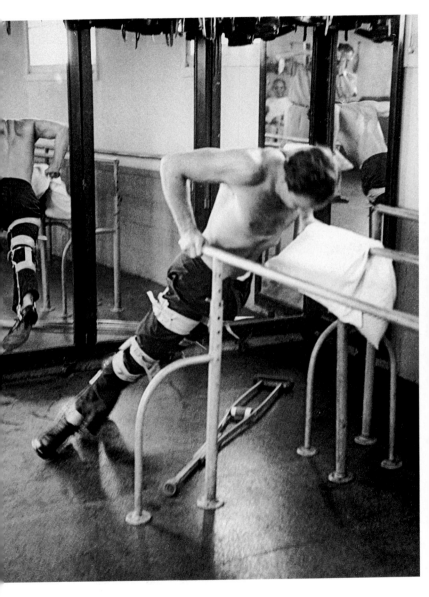

Practicing for his role as a paraplegic in his first film, *The Men*, 1950.

"Friends, Romans, countrymen";
as Mark Antony in *Julius Caesar,* 1953.

Setting a style for a generation: the leather-jacketed
biker in *The Wild One,* 1953.

Rivals and friends: Marlon visits Montgomery
Clift on the set of *From Here to Eternity*, 1953.

On the Hoboken docks, Elia Kazan directs Marlon in
his role as Terry Malloy in *On the Waterfront*, 1954.

Father Barry (Karl Malden) and Edie (Eva Marie Saint) comfort Terry after a horrific beating—the first of many in Brando films.

Marlon and friend at their Los Angeles home, 1954.

Two icons at their zenith: Marilyn Monroe and
Marlon Brando attend a Hollywood party, 1955.

BELOW LEFT: As the Okinawan narrator Sakini in
The Teahouse of the August Moon, 1956.

BELOW RIGHT: Wife #1: the pseudo-exotic Anna Kashfi
(née Joan O'Callaghan), 1957.

ABOVE LEFT: As Christian, the controversially "humanized" Nazi officer in *The Young Lions,* 1958.

ABOVE RIGHT: Playing Snakeskin Xavier opposite Anna Magnani, in every sense, in Tennessee Williams's *The Fugitive Kind,* 1959.

As the renegade Rio in *One-Eyed Jacks,* the only film Marlon ever directed, 1961.

Wife #2: Mexican actress Movita Castaneda and husband
go formal, 1961.

Wife #3: Tahitian actress Tarita Teriipaia on the set of
Mutiny on the Bounty, 1961.

The activist: attending Dr. Martin Luther King Jr.'s "I Have a Dream" speech in Washington, D.C., 1963.

Brando and Chaplin enjoy a rare laugh on the unhappy set of
A Countess from Hong Kong, 1966.

LEFT: As Sir William Walker, agent provocateur of British imperialism, in *Burn!* (*Queimada*), 1969.

BELOW: Another feline, on the set of *The Godfather,* 1972.

LEFT: Vito Corleone plays with his grandson moments before the old man's death in *The Godfather,* 1972.

BELOW: Cavorting with Maria Schneider in the smoldering international hit *Last Tango in Paris,* 1972.

With his fellow superstar and biggest fan, Jack Nicholson,
in *The Missouri Breaks*, 1976.

The only two actors to refuse the Oscar, Marlon Brando and
George C. Scott, in *The Formula*, 1980.

racial G.I. romance. And he had minimal regard for the work of director Josh Logan, scheduled to do *Streetcar* until Tennessee Williams had the sense to insist on Elia Kazan. Logan had made a Broadway candy box of James Michener's austere *Tales of the South Pacific*, featuring Oscar Hammerstein II's self-conscious lecture about racism. Marlon thought it was right out of a Sunday-school text, all righteousness and flapdoodle about how children were without racial or ethnic prejudice. Their parents and communities were the guilty parties; the elders were responsible for instructing the young, carefully instructing them to far those "whose skin is a different shade." In context, the song was effective—one of *South Pacific*'s subplots concerned an interracial marriage. Outside the theater, though, it was just a lecture set to music.

Yet his own attempt to dramatize the Asian situation had been just as ungainly. And unlike *South Pacific*, it had not been greeted with approbation and SRO houses. The star of *Teahouse*, wrote Marlon's most indulgent critic, Bosley Crowther, "looks synthetic. A conspicuous make-up of his eyes and a shiny black wig do not imbue him with an oriental cast. And his manner of speaking broken English, as though he had a wad of chewing gum clenched between his teeth, is not only disconcerting but also makes him hard to understand. . . . His Sakini is less a charming rascal than a calculated clown."

Bad reviews notwithstanding, Marlon remained obsessed with Asia. In *Sayonara*, adapted from another Michener story, he saw a chance to redeem himself, to make a valuable film about America's blighted racial history. And in the process, to get a $300,000 salary at a time when Pennebaker needed money to underwrite its own productions. But first his demands had to be met: a) the script needed work; and b) Logan had to show him that he was the right man to direct this moral fable. A and b were quickly satisfied. Warner Bros. was delighted to have landed the number one box-office star, and so were Logan, producer William Goetz, and screenwriter Paul Osborn. Marlon derided the ending, where Major Gruver leaves Japan and abandons his adored Japanese girlfriend. He said it smacked of *Madame Butterfly*. They agreed. Something would be done about that; on Marlon's orders *Sayonara* would dare to be different. After all, this was 1956, not 1856. Of course the romance of the major and his beloved *had* to end at the altar. What a grand idea. Why didn't we think of that?

Marlon now wanted the job badly—so badly he convinced himself that Josh Logan was ideal for the assignment. His rationale: During a visit to Logan's luxurious East Side apartment, Marlon sermonized about the need to treat the Japanese with respect and dignity while Logan gardened on the terrace, tidily pruning leaves from his plants. "Anyone who cares that much about living things," Marlon deduced, "must be a sensitive person." It was an example of Lorenz Hart's lyrical insight about the self-deception that believes the lie.

In fact, Logan was not an insensitive figure. But he was also driven and disturbed, the casualty of serial nervous breakdowns. Never easy to work with, he would test Marlon severely over the coming months. During the early stages, all was smiles. Logan called Brando "the most exciting person I've met since Garbo." At a press conference in Tokyo, Marlon told reporters, "I welcome the invaluable opportunity of working with Josh Logan, a man who can teach me what to do and what not to do." The director's statement was probably true; the actor's was an outright deception. Logan had promised Marlon carte blanche on script revisions. In a letter to Anna, Marlon described the real situation. At first Logan had been warm and accepting. If Marlon was unhappy with any of his speeches, he was free to change them. "I rewrote the whole damn script. And now they're going to use maybe eight lines."

But Logan did give him carte blanche in another matter. In Michener's novel, Major Gruver hails from Pennsylvania. Marlon insisted on playing the role with a southern accent. To his astonishment, the director responded with delight. He never told Marlon why, but in 1958 the reason became clear. In a three-part confessional in *Look* magazine, Logan spoke of breakdowns, tracing his feelings of remorse and depression back to Louisiana, where he had been raised by a black servant, "my second mother, the queen who ruled the back areas of the house, those permissive places where I was happiest." Then came the day when "I was told she couldn't eat with me or ride in the same railroad car with me. This is the guilty agony that all decent southerners carry inside of them." So Marlon's makeover played directly into Logan's hands. He now saw *Sayonara* as a way to expiate that guilt. Gruver's slow change from spoonbread racist to tolerant American would make him a symbol of the Deep South in the 1950s.

This reworking would have been more effective with a better female lead. Miiko Taka, who played Marlon's love interest, was an American-born amateur, pretty enough but with faulty teeth, no acting experience, and minimal sex appeal. Brando displayed little patience with her, though he was generous to his other fellow actors, assuring the standup comedian Red Buttons that he could play a straight role, and counseling James Garner that every scene in every film has a cliché. "Try to find that cliché and get as far away from it as you can."

On the set in Kyoto, Marlon brought out his familiar arsenal of mischief. He pretended to have broken his arm for a day ("One more picture with Brando and I'll be an old man," Logan sighed). And he holed up in the Miyako Hotel, shunning the cast, scarcely talking to a soul until his father and aunt Betty arrived to watch him perform. Throughout, Marlon engaged in a tug-of-war with his director, sometimes to see who would win the power struggle, sometimes just to egg himself on. One of the film's most affecting scenes comes when Gruver discovers the bodies of his friend airman Joe Kelly (Red Buttons) and the Japanese woman he loves (Miyoshi Umeki), whose culture forbids her to marry an American. The double suicide serves as a profound, life-altering shock, and Marlon insisted that he should play it in a spectacular manner, with howls of sorrow, followed by a smashing of furniture and a tearing of hair. It was as if he had decided to follow Yogi Berra's much-quoted advice: "If you come to a fork in the road, take it." On the one hand, he was still very much the star; put ten people in the same shot and he was the one you watched. On the other hand, his instincts, once nearly infallible, were beginning to play him false. Whatever Marlon's flaws, he had never been vulgar or over the top except when in summer stock. Suddenly he was making hammy, tasteless moves—an ominous turn of events. Happily, Logan stood up to Brando, refused to countenance the changes, denounced Marlon's ideas as amateur theatrics, and redid the scene his way. Major Gruver pushes through a small crowd of traumatized Japanese witnesses, discovers the bodies, stands silently, and then murmurs, "Oh, God." The director's version made the cut.

Logan made many other wise decisions, but the shrewdest of all was one Marlon ignored to his everlasting regret. Truman Capote had persuaded *The New Yorker* to send him on an overseas assignment—to profile Marlon Brando in situ. The previous year Capote had followed an American troupe touring the Soviet Union in a production of *Porgy and Bess*. The prose in *The Muses Are Heard* was faultless, the attitude disparaging. "He'll make us look like idiots," Logan warned, and gave the author a wide berth. Out of perversity as well as curiosity, Marlon made himself available.

Carlo Fiore was on hand when Truman entered the Brando digs, caparisoned in desert shades: tan woolen cardigan, matching corduroy trousers, and suede chukka boots. He carried a disarming gift, a bottle of 100-proof vodka. After some small talk, the little man suddenly launched into a story that should have served as an alarm bell. He and Leonard Bernstein regularly enjoyed tête-à-têtes at Lenny's apartment, during which they eviscerated the reputations of their mutual friends and acquaintances. Unbeknownst to Capote, Bernstein had turned on a hidden microphone. He debriefed Truman, encouraging him to speak of hidden sexual scandals, monetary problems, and family squabbles.

Some time afterward, Capote was invited to a well-attended party at the Bernstein apartment. At the appropriate moment Lenny asked for silence—and then pressed the playback button on his tape recorder. "It was a monologue in maliciousness," Capote remembered. At first the insulted and injured turned on him—how dare he spill such intimate secrets? What kind of creature befriends you only to betray you? But later in the evening the crowd became furious with Bernstein. He was obviously the one who had encouraged Truman, and who edited the tape so that only one speaker could be heard. He was considered more cruel than Truman, who at least had the good grace to look miserable and humiliated. Lenny was laughing out loud. They made their exits, speaking angrily to the host. His stunt had backfired.

Capote's story, coupled with the gift of vodka, "made me suspicious," Fiore would write later. He had a strong foreboding that Truman "would chop Brando up into small pieces, then go around telling people that mayhem was the writer's art."

That's precisely what Capote did. Trading on his own unhappy childhood, he unburdened himself to Marlon, confessional here, rueful there, open about his homosexual encounters, lost loves, and personal liabilities. It was an infallible technique. "The secret to the art of interviewing," Capote was to remark, "is to make the other person think he's interviewing you. You tell him about yourself, and slowly you spin your web so that he tells you everything. That's how I trapped Marlon."

The vodka helped. By the end of the evening, Marlon, whose excesses rarely included booze, had consumed far too much alcohol.

His tongue was thoroughly loosened and Capote got everything he wanted. Although journalists had covered Brando since *Streetcar*, he had always been able to keep them from probing into his psyche. Wisecracks furnished his defense, along with tall tales of amorous adventures and well-rehearsed anecdotes about his childhood. Capote was different. He knew which questions to ask, when to offer the next drink, which buttons to push. The Brando profile, "The Duke in His Domain," ran in the November 9, 1957, issue of *The New Yorker*. That magazine was not in the habit of publishing nonfiction hatchet jobs, and "The Duke in His Domain" occasioned more commentary than anything it had published since John Hersey's *Hiroshima*.

Less than a third of the way into the piece, it becomes clear that alcohol has loosened Marlon's tongue, exactly as Truman had planned. The interviewee complains about his oversensitivity, advising the interviewer to be numb to the miseries of this brutal world. Otherwise they will have their way with him—as they have had Marlon Brando. Once in a while there are remissions; psychoanalysis has been of some aid. "But still, the last eight, nine years I've been pretty mixed up, a mess pretty much."

It is evident from the piece that Capote considers the actor a self-absorbed monologuist and something of a hypocrite, contrasting Marlon's high-minded ambitions with a recent proposed Pennebaker film, a commercial Western entitled *A Burst of Vermilion*. Capote goes on to describe, in considerable detail, the squalid condition of Marlon's room, with uneaten food and soiled clothing scattered about, along with undigested books of Eastern philosophy. Encouraged by Capote, Marlon indiscreetly runs down both parents, but focuses mainly on Dodie and her habit. He wanted to take care of her, he claims in bathetic tones, have her move in with him in Manhattan. But his love was insufficient. "I couldn't take it any more—watching her breaking apart, in front of me, like a piece of porcelain. I stepped right over her. I walked right out. I was indifferent. Since then, I've been indifferent."

Indifferent about his ascent, certainly. Success as an actor, he goes on, is a meaningless thing. Celebrity leads nowhere. He has a good mind to abandon the whole hollow career. Because in the end "you're just sitting on a pile of candy gathering thick layers of—of *crust*." Worst of all, in Capote's eyes, is Marlon's dismissal of live theater. That this once-great, now self-indulged performer could put down a three-thousand-year-old art form in favor of movies was too much to bear (although Capote had accepted Hollywood money for the script of *Beat the Devil* and would appear as an actor in *Murder by Death*).

The conclusion is particularly unkind, treating its subject as a man-child who has fooled the world even as he has deceived himself. The interview over, Capote takes his leave to wander the streets of Kyoto. Suddenly he encounters Brando again, squatting like a Buddha on a garish sixty-foot poster advertising *The Teahouse of the August Moon*. "A deity, yes; but, more than that, really, just a young man sitting on a pile of candy."

Marlon was livid when he read the piece, and wondered whether he ought to sue Capote and *The New Yorker* for character defamation. Lawyers wisely discouraged that idea, and he contented himself with dreams of throttling the writer. Forget about it, advised Logan. "You should have killed him *before* you invited him to dinner." Theoretically, the article shouldn't have provided much of a detour in Marlon's life and career. How damaging could a biographical article be, even if it was written by the shrewdest craftsman in the business? But it did make a difference. Marlon had been portrayed as a windy clown, a fool with too much money and not enough character. Actors who envied his high position were emboldened to criticize him, comedians jumped on his mannerisms, and critics spotted egregious flaws in his work. In 1958, after several months of battering, Marlon wrote a letter to Capote, complaining of the damage done to an innocent who trusted a journalist. "Here is the inevitable communication," he began, attempting to ape the author's polished style. Now that he had time to reflect, he realized that an amalgam of vanity and "unutterable foolishness" had deluded him into thinking their conversation was private.

Capote saw no reason to reply; the mission had been accomplished to his satisfaction. As Truman's biographer Gerald Clarke notes, Brando's "soul could not have been more public if it had been on exhibition at Madame Tussaud's." Despite the mockery and denigration, however, Marlon enjoyed the last laugh—at least as far as his bank account was concerned.

When *Sayonara* opened at the end of 1957, *Time* labeled it a "modern version of *Madame Butterfly* which has gained in social significance but lost its wings," adding with a portmanteau word that the film was marred by "too much Brandoperatic declamation." *Newsweek* found *Sayonara* a "dull tale of the meeting of the twain." Fans disagreed. Star power and that traditional studio favorite word of mouth made the movie a nationwide hit. Jay Kanter had negotiated a profitable contract: Ten percent of the gross went to Marlon. It would be enough to put him in the millionaire category. For the moment, at least, Pennebaker Productions had been redeemed.

The judgment of Brando's peers, of course, was something else entirely. Here Capote had done considerable damage. On Oscar night, Miyoshi Umeki won for Best Supporting Actress and the reformed standup comedian Red Buttons got his statuette for Best Supporting Actor. Marlon, nominated for the fifth time as Best Actor, got nothing. Alec Guinness took the prize for his performance in *The Bridge on the River Kwai*. Another award was granted that night, but few home-grown filmmakers paid attention. Federico Fellini's film *Nights of Cabiria* won for Best Foreign Language Film. It was the second time one of his movies had been cited. The previous year *La Strada,* starring Anthony Quinn, had taken the prize. Remembering Ingrid Bergman, the Hollywood elite gave the Cinecittà products a smattering of emotionally distant applause. As far as they were concerned, such products starred Italian stallions, busty signorinas, and aging American actors trying to give their careers a jolt. Such foreign films had comparatively small grosses and therefore were of interest only to New York cineastes and snobs.

Marlon now made a point of denigrating the whole idea of prizes; as he put it, "I never believed that the accomplishment was worth more than the effort." This cool, ironic statement veiled his true feelings. After the Academy snub he felt an urgent need to take back the hill. An adaptation of Irwin Shaw's bestseller *The Young Lions* came to his attention and he passed up other opportunities to star in it. The book was Shaw's entry in the Great American War Novel sweepstakes, competing directly with Norman Mailer's *Naked and the Dead* and James Jones's *From Here to Eternity.* His was by far the glossiest and most calculated. The winding plot concerned the lives and fortunes of three men in World War II: Noah Ackerman, a sensitive Jew from New York City; Michael Whiteacre, a WASP movie producer; and Christian Diestl, a proud young German officer. The three men are like far-apart images on an inflated balloon. Slowly Shaw lets out the air and draws them closer and closer until they meet in a shattering finale. The casting of the trio was at once classic and bizarre. Noah would be played by Montgomery Clift, but this was not the same actor of the early 1950s. Screening the public from his homosexual liaisons, he now moved in a small circle of intimates. Elizabeth Taylor was one of his few female friends, and it was at a party in her mountain house on May 12, 1956, that he had drunk too much, not for the first time. As he had proceeded uncertainly down the hill, he suddenly lost control of his car. It picked up velocity, skidded, and rammed full speed into a telephone pole. One of the attendees saw the accident from his rearview mirror. He sped back to the house, frantically calling for an ambulance. Taylor shrieked, "I'm going to Monty!" and ran down the steep hill. Patricia Bosworth, Clift's biographer, states that the actress was "like Mother Courage. Monty's car was so crushed you couldn't open the door, so Liz got through the back door and crawled over the seat. Clift pantomimed weakly to his neck. Some of his teeth had been knocked out and his two front teeth were lodged in his throat. She reached deep and pulled them out." He was taken to Cedars of Lebanon, where doctors operated on a broken nose, fractured jaw, and facial lacerations. The patient had also suffered a severe cerebral concussion and back injuries. Nine months later, his face reconstructed and body healed, Clift had returned to the set of *Raintree County*. But he was not the same man physically or psychologically. So began what was to be called the longest suicide in Hollywood.

Whiteacre would be played by Dean Martin, whose film career had suffered from the breakup with his clownish partner, Jerry Lewis. The light comedian Tony Randall had been a strong candidate for the part, but Clift preferred Martin, and Marlon went along with the choice. Their nods were good enough for director Edward Dmytryk. Marlon was cast against type as the German. In keeping with his developing view that evil was relative and that any nation or group was capable of monstrous crimes, he welcomed the chance to play a Nazi with dimension and sympathy. His views ran directly counter to those of the unforgiving. In an essay about cant, Vladimir Nabokov evoked the Russian word *poshlost* to describe "bogus profundity," emotion that posed as thought. A favorite instance: "We all share in Germany's guilt." Irwin Shaw was another who had no sympathy for the devil. In his short story "Act of Faith" Shaw put his attitude into the mouth of Major Segal, a Jewish-American soldier conversing with a captured German officer.

"Segal," said the major, "after this war is over, it will be necessary to salvage Europe. We will all have to live together on

the same continent. At the basis of that, there must be forgiveness. I know it is impossible to forgive everyone, but
there are millions who never did anything. . . ."

"Like you?"

"Like me," said the German. "I was never a member of
the party. I lived a quiet middle-class existence with my wife
and three children."

"I am getting very tired," Segal said, "of your wife and
three children."

Marlon plowed ahead regardless; he intended to remake Christian,
give him more dimension than he had in the book, use him to deny the
concept of national character. When the troupe went off to Paris for
the filming, Marlon held a press conference. "Naziism," he stated, "is a
matter of mind, not geography . . . there are Nazis—and people of
good will—in every country." V-E Day lay a dozen years in the past,
and both Dmytryk and screenwriter Edward Anhalt were willing to
soften Shaw's original intent. Still, it was the star who took the biggest
hit when the novelist learned what was going to become of his German
officer.

It all began in a Paris restaurant, where a cup of hot tea spilled on
Marlon's trousers. He screamed in agony and was promptly sent off to
a hospital. Recuperating, he called Anna, elaborating on what had happened. She suggested a headline: BRANDO SCALDS BALLS AT PRINCE
DE GALLES. He laughed as he winced. The third-degree burns took a
long time to heal, though, and the stay did little to sweeten his disposition. Nor did a subsequent meeting with Clift. Brando told his fellow
actor that he knew all about alcoholism; he didn't want to see a man
he admired go down that path. Had Monty tried psychotherapy? Clift
was insulted—look at Marlon, at least twenty pounds overweight;
didn't he have a *food* problem? Monty continued to deny his habit even
while consuming double vodkas, and distanced himself from further
inquiries. By the time Marlon sat still for a televised interview with
CBS correspondent David Schoenbrun, he was in a sullen and confrontational state. So was the other guest, Irwin Shaw. When their host
asked about the upcoming film, Shaw replied that Marlon, like most
actors, was incapable of playing flat-out villainy. Instead, he wanted
Christian to be what fellow war novelist Merle Miller called "a cuddly

German." Infuriated, Marlon said that Shaw was ignorant, that he had no idea of who Christian Diestl really was. Yes, it took a writer to put him on the page, but only a performer could breathe life into the man: "Nobody creates a character but an actor. I play the role; now he exists. He is my creation." With matching self-inflation Shaw told Brando he was a monument of ignorance. The former playwright marred a lot of former friendships when he went on to define an actor as nothing more than a container. "You have to pour ink into the goddam fool to get anything out of him."

Marlon was no less competitive when filming got under way, except that his focus shifted from Shaw to Clift. Over the course of several films he had told everyone within hearing range that acting was only a sideline. It afforded him "the luxury of time." He was required to do a movie once a year for three months at the most, "which paid me enough so I didn't have to work again until my business manager called and said, 'We've got to pay your taxes at the end of the year, so you'd better make another movie.'" Once more, statement and reality were at odds. On the set of *Lions,* he studied Monty at work, trying not to show his interest, but giving the show away as he stared intently. Irked, Monty instructed Dmytryk, "Tell Marlon he doesn't have to hide his face when he's watching me act." In a turnabout, the next week he cased Marlon, now sporting bleached-blond hair and the accent of an educated German. Clift watched two takes. Unimpressed, he informed the director, "Marlon is sloppy—he's using about one tenth of his talent."

The stars appeared in only one scene together, and most of the time the competition was not between actor and actor but between actor and addiction. Monty alleviated his psychic and physical pain with fruit juice laced with powdered Demerol and bourbon. Marlon was obsessed with lunches, dinners, and snacks, consuming large meals on his off days, then crash-dieting so he could cram into his military uniform.

When the shooting was over in Europe, the entire crew left for the States. The movie's climactic North African battle scenes were filmed in the California desert. In a concluding scene Marlon was required to ride a motorcycle, with his captain straddling the back of the bike. The German officers are exhausted, and Diestl tries to stay awake by saying anything that comes to mind. Marlon saw a chance to address one of his favorite topics: the history of racial injustice in the United States.

He called Dmytryk aside. Wouldn't it be a great idea if Diestl recited a litany of prejudicial incidents as he rode? To humor Marlon, the director asked for a one-page monologue. Marlon returned with a ten-page screed. In it he went on about the Scottsboro Boys, nine blacks who were framed in 1931 for rapes they didn't commit, as well as details about the government's genocidal treatment of the American Indian. Dmytryk read on. As gently as possible, he informed Marlon that the speech wouldn't work in the context and tempo of the picture. Undeterred, Marlon came up with another suggestion. Christian Diestl was to die at the finale, shot by Michael Whiteacre. What if he were to tumble forward into barbed wire, his arms out, his body limp, as in a crucifixion? This was too much for his costar. When Monty overheard the proposal he told Dmytryk, "If Marlon's allowed to do that, I'll walk off the picture." The director intervened. In the end, Marlon was not allowed to impersonate Christ, and Monty didn't walk off the picture. Christian simply tumbled forward, and lay dead, facedown, in a pool of muddy water. He kept his face in the liquid so long the technicians thought something really did happen to him. As they ran down to the prostrate figure, Marlon suddenly rose. With great satisfaction he informed them, "I could always hold my breath longer than anyone else."

3

As *The Young Lions* concluded filming, a pressing matter arose. Marlon's main girlfriend, Anna Kashfi, weary of his notorious affairs, ranging from France Nuyen, the soon-to-be star of *The World of Suzie Wong*, to his longtime girlfriend Rita Moreno, played her trump card. She was pregnant. Marlon was at once intrigued with the idea of fatherhood and intimidated by visions of a wedding. Carlo Fiore had never been a fan of Anna's; he advised Marlon to give her everything but his hand. Marlon reminded him, "But it's my child, too." Translation: Abortion was unthinkable, illegitimacy unbearable, marriage inevitable.

The wedding was held at the home of Marlon's aunt Betty, in Eagle Rock. Among the attendees were Jocelyn and Eliot Asinof, Marlon senior, even though Marlon had initially refused to have the old man—

"I'll bury him before I do"—as well as Anna's friends western novelist Louis L'Amour and his wife. Marlon wore a dark blue suit; it contrasted with his still-bleached hair. Anna was dressed in a sari. That costume was to be her undoing.

Less than a week after the nuptials, a rumor began to make its way around Hollywood. Prowling journalists had made a discovery. The bride was not Anna Kashfi after all. Her real name was Joanna Mary O'Callaghan, and she was not an Indian. She was the daughter of a dark-skinned Frenchwoman and an English railroad worker currently living in Wales. William Patrick O'Callaghan had worked on an Indian railroad when his imaginative daughter was very young. But, he assured the reporter who tracked him down, "there is no Indian blood in our family." Joanna had been a waitress and a cashier before moving to London, where she enjoyed a brief career as a runway model. She changed her name, concocted her illustrious background, went to Hollywood, and won a role in *The Mountain*. Then had come the epochal seduction of Brando, while he thought he was seducing her.

Pondering the vagaries of love, Samuel Johnson remarked, "Were it not for imagination a man would be as happy in the arms of a chambermaid as of a duchess." So it was for Marlon. Formerly he had been bedazzled by the costumes, sandalwood perfume, and subcontinental aura of an Indian houri. When it became known that Miss Kashfi was one more pretender in a city of frauds, his interest rapidly flagged. In this he was backed by Marlon senior, who had thought all along that Anna was a dissembler. His disdain for her was matched by that of Anna's father for Marlon junior, calling him "a bum"—though not to his face. The union was doomed from the start. Nevertheless, the couple bought a place at 12900 Mulholland Drive, a sprawling twelve-room house on two fenced-in acres. Marlon was to live there, off and on, for the rest of his life. Their child, Christian Devi, was born in wedlock on May 11, 1958. The first name was in honor of Marlon's friend Christian Marquand, the second was the Sanskrit word for goddess—Anna had not given up on her story of Indian parentage. O'Callaghan, she insisted, was her stepfather.

According to Anna, Marlon came to her hospital bed and vowed, "From now on, I'll be a perfect husband." No doubt he meant it at the time; the status of fatherhood brought tears to his eyes. It took less than two months for the vow to be broken. Marlon entered the house one afternoon with France Nuyen on his arm. She was youthful and glamorous, Anna recalled, while "I probably looked like the old woman who lived in a shoe." She ran into the bedroom, bawling. Marlon followed, disingenuously asking what had upset her. She consulted her watch and began a countdown. He had exactly thirty seconds to get his girlfriend out of the house. The couple left together. Marlon returned that night, unapologetic.

The marriage held together for a few more weeks. Then in June, Marlon Brando, Sr., remarried. Marlon junior had not been invited to the wedding. His father's second wife was Anichka Paramore, the widowed daughter of a venture capitalist. She bore a strong resemblance to Dodie and she was twenty-eight (six years Junior's junior), and Marlon junior couldn't bear the sight of her. When Senior called from New York on his honeymoon, Anna congratulated him and handed the phone to Marlon. He grabbed it angrily, barked, "Hi, Pop, I hope you'll be happy," slammed down the receiver, and yelled at his wife for making him talk to a man he now despised.

That response was followed by other surly encounters. Matters were not helped by the critical reaction to *The Young Lions*. Montgomery Clift was almost universally lauded: *Time* said the character of Noah Ackerman was "funny and touching"; *Newsweek* found Monty's performance "virtually flawless," and the *Herald Tribune* called him "superb in his inarticulate anguish." On the other hand, *Time* said that Marlon had underplayed his role to such an extent that "only a telepathist could hope to tell what he's thinking." Brando's customary supporter Bosley Crowther was disturbed by the actor's revisionist approach. He told readers of *The New York Times* that Irwin Shaw's "unregenerative Nazi" had been irresponsibly "changed to a very nice young man." The *New Yorker* reviewer agreed with that assessment: As impersonated by Marlon, Diestl had turned into "a poor young mixed-up skier who wishes he didn't have to go around shooting people."

Financial troubles arose. Marlon senior had completely mismanaged Pennebaker's funds, and it was now a company in name only. Yet Marlon junior still could not bring himself to fire his father. Despite a history of antagonism, the men and their wives sometimes dined together after Senior returned from the East, often accompanied by a third couple, Wally and Marilyn Cox, who now lived nearby. *Mister Peepers* had run its course, and the Coxes had moved to the Coast in search of work. The only path open to Wally was a series of guest shots on TV programs, where he often appeared tipsy or out-and-out drunk.

He remained a discreet friend, never speaking publicly of the war between the Brandos. Marilyn was not so reticent. She noted that father and son "couldn't get enough of each other, even though there was no love lost." The strange filial relationship was not to survive much longer.

To salvage Pennebaker's reputation, the company slated several films for production: *The Naked Edge* with Gary Cooper and Deborah Kerr; *Shake Hands with the Devil,* a melodrama about the 1921 Irish rebellion starring James Cagney; and *Paris Blues,* a contemporary jazz-centered movie with Paul Newman and Sidney Poitier. There was no hotter word than *integration* just then. The 1954 Supreme Court decision *Brown* v. *Board of Education* had specifically outlawed the southern tradition of "separate but equal" schools. But the law moved slowly, and three years later Arkansas Governor Orval Faubus defied the courts by keeping a Little Rock high school 100 percent white. To effect integration there, it took an order by President Eisenhower, federalizing the state National Guard to guarantee the safety and security of nine black children as they mounted the steps of the school and entered formerly segregated classrooms. The event was as dramatic as anything since the war, and Hollywood battened on it. "And what did [Stanley] Kramer give us?" Marlon disdainfully asked a friend. *"The Defiant Ones."* That film told of two prisoners, one white (Tony Curtis), one black (Sidney Poitier), manacled together in jail—and, with top-heavy symbolism, after their escape.

Marlon was keenly aware of James Baldwin's appraisal, addressed to the mostly white audience of *Playboy* magazine: The black man is manacled to the white man. When the chains are finally broken, Poitier has a chance to escape, but rather than flee "he jumps off the train and they buddy-buddy back together to the same old Jim Crow chain gang." Baldwin saw the movie twice. Downtown, his liberal friends applauded the brotherhood theme. Then he viewed it in Harlem. His black friends hooted at the screen and cursed Poitier for folding under pressure. Why is it necessary, Baldwin demanded, "at this late date, one screams at the world, to prove that the Negro doesn't really hate you, he's forgiven and forgotten all of it. Maybe he has. That's not the problem. You haven't. And that is the problem."

Marlon refused to play the white liberal's game of guilt and expiation. Poitier would be different in *Paris Blues*—if only Pennebaker could get the money to produce it. That meant Marlon would have to go back to work. Reluctantly, he agreed to appear in a western. It was not *A Burst of Vermilion,* the feature he had been developing for years. This one was entitled *One-Eyed Jacks,* based on the novel *The Authentic Death of Hendry Jones* by Charles Neider. Producer Frank Rosenberg theorized that Marlon had been attracted to the oedipal drama because the villain's name was Dad. In essence it was a revenge story of two outlaws, Rio and Dad, partners in malfeasance. Betrayed by Dad, Rio is caught and jailed. Years later he escapes from prison, thirsting for revenge. Meantime, Dad has gone straight. He's now the sheriff of a small town on the California coast. The first part of Rio's vengeance is the seduction of Dad's daughter. Dad responds by giving Rio a public whipping and breaking his hand. Rio has the parting shot; he kills Dad and rides off with the young lady.

Rosenberg purchased the screen rights to the book and worked out a rough scenario with Rod Serling, creator of the TV series *The Twilight Zone.* Sam Peckinpah was brought in to do a rewrite. Stanley Kubrick, whose powerful black-and-white features *The Killing* and *Paths of Glory* had so impressed Marlon, was signed to direct. Before the set was built Peckinpah gave way to Calder Willingham, author of *End as a Man,* the novel about a soul-destroying military school. But Willingham never made it to the finish line. He was replaced by Guy Trosper—and Stanley Kubrick was replaced by Marlon himself. There were many versions of just what led to Kubrick's firing. Peter Manso's account seems the most plausible. First there was the business of the film's second lead. Kubrick wanted Spencer Tracy; Marlon insisted on Karl Malden, his friend since *Streetcar.* There was also difficulty about a female role. The film was supposed to take place in Monterey, California, during the 1880s. Even then the area had a sizable Asian population, and Marlon wanted his character, Rio, to dally with a Chinese girl. Kubrick asked Marlon who he favored for the role. Marlon suggested his current mistress, France Nuyen. Kubrick had three words for him: "She can't act."

With that judgment, the director supplied the actor with a casus belli—even though Marlon would eventually split with Nuyen and hire another Asian actress. Even if Kubrick had agreed with all of Marlon's choices, however, there was no way he was going to direct this picture. Marlon had another choice in mind—himself. Kubrick was coldly dismissed at a Paramount story conference. The director consoled himself with the way things worked out. If a well-known director had taken his place, it would have implied that Kubrick was short on aptitude or authority. But now that the producer/star had taken over, he told Fiore, "I'm off the hook." That he was, and blithely went off to direct *Lolita* in London. From here on, it was Marlon who was hooked, with all eyes watching.

4

Reporters roamed the outdoor set of *One-Eyed Jacks,* watching Marlon as he ordered his cinematographers to get long shots of the Pacific Ocean. Like a champion surfer, they wrote, the idealist was waiting for the perfect wave. He was doing nothing of the kind, just trying to match the look of some footage he had shot the day before. But Marlon offered no objection to the tales. "I've learned that it's useless to try to suppress stories like that. I don't even bother to deny them. People will believe what they want to believe."

He kept his plans to himself, delphically remarking that "with this film I intend to storm the citadel of clichés." The bromides he had in mind were the classic Western archetypes of swarthy black-hat villains, knight-errant heroes, and virtuous one-dimensional women. To achieve the deconstruction he had in mind, Marlon chose his cast with great care. The young love interest, Pina Pellicer, showed a sensitivity bordering on psychosis. (Tragically, it was not an act; she committed suicide several years later.) Other members included the Mexican actress Katy Jurado, the memorable Other Woman in *High Noon;* Ben Johnson, an authentic cowpoke who had been featured in many John Ford Westerns; Miriam Colon, an Actors Studio regular; and a number of reliable old pros, including Elisha Cook, Jr., Slim Pickens, and John Dierkes. Marlon paid particular attention to Johnson, trying to absorb his Oklahoma accent and laid-back attitude. As he slowly and deliberately went over details, *One-Eyed Jacks* began to leak money. Paramount executives sent notes and emissaries to the set. The burden of their message was simple: The movie was costing $50,000 a day. Marlon replied that he was making a picture not a budget, and kept on his own nonchalant pace. In one scene, for example, he was supposed to be plucking a rose from a bush and fantasizing about Pellicer as Ben Johnson stood by. He took so long, an assistant piped up. "Mr. Brando, don't you think we should get this shot?" That was all Marlon had to hear. He told Johnson in an assumed Western voice, "Ben, go anywhere you want for three or four days, 'cause I'm going to be sittin' on this rock."

Johnson got involved in another expensive scene. He was supposed to argue with one of the saddle tramps and then shoot him when he ran out of words. After repeated takes, Marlon was still unhappy with the henchman's expression. An idea occurred to him. He put the man on a saddle mounted to a piece of wood, began to issue instructions—and then, without warning, smacked him in the face. The hurt, astonished reaction was wondrous to behold, everything Marlon had wanted from the beginning, except for one small matter. He had slapped the actor so hard he knocked off his mustache. The footage was unusable.

As costs skyrocketed, the men from Paramount leaned harder. Marlon not only refused to break; he wouldn't bend. He reminded the men in suits that this was an expansive era. Alaska had just become the forty-ninth state; Hawaii would soon be the fiftieth. People were buying houses as never before. A baby boom was under way. Hell, he had contributed to that. There was a new vaccine for polio. Life expectancy was up. An American satellite circled the earth. President Eisenhower was forever reminding us that we never had it so good. If movies were in trouble, if TV was making inroads, then it was the responsibility of Paramount to make bigger movies, not smaller ones. What was the point in scrimping on a masterpiece?

In the face of his argument they backed off, and a film planned for three months' shooting at a cost of under $2 million turned into an epic that took half a year to make and came in at $6 million. It was not a movie, cracked Frank Rosenberg; it was a way of life. Yet even the longest marathon comes to an end, and *One-Eyed Jacks* wound down on June 2, 1959. This was only phase one. Phase two was the editing of hours of footage. Marlon had almost no experience in a cutting room, and he was losing focus in every sense. The sorrows piled on. His psychiatrist Bela Mittleman, sometimes a charlatan, sometimes a repairman, died after a short illness. The marriage of Jocelyn and Eliot Asinof was breaking up. She had begun to drink hard, Dodie-style. Anna Kashfi Brando was consulting a lawyer, preparing to leave Marlon because of his serial infidelities. The divorce would go uncontested. Given her husband's behavior and schedule, Anna would be granted sole custody of Christian and given $1,000 per month for child support in addition to $440,000 over the next decade for her own maintenance.

What sounded like an amicable arrangement was anything but. Once the separation was put in place, the clash of the exes became frequent and violent. A new lawsuit got under way. One evening, according to Anna, Marlon "brutally beat and struck me." Marlon's version made the encounter into a horror movie: "The door to my bedroom burst open and the plaintiff flung herself into the room and into my bed. I tried to restrain her, but she slapped me and bit me three times. I got her out of the house and then she started to come back in. I spanked her and she went out and got in her car and tried to run over me. I went back into the house and locked the door. She threw a log through one of the windows and came into the house through the window. I held her down on the bed and tied her with a sash from my dressing robe. I then called the police and asked them to escort her home."

In the midst of these legal and physical skirmishes, Marlon senior began to disparage his son's behavior in and out of the office. Junior found the censure intolerable and struck back. The showdown destroyed the last remnants of their relationship. "I was cold, correct and logical," Marlon maintained, "no screaming or yelling—just stone frozen cold." He told the old man that from the earliest days he had left destruction in his wake. His rigidity and selfishness had turned Dodie, Frannie, and Jocelyn into alcoholics. Maybe Marlon senior had a façade of strength and determination, but the truth was that he was weak and incapable of sympathy or empathy. Afterward, the son acknowledged, "I thought the sky was going to fall on me because of what I had said."

The feeling passed. A few days later Marlon received a call from a psychiatrist, advising him that his father had come in with severe depression. He was "on the edge of a precipice." No guilt attended the son's reply: "When he's hit bottom—please call me and I'll see if I can arrange something."

Marlon's other affairs, financial, amatory, professional, proved a little easier to manage. France Nuyen was back on the string; so was Rita Moreno, and there were others. When he was not out with them he wandered alone through the house on Mulholland Drive, moody, introspective, trying to resolve problems that had troubled him since childhood. He ransacked Rollo May's *The Meaning of Anxiety* and *Man's Search for Himself;* Karl Menninger's *Love Against Hate;* Eric Hoffer's *The True Believer,* a little volume of aphorisms by a longshoreman-turned-philosopher. The son of German-Jewish immigrants had caught

the imagination of liberal and conservative thinkers, not least because
he himself had almost no formal education, yet managed to discern the
nature and origins of mass movements. He argued convincingly that
the totalitarians of the twentieth century, notably Hitler and Stalin,
began as men with feelings of self-hatred. They became successful
because their programs offered cowards and nobodies a sense of significance. Marlon, who felt a kinship with all autodidacts, marked up the
book with exclamation points and arguments; the author's aperçus were
at once intriguing and disturbing. He could go along with some:

· "The vanity of the selfless, even those who practice utmost humil-
ity, is boundless."
· "The less justified a man is in claiming excellence for his own self,
the more ready he is to claim all excellence for his nation, his religion,
his race or his holy cause."
· Failed artists (like Hitler and Mussolini) are "the most violent
extremists in the service of their holy cause."

But he had trouble with the notion that the "segregated Negro in
the South is less frustrated than the nonsegregated Negro in the
North." Try that on Rosa Parks and Dr. Martin Luther King Jr. One
way or another, Marlon would have to address the subject of race in the
United States—if only he had the time. Things always seemed to get in
the way. Every day, for example, new scripts arrived by mail or messen-
ger. He could discard most of them. Not all, though. Not the one by
Tennessee. After Williams's play *Battle of Angels* died in Boston in
1940, the playwright revised it and retitled it *Orpheus Descending*.
This modern setting of the Orpheus and Eurydice legend opened on
Broadway in 1957, starring Maureen Stapleton and Cliff Robertson.
Panned by most critics, it lasted for a mere sixty-eight performances.
But Williams refused to quit. He had enjoyed success with *Streetcar*,
and less than a decade later with the film adaptations of *The Rose Tat-
too* and *Cat on a Hot Tin Roof*. He decided that the play, touched up
and furnished with yet another title, would make a splendid feature.
United Artists agreed.

The Fugitive Kind had already attracted the dark, vulpine force of
nature Anna Magnani (leading lady of *The Rose Tattoo*) as Lady Tor-
rance, Williams's ideal for the role of a frustrated middle-aged housewife. The Actors Studio graduate Joanne Woodward would play Carol

Cutrere, a young, slatternly heiress. Marlon was familiar with the play, and liked the script. He could see himself as Snakeskin Xavier, another in a long line of Williams's stud/antiheroes. MCA was brought in to negotiate with United Artists. Marlon expressed his apprehensions about appearing with a Vesuvius like Magnani, nicknamed *La Lupa*— the wolf. "They'd have to mop me up," he predicted. The studio dangled the bait of a $1 million salary. Mindful of alimony bills and Pennebaker debts to be paid, he signed on the dotted line. With that gesture, Marlon Brando became the first American actor ever to receive a seven-figure paycheck. The zeroes after the numeral one did not prevent him from proclaiming his discomfort, not only with the leading lady but with the director.

Sidney Lumet had started as an actor (replacing Brando in *A Flag Is Born* back in the day), switched to directing television, and then made a distinguished film debut with *12 Angry Men*. At the time Lumet was married to Gloria Vanderbilt. They were dedicated New Yorkers, and he arranged to have *The Fugitive Kind* filmed within easy commute of Manhattan. The place he chose was Milton, New York, about an hour's drive from the city. The small town became a stand-in for a Dixie village. Already disoriented, the Italian Magnani got more flustered when she found that Marlon hadn't the slightest interest in her as a woman. The actress had just turned fifty-one. Up to now, she had been considered something higher than beautiful—the essence of the female animal. Even so, the testimony of the mirror and the daily footage could not be denied. Was she still alluring after all these decades before the camera? In her eyes, only Marlon could provide assurance. His memory of their first encounter is ungentlemanly, but rings as true as the one with another aging actress, Tallulah Bankhead.

On a summer afternoon, *La Lupa* managed to get him alone in her hotel room. Without preamble she kissed him feverishly. They rocked back and forth as she tried to lead Marlon to the bed. He saw that she was "in a frenzy, Attila the Hun in full attack." Grabbing her nose, he pinched so hard she released her grasp, and he made his getaway.

In response, the furious Magnani gave him, and everyone on the set, a hard time. Marlon was equally difficult. Woodward resented his pauses and vagueness; the only way she would work with him again, she stated later, "is if he was in rear projection." Cast in a small part, Maureen Stapleton, watching from the sidelines, complained about his halting delivery: "I could make a dinner in all that space."

Williams held his tongue throughout the filming, but the playwright's unhappiness showed on his face. In time he was to pass harsh judgment on Marlon: "Brando's offbeat timing and his slurred pronunciation were torture for Anna, who had to wait and wait for her cue, and when she received it, it would not be the one in the script." Thus, the film was "mutilated by that uncontrollable demon of competitiveness in an actor too great, if he knew it, to resort to such self-protective devices." Generally, reviewers were unhappy with the results. Lumet had opened up the theater piece and evoked fine performances from the rest of the cast, but his efforts could not compensate for the drama's shortcomings. What had seemed poetic on the page once again turned into self-conscious rhetoric: "I tried to pour oblivion out of a bottle, but it wouldn't pour out." Magnani was overemphatic, Brando oversubdued, and Woodward a bit too florid for her own good. Only on one or two occasions did a scene seize the imagination, as in Marlon's defining speech to Lady: "You know there's this kind of bird that don't have no legs, so it can't light on nothing and has to stay all its life on its wings in the sky. I seen one once, and its body was as tiny as your little finger, but its wings spread out this wide, and they was transparent and you could see the sky right through them. The hawks can't catch them because they don't see 'em. They live their whole lives on the wing, they sleep on the wind—and never light on this earth but one time when they die." Marlon had difficulty with this monologue. He was going through a custody fight for his son, and he kept going up on the same spot. "The same line," recalled Lumet, "and bang, he'd lose it." Marlon asked for some time off. The director thought not; the longer Marlon stewed about his offscreen troubles, the worse he would be onscreen. They went through thirty-four takes until both men were satisfied. At that point, the star suddenly hugged the director. Lumet thought it was because Marlon "respected the fact that I hadn't violated him, that I let him fight through it himself and did not try to be a psychoanalytic smart-ass." Their mutual effort caused the scene to shimmer; the rest of the film had nothing comparable to offer.

Released in 1959, *Fugitive* found little critical support. On one coast, the *Los Angeles Times* labeled Williams's personae "psychologically sick or just plain ugly." Back east, *The New Yorker* called the film "cornpone melodrama," and the playwright/scenarist was greeted with catcalls as he left the Manhattan premiere. "I just booed back," he told friends. *One-Eyed Jacks,* released a little over a year later, suffered much the same reception. Paramount had taken over, laboriously paring six hours of footage down to two hours and twenty-one minutes. The result was one of the most striking—and incoherent—Westerns ever made. Its best moments deserved to be mentioned alongside the works of John Ford, and shown alongside *Shane* and *High Noon.* But the commercial editing had come at a prohibitive cost. Some dialogue didn't track; many reaction shots occurred without the proper stimulus. Looking at the result, Malden sounded like the rueful Terry Malloy: "If we'd made it the way Marlon wanted it to be made, like a Greek tragedy, it could have been a breakthrough western. It could have been a classic." After Marlon viewed Paramount's final cut, he sighed, "Any pretension I've sometimes had of being artistic is now just a long, chilly hope." Reviewers expressed bewilderment and the editors of *Esquire* magazine gave it one of their smirky Dubious Achievement Awards: BRANDO ON THE ROCKS. In later years, much too late for the studio bottom-liners, *Jacks* became a cult film, deservedly admired by fans of retro Westerns like *Red River* and *The Searchers.* An odd little book by novelist/screenwriter Barry Gifford is a lyrical defense of the movie. In *Brando Rides Alone,* he concedes that Marlon's thirteenth film is "not a masterpiece," but adds that he would always remember Brando's Rio "suppressing his hatred of the father figure he once loved and trusted who'd thrown him to the wolves. It may well have been the poet e. e. cummings saying, 'How do you like your blue-eyed boy now, mister death?'"

Marlon, whose luck and timing used to be infallible, had lost his way. Nothing seemed to click nowadays. Friends told him about the Dean Martin–Judy Holliday musical, *Bells Are Ringing,* still playing in neighborhood theaters. He caught it one evening and watched Frank Gorshin do a dead-on impression of Marlon Brando as a lost, inarticulate figure. People broke up all around him. He scrunched down in his seat and grumbled. What was wrong with these people? He didn't mumble anymore. It was as if they hadn't seen a damn feature since 1953.

Stockholders, Man the Lifeboats!

1

Federico Fellini's *La Dolce Vita* was released between the terminals of *The Fugitive Kind* and *One-Eyed Jacks,* and like many of his colleagues, Marlon failed to recognize its significance. James Dean was dead and Montgomery Clift incapacitated, but an important new actor had entered the global scene. In 1960 Marcello Mastroianni appeared in his breakthrough role as a world-weary journalist surrounded by materialistic excess. Together, he and Fellini struck a nerve and created a worldwide hit. The Italian performer refused to be taken in by the sudden rush to fame. He told interviewers that Federico had selected him for the role because the picture needed "a face with no personality." Here, Marcello's attitude toward the professional actor posing as *artiste* coincided with Marlon's. Brando: "An actor's a guy who, if you ain't talking about him, he ain't listening." Mastroianni: "An actor is someone who goes out to recite 'To be or not to be' while he's thinking about his lawyer or worrying about the money he has to send to his first wife."

But with all his self-deprecation, Mastroianni knew he was onto something vitally different, just as the young French directors knew that they had just tapped into a fresh kind of cinema with Nouvelle Vague—New Wave—movies like François Truffaut's *The 400 Blows,* and Jean-Luc Godard's *Breathless.*

Had Marlon been more focused, had his career guides been more leery of the collapsing studio system, he might have been a part of these foreign experiments. At the very least he could have found work in challenging, intelligent epics. For despite the recent box-office disappointments, Sam Spiegel believed that Marlon would be an ideal Lawrence of Arabia, made him an offer, and sent him Robert Bolt's vivid scenario. To Peter O'Toole's undying gratitude, Marlon responded: "I'll be

damned if I'll spend two years of my life out in the desert on some fucking camel."

He made misjudgments in his personal life as well. The separation
from Anna Kashfi had gone from bad to impossible. After their divorce
became final she tried to prevent Marlon from seeing Christian, and he
went to court to gain access to his son. He called her "emotionally disturbed." She said he was a lout, whose behavior "tended to degrade
himself and his family in society." Most of her accusations centered on
Marlon's habit of bringing his latest girlfriend around and showing her
off to Christian. The judge restored Marlon's visitation rights, provided
that he didn't do anything to provoke his ex-wife or disturb their child.
Marlon promised to do as instructed—and then promptly took up
flamboyantly with his old flame Movita Castaneda. Anna dismissed this
as a cheap gesture, done only to make her jealous. Actually, there was
more to the affair than that; in June 1960, he and Movita were secretly
married in Mexico. They returned to Los Angeles, but declined to live
as man and wife. Movita was pregnant and soon delivered a child,
Miko. Marlon installed wife and baby in a spacious Coldwater Canyon
house and continued to live bachelor-style on Mulholland Drive.

All this cost thousands per month. There were now two children and
two wives to support. James Cagney's stirring performance failed to
save *Shake Hands with the Devil,* Pennebaker's 1959 film of Ireland in
the postrevolutionary period. The company's next production, *Paris
Blues,* wasn't scheduled to go before the cameras for another year. The
need for cash was dire, and producer Aaron Rosenberg knew it. He
had a question for Marlon: What about a remake of the MGM classic
Mutiny on the Bounty, with Brando in the role of Fletcher Christian?
At first Marlon was unenthusiastic; he didn't believe a simple shot-for-
shot restatement of the old Clark Gable–Charles Laughton epic would
suffice for the modern viewer. However, his curiosity had been
aroused. He got hold of the Charles Nordhoff–James Norman Hall historical novel from which the movie had been adapted. It turned out to
be part one of a trilogy. The first book concerned the actual revolt
against the tyrannical Captain Bligh. The second, neglected volume,
Men Against the Sea, followed Bligh's astonishing survival in a small
boat with a bunch of loyal crewmen and short rations. The third, *Pitcairn's Island,* told of the mutineers in later years: how some enjoyed
their freedom; how others were hunted down, brought back to England, and hanged; how the remaining seamen turned against one

another, resulting in recrimination and murder. The latter portions of the story fascinated Marlon. He agreed to do the film with this proviso: "I want to investigate what happened to the sailors *after* the mutiny. Why did they go to Pitcairn Island and within two years kill each other off? What is there in human nature that makes men violent, even in an island paradise? *That's* what would interest me."

The demand seemed reasonable enough to Rosenberg. He assigned novelist Eric Ambler to do a scenario incorporating all three books and persuaded MCA that this would be the most remarkable Brando film to date. Surely it would be the most remunerative. Playing the part of Fletcher Christian, the star would earn a flat fee of $500,000, plus 10 percent of the gross, plus $5,000 a day for every day the film went past its six-month schedule (practically a guarantee given the complexities of production), plus $10,000 a week to cover overtime expenses. Additional bait was dangled: Most of the movie would be shot on location in Tahiti, the nirvana Marlon had visualized when still a miserable cadet. He succumbed.

Privately, Brando was not so pleased with the man assigned to steer this *Bounty,* Sir Carol Reed. It was hard to believe the studio's claim— that it was aiming for another *Ben-Hur,* MGM's megahit of 1959. Sir Carol's specialty was the intimate psychological drama, not the wide-screen blockbuster. *The Fallen Idol,* for example, explored the mind and loyalties of a boy who witnesses a killing. *The Third Man,* Graham Greene's atmospheric thriller, was basically the story of two men, one honorable and drunk, the other amoral and romantic, who compete for the attention of a woman in depleted postwar Vienna.

A meeting was arranged between director and star; it was not a success. Instead of discussing the material at hand, Marlon went on about the California rapist Caryl Chessman, who had been sentenced to death. This was a story crying out for a film, Marlon insisted, one that could show the folly of capital punishment. Reed hadn't the slightest interest in making such a movie. When the discussion finally got around to *Bounty,* Reed found the actor's suggestions useless. Brando had only the most rudimentary knowledge of Tahiti, derived mainly through old photographs and the paintings of Gauguin. Brando's request for historical accuracy was dismissed out of hand. To defuse the conflict, Rosenberg stepped in, reminding his star that no one in the audience would know or care about what British sailors or Tahitian natives wore in 1789. Moreover, *Bounty* was scheduled for release in two years. At that time it would compete with two other wide-screen extravaganzas: *Cleopatra*, starring Elizabeth Taylor and Richard Burton and directed by Joseph Mankiewicz; and *Spartacus*, starring Kirk Douglas and Laurence Olivier under the direction of Stanley Kubrick. Authenticity was fine for documentaries. But the tale of Bligh versus crew was cluttered with salts and officers. It needed all the sex and spectacle it could get.

Marlon was anxious to get to the Society Islands; he accepted the producer's argument. The events of the first few weeks could have come from an Evelyn Waugh farce. A group of allegedly glamorous Tahitian women—*vahines*, in their native language—had been hired on the spot. Their come-hither looks turned out to be unusable because their teeth were marred by brown stains and streaks, the result of chewing betel nuts. To cover these flaws, they were required to wear temporary dentures. Some five thousand were flown in from the United States. The *vahines* were delighted, took the teeth caps, and vanished to admire themselves in their home mirrors. They went missing for days. An MGM official came up with the solution: Extras were required to pick up their dentures in the morning and hand them in at the end of the day. The sand was equally disappointing. It was black powdered lava, disappointing to the eye and ugly to the camera. Tons of white sand had to be trucked in from a faraway beach.

Nevertheless, there were compensations. The *vahines*, as well as some Polynesian youths, were compliant to the point of passivity. A wink, a nod, and they were in bed with the flirter. Hetero- or homosexual, it didn't matter; there were no obligations beyond the moment of pleasure. This was more like it. Marlon relaxed in an atmosphere of total indulgence, auditioning local women for the role of Fletcher Christian's South Sea inamorata. He settled on a lush, empty-headed nineteen-year-old hotel worker named Tarita. This was the beginning of many disasters for the film. Early on, Tarita had trouble remembering her lines, and her scenes were repeated day after day until she got them right, at a cost to MGM of at least $50,000 per diem. Naturally she bedded down with Marlon, but so did other locals. In this, he was no different from other members of the cast and crew, who slept around more or less at will. Many, including Marlon, contracted gonorrhea and an expensive California physician had to be flown in with serum and antibiotics. Pregnancies forced some young extras to leave; they were replaced by even less talented ladies. A fortysomething technician fell for a voluptuous lass and, alongside her parents, announced their engagement—even though he had been married for more than ten years. Friends eventually persuaded him to give up the fantasy, but it was a hard sell.

Complications continued: While preliminaries got under way, the weather turned foul. Seventeen inches of rain fell one day, and storms were ceaseless. Then there was the problem of the script. Ambler's plot and dialogue were found wanting in character development, and new men were brought in for repair work. First Borden Chase, best known for Westerns, doctored the dialogue and plot; then Charles Lederer, who had earned his first screen credit in 1931, came in to fix the fixes. And then there was the problem of Marlon himself. He adored Tahiti and did everything he could to delay a return to California. On the very first day of shooting he told the director, "I'm sorry to see this day come; it means one day sooner that we'll be going back to the States."

Consciously and unconsciously he made life difficult for his fellow performers, insisting on retakes for nearly every scene. Richard Harris, a hard drinker but a dead-serious actor, was thrown by Brando's improvisatory technique. So was Trevor Howard. As the martinet Captain Bligh he had many scenes with the star, and abhorred Marlon's unpredictability. "You never know where you are," he fumed. "Brando could drive a saint to hell in a dogsled." Squabbles, rewrites, and inclement weather forced more postponements. Having indulged Marlon well past the point of fiscal sanity, MGM finally put on the brakes. Because it was impossible to fire the star, the director took the fall. As a crowd of paparazzi and columnists descended, studio flacks blandly asserted that Sir Carol Reed had decided to move on to other assignments, and that MGM was delighted to welcome Lewis Milestone as the H.M.S. *Bounty*'s new skipper.

Milestone was sixty-five, a durable Academy Award winner whose wide-ranging credits included *All Quiet on the Western Front, Of Mice and Men,* and *Ocean's Eleven.* He was a born survivor, convinced that he could right the foundering ship. Recalling the pacifist spirit of *All Quiet,* Marlon was deeply respectful when they conferred about the picture. Milestone rolled up his sleeves and prepared to take over. He would soon regret his decision. The *Bounty* script was divided into thirds: the mutiny; the life on the island; and the fallout and fatal internecine strife among mutineers. These sections were written by different men at different times and the parts rarely meshed. Marlon continued to be troubled by the personality of Fletcher Christian. Before him loomed the image of Gable strutting in the 1935 film. Clark "was marvelous in a lot of movies," Marlon maintained, but in *Mutiny* "he was just another fellow in a funny hat." To put some distance between the Fletchers, he proceeded to make his mutineer a high-minded, overprivileged fop. That put the wardrobe department in a delicate situation: Marlon's weight fluctuated by the week. At times his belly bulged over his pants (he went through fifty-two pairs), and he insisted on looking taller than his natural height by wearing awkward lifts in his shoes.

All along, Marlon's private life echoed the film production's chaos. After reading about Brando's current affairs in a tabloid article, Rita Moreno made a highly publicized suicide attempt. The overdose of sleeping pills could not have been more ill timed; it occurred in 1961 during one of his short visits home. She was later to describe her state of mind at the time: "There is falling in love and falling in love. You don't want the kind of love where you feel you are falling off a cliff but sometimes you can't tell the difference." Embarrassed and frightened, Marlon refused to comment on the incident then or later. (The ex-lovers would meet again in 1968, this time on the set of a film, where their all-is-forgiven-and-forgotten declarations soon proved to be a lie.)

Rather than face the paparazzi, Brando backtracked to Tahiti. From his South Seas redoubt he phoned Anna Kashfi to tell her he had married Movita, that they had a son named Miko, and that he would like the boys to meet as brothers. Furthermore, he wanted Anna and their son to join him in Tahiti, where racial prejudice was unknown. She wanted nothing to do with the move. "I know why he wants me to move to Tahiti," she commented. "He wants me to be stuck on an island somewhere, and he can come and go as he pleases. It's time he was man enough to assume the responsibility of being a father." And so saying, she opened new court proceedings that accused Marlon of being wholly unfit to raise their child in any way, at any time.

All too soon, these and other factors turned *Bounty* into a book-keeper's nightmare. Production costs for costumes, sets, and plank-and-beam reconstruction of the H.M.S. *Bounty* went into unplanned millions. Scuttlebutt on the picture was distressing; it was said that Marlon couldn't remember his lines and had to have them pinned to the actor opposite him so that he could read the little idiot cards as he went though his scenes. Rumors turned so negative that Marlon felt compelled to speak to journalists. He told a reporter for United Press International that he had little to do with the rising costs of the picture. There had been thirty different versions of the script, but never a final one. He hauled out the various treatments and put them on display. "How can an actor play a character if he doesn't know what will happen to him?" he demanded; those improvisations weren't prompted by frivolity but born of necessity.

No excuses were enough to satisfy MGM or its backers. An investment newsletter warned them, "Stockholders, man the lifeboats! The *Bounty* has sprung a leak!" By the fall of 1961 the stock had dipped ten points. Studio production chief Sol Siegel grumbled to associates about suing Marlon. In his mind the actor had deliberately delayed production so that he could get overtime pay. Siegel added a new grievance: Marlon had tried to subvert *Bounty* by suggesting, with tone and gesture, that Fletcher Christian was gay. Here Siegel was unfair. Going against type, Marlon had attempted to create an exemplar of the upper-class Briton of the period—haughty rather than nasty, effete rather than homosexual. Had he decided to queer the proceedings, however, history would have provided him with ample backing. Sub rosa, the nineteenth-century British naval tradition was often referred to with three nouns: "rum, sodomy and the lash."

The studio's dissatisfaction became a matter of public discussion. Early in 1962, the new President, John F. Kennedy, turned to his White House guest, Billy Wilder. "When in the world are they going to finish *Mutiny on the Bounty*?" he inquired. The director had no answer at the time; a few months later he could easily have supplied one— MGM called him in to help with the picture's finale. None of the writers had supplied a satisfactory ending; Marlon himself had taken a crack at it. Evidently affected by Plato's cave in *The Republic,* Brando suggested a finale with Fletcher sitting at the mouth of an underground retreat. The officer would be shown musing about the dark side of British imperialism. As the chief mutineer mused, shadows of rape, pillage, and murder would move on the stone walls as the British sailors ruined the natives of Pitcairn's Island.

The scene was summarily rejected. Wilder's accepted version had Fletcher Christian exhorting his compatriots to sail back to England and go on trial, pleading for clemency by revealing the harsh conditions of the British navy. The men refuse, attacking him and angrily setting fire to the ship. Mortally wounded, he gives his final speech against a background of flames in paradise. By now Milestone had thrown in the towel. Disgusted with Brando, he refused to direct one more frame. Since the finale was to be shot in Culver City, veteran director George Seaton volunteered to take over for the last few days. Marlon argued for a death scene in which he would lie on a bed of ice to give him the authentic chill of death. Permission was granted. Afterward Seaton was all the more grateful that he had insisted on a clause in his contract. Like Billy Wilder's and Carol Reed's, his work on *Bounty* would go uncredited.

2

During the waning days of production, Milestone granted an interview to Bill Davidson, then researching a piece about the making of *Bounty*. The article ran in *The Saturday Evening Post* of June 16, 1962, ballyhooed in ads, and augmented by a cover showing Marlon as a beefy Fletcher Christian. If the photograph was unflattering, the prose was devastating. The headline read SIX MILLION DOLLARS DOWN THE DRAIN: THE MUTINY OF MARLON BRANDO. Inside were quotes from the director. Marlon's reckless self-indulgence was responsible for "months of extra work" and millions in unnecessary expenses. Milestone seemed to gather rage as he went on: "The movie industry has come to a sorry state when a thing like this can happen." Its executives "deserve what they get when they give a ham actor, a petulant child, complete control over an expensive picture."

Davidson went outside the crew of the *Bounty* to consult Robert Wise, editor of *Citizen Kane* and Oscar-winning director of the lavish but highly disciplined musical *West Side Story*. Wise cited another troubled production, the still-incomplete *Cleopatra*. Originally budgeted at $2 million, it had cost Twentieth Century–Fox a reported $40 million with no end in sight. The first director, Rouben Mamoulian, had been forced out with almost nothing to show for his time. The reason: Peter Finch, who had been signed for only six months, had left to fulfill a prior commitment. The new Caesar was Richard Burton, the

Welsh baritone with "the best pipes in Hollywood," according to his press agent, and a penchant for heavy drinking. The female lead, Elizabeth Taylor, was then considered the most beautiful woman in the world—"violet eyes to die for," claimed *her* press agent. Like Marlon for *The Fugitive Kind*, she had been guaranteed $1 million up front, with extras to compensate for production delays. That sum had already ballooned to $6 million, with more money en route. There were all sorts of reasons for the skyrocketing costs. Taylor had taken ill, and was shipped off to a hospital, where she was reported to be near death, only to make an astonishing recovery, bounce back into her golden costume, and go on with the show. Once healthy, however, she proved even more expensive than when she was bedridden. To the distress of Taylor's husband and Burton's wife, the two stars engaged in a steamy tabloid affair that would ultimately lead to two divorces, a Liz-and-Dick marriage, a Liz-and-Dick divorce, followed by a Liz-and-Dick remarriage. The Burton-Taylor story became a much larger epic than the one being filmed. *Bounty* had merely crippled MGM; Fox was nearing bankruptcy. In an unsigned *Time* cover, John McPhee asked the same question of Burton that had been asked of Brando the previous year. "Does he want to be the richest actor in the world, the most famous actor in the world, or the best actor in the world—and in what order? Or just a household word?"

The complications surrounding Brando and the *Bounty,* and the off- and onscreen excesses of *Cleopatra,* said Wise, "might well mark the end of the star system as it exists in Hollywood today." The superstar monopoly—"the monster that we created ourselves out of fear of television—has now become such an expensive luxury and so loaded with trouble that it's just not worth it."

Testimony from two important directors would have been damning enough, but the *Post* decided to weigh in with its own unsigned editorial. Both Marlon Brando and Elizabeth Taylor, said the editors, should be exiled to Tahiti. After that, *Bounty* and *Cleopatra* "could be merged and sent back thirty years from now when we might be more sympathetic to these examples of National Vulgar. The only hitch we can see is that Tahiti, once burnt by Brando and the *Bounty,* might be unwilling to accept such important émigrés. In that case, we recommend sparsely inhabited but nearby Bora-Bora, an island whose very name onomatopoeically suggests our reaction to both stars."

Marlon's response was volcanic. Not since Truman Capote's *New Yorker* profile had he been so shaken and outraged. On that occasion he had allowed friends to talk him out of seeking justice in a courtroom. Not this time. "My son will soon be starting school," he told his attorneys. "I don't want him to have to answer questions about what a kook his father is." They initiated a $5 million lawsuit against the *Post*, accusing the Curtis Publishing Company of libel. The action forced Marlon to make other moves as well. He bypassed Sol Siegel and went straight to the top, confronting MGM president Joseph Vogel at his New York headquarters. There he turned on the Brando charm, appealing for a statement that would free him from the charges of sabotage and self-indulgence. He thought his plea effective; in fact the case had been made before he entered the room. Vogel was well aware of the lawsuit and wanted no part of it. But he needed to keep Marlon happy and cooperative until *Bounty* opened. It would not do to have both director *and* star knocking the picture. Therefore he issued an official statement: Contrary to uninformed reportage, Marlon Brando "performed throughout the entire production in a professional manner and to the fullest limit of his capabilities." The result was "the finest portrayal of his brilliant career."

Vogel had performed an effective bit of jujitsu. To boost his image as a cooperative team player, Marlon was now obliged to attend the openings of the film on both coasts. He showed up at the Egyptian Theatre in Los Angeles with Movita on his arm; Rosenberg accompanied Tarita, who had returned from Tahiti with Brando, and who was then in the early stages of pregnancy. Audience reaction to the film was mild but not hostile. Things were much worse at Loew's State in New York. When the houselights went up, someone caught sight of the star and booed. More catcalls ensued. Unlike Tennessee Williams, Marlon did not boo back; he simply retreated through a side door. The reviews were no kinder than the Manhattan ticket holders. *Mutiny on the Bounty*, said *Time*, "wanders through the hoarse platitudes of witless optimism until at last it is swamped with sentimental bilge." *The Saturday Review* cited the film as an instance of Hollywood's death wish: "*Bounty* and *Cleopatra* are the auguries by which the entire industry will chart its future course." Though it obviously pained him to say so, Bosley Crowther informed *New York Times* readers, "Brando puts tinsel and cold-cream into Christian's oddly foppish frame, setting him up as more a dandy than a formidable ship's officer." The British press lay in wait, then pounced: "Marlon Brando," said the *Telegraph,* "sounds as if his part had been dubbed by a subaltern at Sandhurst." Several journalists made fun of the way Christian addressed "Cept'n Blah."

Undeniably, Marlon had brought this on himself. Only decades later could the actor's work be judged on its merits rather than on his extracurricular extravagances. There are aspects of his Fletcher Christian to be disparaged, but there is also much to be admired. His disdainful, upper-class attitude is lively and intelligent, and his character grows subtly from a perfumed coxcomb out of a Rowlandson caricature to a complicated figure capable of moral outrage when he sees the skull beneath the skin of career officer Captain Bligh. Like all men of elevated background, Christian is a believer in class distinctions. The idea of mutiny changes from anathema to possibility and, finally, inevitability in the face of cruelty and oppression. His life is wrecked in the process. Yet all along the chief officer retains something none of the others have: a sense of humor. At the beginning of the film he loftily dismisses the *Bounty*'s mission—to bring back samples of the breadfruit tree. These, it is pointed out, could turn out to be cheaper than bread itself, thus feeding the English factory workers at a fraction of the current cost. Christian summarizes the situation: The *Bounty* has set sail going "halfway 'round the world on a grocer's errand." When the crew begins to grow restive and one of the more odious sailors rats on a shipmate, Christian inquires, "Is there anything else you wished to discuss—early Renaissance sketching, perhaps?" In that line Marlon brought contempt, hauteur, and a twinkle far beyond anything in the Gable rendition. As *Mutiny on the Bounty* winds down, Fletcher Christian sounds his own epitaph: "I did what honor dictated, and that belief sustains me." The self-conscious line hangs in the air for a moment; then he adds, "Except for a slight desire to be dead, which I'm sure will pass." Christian's ironies are threaded through the picture; those who wrote that Marlon had no grasp of comedy failed to comprehend what he was attempting to do in *Bounty,* and what a bravura and emotionally consistent performance he gave. Arthur Penn would be one of Brando's directors in a few years; he and film critic Richard Schickel spoke up for Marlon's full-length portrait. Schickel called it a "delicious performance, wonderfully comic, and socially acute." To Penn, Brando's Fletcher Christian "was a terrific work of art." They applauded in an empty house.

3

An old *New Yorker* cartoon pictures a human executive trying to persuade his elephant client. "It's a fabulous deal," he explains. "You'll make peanuts." In 1962, the executive was played by Jay Kanter, the pachyderm by Marlon Brando.

After taxes, alimony, child support, and various expenses, Marlon was close to broke. Aware that his case would be costly and probably hopeless, he had abandoned the lawsuit against the *Post.* Joseph Vogel had been sacked by the board of MGM, largely because he had cut Brando too much slack. The failure of Marlon's last three films thrust him into a deep depression. As he treaded water, the self-styled Dream Factory, the Hollywood of double bills and seven-picture contracts and More Stars Than There Are in Heaven was being dismantled. American International, a new studio with a string of low-budget horror movies to its credit, started working with focus groups. Its aim was simple: to please teenagers with a series of low-budget, high-profit "Beach Blanket" pictures. The all-powerful Production Code, in place since the 1930s, was losing its authority, picture by picture. In 1953, *The Moon Is Blue* had shocked the country by using the words "virgin" and "seduce," and since then every scenarist knew the Code's three general principles by heart:

1. No picture shall be produced which will lower the moral standards of those who see it. Hence the sympathy of the audience shall never be thrown to the side of crime, wrong-doing, evil or sin.

2. Correct standards of life, subject only to the requirements of drama and entertainment, shall be presented.

3. Law, natural or human, shall not be ridiculed, nor shall sympathy be created for its violation.

To articulate those principles ten years later was to engender laughter and disparagement. According to historian Ethan Mordden's appraisal of 1960s features, a new Ten Commandments made their way into the filmmakers' credo:

1. Thou shalt treat with irreverence that great American taboo, religion.

2. Thou shalt question the fairness of the American political system.

3. Thou shalt question even the values of that most sacred place of all, Hollywood itself.

4. Thou shalt despise even war-making.

5. Thou shalt question the beauty of marriage.

6. Thou shalt question even the very nature of romance.

7. Thou shalt be sympathetic to psychotic heroes.

8. Thou shalt make merry comedies about disgusting people.

9. Thou shalt deal most honestly with sex in all its varieties.

10. Thou shalt deconstruct heroism.

The Hollywood of the 1960s began with Alfred Hitchcock's perverse black-and-white horror movie *Psycho* in 1960, followed by *Dr. No*, the first blondes-and-violence James Bond film, released in 1962, followed by John Frankenheimer's paranoid thriller *The Manchurian Candidate,* and the decade's last well-received and remunerative blockbuster, *Lawrence of Arabia.* New leading men were on the rise. Paul Newman, an intelligent young actor with some of Marlon's brooding quality, had taken center stage with *Somebody Up There Likes Me* and *The Hustler;* and the open-faced brother of Shirley MacLaine, Warren Beatty, had made a sensational debut in the 1961 film *Splendor in the Grass,* directed by Elia Kazan. And there was a great buzz about the Englishman Peter O'Toole. In this new firmament—much of it composed of young men who had been riveted by Marlon's early performances—the Brando star had begun to drop. Scripts stopped coming to the Mulholland Drive mailbox. His bank account was drained by the business, by his father, by his ex-wives. He was overweight again and in poor shape, the barbells and exercise outfits gathering dust in a corner of his bedroom.

Marlon's private life was at its most chaotic and ruinous point. He had to support his ex-wife, Anna Kashfi, and their son, Christian, plus the current Mrs. Brando, Movita, the mother of Miko. But he had lost interest in wife number two as well as wife number one and was currently involved with the Tahitian Tarita. The couple planned to wed as soon as he could extricate himself from his current marriage. If Marlon was to jump-start his professional and private lives, he needed a guaranteed cash flow, and he needed it now.

Kanter was just the man to provide it. In the early 1950s the Anti-Trust Division of the U.S. Department of Justice had forced film studios to divest themselves of movie theaters; in the early 1960s it forced companies like MCA to make a choice. They could be either agents or producers, but not both. MCA chose production. Like most of his fellow ten percenters, Kanter released his clients and opted for an office at Universal Studios, an MCA subsidiary. In that capacity he offered to rescue Pennebaker by purchasing it for $1 million. As added bait he agreed to back a film Pennebaker had optioned three years before, *The Ugly American.*

Eugene Burdick and William J. Lederer's 1958 book followed the map laid out by Graham Greene in *The Quiet American,* published three years earlier. Both novels were indictments of U.S. foreign policy in Southeast Asia. Greene's antihero is a well-meaning young American official in Saigon whose idealism becomes responsible for death and chaos. "Innocence always calls mutely for protection," wrote the author, "when we would be much wiser to guard ourselves against it; innocence is like a dumb leper who has lost his bell, wandering the world, meaning no harm." *The Ugly American* takes place in the fictive country of Sarkhan, and throughout, the novel denounces the U.S. State Department's history of corruption and incompetence. "A mysterious change seems to come over Americans when they go to a foreign land," observes a Burmese journalist. "They isolate themselves socially. They live pretentiously. They're loud and ostentatious. Perhaps they're frightened and defensive, or maybe they're not properly trained and make mistakes out of ignorance."

Marlon had come to much the same conclusions during his own trips overseas. The story of the Ugly American would give him another chance to make a political commentary in the guise of entertainment— if he could find backing and distribution. MCA persuaded Universal that Marlon was still a box-office draw, and that those who read the Book-of-the-Month Club selection and bestseller would turn out for the movie. In due course a contract arrived. Its provisions were not quite what Marlon had in mind: He would get $270,000 in salary, a far cry from his earnings in the halcyon days. But Universal would guarantee a number of other features to be named later. No other offers came close. Backed into a corner, Marlon signed.

There were no ulterior motives behind the deal. Kanter maintained a fervent belief in his old client. In his eyes Marlon was a misunderstood, first-class talent who simply needed a few good properties to put him back on top. Universal would supply them. The problem, which Kanter failed to realize, was the supplier itself. No matter how high Kanter had risen, he was still a member of the Universal team. All members of that organization were expected to obey two guiding principles:

1. Films must come in at or below budget.
2. At all costs, those features must aim to please the largest possible audience.

In short, an inappropriate place for a maverick actor. "Career-wise," said a friend, looking back, "Marlon's contract amounted to a ten-year prison sentence."

Not at first, however. Stewart Stern, the scenarist responsible for *Rebel Without a Cause*, would write the script for the new Brando film, and George Englund, a businessman-turned-producer, would direct. Englund had never directed a movie, but he had financial interests in Pennebaker and Marlon trusted him. Kanter gave the personnel a green light.

Marlon yearned to make the film entirely on location in the Far East. He settled for a month in Thailand, and the rest of the time in Hollywood, acting on Universal's soundstages. This time out he made few demands, but one of them was not negotiable. Jocelyn Brando would play a part, no matter how small, in the picture. There was more than family feeling here. His sister had fallen on rocky times. She was a single mother again, with two boys to raise. Except for the first few years, getting work had been difficult for two reasons: She was drinking hard, and she had been on Hollywood's political blacklist since the late 1950s. Like her brother, she had been a sponsor of the Waldorf Peace Conference, but unlike him, she and her ex-husband Eliot Asinof had been involved with other left-wing causes. When the blacklisters demanded a mea culpa she gave it to them in the form of a letter that stated she was a naïve pacifist, not an angry ideologue. In the first years of the Cold War she had gone along with a crowd of better-Red-than-dead activists, and paid the price for her inexperience.

The declaration seemed to satisfy the HUAC. Still she had trouble finding roles, and Marlon felt he had to do more than send her checks; he had to get Jocelyn back on track. He cast her as the altruistic director of a children's hospital. Marlon put on his good-brother face, insisting that Jocelyn had "the true talent in our family." The statement made excellent copy and the film got started in a whirlwind of good publicity. *The Ugly American* needed all the ink it could get. In Hollywood, the crusty old mogul Samuel Goldwyn, who had stood up to the blacklisters in his day, denounced the film as unpatriotic even before the cameras started to grind. And on the Senate floor, William J. Fulbright, chairman of the Foreign Relations Committee, condemned the new Brando project: Just as the book was unworthy of an American publisher, the movie would be unworthy of an American studio.

Belligerently, Marlon fired off a response. "Halfbright," as he referred to the senator, ought to be aware that "there are few countries where a film like this could be made. It couldn't be done in France, the one-time citadel of freedom. Certainly not in Russia. Only America, England, Sweden, and a few other countries would permit such freedom."

Righteous as those words were, they made the cast and director uneasy; they were afraid Marlon would bring his irritation onto the set. They were pleasantly surprised to see him reborn as a total professional, arriving early, his lines memorized, his performance polished. To be sure, he called for many retakes, but this was his customary pursuit of perfection and a small price to pay for such gentlemanly deportment. Privately, though, he remained the same old Marlon. Stewart Stern spoke of the many times that groupies came to the set, surrounding him after work. "He would stop and say, 'Listen, who do you think you're asking for this autograph? You don't know me. I don't know you. It's an invasion of who I am to expect me to do this. I have no interest in it and don't know why you have an interest in having an autograph from someone you don't know. What possible use could it be?'"

And in an uneasy memoir, George Englund referred to an evening when he visited a business couple and some other guests at their Pasadena home. He thought to bring Marlon along, assuming that the pair would be impressed by a movie star. The initial chatter was convivial. The group was finishing their entrées when Marlon turned to his hostess.

"What size are your moons?" he inquired. " 'The brown areas

around your nipples, what are they, about silver-dollar size?' He held up a circle with thumb and forefinger as he munched. She flushed. Marlon waited, pleasant.

" 'Let's see them,' he said.

"Maximum disarray in the room."

To crack the tension, Englund tried a little levity. He said that it was unseemly to have the hostess expose herself at the dining table; for that, she needed an arena and a saxophonist to play stripper music in the background. The tactic worked. To everyone's relief, "Marlon didn't persist, but he'd gotten the animals moving around—everyone at that table had a mental picture of something he'd have said was preposterous only a moment before."

Perhaps it would have been better to have that eccentricity displayed on the set instead of at the dinner table. Playing the WASPish, condescending Harrison Carter MacWhite, journalist-turned-ambassador, Marlon was the embodiment of a government pawn who mistakes himself for a bishop. He was also less than compelling for the first time in his career. The plot was of little help: MacWhite is given the appointment because he got to know Sarkhan during World War II. He begins as a mouthpiece for American business interests, brainwashed into thinking that his old Sarkhanian acquaintance Deong is a Communist bent on taking over the country. In fact Deong is an anti-Communist. He is also anti-imperialist, convinced that both the Marxists and the capitalists, left to their own devices, would destroy his country. In the end, Deong is killed by Red assassins, and MacWhite, made aware of the arrogance and ignorance of the State Department, resigns his post. The Cold War is irrelevant to America's moral duty, he concludes; regardless of politics, the American people must battle "ignorance, hunger and disease because it's right." When he takes his bland, inarguable message back home, he is ignored. When he tries to appeal to the American public on television, they switch off the program. This indifference, on high and down low, will soon consign an entire region to flames.

These two portraits of ugly and silent Americans were prophetic, but few heeded their dark messages. The Sunday *New York Times* book reviewer judged Greene's "caricatures of American types" to be "as crude and trite as those of Jean-Paul Sartre," and *The New Yorker* called the book a "nasty little plastic bomb." By the time Brando's movie was released, the war in Southeast Asia had heated up, U.S.

advisers were on the scene, a young and vigorous president had energized the nation, and negative overviews of American policy, foreign or
domestic, were yesterday's news. Even then, a display of Brando's force
and originality might have given the film a chance. It was nowhere to
be seen. Marlon's ability to compartmentalize, to shut off the disagree-
able parts of his life, had vanished. He became an embodiment of the
French proverb "I have so much to do I am going to bed." With all the
financial obligations to women, to the island, to employers and employees, he had simply shut off his talent. Even his comrade and director
could do nothing to awaken him; Englund called Marlon's performance in one scene, shot twenty-seven times, "nearly inert" in every
take, and he was being friendly. In addition, the star had surrounded
himself with a troupe of lesser performers, Jocelyn not excepted. This
was the equivalent of a CEO flanked by weak vice presidents who dare
not contradict his whims. Such maneuvering rarely works in the private
sector, and in film and theater it is almost always catastrophic.

Before Universal's publicists could get any traction, a news event
displaced gossip about all films and filmmakers. On the night of August 4, 1962, concerned by a hysterical phone message, Marilyn Monroe's psychiatrist made a house call. When no sound issued from her
bedroom, he broke down the door and found his patient dead of a barbi-
turate overdose. Conspiracy theorists immediately went to work. It was
known that John and Bobby Kennedy had more than a passing interest
in the most famous blonde in the world. It was also known that she had
just been fired from the film *Something's Got to Give* for her habitual
lateness and inability to remember lines. Was she killed by the studios
or the politicos? Were the rumors correct? Did the FBI confiscate her
notebook and phone records? Or was John Huston right when he
grumbled, "Marilyn wasn't killed by Hollywood. The girl was an addict
of sleeping tablets and she was made so by the goddamn doctors."

Marlon was less shaken by the speculations than by the fact of her
sudden death. He and she had never enjoyed more than a brief
encounter, but their lives ran along parallel lines. Each was considered
the ultimate sexual presence onscreen. Both were known to be trouble
on the set, financially improvident, distrustful, victimized by the flaws
they had carried with them since their traumatic childhoods. And both
were assumed to be supernovas, fading into myth as viewers watched.

Monroe was not known for shrewd insights, but her brief summary
of Marlon Brando and Montgomery Clift had been astute: "They don't

plan their careers too well. They're not ambitious enough for their talents." Marlon knew of that remark and agreed with it, but never had a chance to tell her how right she was. Now that Marilyn was gone, he felt the need to write about her, and, in a way, *to* her. When the news of the actress's demise hit the wires, he remembered, "Everybody stopped work, and you could see all that day the same expressions on their faces, the same thought: 'How can a girl with success, fame, youth, money, beauty . . . how could she kill herself?' " They simply couldn't believe that the ballyhoo and hype wasn't truly important to Marilyn Monroe, "or that her life was elsewhere."

Marlon believed his own life was elsewhere. In the spring of 1963, he and Kazan paid a call on Clifford Odets, in the last throes of cancer. The visit was almost unendurable. Afterward, Kazan wrote, Marlon spilled his guts: "Here I am, a balding, middle-aged failure. . . . I feel a fraud when I act. . . . I've tried everything . . . fucking, drinking, work. None of them mean anything. Why can't we just be like—like the Tahitians?" But going back to Tahiti was not an option just then; nor was the secondary life he wanted, a life devoted to social causes. He had a Pennebaker film to sell. Marlon shook off the self-doubt and depression and plugged *The Ugly American* in Washington, D.C., Chicago, and Boston, as well as Japan and Hawaii. He hit the TV talk shows and patiently sat for interviews. "I have kids growing up," was his rationale for making the hated publicity tour. "The children made me realize I have a duty to perform." Initially, the cooperative attitude paid off. For if Marlon's Fletcher Christian had been mercilessly panned, his Harrison Carter MacWhite won a few hearts, including two critics, who endorsed its tepid editorial. In the spring of 1963 the dependable Bosley Crowther reported that "Mr. Brando moves through the whole picture with authority and intelligence, creating an 'ugly American' that provokes dismay but sympathy," and the *Daily News* found the role of Ambassador MacWhite to be "one of Brando's best performances." Theirs were dissenting voices. The general view was expressed by *Time:* The leading man "attempts an important voice, but most of the time he sounds like a small boy in a bathtub imitating Winston Churchill. . . . Through the stuffed shirt peeps the T-shirt, and at his most ambassadorial moments Marlon is unmistakably a man who longs to scratch. The customers will probably feel the same. It's the natural reaction to a lousy picture."

The Ugly American died at the box office, completely overwhelmed that year by a slew of better films, including *The Birds; Tom Jones; From Russia with Love; Hud,* starring "the new Marlon Brando," Paul Newman; and, predictably, *Cleopatra.* Because of that epic disaster, Fox had been forced to sell off 176 acres—almost the entire back lot—to real estate developers. They would call it Century City; the columnists and fans of old-time films, aware that this was the end of Hollywood's long line of sword-and-sandal epics, called it heart-breaking.

In Marlon's private life, pandemonium ruled supreme. Since the marriage with Movita was in name only, she took up with another man. Her legal husband continued to prowl. After one encounter he was accused of fathering yet another child. A laboratory test showed that this time, at least, he was not responsible for the pregnancy. But the newspaper stories made Marlon Brando out to be incorrigibly juvenile and irresponsible. Meanwhile, Anna kept at him in court, labeling him "morally unfit," and intensifying their custody battle. Tarita's child was far away in a benign climate and tranquil surroundings. His half brother was not so fortunate. Miko had become a total misfit, anxious to be noticed by a father who was more of an absence than a presence in his life. He was a terror with visitors and babysitters. These included Wally Cox and his wife, who couldn't stand the boy and said so. They were simultaneously saddened and relieved when Marlon confessed, "I don't much like him either." At the same time, observed a friend, Christian had turned into "a little devil." This was not meant to indicate a mischievous kid out of an *Our Gang* comedy. The youth was cruel to pets and made angry messes with his food and toys. He seemed beyond discipline—then abruptly morphed into the soul of goodness when his father entered the scene.

There is no sadder summary of that time than George Englund's. After he was divorced from Cloris Leachman, he saw his second son, Bryan, become fatally drawn to illegal drugs. Attempting to intervene, he found Brando restive and unhelpful. "I think Marlon didn't like what he perceived as my authoritarian way with Bryan," Englund rue-fully noted; Marlon Brando, Jr., still winced from an "old sensitivity to his own father's angry authority."

It was as if nothing had been learned in all the intervening years: Marlon senior's coldness and brutality had been replaced by Marlon junior's inattention and self-indulgence. It would be ten years before these shortcomings came back to haunt Brando with a terrible vengeance. But the stage was already set for failed fatherhood.

4

Stanley Shapiro served his apprenticeship in radio and television, where he learned the basics of situation comedy. He made an easy transition to films, establishing himself as a master of well-constructed farce, most notably with the Rock Hudson–Doris Day feature *Pillow Talk* and two Cary Grant pictures, *Operation Petticoat* and *That Touch of Mink*. His new script, *Bedtime Story,* had great promise: Two cads ply the Riviera looking for rich women. Originally rivals, they unite to steal the fortune of a soap heiress. But she is something of a con artist herself . . .

Shapiro wanted Cary Grant and Rock Hudson for the roles. Both had other commitments. Marlon read the script and got intrigued with the idea of playing Freddy Benson, an unscrupulous American charmer. David Niven was recruited to impersonate the smooth-talking charlatan Lawrence Jameson. The scenarist was glad to have Niven aboard; the Briton was an accomplished farceur. But Brando came with a lot of baggage. On the first day Shapiro confronted him: "I've heard some wild stories about you. I don't know whether they're true or not. But when we work together I'd like to have an understanding: one, that you'll be on the set on time; two, that you'll know your lines." Marlon was all bonhomie and assurance: "Look, a lot of what you've heard was not true. A lot of what you've heard *may* be true—but I had my reasons. You don't have to worry."

That guarantee held. He was motivated to be on his best behavior; for one thing Marlon knew Niven from the early days in Hollywood and wanted to impress him. "Working with David," he remembered, "was the only time I ever looked forward to filming. I just couldn't wait to wake up each morning and go to work so he could make me laugh." For another, he knew that Shapiro and first-time director Ralph Levy were not alone in their concerns about the bad Marlon. Class A scripts would not come his way until he repaired his reputation. Save for a few memory lapses, and a tendency to take the comic pacing *a lento* instead of *con brio*, he was the consummate screen actor. For perverse reasons he especially enjoyed a bit in which, to separate a woman from her money, he had to pretend to be paralyzed below the waist. To prove the point, Niven, his partner in crime, belabored Marlon's legs with a cane while the canee maintained a poker face. The scene was not merely masochistic, it was a cruel comment on his paraplegic role in *The Men*. Marlon was going the impressionists one better: If they were going to do parody, he would do *self*-parody and leave them speechless.

In his personal life, the backsliding continued. Unable to curb a ravenous appetite for junk food, Marlon gained twenty pounds during the filming; a beach-front scene had to be excised because his stomach bulged over the waistline of his bathing suit. And on some afternoons, he had a distracted air. Those who suspected drink or drugs were wrong. Marlon was experiencing his latest intoxication—a renewed concern for social justice.

With all the tergiversations of life and career he had never got away from the burdened, guilt-haunted childhood; as Frannie wrote: *When you were seven or eight you were constantly bringing home starving animals, sick birds, people you thought were in some kind of distress.* Men, women, children were out there suffering, deprived, disenfranchised, and he was in here getting fat and rich for doing . . . what? Speaking a few lines, making a few gestures. It was time to make other kinds of gestures, speak other sorts of lines. Time to make a difference. He had been sitting around too goddamned long.

The civil rights movement didn't wait until the 1960s to begin—the desegregation of the armed forces during Harry Truman's administration and the integration of southern schools under Dwight Eisenhower's were markers of a new America. Still, it was the election of John F. Kennedy—with crucial support from African American voters in the key states of Illinois and Texas—that energized the nation. Sit-ins took place at segregated lunch counters. As David Halberstam wrote, "The Negro, according to the Southern myth, is content. Even the young ones. The myth has exploded with the sit-ins." After hundreds were arrested, Halberstam asked what would happen if the undergraduates at Tennessee State were expelled for their part in the sit-ins. "Then we'll close the school," replied Willie Stewart, one of the leaders. "We'll all go out together. If we all stick together they can't stop us no matter what is handed down from whom."

Dr. Martin Luther King Jr.'s advocacy of civil disobedience gave

Gandhi's philosophy an American translation. It was provided impetus by the Justice Department, under the direction of the President's brother Attorney General Bobby Kennedy. But it moved too slowly to satisfy the radical advocates of black self-determination. New names cropped up—Sonny Carson, Elijah Muhammad, Malcolm X, the Black Panthers. Marlon diligently followed their progress. He would sometimes stay in his dressing room for hours chatting with civil rights activists while the rest of the cast waited around. He was determined to get involved somehow, either personally or by means of future films. This new passion brought him into contact with an old classmate at Stella's studio, the African American singer and actor Harry Belafonte. He and Belafonte attended meetings with Dr. King and other minority leaders—Chicanos pushing for the rights of Hispanic laborers, Native American leaders addressing the country's long history of broken treaties and false promises.

Marlon wangled a dinner invitation to the White House, where he hoped to present his ideas for a just society. But at mealtime, President Kennedy deliberately kept the conversation away from politics. As Marlon attacked the pasta, Kennedy challenged him: "Marlon, have you gained weight? Looks like you've put on a few."

"Nary an ounce."

Kennedy grinned. "Then the CIA sent up some wrong information."

Marlon bet the President that JFK weighed more than he did. A bathroom scale was brought to the room. Brando checked in at 187 pounds. Kennedy was eleven pounds lighter.

"Get some food into this man," Marlon told the other guests. "You can't lead the country at a hundred seventy-six."

The presidential laughter put everyone at ease. On another, more appropriate occasion, Marlon figured, he could speak to JFK and his brother Bobby about civil rights and Indian affairs. They were decent, progressive men. The kind he could talk to.

1963–1967

The Snake in Eden

1

Marlon resolved to be an *homme engagé,* separating himself from those "Bel Aire dissenters," who rarely left their gated communities except to go on location. He returned to a Pennebaker project that had been in the pipeline for too long. As he envisioned it, *Paris Blues* would not only be an entertainment, but a political and social statement. It boasted impressive credentials. Martin Ritt, a director who had been blacklisted for his pro-labor stance, was to guide the outstanding cast. The male stars, one black, one white, were Sidney Poitier and Paul Newman; the jazzmen's respective girlfriends Diahann Carroll and Joanne Woodward. The narrative would follow the Americans as they fled to Paris to find cultural and artistic freedom. So far, so beguiling. But halfway through, these ingredients failed to jell. Poitier's boilerplate speeches about racism and Newman's about the meaning of serious music stopped the action cold. No one was convinced by the finale, in which Newman opts to give up his romance to stay in Paris, and Poitier elects to go home to fight the good fight for equality. When the reviews called *Paris Blues* "well-intentioned," praised Duke Ellington's score as better than the acting, and called the direction "uninspired," Marlon knew that Pennebaker had struck out. "God," he told a friend, "let no one ever call me 'well-intentioned' again. Those are killer words. Nothing can survive them."

To assure the world that his motives were stronger than his movies, Marlon took the stage of the Apollo Theater in Harlem, helping to raise funds for a march on Washington. That spring he went on to protest segregation in Alabama, walking side by side with black leaders and a handful of like-minded actors, among them Paul Newman and Anthony Franciosa. The Goodyear Tire & Rubber Company in Gadsden, Alabama, had been accused of racist hiring policies; Marlon appeared at the factory gates, identifying himself and his colleagues as "devoted and peaceful representatives of goodwill, not as agitators, interlopers or interferers." A crowd had gathered by this time, and the hecklers drowned out the few who dared to cheer.

In a matter of weeks Marlon was persona non grata throughout Dixie. He expected no less; justice had a cost, and he was quite willing to pay the freight. To deepen his commitment to the black cause, he tried to get close to Dr. King spiritually and physically. The black leadership kept him at arm's length, but on August 28, 1963, he stood a few feet back from the speaker when King gave his "I Have a Dream" speech at the Lincoln Memorial. Marlon repeated the words of the leader, "Free at last! Free at last! Thank God Almighty, we are free at last!" painfully aware that a white film star would always be considered an outsider in the movement.

Never mind; there were other groups battling for civil rights. Perhaps, Marlon thought, he could be of greater aid to them. The American Indian Movement, for example. The double-crossing of the tribes was an old, sad story, but you would never know it from the classic oaters. There they were wild-eyed savages, much given to ambushing cowpokes, downing firewater, and talking about how the white man spoke "with forked tongue like snake." On the set of *One-Eyed Jacks* he and Ben Johnson used to kick around the idea of a movie about the real Indians and how they really talked and felt and suffered. Johnson was part Cheyenne; he knew American history better than most. Over at Warner Bros. John Ford had a picture in production, *Cheyenne Autumn*. It was supposed to cover the trek of a defeated people—maybe Ford's way of acknowledging all those John Wayne films he'd directed where all "Injuns" are murderers and rapists and kidnappers. ("Livin' with Comanches ain't bein' alive," says the Duke in *The Searchers*. "A human rides a horse until it dies, then he goes on afoot. Comanch comes along and gets that horse up, rides him twenty more miles, then eats him.")

Friends on the Left questioned Marlon about his new awareness. After all, he had made a Western and it didn't do a damn thing for Native Americans. Yes, he conceded, but that was before the sixties, before the freedom rides, the new implacable itch for justice. Maybe the blacks regarded him with mistrust, but the Native American activists seemed okay with a movie star. He would make common cause with Native Americans, be a bridge to the powerful men and women who cared deeply about minority rights. He knew key figures in Hollywood and New York. Come to that, he knew the President.

Three months later, John F. Kennedy was shot to death in Dallas. Like the rest of the country, Marlon went into shock. His recovery was slow, his outlook confused and unfocused. He had trouble dealing with simple things like weight-watching, and complex ones like repairing his troubled vocation.

Studio executives referred to him as "box-office poison," and not without reason. The last two Brando pictures had bombed, and *Bedtime Story* was greeted with very mixed reviews. A few critics were kind; Crowther praised "Mr. Brando's mischievous glee," but Judith Crist, the *Herald Tribune's* full-throated film critic, was closer to the general opinion when she called the film "a vulgar soporific for the little-brained ones." When *Bedtime Story* opened in the deepest South in late-summer 1964, because of Marlon's speeches in Alabama the Brando name was expunged from lobby cards. For all the moviegoers knew they had bought tickets to a David Niven picture. The Brando luster had dimmed, a fact, said a rueful Pennebaker executive, "evident to him as well as everyone else." Once more Marlon was faced with two choices: fight or flight. And once more he chose to fly. The Native Americans would have to wait. He had to get out of town. Way out of town. To the South Sea islands.

2

Fleeing to Samoa in search of health, the tubercular Robert Louis Stevenson had described his surroundings: "We dine in state—myself usually dressed in a singlet and a pair of trousers—and attended on by servants in a single garment, a kind of kilt—also flowers and leaves—and their hair often powdered with lime. The European who came upon it suddenly would think it was a dream." Paul Gauguin, abandoning Paris for Tahiti, wrote of his new liberty: "Seen from my bed, by the moonlight that filtered through them, the lines of reeds some distance from my hut looked like a musical instrument. I fell asleep to the sound of that music. Above me the great lofty roof of pandanus leaves, with lizards living in them. In my sleep I could picture the space above my head, the heavenly vault, not a stifling prison. My hut was space, freedom." In *The Moon and Sixpence,* Somerset Maugham's fictive portrait of Gauguin, a retired French captain described his paradisiacal island home: "We are very far from the world—imagine, it takes me four days to come to Tahiti—but we are happy there. . . . Our life is simple and innocent. We are untouched by ambition, and what pride we have is due only to our contemplation of the work of our hands. Malice cannot touch us, nor envy attack. . . . I am a happy man."

Marlon used to envy those men. Now he could go them one better. There was a coral atoll in the region of Tahiti—a dozen small islands called Tetiaroa—and it was for sale at a bargain price. Authorities had no taste for allowing these unspoiled isles to slip into the hands of an American, but he turned on the charm and began a series of long and complex negotiations. While they progressed, he built a small house on a Tahitian shore. Tarita and their son, Simon Teihotu, moved in with him. They went native, beachcombing, swimming, letting go. It was true that Papeete had been overtaken by tourism—the caricaturist Al Hirschfeld called it "Bridgeport with palms." But the outlying archipelagoes remained as unspoiled as they were in the days of Captain Cook's South Sea voyages two centuries before. Historian Alan Moorehead's description held true: "The bright festoons of coral, yellow, pale heliotrope, pink and blue, and the myriads of fish, brighter and more fantastic even than the coral itself, some with streaming ribbon-like tails, others streaked and colored like butterflies, shoals of minute minnows that advance and retreat in a pale blue cloud, the occasional turtle, the slimy water-snake, crabs that inhabit shells and clams with scarlet and cerulean lips that close upon their prey and never let go."

A more dangerous snake in this Eden was debt, the reason Marlon had to keep his eye on the clock. From here on, money would take on a variety of meanings. In theory he should not have felt guilty about a large salary: There were three households to support and children to raise. Capital would reduce the sheaf of bills that stuffed his mailbox every month. But he had read voraciously, and was familiar with Freud's dictum that "in dreams and in neuroses . . . money is brought into the most intimate relationship with dirt." It was no wonder that people referred to the "filthy rich," and, at least on paper, Marlon Brando now belonged in that reviled and envied group. If this was not guilt-producing enough, he also knew, and to some degree concurred with, Marx's feeling that money was a distorting power, transforming "love into hate, . . . virtue into vice, . . . intelligence into idiocy." Attached to this was a general malaise, a feeling that something had gone wrong in the center of his life. No therapist had been able to turn things around. There were times when he quoted Macbeth to friends: "Canst thou not minister to a mind diseased,/Pluck from the memory a rooted sorrow?" At other times he spoke about throwing it all away, the career, the family, everything. But on clear days he acknowledged that the dilemma of money versus freedom, security versus caprice, was insoluble. He guessed it was the same for every man.

And so in the summer of 1964 he flew back to Los Angeles to report for *Morituri*. Marlon was to play Robert Crain, a wealthy, complacent engineer waiting out World War II in neutral India. Crain's life there is a fraud: The fugitive has a Swiss passport, but is actually from Germany. His real name is Schroeder, and his ostentatious pacifism is not born of principle but of cowardice. Enter Colonel Statter (Trevor Howard), an officer from MI-5. British intelligence knows Crain's true identity and presents him with two options. The German can be returned to the fatherland, where he is a marked man. Or he can become a double agent working for the Allies. Crain chooses column B.

On paper the picture had much to recommend it. *Morituri*'s director was to be Bernhard Wicki, a German who had recently directed the bleak, much-praised film *Die Brücke* (*The Bridge*). The drama followed six romantic, doomed German schoolboys drafted into the Wehrmacht in the last days of the war. The youths receive one day's training before being assigned to defend a small span across an insignificant river. Children who were playing cowboys-and-Indians only a few weeks before are helpless against the lethal onslaught of American tanks and ordnance. Marlon found the director's antiwar views congenial, and when Wicki agreed to cast William Redfield and Wally Cox in small parts, the deal was sealed.

Once more Marlon invested his part with personality and considerable depth of feeling. Crain has been a decadent adult; now, following British orders, he must pretend to be a Nazi officer. He boards a cargo ship bound for Germany with one intention: to make sure her cargo of rubber—enough to equip an entire panzer division—never reaches its destination. The ship's chief officer is one Captain Mueller, played with gusto by Yul Brynner, an actor Hollywood found difficult to cast. Marlon thought he knew the reason after Wally Cox mused, "I wonder what Yul would look like if he ever put his legs together." That was because the actor was forever posturing as he did on Broadway, playing the Siamese potentate in *The King and I*. Marlon found Yul's first scene to be stagy and artificial. But he was astonished to see how effective it turned out to be, thanks to some deft illumination. "I had never paid much attention to lighting," he remarked, "and it made me realize that the man who sets it up can do a lot for your performance or break your neck if he wants to."

Yet with all the technical craft, two strong actors, and a good supporting cast, *Morituri* was slowed by heavy subplotting. A Jewish girl, Esther (Janet Margolin), is taken aboard from a Japanese submarine, along with several American POWs. Esther is less a person than a symbol of her people, violated in a concentration camp and, now, on this Nazi vessel, endangered once more. Captain Mueller is a career officer, disdainful of the Nazis and proud of his son, also an officer in the German navy. Crain does the work a spy is supposed to do, but has a withering contempt for any combatant: "All war is idiotic." The crew is composed of degenerates, open-faced recruits, and career seamen, the typical assortment necessary for war pictures since *The Big Parade* in 1925. Moral ambiguity is the theme of the day. The captain is gratified to hear that his son has sunk a ship—only to find that it was a floating hospital. He falls apart. Esther is gang-raped again, goes mad, and is ultimately slain during a gunfight. All this is too much weight for such a fragile vessel. A pity, because Marlon's German accent is wholly persuasive, as is his progress from effete poseur to reluctant hero. Crain's diatribes against war are no less convincing than James Donald's at the end of *The Bridge on the River Kwai* ("Madness! Madness!"). On the other hand, that film had strong dialogue, an epic structure, and David Lean's firm direction. *Morituri* suffered from a lack of coherence and a dearth of badly needed understatement. Marlon was to liken the making of the movie to "pushing a prune pit with my nose from here to Cucamonga."

Part of the pushing was done to satisfy Twentieth Century–Fox's publicity department. For this assignment Marlon essayed a role he disliked: the Gracious Brando. Just before *Morituri* opened he sat with unaccustomed calm at the Hampshire House in New York, posing for photographers and affably fielding questions from local and international paparazzi. The documentary filmmakers Albert and David Maysles were on hand to record the encounters, later released as a twenty-eight-minute short, *Meet Marlon Brando*. Predictably, Marlon flirts with a female correspondent, flashing his killer smile and inquiring about her background. ("It's unusual to find somebody as beautiful as you who is also a college graduate and seriously interested in world affairs and studying law.") A fawning journalist comments on his versatility and popularity and Marlon compares himself to a hula hoop—a fad destined to fade. But when a French reporter asks him a question, Marlon recognizes the accent, grows serious, and replies in fluent Parisian argot—obviously the time with Christian Marquand was not entirely spent in pursuit of romance. When a local radio personality makes a remark in German, Marlon answers him in grammatical Deutsch. Even though he makes it evident that fools will not be suffered gladly, his tone is never less than civil. He presents the image of a thoughtful, if playful gentleman who has read widely and challenges the received wisdom of his time.

Understandably, Marlon's fellow actors, particularly those who had recently shared soundstages with him, had trouble reconciling two opposing images. Could this sophisticated and patient interviewee be the same man who insisted on altering scenarios, who used cue cards as if he were subject to chronic memory loss, who wrangled with studios, and who generally made a private and public nuisance of himself? It could indeed. Few, in show business or out of it, recognized that Marlon was still on a search, perhaps an Ahabian one, to act onscreen, in his words, "the way it's never been done before." To keep delivering, even in middle age, a fresh, second-by-second realization of character. Like the rest of the young actors, Paul Newman watched in wonder and exasperation: "I'm angry at Marlon. I have to break my ass to do what he can do with his eyes closed." That was because Brando made it look easy. It was anything but. Marlon's attempt to live in the moment (and *only* in the moment) was difficult for colleagues to understand, much less to imitate. His ways sullied male friendships and made normal relationships with women impossible. But by this point he could do nothing else, and even in his worst performances, something of the genius Kazan had spotted so long ago was still hard at work. Elaine Stritch summarized it well: "There was never anyone remotely like Marlon Brando. Thank God."

3

As far as the Puyallup tribe was concerned, Marlon played his greatest role at the spot where Interstate 5 passes over the big river, leading down to Tacoma's Commencement Bay. In 1964 Washington State game wardens had hardened their stance against the tribe, arresting dozens of members. Their crime: taking salmon out of waters their ancestors had fished for over a century. It was one more instance of the federal government going back on treaties guaranteeing Indians the right to fish and hunt on ancestral lands, rivers, and lakes. According to SuZan Satiacum, wife of the Puyallup chief, "All kinds of authorities were coming down to the river and attacking us. And not just the game wardens, it was anyone with a badge." Their actions were met with total indifference. "Nobody—the newspapers, TV—nobody would want to hear what the Indians wanted to say."

The tribe was shrewd enough to hire a consultant, someone who knew how to reach a wider public. The adviser heard about Marlon Brando's interest in the plight of the American Indian and managed to get a message through. To the Puyallups' astonishment, Marlon not only sent money, but turned up in Tacoma, walking the bank of the river with a sympathetic clergyman. They borrowed a rowboat, set out a drift net, and caught a small salmon as part of a "fish-in," modeled on the sit-ins down south. One catch was all it took. When Marlon returned to the shore he was arrested and taken to the Pierce County jail. Anxious to avoid adverse publicity, the county prosecutor released the celebrity on his own recognizance. But the point had been made. "His appearance kind of gave the Indian people more backbone," said another member. "When Marlon showed up, then we knew the word was out all over town—and it made us braver." Their new hero did more than supply money. He gave interviews that left no doubt about where he stood. "Christ almighty," he told a *Newsweek* reporter, "look what we did in the name of democracy to the American Indian. We just excised him from the human race. We had four hundred treaties with the Indians and we broke every one of them." When another Washington tribe, the Nisquallys, staged their own fish-ins, Marlon urged his fellow performers to show up. Comedian Dick Gregory flew to the Northwest to lend support; so did Peter and Jane Fonda.

The tribes gave Marlon what the black civil rights movement could not. African American leaders had let him know that he could only be on the sidelines of their struggle; he was too rich, too famous, too Caucasian to join them at the front. In contrast, the Puyallups, the Nisquallys, and others were grateful for his aid, welcoming this prominent white actor into their company. It was with the American Indians that he developed the strongest connection; they became the focus of his compassion, the antitoxin to his contaminated celebrity.

4

In the spring of 1965, Marlon took his new and very temporary girlfriend—a Dutch immigrant named Honey—on a drive to Arizona. Indians were very much on his mind, and they stopped at a Navajo reservation. He sought out a medicine woman and attempted to palaver with her. He could see that she had no idea who he was, and on a whim asked for an appraisal. The old lady ran her eyes over his face and body. Through an interpreter she said that alcohol had played a large part in his life. She added that he was about to be struck by lightning.

"As she said it," he remembered, "I felt a strange sensation streak through my nervous system."

"Both your parents are dead," she stated.

"No, one of them is dead—my mother—but not my father."

Within minutes he was summoned to the tribal office; a call had just come through for Mr. Marlon Brando. Fran was on the phone. Marlon senior, who had been suffering from cancer for the past several months, had passed away minutes earlier. "We both laughed," said Junior, "and I said, 'And not a moment too soon.'" No one could tell how deeply the death resonated with Brando junior. On the surface, at least, he handled it with characteristic dissembling.

Marlon and Honey drove straight through to Los Angeles. At the end of the long drive they collapsed in bed. As he drifted off, Junior summoned up an image of Senior walking toward the edge of eternity. Just before the old man disappeared forever, "he stopped and looked back again, turned halfway toward me and, with his eyes downcast, said: *I did the best I could, kid.*"

After Marlon senior's death, Junior paid a forensic accountant to examine his father's investments. The report was grim: Senior's secrets had gone with him to the grave. Evidently he had deposited cash in banks under a variety of false names. W. C. Fields had done the same thing a generation before, under the monikers Otis Cribblecobble, Mahatma Kane Jeeves, and who knew how many others. Not a single explanatory note was found in Senior's papers or belongings. No doubt some of his accounts had gathered a lot of interest over the years, but neither Marlon nor anyone else could cash them in. All but one of his father's financial ventures had been futile. Some money had been invested in a group of gold mines, and not long after his death the price of gold shot up. Had Marlon senior held on to the shares he would have realized a profit. But a year before, he had panicked and dumped them at a loss. Even after death, the father continued to deplete the son.

The story of Junior and Senior made a fruitful field for psychiatrists; for years the doctors tried a series of therapies. Yet Marlon probably received more aid from his sisters than from professional counselors. A letter from Fran, for example, got him back on track after Senior's funeral. She reminded him that their paternal grandfather had been "a mean-spirited, rigid, terrifying martinet of a person who had made life so unbearable for our grandmother that she ran off when Poppa was just four years old. Left him abandoned. Left him to a miserable, loveless and terrified childhood with a self-righteous, loveless disciplinarian instead of a father. That was our father's wound and terror from which he never recovered. He grew up to be six feet tall, and inside his strong masculine presence was a very complicated, troubled and isolated person at odds with himself and often with the world."

Marlon held on to the letter, reading it over and over when the dark moods descended. They were hard to shake; at this moment he felt trapped in the Dark Ages of a career, and his instincts did not play him false. The beaches of Tetiaroa were the sole positive note in a cacophony of misbegotten marriages, bewildered children, and unsuccessful films. Contributing to the sadness was the schadenfreude of journalists who seemed to get a special kick out of his failings.

There was nothing unique about it; from the early days of silent movies, critics and feature writers had derived great amusement from two points in a film star's career—the rise, when they competed for interviews and wrote gushing features, and the decline, when they took down the once-famous in excruciating detail. Marlon made no protest when it happened to him. He had done no harm to those journalists who had found pleasure in his performances and who had been at his feet only a few years before. He would have been within his rights to utter some public statement about their perversity and ingratitude. None was forthcoming. As he saw it, the paparazzi were simply amplifying Marlon senior's evaluation of his son as worthless. If the old man was right, if an actor's life was essentially a sham—as Marlon junior had been stating all along—what was the point in fighting the truth? Let the Hollywood sharks have their way; he would swim in another sea.

Turning away from Los Angeles, Marlon renewed his efforts to buy the little chain of islands. In the back of his mind was a plan to turn them into a resort. Every time he visited the region he felt a new vigor and peace; surely there were thousands who would get the same effects, people in need of renewal, people respectful of other cultures and of the ever more fragile Tahitian environment. He saw the benefits to his son Christian when he flew him there in the early 1960s, and he wanted to bring him back. For by 1966 Anna's instability had worsened, and the parental drama, played out in courtrooms and living rooms, had piled on more misery. The twelve-year-old Christian retreated into himself. A textbook example of the syndrome pediatricians called "failure to thrive," he was angry, underweight, and manipulative, repeatedly lashing out at classmates and at his mother. Marlon, playing the paternal savior, escaped the anger, and Anna, burdened with physical and psychological problems of her own, allowed him to take Christian off to Tahiti. There the two played in the sun and made life into a vacation. The boy grew tan, filled out, and learned something about self-control.

It was not to last. When father and son got back to the States, Christian returned to his mother's house in Los Angeles, and she went back to court to regain full custody. As the judge listened, Marlon acknowledged his own shortcomings. But he predicted that Christian would suffer far more from living with his mother than from being with his father. Anna's instabilities were well masked; her plea was granted. Marlon furiously denounced the decision as "barbaric"; once outside, he repeated the word to reporters.

Now there were even more bills to be paid and, therefore, more films to be made. Next on the docket was *The Chase,* a melodrama with an unassailable pedigree. Lillian Hellman had adapted Horton Foote's stage play for the screen. The producer was Sam Spiegel, three of whose films—*On the Waterfront, Lawrence of Arabia,* and *The Bridge on the River Kwai*—had won Academy Awards for Best Picture. The director was Arthur Penn, who had climbed rapidly from television to the legitimate theater. His work on Broadway included a string of hits, some of which were *The Miracle Worker, Two for the Seesaw,* and Hellman's own *Toys in the Attic.* Marlon's costars included four escalating newcomers—Robert Redford, James Fox, Robert Duvall, and Henry Fonda's saucy daughter, Jane—abetted by the reliable character actors E. G. Marshall, Miriam Hopkins, and, thanks to Marlon's lobbying, his sister Jocelyn.

The first inkling of disorder came from the script. Foote was a local colorist first and a polemicist second. Hellman was all politics all the time. Blacklisted for refusing to give HUAC the names of fellow travelers, she continued to pose as the Joan of Arc of the Left, at once intrepid and mendacious, lashing out at the know-nothing Right but forever covering up her defense of Stalin in the 1930s; advocating free speech, but refusing to acknowledge her attempts to silence Leon Trotsky and his followers when they tried to present their side of the Russian revolution. Customarily, Hellman kept her views apart from her stage and film works, but with *The Chase* she saw an opportunity to fuse current events with fictive ones. Kennedy had been assassinated in Dallas three years before; the film represented her delayed reaction to that event. The melodrama took place in a Texas town full of overdrawn bullies and cowards. They were meant as an indictment of the United States in the manner of D. H. Lawrence, who saw the American soul as "harsh, isolate, stoic and a killer." Marlon was the good man in the center, a drawling, well-intentioned sheriff with a distaste for violence. The plot, like that of *High Noon,* concerns the return of a local malefactor and his effect on a small town. Bubber Reeves (Redford) escapes from jail and heads home to settle old scores. A lot of folks have reason to fear his return. They had crossed the young man in earlier times, framing him for a crime he didn't commit. In addition, Bubber's wife, Anna (Fonda), has been carrying on with Jake Rogers (Fox), son of the plutocratic Val Rogers (Marshall).

Every corner swarms with caricatures. Fat middle-aged bankers slaver over teenage girls partying next door. Migrant workers are paid off with broken-down TV sets instead of the wages they've earned.

Lower down on the food chain a group of vigilantes gather, armed to the teeth, spouting racist and loutish comments, determined to gun down Bubber as soon as he shows his face.

Sheriff Calder is all that stands between evil (95 percent of the citizenry) and the desperate and guileless Bubber, who gets arrested before any trouble can start. Then, in a series of overheated incidents, the townsfolk overwhelm Calder and beat him mercilessly—the requisite massacre in Brando films since *On the Waterfront*. For lagniappe they also assail a black convict in his prison cell. A killing, deliberately evocative of the Lee Harvey Oswald murder, takes place when the handcuffed Bubber is led off to jail. All along, a Texas-accented Greek chorus—a real estate salesman and his wife, played by Henry Hull and Jocelyn Brando—comment on the procession of violent and/or degenerate incidents.

What had started as a sensitive social document became a stew of clichés. Hellman's dialogue rarely rose above the level of comic strip ("Shoot a man for sleepin' with someone's wife? Half the town 'ud be wiped out"), and Penn never did get full control of the proceedings. This despite Marlon's lack of onscreen vanity—the gut-over-the-belt sheriff needed no padding around the waistline—and the technical advice he whispered to the director. Penn had earned his respect by quietly and professionally going about his business, neither coddling nor prodding the star. On set Marlon insisted, as usual, that the actor's "art" was nonexistent. But his diction and movement gave the lie to that attitude, and so did his suggestion that the beating could be filmed in an "undercranked" slow-motion style, then projected at a normal tempo. That scene became one of the movie's most persuasive incidents. For a moment it seemed that the old, exciting Brando might be reasserting itself under Arthur Penn's careful management.

And then, in the great Hollywood tradition, Spiegel brought in three writers to rework the scenario to his satisfaction. Their contributions served to make the disarray worse. Penn had intended to edit *The Chase* in New York, where he had other commitments. The producer wouldn't hear of it; the raw footage was flown to London, where he could personally supervise the cutting. Hellman washed her hands of the whole business. In her view the script had been "mauled about and slicked up." Slicked up, no doubt. But her contempt for the South, where she was raised, and her sour view of the U.S. justice system ("If

you knew what I know about American prisons, you would be a Stalin-
ist, too") did their own mauling without any outside interference.

By the time Penn journeyed to London, Spiegel had pared *The
Chase* down to his satisfaction. The director was mortified: Almost all
of Brando's most brilliant moments—the best material in the film—had
been left on the cutting-room floor. "It was the performance Marlon
had given," Penn was to recall, "but stripped of all his improvisation.
It was like, 'You want the scene? Here it is, as written. This is the
dialogue.'"

Absurdly plotted, loud, inert, the film opened to bewildered audiences. They dwindled by the day. The critical consensus was uniformly
hostile. *Time* found *The Chase* a "shockworn message film top-heavy
with subtle bigotry, expertly exploiting the violence, intolerance and
mean provincialism that it is supposed to be preaching against."
Pauline Kael, *The New Yorker*'s assertive critic, thought the movie a
portrait of "the mythical America of liberal sadomasochistic fantasies,"
a "hellhole of wife-swapping, nigger-hating and nigger-lover-hating,
where people are motivated by dirty sex or big money, and you can tell
which as soon as they say their first lines." Many people blamed Texas
for the assassination, she pointed out, "as if the murder had boiled up
out of the unconscious of the people there—and the film exploits and
confirms this hysterical view."

The long, complicated interplay of film critic and film actor had just
begun.

5

In the March 1966 issue of *The Atlantic*, Kael cruelly appraised Marlon
Brando in decline. She tagged him as one more superstar who had
become a clown. The standard palaver had it that great comic artists
like Charlie Chaplin and Buster Keaton always wanted to play Hamlet.
But over the past several decades, she wrote, the tide had reversed.
Our Hamlets, like the gin-soaked John Barrymore and the ego-
besotted Marlon Brando, had become "buffoons, shamelessly, patheti-
cally mocking their public reputations."

In his rebellious days, Marlon "was antisocial because he knew society was crap; he was a hero to youth because he was strong enough not to take the crap." And now look: America's most forceful and promising screen actor had turned into a self-deriding caricature.

A century before, Ralph Waldo Emerson had charted the American artist's downhill process. "Thou must pass for a fool and churl for a long season." According to The New Yorker's cinema critic, "We used to think that the season meant only youth," a time before actors could be expected to prove their talents. "Now it is clear that for screen artists, and perhaps not only for screen artists, youth is, relatively speaking, the short season; the long one is the degradation *after* success." In a few years Kael would offer a hysterical overcompensation for this judgment. But she was not wrong in 1966. Marlon did find himself in serious decline, and not all of it was of his doing. By the mid-1960s, Hollywood's vitality made itself known on the little screen, not the big one. On television the very worst of show business was on display every single day.

Five years before, Newton Minow, chairman of the Federal Communications Commission, had shocked the National Association of Broadcasters by condemning American television. Once there had been broadcasts, in *prime* time, of Arturo Toscanini leading the NBC Symphony. There had been CBS's high-minded program Omnibus, the home of James Agee's documentary about Abraham Lincoln, Leonard Bernstein's lively programs introducing the young to classical music, and William Faulkner's guided tour of Oxford, Mississippi. Now viewers were subject to "a procession of game shows, violence, audience-participation shows, formula comedies about totally unbelievable families, blood and thunder, mayhem, violence, sadism, murder, western badmen, western good men, private eyes, gangsters, more violence and cartoons. And, endlessly, commercials—many screaming, cajoling and offending"—the intolerable driving out the worthy. Minow's summary of daily and nightly TV: "a vast wasteland," the term ominously echoing T. S. Eliot's image of modern society—"A heap of broken images, where the sun beats."

That wasteland was to become more arid in the next five years. By that time, Marlon sensed that no amount of mannerly compromising, no act of conciliation, no truckling to the powerful, would get him better scripts or a galvanizing director. TV was in the saddle and rode Hollywood. He and the film business were both in crisis, and neither knew what to do about it.

Marlon, as he always did when troubled, retreated into himself, growing more remote from his children and more critical of his friends. Women still found him attractive, but not many were willing to pay the price of a lengthy relationship—the emotional cost was prohibitive and the demands outrageous. At one dinner party he suddenly interrupted the proceedings by daring everyone to strip to the skin. Some did, some refused. One woman burst into tears. Marlon removed all his garments, plucked a lily from a nearby vase, stuck it in his rectum, and exited. The evening was considered more annoying than offensive; Marlon's social high-wire act had grown tiresome. The only bright spot in his life seemed to be the negotiations for Tetiaroa: Every day brought the two sides closer to an agreement. But everything else could be summarized in an exchange with the Canadian director Sidney Furie, assigned to Marlon's next feature, a Western entitled *The Appaloosa*:

FURIE: I'm really looking forward to this picture. I consider it a real privilege to be working with you. . . .
BRANDO: Bullshit.

Why did he go on the offensive? Marlon couldn't say. He only sensed that something was askew about this feature. It wasn't the externals—he felt easier in the saddle these days, and the film schedule was undemanding. It was the style of the film that seemed wrong, and he had no idea how to fix it. His gaze was turned inward at a time when it should have been looking overseas.

In the 1960s Italian studios shot dramas in the Spanish desert region of Almería, an area reminiscent of the American Southwest. Marked by a crude vitality, they featured snarling, slit-eyed villains and taciturn heroes, minimalist photography, and the stark background music of human whistles and stallions' hoofbeats. Hollywood producers mocked Sergio Leone's unsubtle direction—until the "spaghetti Westerns" caught on with fans. Made for a pittance, the movies demythologized a genre and hauled in millions throughout Europe and the United States. In the process they jolted the careers of Clint Eastwood, Eli Wallach, Lee Van Cleef, and other American actors. During this period Marcello Mastroianni, whose career ran parallel to Marlon's, starred in several flops—*The Poppy Is Also a Flower*, made for American television, for example; and *Spara Forte, Più Forte, Non Capisco* (*Shoot*

Loud, Louder . . . I Don't Understand), costarring Raquel Welch; and *Diamonds for Breakfast,* a misguided British production. Yet he also worked for Visconti in his adaptation of the Camus novel *The Stranger,* and made more movies paired with his vibrant costar Sophia Loren. Marcello loved to work and never put down his director, nor did he shy from roles of hapless men, antiheroes, and failed lovers. He continued to learn and grow while Marlon marked time in his native country, waiting for a miracle to occur. *The Appaloosa* would not fill the bill.

In contrast to the Italian product, Furie's Western was marred by fussy, elaborate camerawork and ostentatious direction. The director's previous pictures *The Leather Boys* and *The Ipcress File* reflected the syncopations of the 1960s; swinging London had earned him a reputation for a glossy with-it style. He was the wrong man to direct a Mexican border drama about an unwashed saddle tramp, Matt Fletcher (Brando), and a surly *bandito,* Chuy Medina (John Saxon), as they fight over a woman (Anjanette Comer) and the steed of the title. Unsurprisingly, Marlon attempted to undermine Furie at every turn. Furie responded with a withering appraisal. The key to Brando, he told studio personnel, is that he "loves chaos. You simply can't get past 'B' in a conversation with him and you can't get him to discuss a script rationally. He's disorganized, no discipline at all." What griped Furie most of all was Marlon's social conscience.

The actor would sit still for hackneyed dialogue. At the same time he refused to act in any scene that, in his view, denigrated Native Americans. On Marlon's orders, twenty-five pages of Indian fights were bluepenciled, every one of them crucial to the action. What remained were a series of stand-alone confrontations with Medina. These included a hand-wrestling scene complete with scorpion waiting to bite the loser, and the now-unavoidable moment of sadomasochism, this one featuring the hero roped and dragged over rough ground and through a stream before rising to exact his bloody revenge.

Earlier Kael had decried the "open season on Brando." Now she was an integral part of it. Her review of *The Appaloosa* found him "trapped inside of still another dog of a movie. . . . Not for the first time, Mr. Brando gives us a heavy-lidded, adenoidally openmouthed caricature of the inarticulate, stalwart loner." Her fellow reviewers piled on; Marlon was variously "somnambulistic," "pretentious," and "vaporous." *The Washington Post* sent up a distress signal: "Brando's self-indulgence over a dozen years is costing him and his public his talents." Marlon acknowledged as much, adding another three years to the count: "The last fifteen years of my life seem never to have happened; they've just gone up the chimney without any impression or impact on me at all."

Two men thought they knew what had happened to Marlon, and how to rescue him. In *Cosmopolitan,* film critic Hollis Alpert beseeched the star to return to Broadway for renewal. William Redfield went Alpert one better. The actor had been cast as Guildenstern in the celebrated 1964 production of *Hamlet* at the Lunt-Fontanne Theatre, with Richard Burton in the title role. He had also appeared in seven movies, one with Marlon. But for all that, Redfield worshipped the legitimate stage, dismissing film as trivial and destructive to the soul. In the book *Letters from an Actor,* published in 1967, he wrote ruefully of his colleague, remembering what had been and was no more:

"We who saw him in his first, shocking days believe in him not only as an actor, but also as an artistic, spiritual, and specifically American leader." Technically, Laurence Olivier "drew rings around him, but Brando's heartbeat was stronger. As Richard Burton has said of Brando, 'He surprises me. He's the only one who does.' That he should say it of his film work leaves me dismayed, but on stage it was certainly true." Jacob Adler, Stella's father, used to dismiss a certain kind of Yiddish-theater ham: "He used to be an actor, but now he's only a star." By Redfield's reckoning, that was exactly what had happened to America's most promising leading man. Brando, he predicted, would not reclaim his stature until he went back on the boards.

That event was about as likely as Marlon's taking up ballroom dancing. He was never much for looking in the rearview mirror. "If I've sold out, so be it," he sighed to a friend. "In for a penny, in for a million." That sum was a bit off; nonetheless his next assignment paid decently, and put him under the baton of the most famous name in cinema. At the age of seventy-seven the director was well past his prime and known to be imperious and crotchety. Marlon signed without misgivings; who could refuse Charlie Chaplin?

Charlie had written *A Countess from Hong Kong* in 1938 for his then-wife, Paulette Goddard. It was never made. The scenario had not aged well, nor had its personae. Still, *A Countess from Hong Kong* had a lot going for it besides Brando and Chaplin. Sophia Loren was the costar, abetted by Tippi Hedren, breaking away from the kind of glacial blonde roles Alfred Hitchcock had given her in *The Birds* and *Marnie;* and by Margaret Rutherford, one of Britain's greatest comic actresses. It was up to them to enliven an elemental plot.

Since the Revolution, a beautiful White Russian princess has been supporting herself in Hong Kong as a taxi dancer (i.e., prostitute). Frantic to begin a new life, she sneaks aboard an ocean liner and into the stateroom of a married American senator, hoping to enlist him in her cause. The senator righteously objects to the stowaway's presence, and then, by degrees, succumbs to her wiles.

The world had revolved many times since the late 1930s; Depression, World War, the New Deal, the Fair Deal, the Korean conflict, the War on Poverty, the civil rights movement—all had passed or were passing in review, and everyone had been changed by the cascade of events. Everyone except Charlie. He still clung to the idea of a comedy of manners, with static camera work and big stars making grand entrances. No one dared to tell him that a generation later his gossamer had turned to cobwebs. Hedren watched her part, as the ambassador's wife, shrink to microscopic proportions. She honored her contract nonetheless. Marlon knew that the plight of White Russians had become as obsolete as two-reelers. But he, too, put his concerns aside, convinced that Chaplin was the greatest genius in the history of motion pictures.

In the beginning he was amused to work alongside Sophia Loren, who had risen from Neapolitan sex goddess to Academy Award–winning actress in the stark wartime drama *Two Women.* A few weeks into the London-based production Marlon realized that he had made a disastrous misstep. The industry publications were full of stories about new talents and fresh approaches. Not a word about Charlie's latest activity. To the editors, Chaplin was old news, and his actors archaic by association. As the director/scenarist/composer imposed his will on an uncomfortable cast, Mike Nichols was busy directing *The Graduate,* Arthur Penn *Bonnie and Clyde,* Luis Buñuel *Belle de Jour,* and Jean-Luc Godard *Weekend,* features that would attract young audiences and shake the foundations of Hollywood, just as Brando's early films had in their day. The action had gone elsewhere, leaving Charlie and his cast in the dust.

Suddenly aware of what had happened, Marlon became irritable and unruly. In a close-up he asked Loren in a whisper if she knew there were black hairs growing out of her nose. She never forgave him for that, or for pawing her. Their lack of chemistry was apparent in every exchange. Charlie was to recall, "I had to keep reminding them it was a love story. The antipathy between the two stars was evident on the screen when each clasped the other as if embracing a werewolf." Chaplin had always preferred small movements and sharp exchanges of dialogue; Marlon's trademark gestures and hesitations drove him wild. Urged on by Loren, he confronted the star before a group of technicians and actors. "If you think you're slumming, take the next plane back to Hollywood. We don't need you." Marlon responded tersely: "Mr. Chaplin, I'll be in my dressing room for twenty minutes. If you give me an apology within that time, I will consider not getting on a plane and returning to the United States. But I'll be there only twenty minutes."

Chaplin knocked on Marlon's door a few moments later, expressing the requisite remorse. Reconciliation followed, and there were no further incidents. Nor were there any high moments. Chaplin, convinced that order had been restored, continued to direct with close-minded authority, giving the cast line readings and showing the exact body movements he wanted. Nothing had changed since the palmy days of the 1920s, when an actor inquired: "How shall I play this, sir?" and Charlie replied, "Behind me and to the left." Miserable with each other, disappointed in their director, Loren and Brando mugged and posed. The remainder of the cast, including Chaplin's son Sydney, simply carried out orders and hoped for a miracle. It never came. The picture was dead on arrival and treated that way by the press. This was Chaplin's last film, and one that did him no credit. Indeed, scenarist/historian William Goldman made the movie into a curse. Berating followers of the auteur theory in *Adventures in the Screen Trade,* he fumed, "I wish them all a very long life on a desert island with nothing but [A] *Countess from Hong Kong* for company."

6

As the 1960s barreled on, journalists assigned more space to Marlon's image than to his acting. The Beatles used his biker image on the cover of their new album *Sgt. Pepper's Lonely Hearts Club Band.* Newspapers ran photographs of the overweight star with numerous dates,

ranging in age from the late teens to the early forties, and the tabloid
News of the World headed an awed article, BRANDO: AS A LOVER HE
SEEMS TO BE WITHOUT EQUAL IN CONTEMPORARY FILM HISTORY.
Some of the women, stories noted, had remained friends; others
wanted nothing to do with him. To Marlon, none were of significance.
Then again, neither were the films he had made in this decade. Long
before, the Adlers had taught him the Yiddish word for trash: *shund*.
That was the label he gave to his 1960s efforts. Every so often there
was noise about giving it all up and retreating to the South Seas. No
one believed it this time—including Marlon. Well aware that he had
been marked as a dilettante for his on-again off-again interest in social
justice, and troubled by the abysmal state of his career, he abruptly
took off for India with an eight-millimeter camera in hand. An almost
medieval famine had struck the northeastern state of Bihar. Thousands
of untouchables were dying, and Marlon intended to make a documentary that would move the hearts of the Western world. "The Bihari children I filmed," he wrote, "were emaciated and covered with lesions
and scabs. In many villages cows had chewed the thatch off the roofs
because they had nothing to eat, and people were so thin it seemed
incredible that they could walk. If you touched the cheek of a child, a
hollow spot remained in her flesh after you removed your hand; the
skin had no resiliency and was like that of a cadaver." On his last day of
filming, a little girl died as he watched helplessly. Marlon broke down
and cried. He rushed home, rushed to get the film developed and
edited, then took it to UNICEF personnel in Los Angeles. According
to historians William Russo and Jan Merlin, the UN people viewed
Marlon's work "and grumbled that the star's film resembled discon-
nected tourist views and couldn't be integrated into any documentary
because his film stock and compositions were so amateurish."

Undiscouraged, Marlon then took the footage to Jack Valenti, aide
to Lyndon Johnson. Valenti assured him that the President would view
the film. If he did, nothing came of it. Marlon shopped his work around
Hollywood. Everyone was deeply moved; no one offered to lift a finger
on behalf of the Biharis. Television networks were next; the reels were
screened for a CBS programmer.

"It's an effective film," said the executive, "but we can't use it."

"Why not?" Marlon demanded.

"Because our news department produces all its own stuff; we don't
requisition or use outside documentaries."

"Why not? I was there. What I'm showing you is the truth."

"Well, we have policies we have to follow, and we can't make exceptions."

From NBC came an identical response. Marlon thought he knew the reason why. "In the United States," he resentfully concluded, "we've always had our own untouchables—American Indians, blacks, homosexuals. Who knows who will be next?"

A week after the turndown, an unexpected phone call from Ireland: Marlon had spoken up for blacks and Indians, and John Huston was about to give him an opportunity to represent the third category of the oppressed. The director was holed up at his Hibernian estate, pondering an adaptation of Carson McCullers's southern-gothic novella *Reflections in a Golden Eye*. One of the main roles had been cast for over two years. Elizabeth Taylor couldn't wait to play the spectacularly neurotic female lead, Leonora Penderton. As for the role of her husband, suppressed homosexual Major Weldon Penderton, Huston had a list of candidates: Marlon Brando, Rod Steiger, Richard Burton, Robert Mitchum, Lee Marvin. They had all refused, and that was just fine with Taylor. Who was more fitting for the role than her closest male friend, Montgomery Clift? Besides, Monty needed a comeback; he had been absent from the screen since Huston's biographical film *Freud* in 1962. For the actor had never really recovered from his fateful automobile accident, and since then had slid backward into drug and alcohol abuse. The victim of mood swings, circulatory ailments, and botched plastic surgery, he rarely left his Manhattan town house and avoided all but a few close associates. The lawyers at Warner Bros. knew about Clift's precarious health; they deemed him too risky to employ. Taylor overrode their objections by writing a personal check for an insurance bond. Her generosity and loyalty were admirable but insufficient. Before negotiations could get under way, Clift suddenly died of a heart attack on July 23, 1966. He was forty-five. Biographer Patricia Bosworth sorrowfully records that the mirror told him what kind friends would not. At the time of Monty's death, "he looked like an old man."

The tragedy spurred Huston on. He was in need of a comeback after the failure of *The Bible*, his gaudy and tasteless adaptation of the Old Testament, and, starting at the top of his list, he asked Marlon to have a face-to-face chat about the film—just talk, no strings, no commitment. The director would pick up the tab for the round-trip airplane ticket, as well as all other living expenses. Marlon accepted. Huston's son Tony interpreted this as a yes; what actor would make a five-thousand-mile journey just to refuse a role? His father knew better. Marlon was notorious for quixotic gestures that ended in nothing. The documentary about the untouchables, for instance.

Few men could be as charming as Huston when he wanted something, and he wanted Marlon. The sixty-two-year-old director put on a mask of paternal benevolence. He appealed to the listener as script adviser, intellectual, fellow artist. Marlon matched the confidence man trick for trick. He made a big show of mulling over Huston's proposal, taking a long walk in some faraway fields before making his decision. It was particularly rainy that night, even for Ireland. After an hour Tony and his sister, Angelica, drove out looking for him. "We found him two miles away," Tony reported. "He knew exactly where he was and he wouldn't get in the car. He was having a wonderful time." An hour later, having squeezed the last drop of suspense from the situation, Marlon returned, dried off by the heat of a glowing hearth, and announced, "Yes. I want to do it."

Filming began at a military installation on Long Island. Huston kept most of the press at bay, but a *New York Times* reporter managed to get to Marlon, and found, to his surprise, that the actor was open to questions. Asked why he had chosen to play the role of Major Penderton, he cracked, "Seven hundred and fifty thousand dollars plus seven and a half percent of the gross receipts if we break even." The smile vanished as he added, "Then, the attraction of a book by Carson McCullers. As for the part itself, it's hard for me to be articulate about acting. What can you say about a certain moment or expression? It's like Chaplin chewing a rose and looking . . . there at the end of *City Lights* . . . or that final cry by Olivier in *Oedipus Rex*." The reporter looked for a trace of irony. There was none. In that last sentence, Marlon had let down his guard. Whatever problems he had experienced with Charlie Chaplin, he still held him in awe as a performer, as he did Sir Laurence. There would be no put-ons this time out; *Reflections in a Golden Eye* had Brando's full attention.

Two weeks later he and the rest of the company, including Julie Harris, Brian Keith, and newcomers Robert Forster and Zorro David, were in Italy. The bulk of filming took place at the De Laurentiis studios in Rome. *Reflections* was an American story, but Taylor had insisted on filming overseas for tax reasons, and no one argued with

Liz, the number one box-office draw of her time. However, those who expected her to be self-indulgent in other ways had a surprise coming. Taylor had been in films since the age of ten; this was her thirty-seventh feature, and two of those had won her Academy Awards for Best Actress. Flamboyant romantic adventures notwithstanding, she was a consummate professional. "Elizabeth comes to the set beautifully prepared," Huston remarked in an awed tone. "If she does a scene six times, there'll be six renditions that are almost exactly alike. That sort of attention and concentration deserves some attention itself." Brando's technique was the polar opposite of Taylor's. Directing an early scene, Huston noted, "I could have said, 'That's it,' as I often do; but knowing Marlon and the way he works, I said, 'Let's do it again.' We did it three times, and each time was different; any of them could have been used. I've never seen any other actor do that."

Fireworks should have resulted when these costars faced each other, but that's not what happened. Early on Taylor did get annoyed with Marlon's slurred southern accent. She referred to him openly as "Mr. Mumbles." When that didn't work she summoned him to her dressing room and, before a startled Richard Burton, stated, "Young man, just remember you are only a replacement for Montgomery Clift." The criticism stung, but Marlon knew it was the truth. He *was* a second choice for Major Penderton. Thereafter, he not only behaved himself on the set, but spoke with greater clarity and started to create a pathetic and deeply conflicted character. Aware of Marlon's womanizing, which far exceeded his own, Burton initially distrusted his wife's costar. As he watched the film grow before his eyes, he changed his mind. "Marlon's immorality," Burton wrote in his diary, "his attitude to it, is honest and clean. He is a genuinely good man I suspect and he is intelligent. He has depth. It's no accident that he is such a compelling actor. He puts on acts of course and pretends to be vaguer than he is. Very little misses him as I've noticed."

As the weeks wore on, Huston found that the actors were the least of his difficulties. He had a grand notion of giving the film an odd, unsaturated look until all that the viewer's eye saw was black, white, and an almost golden-yellow tone. Warner Bros. production chiefs were nervous enough about the project without this additional frippery. They would never have agreed to make the picture except for Huston's powers of persuasion—plus the credentials of three Oscar-nominated players (Taylor, Brando, and Harris). Even then, a company official kept saying that the plot gave him the willies and it would give audiences the willies, too; no wonder Tennessee Williams was such a McCullers fan.

The executive could hardly be blamed for his fears. Very few readers were comfortable with the novel. On its first page, it reads, "There is a fort in the South where a few years ago a murder was committed. The participants in this tragedy were two officers, a soldier, two women, a Filipino, and a horse." McCullers proceeded to elucidate, and, in the film adaptation, so did Huston. Major Penderton is a heavily closeted gay man married to Leonora, a nymphomaniacal horsewoman. She is carrying on with the major's superior officer, Lieutenant Colonel Morris Langdon.

And this is merely the first layer of complications. Langdon's wife, Alison (Harris), lost a baby some time back, and in a horrific act of self-abnegation cut off her nipples with a garden shears. Alison's down time is spent with Anacleto, an effeminate Filipino houseboy (David). Amid all this, Penderton suppresses his true desire—for a handsome G.I., Private L. G. Williams (Forster). Unaware, the soldier nourishes a secret lust for Leonora, standing for hours outside the Penderton house at night, and, on occasion, sneaking in to fondle her underwear. Violence, always hovering over these six, breaks out in a series of incidents, some ludicrously symbolic, others poignant, until the deadly finale, when the major discovers the unbearable truth about Williams's desires—and his own.

In addition to experimenting with color, Huston built the film out of set pieces: elliptical, threatening conversations; Leonora's fascination with whips; her mastery of a sexually powerful white stallion—the very horse that so intimidates her husband; an automobile crash in which all eyes turn toward the noise—save for the major's, which never swerve from the face of Private Williams.

None of this could hide a central fact: The two leads were miscast. Taylor was far too glamorous and canny to be the airheaded strumpet she was impersonating, and Brando had too much power and guile to play so clueless a figure. Strangely enough, their flawed interpretations gave the film its peculiar strength. Elizabeth worked diligently to make her Leonora credibly repugnant; Marlon became absorbed with his character's hidden apprehensions and rages, and vanished into the role. His work was subtle, layered, and completely honest, his best effort since the late 1950s. Weldon's primping before a mirror, for example, applying cold cream to his anxious face in anticipation of a visit from the beloved—while that very figure is headed for the lady in the adjoining bedroom—are moments no other actor would have dared go for in 1967. To Julie Harris, "It was almost as if he was exploring his own sexuality, yet his work was so beautiful and pure there was no telling where it came from."

She was profoundly right about his performance. Everyone at Warner Bros. agreed that *Reflections* did indeed have a ton of star power. But no one at the studio knew how to sell the film. Given its edgy subject matter, the promotion department opted to go downmarket with titillating posters: "Most women in her situation would do the very same thing! They just wouldn't do it as well—or as often!"; "In the loosest sense he is her husband . . . and in the loosest way she is his wife!"

Nothing worked. Critics were generally dismissive. *Time* had little use for its "gallery of grotesques." *Newsweek* said the movie was "devoid of style and grace." If Huston expected recognition from the cineastes at *Film Quarterly,* he was to be bitterly disappointed. The periodical dismissed the "McCullers brand of Southern decadence," because it "lacked the Mr. Showmanship flamboyance of Tennessee Williams." As for the "tepid Major-loves-Private plot," it might "just as easily have happened at Fort Ord, California." On the *Today* show, the most popular morning TV program in America, millions of viewers watched Judith Crist's annihilation: *Reflections* "has one possible virtue: it will send you right back to the book because one can't imagine that the perceptive novel had nothing more to offer than nutty people and pseudo pornography. . . . An embarrassment for all concerned." Pauline Kael reversed engines here; at a meeting of the New York Film Critics she nominated Brando for Best Actor. The praise came too late. Panicked, Warner Bros. had reissued *Reflections* in standard Technicolor one week after the regular opening. That further weakened the film's distinction, and it faded away.

In a sense, Marlon was vindicated. He had stated for the record that acting was "a bum's life in that it leads to perfect self-indulgence. You get paid for doing nothing, and it all adds up to nothing." And here was the proof. He had allowed some long-hidden part of himself to be on exhibit. He had been a pro, studied his lines, given no one any trouble. In every difficult scene he had revealed the vulnerability and confusion beneath his rough pose. And what did it get him? Hoots, snickers, oblivion. Well, let the critics and crowds have their way. If they thought

Reflections was kinky, if they believed Brando had touched bottom in his latest film, they had no idea how appalling *shund* could be. He was about to show them.

After the fish-ins, few doubted his devotion to the cause of the American Indian. The African American movement was something else entirely. A new group was getting started in Oakland just then: the Black Panthers, founded by Huey P. Newton and Bobby Seale, calling for militant resistance to racism. Heavily influenced by the post-colonial philosopher Frantz Fanon, Newton held that ordinary blacks—"the brothers off the block," as he put it—were as important to the Panthers as the lumpen proletariat was to Marx.

"If you didn't relate to these cats, the power structure would organize those cats against you." Given this concern with ghetto dwellers, the organization had no time or room for white people, none of whom were deemed trustworthy anyway. This served to make the Panthers more attractive to Marlon; he found something impractical, outrageous, and romantic in their angry declarations, and resolved to learn more. For now, though, he knew an outsider hadn't a prayer of entering their meetings, let alone their ranks.

1967–1970

Eleven Turkeys in a Row

1

The upheavals of the 1960s were old news to Marlon. He watched, amused, as an emerging generation rejected the old moralities and proclaimed itself the vanguard of a sexual revolution. Big deal; he had been a sexual revolutionary since his earliest days in New York. The rise of the New Left also failed to move him; he had been agitating for minority rights before these youths were out of their playpens.

In other ways, though, Marlon saw that he was being outdistanced and made irrelevant. The Vietnam War, begun quietly in 1964, had fatally enlarged. Eighteen-year-olds were being drafted, and the slogan "If you're old enough to die for your country, you're old enough to vote" empowered youth in a new way, and drove their parents to argue against America's role in Southeast Asia. Chanting "Hey, hey, LBJ, how many kids did you kill today?" antiwar protesters drowned out President Lyndon Johnson's claims that his projects—the Great Society and the civil rights acts—changed the country for the better. Different terms entered the language: the Establishment—an umbrella term meaning anyone in authority; Fascist pigs, a synonym for the police; "tune in, turn on, drop out," advertising the benefits of illegal hallucinogens. None of this was in Marlon's lexicon. He felt marginalized, fortysomething at a time when bumper stickers read DON'T TRUST ANYONE OVER 30.

There were two ways around this. One was to do films that addressed the main currents of American thought. The other was to get personally involved in the new politics—those of the Panthers, for instance. He made a list of priorities and took them in order. The career came first; no point in dropping out like some druggie in Haight-Ashbury, or yelling slogans in a crowd of nobodies. Besides, he convinced himself, the money and celebrity could work wonders for the causes that needed help. That needed *him*.

Problems attended this decision. For Hollywood was undergoing its own collisions of reality and fantasy just then, and these reflected the ones in the outside world. Paramount had been acquired by Gulf + Western. In 1976's *Silent Movie*, Mel Brooks would caricature that company as Engulf + Devour, and it was not much of a stretch. Charles Bluhdorn, the driving force behind G+W, was an acquisitive type-A executive, a shark who could never rest. His company had seven divisions: manufacturing (automobile and airplane parts); distribution (warehouses and outlets); metals (zinc mines); agricultural (vegetable and citrus fruit processing); consumer products (Dutch Masters and Muriel cigars); forest and paper products (towels, paper plates); insurance, financing services, and banking (Associates Investment Company, Capital Life). By obtaining Paramount Bluhdorn could create a new division, Leisure Time. As Bernard F. Dick demonstrates in *Engulfed*, a study of corporate Hollywood, Bluhdorn was both fan and manipulator: "He delighted in visiting a set and posing with a star. Then there was the special kind of power that comes from owning a studio: the power over those who create mass entertainment but lack the autonomy that all filmmakers crave yet rarely achieve. Thus, Bluhdorn could run Paramount on the creative energy of others." Paraphrasing Lord Acton's aphorism that power corrupts and "absolute power corrupts absolutely," critic Kenneth Tynan stated that "power is delightful, and absolute power is absolutely delightful." So the leaders of conglomerates thought and acted. Taking the example of Gulf + Western, Kinney Services, based around parking lots, grabbed Warner Bros. United Artists merged with the Transamerica Corporation. Traditions washed away in a flood of MBAs and bottom-line accountants.

The new corporate heads wanted to change the way films were made and sold, and they wanted to entice youth back to the film palaces. Yet these men and women were raised on the movies of Goldwyn and Warner and Zanuck and Zukor, and they were still in love with the images of the past. Should their movies comment on the moral chaos of contemporary America? Or should they look backward to the glory days of pure entertainment?

By 1968, a number of features had begun to reflect this dilemma. Two hits directly echoed the current social unrest and seemed poised to invigorate the industry with a new comic force (*The Graduate; The*

Producers). Two others were moral fables cloaked as science fiction (*2001: A Space Odyssey; Planet of the Apes*). A fifth looked at American violence without condemning its strangely attractive characters (*Bonnie and Clyde*). At the same time, though, the retro musical genre showed its age (*Chitty Chitty Bang Bang; Funny Girl*). And sweaty, achingly unfunny comedies (*Don't Raise the Bridge, Lower the River; Candy*) gave the lie to the tag line in many full-page ads and billboards: "Movies Are Better Than Ever." Judging by the last film, they were worse. Much worse.

Of all the trash to unreel that year, no film was more appalling than *Candy*. Directed by Marlon's old *copain* Christian Marquand, it was based on a ten-year-old chichi sendup of *Candide* by the nose-thumbing novelists Mason Hoffenberg and Terry Southern. This time out, the protagonist was female, exploited by a parade of sexual predators without ever losing her innocence. Filmmakers had stayed away from the novel because of its tittering faux-pornographic style. But in the anything-goes 1960s ABC-TV backed a screen adaptation, assuming that it would attract a young audience. To further assure the picture's success, it was loaded with celebrities, including the Beatle Ringo Starr, Richard Burton, John Huston, Charles Aznavour, and Marlon Brando, much as *Casino Royale* had boasted the star power of Peter Sellers, David Niven, and Woody Allen.

Apparently no one in charge noticed that the James Bond spoof, released only one year before, had been a major bomb. So was *Candy*. Most American critics found Buck Henry's adaptation smug and wit-free. The movie, observed the *Times*'s bright new reviewer Renata Adler, managed "to compromise, by its relentless, crawling, bloody lack of talent, almost anyone who had anything to do with it." After eviscerating Richard Burton for a "lack of any comic talent whatsoever," John Huston and Ringo Starr for being "humorless," and Charles Aznavour for performing "uncrisply and badly," Adler relented when she came to Brando. As "a Jewish guru (the film has an ugly racialism and arrested development, frog-torturing soft sadism at its heart)," he was "less unendurable because one is glad to see him on the screen, in anything, again."

Marlon knew the picture would be a turkey before he ever uttered a line. He had taken the job because of his friendship with Marquand, and because a few days' effort would bring him a salary of $50,000. He needed every cent. Negotiations for Tetiaroa had been concluded in his favor, at a purchase price of $70,000. That was a onetime cost; more expensive were the bills coming in from Anna and Movita. The second Mrs. Brando had filed for divorce, demanding child custody as well as costs for upkeep of home and wardrobe. During the filming of *Candy,* Marlon asked fellow actor James Coburn if he had any children. Coburn, also a divorcé, said that he had two kids but that he didn't get to spend much time with them. "I don't either," lamented Marlon, "and I don't know how they're going to grow up."

Only Marlon's ability to compartmentalize kept him afloat. In her elegant memoir *Off the King's Road,* Phyllis Raphael, then the wife of a film producer, writes of an evening she and her husband spent with Marlon and Rita Hayworth. The time is 1968, the place a fashionable Westwood restaurant. No longer a sex symbol, the actress is ill and weary; only a few hints of the old glamour can be discerned. Yet that night the star pays court to her even as he slyly romances Raphael. "Marlon Brando in a brown velvet jacket with a black broadtail collar has his arm draped around Rita Hayworth's shoulders, but his knuckles—light as a firefly's wings—are tracing the upper flank of my left arm." No one else at the table can see Marlon's hand, but, she goes on, "his touch is heating up my skin like a sun reflector in the California desert." And all the while he delivers a paean to Hayworth, what a sensitive actress she was, how her Stanislavski technique helped to mold his work. Hayworth leans back, "suddenly younger, even glowing. He'd moved her into the spotlight." All the while, Marlon has other plans in mind. As the dinner concludes, he speaks to the younger woman: " 'Phyllis,' he said in his soft, buttery whine, 'I live on Mulholland. Up at the top, honey. You can't miss it. Why don't you come over later? I'm always up late.' " The invitation is not accepted, but she finds herself secretly covering the spot where she had been caressed, as if she could "save what was left of him from blowing away."

Manifestly the seducer had not lost a step. Professionally, however, *Candy* had put him in the subbasement of his career. If Marlon didn't care to count, others did. It was all over town that Brando had made eleven consecutive commercial flops. Paradoxically, the only way he could break the string was to make a twelfth. It was a modish thriller in the French Nouvelle Vague style, entitled *The Night of the Following Day.* By agreeing to star in the film, he would discharge his final obligation to Universal.

The director was Hubert Cornfield, whose previous credits included such bottom-of-the-bill pictures as *Plunder Road* and *Lure of the Swamp*. Marlon of course distrusted the man on sight. To further roil the proceedings, he maligned the script as "arty and nonsensical." He had a point. In rural France four schemers grab an adolescent heiress and hold her for ransom. The quartet includes Marlon, at his thinnest in ten years; onetime girlfriend Rita Moreno; Richard Boone, best known for his TV series *Have Gun—Will Travel;* and Jess Hahn, a veteran heavy.

To compensate for a profound lack of plot and character development *Night* leaned on visual style. This it had in overplus: bleached-out interiors, an abandoned beach at sunrise, harrowing music, odd outfits. Perhaps the oddest were the blond wig worn by Moreno in her role as a scheming airline stewardess and by Marlon in his role as a devious chauffeur. Missing were credibility and narrative drive. Everything was ominous; nothing made sense. The last scene was a duplicate of the first—the heiress looks at the solicitous flight attendant. Had the kidnapping taken place in her imagination? Or is she foreseeing the horror to come? Marlon let it be known that *Night* made about "as much sense as a rat fucking a grapefruit." His hostility carried over to the set. From the first day, some actors said they could feel a palpable tension between Marlon and his old girlfriend. Perhaps as a protective barrier Moreno had brought along her husband, a New York–based cardiologist, and their infant son. In the view of the more cynical and observant actors, however, that barrier had been painfully breached. To them, evidence of Marlon and Rita's old attraction and revulsion was clearcut, particularly during a pivotal scene. The chauffeur was to accuse the stewardess of drug abuse. Her denial would trigger a brief physical skirmish. In rehearsals Rita feigned a smack across Marlon's cheek. But when Cornfield shouted, "Action!" her private resentments suddenly went public. She slapped her costar hard across the face. Astonished, Marlon retaliated by striking her with furious and inappropriate force. She burst into tears, the two tussled furiously, and the cameras recorded it all. "You're through, you dumb bitch! You've had it!" Marlon shouted at the end of the scene, and it was not stated in character. This exchange made the final cut. The director tried to restore calm, but he was too inexperienced to assert any meaningful authority. In the final days, at Marlon's insistence, the second lead took the director's chair. Richard Boone restored order, commanding the cast with a severity Cornfield had never displayed. It was not enough. The star's mental afflictions were never more apparent. Once again he seemed to hold two conflicting ideas in his head: a) his colleagues must not be injured by his behavior—it was incumbent on him to make *Night,* with all its shortcomings, the best it could possibly be; b) all authority figures, even a good guy like Boone, must be defied and betrayed. After two days of unsatisfactory takes, Boone accused him of "phoning in" his lines. Marlon responded by inventing new speeches and making faces as the cameras rolled.

The end result was irreparable. As soon as the film wrapped the cast scattered, anxious to get as far away as possible. They had wasted their time and effort on yet another Brando movie gone awry. It didn't matter whose fault it was; none of them would willingly work with him again. Universal pieced the mess together and released it quietly. One friendly review appeared in *Time,* no doubt triggered by that scene of unrehearsed malignity (Brando's "powers remain undiminished by intervening years of sloppiness and self-indulgence. It is good to have him back"). The rest of the assays were appropriately withering. The *Los Angeles Examiner* said the dialogue was so incoherent it must have been improvised on the spot. In *The New Yorker,* Pauline Kael stated that Marlon "had never been worse or less interesting, not even in *A Countess from Hong Kong.*" And in the Chicago *Sun-Times,* Roger Ebert inquired, "Should Brando really be wasting his time on this sort of movie?" No one knew the answer better than Marlon himself.

2

In the May 1968 issue of *Jet* magazine, Louie Robinson headed his article WHY MARLON BRANDO QUIT FILM FOR CIVIL RIGHTS. With the knowing tone of an insider, Robinson told his readers that the actor's decision had been made immediately after the assassination of Dr. Martin Luther King, Jr., on April 4, as the civil rights leader stood on the balcony of the Lorraine Motel in Memphis. The murder triggered riots in more than a hundred cities across the nation, and five days later President Lyndon Johnson declared a day of mourning. Flags flew at half mast as a crowd of three hundred thousand paid their last respects. At the funeral, King's haunting sermon was broadcast. In it he forecast his own death and asked that no mention of his awards and honors be made. All that needed to be recollected were his attempts to "feed the hungry . . . clothe the naked . . . be right on the [Vietnam] war question," and "love and serve humanity." The soul singer Mahalia Jackson sang his favorite hymn, "Take My Hand, Precious Lord," as a nation wept.

During this period, wrote Robinson, Marlon "made one of the strongest commitments to furthering Dr. King's work. White, wealthy and still a major star, the forty-four-year-old Brando would seem to have the most to lose and the least to gain. Yet, shortly after Dr. King's death, Brando announced that he was bowing out of the lead role of a major film [*The Arrangement*] which was about to begin production, in order to devote himself to the civil rights movement."

It was true that in the wake of national grief Marlon did appear on ABC-TV's *Joey Bishop Show*, where he reflected, "If the vacuum formed by Dr. King's death isn't filled with concern and understanding and a measure of love, then I think we're all really going to be lost here in this country." And he did bow out of a starring role in *The Arrangement*, which would have reunited him with Elia Kazan, whose novel the movie was based on, and who was directing. But rhetoric aside, he had no intention of quitting filmmaking. He thought to carry on Dr. King's legacy through the use of movies. Robinson did not know this, nor would he have understood it. Nor would Kazan. Nor, for that matter, would Marlon, who was making the whole thing up as he went along, infuriating everyone in the process.

One of the angriest was Gadge. With his novel, Kazan had proved Oscar Wilde's observation "Man is least himself when he talks in his own person. Give him a mask, and he will tell you the truth." The narrator is Eddie Anderson (read Elia Kazan), a charming, wealthy, corrupt, and ultimately destructive figure. The adman's life has been a series of disloyalties and duplicities en route to the top. His unhappiest victim is Eddie himself—the poor but promising writer who sold out to Mammon and now looks back on a spilled life. Written with gusto and promoted tirelessly, *The Arrangement* rose to the top of the bestseller lists and stayed there for nine months. "Who better to direct the film adaptation than me?" Gadge asked rhetorically. "And who better to play me than Marlon?" Aware of Brando's flops and compromises, he elaborated on his choice: All Marlon had to do was to "come and be photographed. Talk about typecasting!" To that end, the director wrote a glowing and, he thought, persuasive letter to the actor, entreating him to lose weight and regain the old fire in the belly: "If you really want to, you can be a blazing actor again. The wanting is the hard part." Marlon evinced some interest. Heartened, Gadge scheduled story meetings and even set up an appointment with a wig maker. He wanted Brando to look more like the Anderson of the book, and Marlon went along. It was all a feint. Biographer Richard Schickel points out that "in the end Brando betrayed Kazan." If Marlon had ever been tempted by the notion of working with Gadge again, *The Arrangement* was certainly not what he had in mind.

On the afternoon of April 4, 1968, the actor called the director and asked him to drive over to the house on Mulholland. Kazan could hardly be blamed for assuming that this was to be a creative meeting, a discussion of how the role of Eddie Anderson might be interpreted. He never got to the front door. Marlon met his car in the driveway and, as Gadge got out, began an intense monologue. Dr. King had been murdered, gunned down on the balcony of a Memphis hotel. How could anyone think about filmmaking at a time like this? Marlon went on at length and in detail: The conditions of race and economics could not continue, America must change or die. The rhetoric so hypnotized Kazan that he scarcely noticed he was being led back behind the wheel. Before he could turn the ignition key, Gadge was informed that Marlon wouldn't—indeed, couldn't—be in *The Arrangement*. The director slowly drove away. As he did, he watched Marlon in the rearview mirror. Slump-shouldered, the actor entered his house without looking back. The two men never spoke again.

Marlon didn't mention that he had also turned down a lead part in *Butch Cassidy and the Sundance Kid*. He was through with trivia, he told his agent. The only film he wanted to do was *Queimada*. Since the release of *The Battle of Algiers* two years before, he had been intrigued with the idea of working with Gillo Pontecorvo. The director had shown the world his radical sympathies and had come away with awards and legions of new admirers. *Algiers* had the persuasive, hand-held-camera feel of a documentary. Never, not even in newsreels, had there been a better and more honest portrait of the ruthless Arab agitators and the vindictive occupying army of France. It was no wonder that *Time* had described this work as "a blueprint for revolution." Feelers were sent out and Pontecorvo and Brando met. "Our ideas were in the same political sphere," the director announced afterward. "While I am an independent Italian left-wing thinker, he is an independent left-wing American thinker. We both liked the idea of an ideological adventure film. He was concerned with the idea of film as medium serving a political purpose."

Set in the mid-nineteenth century, the script followed the doomed relationship of two men, a black revolutionary, José Dolores, and Sir William Walker, a high-toned, amoral British mercenary ("I don't know what I believe or what I should do, but whatever I do, I will do it well"). Walker's government sends him to a Caribbean island controlled by Portugal, a waning colonial power. Long before, the Portuguese had slaughtered the native Indian population, taken full control of the sugar plantations, and imported African slaves to work them. Sir William embodies Hamlet's observation that "one may smile, and smile, and be a villain"; superficially friendly to the administrators, he is in fact Queen Victoria's agent provocateur sent to stir up trouble among the slaves. Concentrating on the charismatic Dolores, Sir William encourages him to overthrow his masters. In time a violent rebellion does take place, forcing the Portuguese to flee. Into the power vacuum rush the British, full of empty promises to the insurgents.

A decade later, Dolores and his fellow workers come to realize their appalling mistake: They have only traded oppressors. Another rebellion is in the making, this one against the British. Her Majesty's colonial administrators, aware that the slave organizer is now the most dangerous man on the island, send Sir William back. He is to track down Dolores and have him eliminated. A true mercenary, Sir William carries out his orders. But Sir William's is a Pyrrhic victory. Moments later his own death occurs at the hands of another guerrilla, a young black man who will replace the fallen leader and lead the rebels to victory.

As Marlon studied the scenario he felt an old itch. For the first time in years he stopped going through the motions of rehearsal, and now started ransacking libraries for material on imperialists and the subjugated. He had already determined the sound and posture of William Walker: He would be an arrogant upperclassman with a kind of Fletcher Christian accent. But what were Sir William's inner feelings about the sway of empire and those who resisted it at the cost of their lives? And just who were these rebels? Did they have any relation to the antiwar demonstrators and self-styled revolutionaries of the 1960s? In search of answers, he flew to Oakland. An intermediary arranged a meeting with Bobby Seale, cofounder of the radical Black Panthers, and Eldridge Cleaver, the Panthers' minister of information. Marlon had read Cleaver's collection of incendiary essays *Soul on Ice,* written while the author was in jail for assault with intent to murder. Marlon's old racial consciousness was reawakened. He couldn't take his eyes off Cleaver; the man seemed to be a Dostoyevskyan hero in another skin, in another country. They talked until nearly 4 a.m. By then the listener had become a disciple, convinced that at "a fundamental level all the Panthers really wanted was respect as human beings." Sitting nearby was Bobby Hutton, the seventeen-year-old secretary of the Panthers, who impressed Marlon as a poised and "beautiful boy who could have been my own son." Two weeks later, Hutton was dead, shot by police when they raided a house where he and Cleaver were holed up. The killing of the unarmed Hutton, Marlon decided, "confirmed everything I'd heard during that long night." The next day he flew back to Oakland. James Farmer, the head of CORE, seemed to be in charge of things and made no secret of his disdain for Marlon. ("They told me that he despised me because I was just another knee-jerk white liberal to him.") The dilemma was intolerable: It was one thing to be hated by integration-hating whites in Alabama, and quite another to be held at arm's length by the very people with whom he identified so strongly. A minister addressed mourners at Hutton's funeral. Then Marlon spoke, attempting to convince the audience that he and they were on the same page. "The preacher said that the white man can't cool it because he has never dug it. I'm trying to dig it, and that's why I'm here. You've been listening to white people for four hundred years, and they haven't done a thing. Now, I'm going to begin right now informing white people what they don't know."

It was a strained effort and it did nothing to change Farmer's mind, or to convince another Panther minister, H. Rap Brown, that the speaker was any more than a rich interloper dealing with his Caucasian guilt. Seale was not as hostile, but maintained an emotional distance. Marlon redoubled his efforts. The house on Mulholland became a retreat for radicals who were passing through town. Much talk about revolution occurred in that living room, and the host spoke once again about abandoning show business and joining the liberationists full-time.

A monograph put him back on the career track. Cleaver's autobiography, *Soul on Ice,* states that he "fell in love" with an English translation of the "Catechism of a Revolutionary." This inflammatory work was written by once notorious, now half-forgotten Mikhail Bakunin, architect of nineteenth-century Russian anarchism. Cleaver had the pamphlet reprinted cheaply, so that all Black Panthers and their supporters could own a copy. It was a tactical blunder: "Catechism" shed plenty of heat but precious little light. Bakunin's main thrust was an insistence on revolutionary "purity." If, for example, patricide and matricide were required of an insurrectionist, then without question he should slay his parents for the higher cause. Whether the Panthers were to take this statement literally was arguable. One thing was certain, though: Marlon did. He called Seale and said he "couldn't roll" with murder. Quite a few agreed with Marlon, but none would speak out against a fellow Black Panther. Some of them made halfhearted attempts to get the actor back in the fold, but essentially Marlon's association with the organization was at an end. He never went public with his severance from the Panthers, but began to edge closer to the charities and institutions of the late Dr. King. In the process he went on NBC's *Tonight Show* to tell Johnny Carson and some forty million viewers of his intention to tithe himself. From now on, 10 percent of his salary would be donated to King's Southern Christian Leadership Conference. On the spot, Carson made the same pledge.

This talk of earnings implied that Marlon would soon be back on the screen. And in December 1968 he did indeed take off for South America, where most of *Queimada* would be filmed. As the journey began, the clown in Brando asserted itself at exactly the wrong time. Bearded and long-haired for the role of Sir William, he posed a question for the flight attendant at Los Angeles International Airport: "Is this the plane for Cuba?" Terrified, she informed the pilot that a hijacker might be on board. He notified the airport police. Marlon was swiftly removed from the aircraft and brought to an interrogation room. There, someone recognized him: "My God, it's Marlon Brando!" Profuse apologies followed. Chastened, Marlon went home, then quietly took off for Cartagena. He was three days late for his entrance into Hell.

3

Gillo Pontecorvo was, in Marlon's view, "a complete sadist." He was also a Communist, a fetishist, and a hypocrite. All this would be revealed on a day-by-day basis.

Cartagena is situated eleven degrees north of the equator. In the winter, the city's average temperature is about eighty-eight degrees Fahrenheit, and on many days the thermometer goes higher. When filming began, Marlon and Gillo made an elaborate show of courtesy and deference. As the work proceeded, the politesse evaporated. Tempers lacerated in the unrelenting heat and humidity, and small disputes spiraled into major confrontations. Gillo insisted on multiple takes without explaining what he was after. After the tenth shot of a facial close-up, Marlon strapped a chair to his rear and continued to do the scene his way, then after each take lowered himself to the ground. The director, a doctrinaire Marxist, made a countermove, inserting passages that were straight out of *The Communist Manifesto*. Marlon found them anachronistic and lumpy. He refused to read them. Gillo insisted. Marlon got hold of a copy of *The Wall Street Journal*. Every time he sat down he intently perused the editorial page. Gillo, Marlon noted, detested the paper "as a symbol of everything evil. After scores of takes, he finally gave up; I'd worn him out." The match had many rounds, however, and Gillo won his share of them. Sometimes, Marlon complained, the director wanted "a purple smile." Instead "I gave him a mauve smile." Gillo continued to reshoot "until he got exactly what he wanted, even if I got a dislocated jaw in the meantime."

Bandits roamed the outskirts of Cartagena and made frequent forays into the city. Nervous crew members acquired firearms. Pontecorvo roamed around with a holster on his belt, the pistol loaded and ready to fire. Marlon didn't bother with sidearms. He remained on the set or near it, save for weekends, when he was conveyed to the airport by an armed driver. From there, he flew to Miami and then on to Los Angeles for rest and relaxation while everyone else sweltered.

He was not always so self-centered. As the filming went on, Marlon noticed something peculiar. Gillo had hired a large group of black Colombians to act as slaves and extras in crowd scenes. These men were served different food from the white members of the company.

"That's what they like," Gillo explained. "That's what they always eat."

The answer did not sit well with his star. Marlon nosed around and made an unpleasant discovery. Despite his protestations, Gillo was just trying to save money: Meals for *los negros* were cheaper to buy and easier to prepare, and the men were afraid to complain. More damning revelations followed: Almost without exception, the white extras were being paid more than their black counterparts. Confronted with the facts, Pontecorvo pleaded guilty. But he insisted that if all were treated equally the Caucasians would walk off the set. Marlon heatedly accused his director of racism. Had he forgotten that *Queimada* was based on the terrible exploitation of dark-skinned people? "Gillo said he agreed with me," Marlon remembered, "but he couldn't back down; in his mind the end justified the means.

" 'Okay,' I said, 'then I'm going home. I won't be a part of this.' "

He arranged to be driven to the local airport. As passengers prepared to board the plane, a messenger called out Marlon's name. The young man presented a letter from Pontecorvo promising to equalize all pay and food. It was the Chaplin capitulation all over again, this time in Spanish.

Several months down the line Marlon and Gillo went to war again. For thirty-six weeks the set had been plagued by difficulties. Some were circumstantial—petty thievery, unrelenting heat, tropical rashes, dysentery. Some were self-induced, ranging from rampant drug use, especially by the camera crew, to Pontecorvo's indifference to suffering—provided that it was not his own. The snapping point occurred on a particularly molten morning, when Gillo insisted on forty takes of the same scene. Fuming, Marlon performed them all. At the conclusion, he silently walked off the set and flew home to Los Angeles.

In a few days Marlon sent word to Alberto Grimaldi, the film's Italian producer. The star would not return to Colombia under any circumstances. No point in apologizing, wheedling, or threatening; his demand was not negotiable. Find a more habitable workplace or forget about finishing the picture with Brando. The producer and director had no options. They scouted locations with compatible light and background, settled on Morocco, ran the choice by Marlon, and won his grudging approval. Filming resumed, one month behind schedule. Later Pontecorvo admitted that he "shouldn't have been so stubborn. I should have realized that Marlon was not in the mood and put off the scene for another day." His obstinacy was to cost the production an additional $700,000, and to virtually guarantee the movie's unprofitability.

And yet in those last days there occurred one moment of grace, and it was enough to justify all the skirmishes and miseries. At the denouement, Sir William vainly attempts to persuade Dolores to choose freedom over martyrdom. The scene was overlong and ineffective as written. In a sudden burst of inspiration, Pontecorvo slashed the dialogue. In its place he would use Bach's mournful partita "Come Sweet Death" to convey the tragic quality of the scene. Without informing Marlon of his decision, he gave the actors their abbreviated dialogue. A recording of the music played as they went through their paces. "Since Brando is like an ultra-sensitive animal," said the director, "he was so moved by the music that he performed one of the most extraordinary scenes he ever played." The crew agreed; they burst into applause afterward. Marlon knew that something unprecedented had been filmed that day. He dared to hope that *Queimada* might do everything he wanted: simultaneously making a moral declaration and restoring his image as a serious and concerned performer.

Once filming was done, the opponents put on masks of collegiality. Pontecorvo designated Marlon "the greatest actor of the contemporary cinema," although he followed this with a sly reference to his on-set behavior: Brando is a man who "with one expression covers more than ten pages of dialogue. And he is the only one who can do it. His eyes simultaneously express sadness, irony, skepticism, and the fact that he is tired."

Marlon took a lot longer to acknowledge his debt. During the last days he told a *Life* reporter he "really wanted to kill" Pontecorvo.

"But why?" inquired the journalist.

"Because he has no feeling for people."

Another question: "Have you ever tried to kill anybody?"

"I once tried to kill my father. Really." He stopped to consider his hostility to the director. "I always used to imagine I was killing him by pulling out his corneas." It took twenty years before resentments had cooled enough for a mellower Marlon to revise his opinion. In his memoir he called the bête noire "one of the most sensitive and meticulous directors I ever worked for."

Had the film thrived, Marlon and Gillo might have reconciled. It did not. Released in the United States as *Burn!*, the film was severely edited—twenty minutes were cut out, resulting in a lapse of coherence and some awkward links in the story. It got a hostile reception. *The New York Times*'s new movie critic, Vincent Canby, advised readers that Brando was almost always worth watching: "You should enjoy seeing him here, using that Fletcher Christian accent and, towards the end of the film, looking very much like the late Ernest Hemingway, a tired and tragic hero whom life has somehow double-crossed." A pity the rest of the feature was only "the sort of prole pageant in which

characters always seem to be conceptualizing great issues, mostly freedom, as they pass in front of history, as if it were a scenic view, instead
of moving in and out of it."

In a thoughtful *New Yorker* piece, Pauline Kael gave with one hand
and took away with the other. Marlon's performance delighted and
confused her: "The oppressor as cynical clown is an entertaining idea,
and perhaps the audience needs his foppish foolery." However, "When
the role is played with Brando's bravura, so that Sir William becomes a
daring white loner who loved and betrayed the blacks, it's a muddle,
because we simply don't understand his motives or why he is so zealous
in crushing the rebellion." Other reviewers were generally dismissive,
assessing Marlon's role as "rudderless" and condemning the movie for
its Marxism 101 approach to colonial history. The overheated *Burn!*
contrasted harshly with the austere brilliance of *The Battle of Algiers*.
Like too many Brando movies of the 1960s it went away quietly. Pontecorvo never again directed a full-length film, and Marlon described
himself as truly "washed up and unemployable."

From here on, he decided, all his time, energy, and money would be
devoted to making Tetiaroa into an Eden. Settling down with his pregnant wife Tarita, he would oversee a showplace of irreproachable
beauty complete with airstrip and lobster farm. Like so many others
before him, Marlon made the mistake of believing that serenity and
fulfillment worked their way from the beach to the brain. Alas, just the
opposite was true. He knew the poems of Wordsworth, and acknowledged later that the Briton had said it best:

> Not in Utopia, subterranean fields,
> Or some secreted island, Heaven knows where!
> But in the very world, which is the world
> Of all of us,—the place where in the end
> We find our happiness, or not at all!

4

The late sixties had seen the assassinations of John and Robert
Kennedy, Martin Luther King Jr., Medgar Evers, and Malcolm X;

racial disturbances on both coasts; the early seventies, the shooting of Kent State University students protesting the Vietnam War. Violence had become, as H. Rap Brown insisted, "as American as apple pie." Richard Nixon packaged himself as a counterweight to civil disturbance, and he made his sale. The last year of the decade began with the Republican being sworn in as the thirty-seventh president of the United States. Less than two hours later, groups of demonstrators shouted antiwar slogans and hurled rocks and beer cans at the heavily guarded presidential limousine. The events were emblematic of a nation divided, with the gaps widening month by month. The death of former President Dwight D. Eisenhower underlined the difference between those who had put his vice president in the White House and those who were subject to the army draft and went out in the streets and on the campuses to demonstrate, singing Bob Dylan's "Subterranean Homesick Blues," with its ominous lyrics "You don't need a weather man / To know which way the wind blows." Popular culture mirrored this conflict of ideas and ages: Smooth, mindless entertainment like *Butch Cassidy and the Sundance Kid* did well; so did *Medium Cool,* with its footage of police violence during the 1968 Democratic convention in Chicago. In the Broadway theater, the musical *1776* celebrated America's Founding Fathers—and the revues *Oh, Calcutta!* and *Hair* defied the traditional taboo against obscenity and full-frontal nudity in popular mass entertainment. On the nonfiction best-seller list, *The Emerging Republican Majority* vied with *Custer Died for Your Sins: An Indian Manifesto.* And among the novels were *The Gang That Couldn't Shoot Straight,* a farce about organized crime, and *The Godfather,* Puzo's deadly serious examination of the same subject: "No matter how poor or powerless the supplicant, Don Corleone would take that man's troubles to his heart. And he would let nothing stand in the way to a solution of that man's woe. His reward? Friendship, the respecful title of 'Don' and sometimes the more affectionate salutation of 'Godfather.' "

Unwittingly, Puzo tapped the public's desperate appetite for rationality and control—even at the hands of criminals. Readers, battered by too much news, too much information about strife at home and abroad, made *The Godfather* a phenomenal bestseller. It was as if they needed to believe a Vito Corleone existed, that violence made sense if you looked at it a certain way, that, for example, a Mafia don could exact revenge against wrongdoers, seeking his own kind of justice, controlling vast swatches of modern life from his living room. Puzo had served a long apprenticeship as a freelance journalist, writing stories and articles for men's magazines like *Stag* and *Male,* as well as articles for such upmarket publications as *Redbook* and *Holiday.* His first three books were well received by critics and ignored by the public. With a gambling habit and four children and a wife to support, he determined to write a work of purely commercial fiction. Though Puzo knew no gangsters personally, he had heard stories about the Cosa Nostra for years, tales of brutality and loyalty, of stone killers who would murder in the evening and attend mass the following day, of felons in high places and senators on the take. Using the central figure of Don Corleone, he constructed a strong Italian family whose business happened to be crime. A world rose up from his typewriter. He filled it with recognizable capos, dons, and hit men, politicians, movie actors, and studio big shots. Puzo emphasized *la famiglia*'s intense loyalties to children, women, and friends, and its lethal approach to those who would poach on its turf. Nicholas Pileggi, the most intrepid investigator of Italian-American criminals, noted that while *The Godfather* romanticized and exaggerated the Corleones' power and their influence on legitimate business, "it humanized rather than condemned them. The Godfather himself, for instance, was shot because he refused to deal in the dirty business of narcotics." Michael Corleone, Vito's college-educated, war-hero son, assumed his father's mantle "not out of greed, but from a sense of responsibility to his father who, for all his illegal activities, was a far more honorable man than all the crooked cops, venal judges, corrupt politicians and perverted businessmen who peppered the plot."

As he described the Godfather, Puzo kept the image of one man before him: Marlon Brando. It was a fantasy, he told himself; Marlon would never go near such a story. And who knew if a movie would ever be made of the book? Still, an author could dream. . . . All the while Marlon was in his South Seas retreat with wife, son, and new daughter, Cheyenne, with irregular forays to Mulholland Drive to tap into his bank account. He knew what the industry thought of him: If Brando could get work at all, said the smart money, it would be for second-rate directors with third-rate material. Indeed, the only valid script that had come Marlon's way in the late 1960s was a modified horror film to be directed by Michael Winner. The Briton's last few movies had been sledgehammer farces like *The Jokers* and *I'll Never Forget What's-'is-name. The Nightcomers* looked to be number twelve on the bomb rack.

In 1970, shortly after Marlon signed the contract for that feature, Paramount hired thirty-one-year-old Francis Ford Coppola to write and direct an adaptation of *The Godfather.* He was not the studio's first choice; Arthur Penn had been a front-runner, as had Franklin Schaffner and Fred Zinnemann. When those old pros turned down the chance, the front office settled on Coppola. It was hardly a shot in the dark. Coppola had written the greatly admired script for *Patton.* But this credential was only a part of his attraction; he was very green, and the studio intended to use him as their marionette, controlling every move.

Paramount gave Coppola a hard time about everything. The front office wanted Robert Redford, Ryan O'Neal, Dean Stockwell, or Martin Sheen for the role of Michael Corleone, the Don's favored son—anybody but Coppola's first choice, the unknown Al Pacino. As for the Don, recalled the director, "Ultimately they said, 'What about the Godfather?' " They suggested Orson Welles, George C. Scott, Edward G. Robinson. Coppola kept shaking his head. One of them had an off-the-wall proposal: What about Carlo Ponti? At the time Ponti was known for two things: He was a highly successful producer of Italian and international films, and he was the husband of Sophia Loren. Short, balding, resolutely unglamorous, he had never acted in his life.

That hardly seemed a liability to Robert Evans, Paramount's production chief. Evans could have had a career in the garment industry; his family's company, Evan-Picone, was one of the most prominent fashion houses. Robert wanted no part of it, however; people told him he was handsome enough to be a movie star, and he believed them. After a few roles it became obvious that his talents lay elsewhere, and he switched to the producer track. In the last year he had gained considerable velocity, having shepherded *Love Story* from weepy paperback to blockbuster film. "Bob was execrable on screen," said Peter Bart, vice president of production. "But you could go to the bank on his instincts." Paramount did exactly that, and grossed millions. These days few people dared to contradict Evans.

Coppola was one of them. "I said, 'I don't want a real Italian for the part of the Godfather. I want either an Italian-American or an actor who's so great that he can *portray* an Italian-American.' " And who would that be? Evans inquired. Coppola named the two men he considered the greatest actors in the Western world: Laurence Olivier and

Marlon Brando. Inquiries got under way. Sir Laurence was said to be very ill; acting was the last thing on his mind just now. The field appeared to be clear for Marlon. Coppola rationalized the situation: Brando would be even better than Olivier because Puzo had always had him in mind, and because younger actors held the man in awe. On this film they would give the performances of their lifetimes. The director's pitch left Stanley Jaffe cold. He was a second-generation mogul (his father, Leo, had been the president of Columbia Pictures) and he was not going to be pushed around by creative types. "As the president of Paramount Pictures," he said loftily, "I want to inform you that Marlon Brando will never appear in this motion picture and I instruct you not to pursue the idea anymore."

Upon hearing that declaration, Coppola fell from his chair to the carpeted floor, writhing and clutching his chest. "I give up," he groaned theatrically. "You hired me; I'm supposed to be the director. Every idea I have you don't want me to talk about. Now you're instructing me that I can't even pursue the idea. At least let me pursue it."

The Paramount people exchanged glances. The young man might be full of himself, but you had to admire his chutzpah. They consulted and then gave in—with three provisos. One: Marlon had to do the film for *bubkes*—literally "beans" in Yiddish, but translated more accurately as very little money. Two: Brando had to put up a cash bond. If he caused delays in shooting, his insurers, rather than Paramount, would pay for it. Three: He had to do a screen test to assure everyone that at forty-seven he could play a *capo di tutti i capi* twenty years his senior.

Number three was the hardest; Coppola tackled it first. Puzo had sent Marlon a handwritten letter a few weeks back: "I wrote a book called *The Godfather*. I think you're the only actor who can play the Godfather with that quiet force and irony the part requires." He followed it up with a phone call. Marlon allowed that he wanted the part; he saw the story as "about the corporate mind, because the Mafia is the best example of capitalists we have." By then Puzo figured he had a sure thing—if only Paramount hadn't insisted on the screen test. How could anyone ask Marlon Brando to try out for anything? Coppola thought about it, called up the actor, and meekly offered, "Mr. Brando, don't you think it would be a good idea if we fooled around a little bit, and do a little improvisation for the role, and see what it would be like?" Marlon said that would be fine.

At 7 a.m. the next day Coppola arrived at Mulholland Drive with a small crew and a selection of props—small Italian cigars, an espresso cup, pieces of cheese, appetizers. A housekeeper ushered them into the living room. Brando entered in a kimono. He had "long flowing blond hair and a ponytail," the director remembered. "Very handsome." Marlon looked at the cheese and took a bite. "These old guys," he said, "their collar is always creased like this." Then he rolled up the ponytail, took some shoe polish, and colored his hair black. On his instructions, a makeup man penciled in a little mustache and darkened the creases around the actor's mouth and eyes. Marlon stuffed facial tissue in his cheeks, wrinkled his collar some more, put on a jacket, lit a cigar, tightened his diction—and turned into Don Corleone. One of the cameramen showed him a playback of the videotape. He was pleased at his bulldog appearance, "mean-looking, but warm underneath." Coppola knew he had captured something invaluable that morning. He also knew that nothing would be accomplished without a go-ahead from Gulf + Western, Paramount's parent company. A viewing was arranged for G + W's volatile president, Charles Bluhdorn. In the immense New York office, Coppola ran the footage of Marlon as he had first appeared, surferlike, blond, and indifferent. "No, absolutely not," the CEO decreed. After Brando's hair was darkened and his face and carriage assumed a different persona, Bluhdorn did something very rare: He changed his mind. Evans came in, inspected the later footage, and didn't recognize Marlon: "He looks Italian, fine. But who is he?"

"The word goes back to Los Angeles," said Coppola, "that Charlie thinks the screen test of Brando is incredible. I jumped over five guys that way." The ones he couldn't jump over were the Mafia wiseguys. For sixty-seven weeks they had suffered while the Puzo novel stayed on the goddamned *Times* bestseller list. It gave them a bad image, what with the killings and the extortion and the hookers and the contraband. And now Paramount was going to make a *Marlon Brando* picture of it? They had a lot of problems with that, with this punk kid Francis, with his Italian name, no less, and with his star. Who the hell did Brando think he was? A cheapie, a has-been. Somebody ought to take care of the situation, Cosa Nostra–style.

1971–1972

How Did God Go About His Work?

1

Marlon needed *The Godfather* as much as *The Godfather* needed him. Perhaps a bit more. The list of recent and not-so-recent failures was long and painful to contemplate. *The Fugitive Kind:* one of Tennessee's mistakes, and unprofitable to boot. *One-Eyed Jacks:* his sole directorial attempt, a flameout. *Mutiny on the Bounty:* universally panned, wasteful, a neutron bomb. *The Ugly American:* purposeful, decent, Jocelyn got work, nobody cared. *Bedtime Story:* David Niven an avalanche of laughs; the picture a fiasco. *Morituri, The Chase, The Appaloosa,* all letdowns. Who was it called the sixties "a slum of a decade"? Well, these were a big part of the big dump. *A Countess from Hong Kong:* bad Brando and no business. *Reflections in a Golden Eye:* good Brando and no business. *Candy:* garbage. *The Night of the Following Day:* incoherent. *Queimada:* the best Brando, noble, memorable, circling the drain. Why did he make them all? It was hard to remember sometimes. A combination of debt, women, kids, and on rare occasions a belief in the material.

Would *The Nightcomers* be one more on the list? He had every reason to think so. The movie was designed as a prequel to Henry James's eerie ghost tale *The Turn of the Screw.* It needed a subtle hand, and Michael Winner was alleged to have lobster claws. Marlon would play Quint, the gardener of a British estate. Gruff, unmannerly, Quint is less interested in his duties than in seducing the estrous governess, Miss Jessel (Stephanie Beacham), supervisor of two recently orphaned children. The scenario concerns the servants' sadomasochistic affair and the effect it has on all around them—especially the orphans. Marlon approached his character with care, not least because he wanted the news to get around: Brando is behaving himself. Brando knows his lines cold. Brando can do an Irish accent. Brando is not causing delays.

Filming took place in a large country house, and Winner set aside a dining room just for Marlon and whatever guests might be visiting him. Marlon objected; he hated class distinctions and wanted to eat with the rest of the crew. Said Winner, "I am sorry to say this, but the crew do not wish you to eat with them. They are much happier in the next-door canteen eating on their own and not worrying about the overpowering presence of their employers and a major star." Thereafter Marlon ate in his dressing room or trailer. The dining room was taken by Winner.

Marlon's demeanor got good marks from the beginning; in her diary Beacham remarked on Marlon's increasing girth but called him an "amazing talent," even with his proclivity for monkeyshines. She was deaf in one ear, and Marlon had gotten into the habit of inserting flesh-colored earplugs during rehearsals to blot out distractions. They wound up shouting at each other, and then dissolving with laughter at the result. Sometimes Marlon displayed a darker kind of humor. "We had a scene where he tied me to the bed posts with ropes. Suddenly, the bell to break for lunch rang. Marlon got up, and without saying a word, marched off to his dressing-room. I tried to untie myself. I tried and tried, but I couldn't get those knots undone. I couldn't believe it. He had been able to do it so easily. Then some of the crew came to my rescue, but they couldn't untie me either! Finally, someone called Brando who, very calmly, came back to the set and proceeded to untie me with the greatest of ease." She took it in good spirits: The two were seen chuckling between takes.

Crew members witnessed a few head-to-head collisions with the director—Winner was a coarse talent masked as a refined one; Brando, as always, was a fragile ego covered with a hard carapace of fake lechery and vulgar remarks. He was forever grabbing Beacham, to whom he was not attracted, or trying to offend the Jewish Winner by calling him "mein Führer." With all that, the two men came away with warm mutual regard. Marlon said that Winner was always Peter Politesse, the only one who ever talked to him as he preferred to be talked to. *The Nightcomers* suffered from meager distribution and failed to make the hit parade, but that didn't seem to matter to Winner. He was to pronounce Marlon a figure of profound importance: "Before Brando, actors acted. After Brando, they behaved. That is the difference—an extraordinary effect on the history of drama and the history of movies."

And so it came to pass that another director recognized Marlon's extraordinary talent. Meantime, the star remained in the black hole of his career. He stayed there throughout the filming, although every now and then the cast could see glimpses of the old Brando—alongside the one who prevailed most of the time. They watched him veer in a single day—sometimes in a single hour—from ennui to euphoria, from a total rejection of his profession to an artful performance that moved fellow performers to tears. His indifference was not faked, but the result of a self-portrait that could never, ever be erased. If the boy was no good, how could the man be worthy? If people applauded him, if producers paid him, if directors saluted his work, then obviously they belonged to the Club of Phonies. "I ought to know," he told friends. "I'm a charter member." Even so, Marlon couldn't put himself down all the time. There were scenes in *The Nightcomers* when the conflicted actor breathed life into his character, and it was at those moments that he wished his life onscreen to continue, to go on at the highest level. Was it too late?

Just when the industry seemed ready to shut him out for good, Marlon made a last desperate gesture for respectability and stature, in seeking the *Godfather* role. He sought an audience with the higher-ups at Paramount. "You may have heard a lot of crap about how I misbehaved on pictures," he told Robert Evans. "Some of it is true, some of it is not true. But I'll tell you this: I want to play this role. I'll work for it, work hard. It's going to be something special for me." Yet even as he spoke he feared that *The Godfather* could be a washout like the others. So many things depended on luck, timing, other actors, the director, the script, the studio. You just never knew. Never. Jesus, it would be good to break the string.

2

The Italian-American Civil Rights League was founded in April 1970. It posed as an organization much like B'nai B'rith and the NAACP, alerting the country to verbal and physical bias against Italian-Americans. The league's first great cause was the "victimization" of Joseph Colombo, Jr., on a charge of conspiracy to melt down U.S. silver coins into ingots. The arrestee was the son of the reputed mobster Joseph Colombo, Sr. Two months after the league was created, it claimed to have forty-five thousand members; in November, Frank

Sinatra held a benefit concert in Madison Square Garden, solidifying the organization's credentials and its treasury. With a $600,000 war chest, the IACRL felt strong enough and rich enough to go up against Paramount.

As plans got under way for filming, *The Godfather* producer Albert Ruddy received some disturbing mail. Letters (many of them sent from the same post office) decried Paramount's forthcoming adaptation. It was "anti-Italian," "un-American," "provocative," "shameful." With the missives came dark predictions of labor-union demonstrations and stoppages. The Grand Venerable of the Grand Council of the Grand Lodge of New York State's Sons of Italy urged an economic boycott of the film. He called on federal and state authorities to refrain from giving the production any cooperation whatsoever. Protests were not confined to the private sector; Ruddy got mail from New York State congressmen, senators, and judges. One complaint took the high road: "A book like *The Godfather* leaves one with the sickening feeling that a great deal of effort and labor to eliminate a false image concerning Americans of Italian descent and also an ethnic connotation to organized crime has been wasted." So many careers "could have been made into constructive and intelligent movies, such as the life of Enrico Fermi, the great scientist; Mother Cabrini; Colonel Ceslona, a hero of the Civil War; Garibaldi, the great Italian who unified Italy; William Paca, a signer of the Declaration of Independence."

Others took the low road. The Manhattan offices of Gulf + Western were twice evacuated because of bomb threats. In Los Angeles, Al Ruddy took extra precautions. He told police he had a bad feeling about the Mob. Would they please investigate suspicious activity in or around Paramount? In a few days they got back to him: His car was being tailed by person or persons unknown. Ruddy switched vehicles with his secretary. She parked his car in front of her house. In the morning she found it riddled with bullet holes. In Hollywood to collaborate on the screenplay, Puzo enjoyed the perks of a big office, a commensurate salary, and four phones. He soon found that being the father of *The Godfather* came with a curse. At a Los Angeles restaurant he was introduced to Frank Sinatra, generally thought to be the model for Johnny Fontane, the down-on-his-luck singer given a second chance by pledging fealty to Vito Corleone. Sinatra, wrote Puzo with cheery bravado, never looked up from his plate, but "started to shout abuse. The worst thing he called me was a pimp, which rather flattered me. But what hurt was that there he was, a northern Italian, threatening me, a southern Italian, with physical violence. That was roughly equivalent to Einstein pulling a knife on Al Capone."

Ruddy couldn't afford such a jaunty response. As if this were the latest chapter of *The Godfather,* he arranged to plead his case with Joseph Colombo, Jr. That cleared the way for a meeting with Joseph Colombo, Sr. It took place at the Park Sheraton Hotel, and the old man was not alone. In the hotel's grand ballroom were some fifteen hundred members of the league, all of them radiating hostility. Junior informed the audience that Mr. Ruddy had agreed to delete the pejorative words "Mafia," "Cosa Nostra," and all other Italian labels from the script. As a capper, he agreed to turn over the proceeds of the film's New York premiere to the league's hospital fund. This did not elicit the expected response. "I couldn't care less if they gave us two million dollars," Senior snapped. "No one can buy the right to defame Italian-Americans."

What the hell did these people want? Ruddy wondered. He promised, in front of all those assembled, that the *Godfather* film would depict individuals, and that it would never, ever allow the dialogue to defame or stereotype any group. If you think about it, he pointed out, what it really is, is a story of America, of proud, energetic immigrants who overcome bias and poverty. He added another level of assurance. "Look at who's playing the roles." He was about to reel off a laundry list of non-Italians, starting with Marlon Brando and including James Caan, Robert Duvall, Sterling Hayden, John Marley, Diane Keaton, Abe Vigoda. Before he could begin, the senior Columbo interjected: "Who is playing?"

"Lots of people," Ruddy replied.

"How about a good kid from Bensonhurst?"

Ah, so that was it. These wiseguys were star fuckers like everyone else. They wanted in on the casting of a big movie. Fair enough; what was the harm in letting them pick and choose actors for walk-ons and small parts? It was better than bullet holes. He listened as the senior Colombo indicated one delegate, then another and another, as they made suggestions about young men suitable for the screen. Ruddy noted down all the names. By the end of the evening Colombo inserted a pin in the producer's lapel, designating him a captain in the league.

Smiles all around. They continued during the filming in New York. Threats of labor troubles, breakages, and extortions evaporated. Paramount had already been shaken down.

3

Colombo did more than smooth the way at assorted restaurants and bars that would provide *The Godfather*'s backgrounds. He also introduced the lead actors to his associates. James Caan studied their mannerisms and came away awed. "They've got incredible moves. There's tremendous interplay. They toast each other—'*centanni*,' '*salute a nostra*'—all this marvelous Old World stuff from guys who were born here and don't even speak Italian.

"I noticed also that they're always touching themselves. Thumbs in the belt. Touching the jaw. Adjusting the shirt. Gripping the crotch. Shirt open. Tie loose. Super dressers. Clean. Very, very neat."

Marlon, the ultimate mimic, went him one better. He got himself invited to the home of a well-placed mafioso in New Jersey. Some forty people attended a dinner in his honor. He could see the importance of well-prepared food and vintage wine; the manner in which powerful dons spoke in quiet voices; the way the men went out of their way to be gracious to their women, but also how they kept them in secondary roles; the exaggerated politesse to a stranger, albeit a movie star; the overwhelming feeling of *la famiglia*—loyalty to one's own. He took mental notes that were to affect the film and everyone in it.

Two generations before, when Stella Adler's father, Jacob, the Yiddish-theater impresario, became the first Jewish actor to play Shylock on the New York stage, he had studied the role intensely, reaching below the anti-Semitic portrait to find a whole human being with a wide range of emotions and justifications. "Weighty and proud his walk," the actor reasoned, "calm and conclusive his speech, a man of rich personal and national experience, a man who sees life through the glasses of life and eternity. So I played him, so I had joy in him."

Marlon, a devotee of Jacob's widow, Sara, and a pupil of his daughter Stella, had the same urge to turn a standardized villain into a man of dimension and stature. Bearing in mind the Adlerian approach to character, he set out to portray Vito Corleone as a modest, quiet man. As he saw it, the Don was "part of the wave of immigrants who came to this country around the turn of the century and had to swim upstream to survive as best they could. He had the same hopes and ambitions for his sons that Joseph P. Kennedy had for his." As a young man "he probably hadn't intended to become a criminal, and when he did, he hoped it would be transitional." As he says to his son, "I never wanted this for you. I work my whole life, I don't apologize, to take care of my family. And I refused to be a fool, dancing on the strings held by all those big shots. I don't apologize—that's my life—but I always thought that when it was your time that you would be the one to hold the strings. Senator Corleone. Governor Corleone . . . Well, there wasn't enough time, Michael. There just wasn't enough time."

As rehearsals began, Marlon's coworkers gave him a wide berth. Duvall had appeared in *The Chase* with Marlon; he was happy to be cast as Tom Hagen, the Godfather's adopted son, but was not rendered speechless by the opportunity. The others, however, were clearly intimidated. Pacino could barely articulate his feelings: "Have you any idea what it is for me to be doing a scene with *him*? I sat in theaters when I was a kid, just watching him. Now I'm playing a scene with him. He's God, man." Watching the cast behave with such gingerly respect, Ruddy remarked that "in a sense Marlon had created these guys," and Puzo concurred: Marlon was "the one guy with whom they all wanted to act, and here was their chance." They remained stiff and unnatural around their favorite until he began cracking jokes and making faces and "unfroze them. No attitude, no superiority. He was a superstar, all right, but from that point on he was first among equals."

Those equals were consumed by curiosity. Each had his own approach to acting, to climbing inside the character he was to play. But how did God go about his work? What was Marlon's technique? They scrutinized him, watching for giveaways. As Vito Corleone he had them alternately scratching their heads in wonder and laughing at his weird ways. The man they regarded with such fervor had read the novel, had studied the script, and yet knew very few of his lines. He saw to it that cue cards were scattered wherever he did his scenes. They were attached to dishes, to furniture, to cameras, and sometimes written with ink on his palms. By the time Vito Corleone conversed with Luca Brasi, played by the massive wrestler Lenny Montana, the cast had loosened up. They were so relaxed and confident, in fact, that Montana faced Marlon with his back to the camera and opened his mouth. On

Montana's tongue, Caan had attached a piece of tape. It read "Fuck you, Marlon." The cast and star broke up, and the director joined in. Coppola's mirth covered a queasy feeling that Marlon was setting a bad example to the others—a blizzard of idiot cards was the last thing *The Godfather* needed.

Marlon would not budge. Committing lines to memory would make his performance sound like "Mary Had a Little Lamb." "People intuit," he said. "They unconsciously know you have planned that speech." The fact was that "in ordinary life people seldom know exactly what they're going to say when they open their mouths and start to express a thought. They're still thinking, and the fact that they are looking for words shows on their faces. They pause for an instant to find the right word, search their minds to compose a sentence, then express it." It was his way, and that was that. Coppola could only smile, nod, and hope that the Brando method wasn't infectious. To the director's relief it never did catch on with the others, and Marlon's inventions added vigor and originality throughout the months of filming. On one occasion, for example, a confrontation between Vito and Johnny Fontane was going nowhere. It was all too evident that Al Martino was a singer, not an actor, and that his plea for godfatherly help was about as authentic as wax fruit. Upon the next take, Marlon took matters into his own hands:

FONTANE: Oh, Godfather, I don't know what to do. I don't know what to do.

DON CORLEONE: You can act like a man!

The Godfather suddenly slapped Fontane. Martino's face registered trauma and fear, and they were not faked. Marlon pressed on:

What's the matter with you? Is this how you turned out? A Hollywood *finócchio* that cries like a woman? "What can I do? What can I do?" What is that nonsense? Ridiculous.

He imitated the character's whine, Martino straightened up, and the scene took off. Marlon contributed hundreds of other ad-libs and gestures that gave *The Godfather* a chiaroscuro reality. It was he who grabbed a stray cat, stroking it while he gave his lethal orders in a tender, strained voice, and it was he who articulated the line "After all, we're not murderers, whatever that undertaker thinks," pausing then to sniff a rose—a moment that was not in the script. The multiple portraits of authority, warmth, and evil had seldom been projected so effectively. And when a scene with Vito's little grandson was slow and cloying, it was Marlon who peeled an orange, made fangs with pieces of the rind, stuck them in his gums, and made the boy shout with an appealing mirth.

As usual, the power Marlon displayed onscreen was offset by the antics he initiated or provoked. "He was always trying to figure out a way to stop eating," said Caan. "He had this plan." He would say to his assistant, Alice Marchalk, " 'Listen, after nine o'clock I want you to lock up all the cabinets. After nine o'clock no matter what I say don't give me the key.' At nine-twenty he says, 'Alice, give me the key.' 'No.' He says, 'I swear to God I'll fire you.' 'No.' So he went and got a crowbar and just busted all the locks."

"Mooning" became an outdoor sport—Caan and Duvall began to drop their pants and display their buttocks during breaks in the action. Marlon outdid them by dropping *his* pants and mooning the entire company of men, women, and children during *The Godfather*'s elaborate wedding scene. The monkeyshines continued at the crucial moment when Vito Corleone is gunned down at an outdoor market. Guards were supposed to put him on a stretcher and rush the Godfather to a hospital. Marlon arranged to have six counterweights hidden under his blanket. They were used to anchor camera booms, and added an additional three hundred pounds. Recalled Caan: The stretcher bearers "were very big guys, maybe six foot three, two hundred and thirty pounds, weight lifters. They sweated halfway up. One guy's voice climbed three octaves. Their veins stuck out. They couldn't make it. They had to quit." Marlon fell off the stretcher laughing, and gave the joke away.

All this was taken in good grace by the cast, crew, and studio. What Paramount could not forgive was the rising cost of production. The fault, for a change, lay not with the star but with his director. Coppola insisted on his private vision of perfection, with multiple takes and expensive delays. Interiors were built and rebuilt until he got exactly what he wanted. The lighting never seemed to satisfy him. Every film set is rife with rumors; during the frequent down time all sorts of gossip is engendered, some of it total fiction, some of it with grains of truth. The *Godfather* set was no different, just more intense. It was bruited about that the studio wanted to replace the young director (true), and that Kazan was hovering just out of sight, waiting to take over (false). Coppola overheard the scuttlebutt but was defenseless. He would need two major interventions to save his job. When the Oscars were announced for the best films of 1970, *Patton* ran the table. It was judged the best film of the year. George C. Scott won for Best Actor—and became the first performer to refuse his statuette, claiming that the Academy Award ceremonies were little more than a "beauty contest and a meat market." Francis Ford Coppola was only too glad to come onstage and accept *his* award for collaborating on the Best Original Screenplay. Even then he was considered vulnerable. Paramount grudgingly acknowledged Coppola's writing talent, but had deepening doubts about his managerial skills—particularly the all-important ability to stay within budget. Marlon thought it was time to make a stand. He had come to admire Coppola, "Victor Vicarious," as one of the stagehands called him, an indoor type who had suffered from polio as a child and who lived his adventures through the characters he moved around onscreen. Like everyone else on *The Godfather*, from the grips on up, Marlon knew about the threats from Paramount. He confronted Bluhdorn directly with nine words, stated Godfather-style: "If you fire Francis, I'll walk off the picture." Coppola stayed.

Upon completing his work on the movie, Marlon told friends that *The Godfather* was one of the most pleasurable experiences in his career. And after viewing the still-incomplete movie at Coppola's San Francisco office, he spoke euphorically to the press. In his judgment *The Godfather* was flat-out "one of the most powerful statements ever made about America." Coppola had bought the interpretation of the Mafia as ur-capitalists, and, by suggestion, brought in the Cuban crisis, the explosions on campus, the Vietnam War, the corruption around President Nixon, the Central Intelligence Agency, the illicit links between the private sector and the government. "Certainly there was immorality in the Mafia," Marlon reflected, "but at heart it was a business; in many ways it didn't operate much differently from certain multinational corporations that went around knowingly spilling chemical poisons in their wake. The Mafia may kill a lot of people, but while we were making the movie, CIA representatives were dealing in drugs in the Golden Triangle, torturing people for information and assassinating them with far more efficiency than the Mob."

People listened to him in a way they hadn't for more than a decade. The irony was that as the superstar once again took control of his lumbering career, Marlon lost his grip on everything else. Christian Brando had turned thirteen. He continued to live with his mother in a state of confusion and misery; Anna Kashfi had become addicted to alcohol and various pharmaceuticals. Her behavior swerved from ecstasy to melancholia and back again, often within a single day. Christian, influenced by what he saw, had his own problems with substance abuse. On his visits to Mulholland, Marlon saw what was happening; he told the boy he disapproved of drinking and drugs, but added that if he was going to drink bourbon and smoke pot, he could at least do it at home, "in front of me."

At the same time, Marlon's second ex-wife, Movita, was costing him $1,400 per month for court-ordered maintenance and child support. Marlon stubbornly refused to pay, partly because of jealousy—Movita was known to have a new man in her life. But there was another, more urgent reason for his parsimony. Alberto Grimaldi had just initiated a major lawsuit accusing Brando of willfully and deliberately causing delays and relocations in the filming of *Quiemada*. As compensation, the producer was demanding the sum of $700,000. Despite frantic maneuvering by Marlon's lawyers, Grimaldi convinced a judge to have the actor's financial assets frozen. Living expenses would be allowed, but nothing else could be taken from saving banks or securities. The result was that after twenty-six films and several million dollars in salary, Marlon would have to live from paycheck to paycheck, the way he had when he was twenty-four years old. Pennebaker had been sold. Other investments had turned sour. Two ex-wives had their hands out and five young Brandos, ranging in age from one to thirteen, had to be fed and clothed. There was Christian by his marriage to Anna Kashfi, Miko by his marriage to Movita Castaneda, and Teihotu, Rebecca, and Cheyenne by Tarita Teriipaia, the current Mrs. Brando.

And so, having completed his most promising film since *On the Waterfront,* Marlon was still strapped for money, concerned for his children, and uncertain about the future. Emotionally and financially drained, he desperately needed time out at Tetiaroa with Tarita and the kids. But there was no time for a break. He needed cash flow and he needed it now. There was only one way to get it. He would have to make another movie.

4

David Merrick was pleased with his reputation as Broadway's Abominable Showman, the producer with the temper of a warthog and the ethics of a fox. In a notorious 1961 stunt, Merrick rescued a musical panned by every major newspaper critic. Out of the Manhattan phone book he picked seven ordinary citizens who happened to share the reviewers' names. After paying them, he ran their names under an ad for the show. It read, SEVEN OUT OF SEVEN ARE ECSTATICALLY UNANIMOUS ABOUT SUBWAYS ARE FOR SLEEPING. Yet he could be amiable at times, and he had a shrewd eye for talent. Merrick productions included the megahits Gypsy, Oliver! and Hello, Dolly! By 1972 he was rich and ready to invade Hollywood. For his first venture the showman chose an adaptation of Child's Play, the story of dark doings at a Catholic school. He enlisted Sidney Lumet as director and James Mason as one of the professors. Merrick thought Marlon Brando would be ideal as Mason's antagonist. He enticed him with promises of a decent salary and the chance to work again with Lumet, who had directed The Fugitive Kind. At Marlon's insistence, Merrick agreed to find a part for Wally Cox. Marlon and Wally had never quite been out of touch, but only recently had they talked to each other about their personal travails. From mutual friends, Wally heard about Marlon's backstairs fights with his exes; from the same people, Marlon learned about Wally's career nosedive. Since the last broadcast of Mister Peepers, the diminutive clown had suffered a series of reverses. The Adventures of Hiram Holliday, a TV comedy series built around him, failed after one season. The Walrus currently depended on a voice-over role as the cartoon character Underdog, and guest shots on game shows. Marlon knew that his pal was unhappily married and drinking hard. He hoped to put Wally back on track by giving his career a jump-start in Child's Play.

Marlon had not reckoned on Merrick. The producer lionized the performing Brando but had no experience with the editorial one. Marlon had barely arrived on the Westchester County, New York, set when he began to insist on dialogue changes. Lumet was not happy, but admitted that Brando "saw the holes in the story and lack of logic."

Arguments erupted between star and producer as the director sat on the sidelines. "David thrives on conflict," Lumet sighed, "but I do not feel as he does that tension is a spur to creativity." Two days later Marlon was replaced by Robert Preston. "I simply threw Mr. Brando out of my film," Merrick told the *Los Angeles Times*. "He wanted to make basic changes in the story and I could not accept that."

Marlon knew his Shakespeare and counted his sorrows as Hamlet did, not in single spies but in battalions. If he was out, so was Wally, who took the news badly and began drinking again. Merrick spread the word that Brando was more difficult and unmanageable than ever. Alberto Grimaldi picked this moment to pounce. With a combination of guile and promises to drop the lawsuit, he enticed Marlon to play the lead in a new film to be directed by Bernardo Bertolucci.

The son of an Italian professor and cinema critic, Bertolucci had the appearance and demeanor of a leading man. He was instead a filmmaking wunderkind, already renowned for meticulous camera work, use of symbolic colors to emphasize the emotional content of the narrative, and lively, audacious editing. His most celebrated feature, *The Conformist,* took Alberto Moravia's novel and gave it new life, tracking the backward slide of a young man in Mussolini-run Italy who buries his homosexual past and joins the Fascists. The price for his "normality" is a job as assassin. His quarry: a former professor, judged to be an enemy of the state.

A succès d'estime, the feature established Bertolucci as a major European director. He backed away from American offers—he called Hollywood "the big nipple"—but found himself short of money. Grimaldi became his banker and savior. For Alberto could not only supply financing, but supply Marlon Brando by entirely forgiving the star's debt and throwing in a $250,000 salary plus 10 percent of the gross after the movie broke even. Bertolucci was not as excited as the producer had hoped. Jean-Louis Trintignant, star of *The Conformist,* had been his first choice to play Paul, the lead in Bertolucci's new sexual drama. But as Bernardo remembered it, "He told me in tears he couldn't be naked on film. Then I tried Jean-Paul Belmondo, Alain Delon. Belmondo said it was a porn script. Delon wanted to be the producer." So it came down to Marlon after all. As so many others had done, Bernardo approached the American gingerly—he and Marlon had once met in Paris, but at the time the young director had been too awed to speak up. The impression he'd gotten was of a man absurdly reduced in size. Bernardo had seen *Viva Zapata!* as a youth, and in his mind the American was sixty feet tall.

In the fall of 1971 Bertolucci made a house call. He and Marlon went over the broad outlines of the scenario, reshaped to accommodate Brando's appearance and background. Paul, a middle-aged American expatriate, small-time boxer, onetime actor and drummer, wanders the streets of Paris, despondent over the suicide of his adulterous French wife. They had owned a rundown hotel; today his life has lost whatever meaning it had. He learns of an apartment for rent and goes to see it. As it happens, a liberated twenty-year-old, Jeanne, is looking over the same flat. She and her fiancé, a talentless New Wave filmmaker, need a place to live. Paul and Jeanne meet by chance in this gray, unfurnished place—and light it up with a burst of impulsive, semi-clothed sex. Their brief encounter leads to a passionate and unbridled three-day affair.

Marlon had his doubts; Bernardo gently pressed on, attempting to win his listener's confidence, much as Truman Capote had done. Both men wanted something from Marlon; the difference was that the writer had aimed for exposure and humiliation, and the director looked for revelation and art. Bernardo and Marlon conversed for two weeks, first with the Italian speaking of his upbringing, his adolescent fantasies—he dreamed of sex without consequence, having an intense liaison with a woman he didn't know and who didn't know him. He went on about his experience with Freudian analysis and his love of nihilistic literature. Bertolucci was fondest of the novelist Louis-Ferdinand Céline, whose protagonists embraced sex but despised love ("In this world we spent our time killing or adoring, or both together. 'I hate you! I adore you!' As if it were the greatest of pleasures to perpetuate ourselves"), and the sadomasochistic maunderings of Georges Bataille, a writer proud of his moral numbness: "How sweet to enter the filthy night and proudly wrap myself in it. The whore I went with was as uncomplicated as a child and she hardly talked. There was another one, who came crashing down from a tabletop—sweet, shy, heartbreakingly tender, as I watched her with drunken, unfeeling eyes."

Gradually Bernardo induced Marlon to drop his guard and address the anguish of his own formative years. The Brando parents and siblings entered the conversation. Only Marlon's children were left unmentioned; he considered them works in progress and kept his worries and guilt bottled up. They were fit subjects for a psychotherapist, not a film director. The Italian was captivated, both by the disclosures and the secrets: "I had at my disposal a great actor with all the technical expertise any director would require. But I also had a mysterious man waiting to be discovered in all the richness of his personal material." Bertolucci wanted Dominique Sanda to play Jeanne. When she announced her pregnancy he interviewed scores of ingenues until he found one with the appropriate sexual dazzle. Maria Schneider had to meet with Marlon's approval, however, and when Marlon showed up in Paris, great care was given to the way she auditioned before him. At one point Maria was asked to remove her clothes; she obliged without a moment's hesitation, unselfconscious and insouciant. Bernardo dubbed her "a Lolita, but more perverse." Marlon agreed. She was used to that label. The illegitimate daughter of actor Daniel Gélin, Maria had been an unsupervised teenybopper from the age of fifteen, living in Montparnasse communes, swinging with male and female partners, trying her luck as a painter, fashion model, and would-be starlet. Maria and Marlon hit it off immediately. He dragged her off to a zinc bar and advised, "We're going to go through quite a lot together, so let's not talk. Just look me in the eye as hard as you can." The next day flowers arrived with a note from Marlon and from then on, Maria said, "he was just like Daddy." She did not mean to imply an incestuous relationship. Physically, Marlon exerted no appeal. Running her hand down her torso to her midriff, she told a *Time* reporter, "He's almost fifty, you know, and he's only beautiful to here."

As soon as filming began, Bertolucci experienced the problems of every Brando director since Kazan: Marlon steadfastly refused to memorize his part. The customary cards were strategically scattered around the set where they could be easily spotted. Rather than force the star to mend his ways, Bernardo accommodated them. During Paul's monologue over the body of his wife, for example, the widower casts his eyes upward. The edit makes him seem to be petitioning heaven; actually Marlon was looking for a piece of paper overhead, checking out the lines before he spoke them. Schneider was not exactly a director's dream either; she hung around with the friends of her youth, getting stoned at night and showing up late the next morning.

No one seemed to care, least of all Bertolucci. He deliberately excluded her from any discussions of the script. Only Marlon was allowed to add or subtract dialogue as he chose. Bertolucci tried to shoot in sequence, and the first footage was not promising. The opening scene showed Marlon trying to drown out the sound of an overhead train by screaming out, "Fucking God!" That vehement reaction, noted Bernardo, "was Marlon's idea. He started at such a violent pitch, I thought, 'I cannot work with this actor.' My fear lasted all that week. Then Marlon said he was feeling the same thing about me. From then on, everything went very well."

Marlon also went over some scenes with friends at his rented *rive gauche* apartment. Christian Marquand saw that "forty years of Brando's life experience" was going into the film: "Brando talking about himself, being himself. His relations with his mother, father, children, lovers, friends." In one such interlude, Paul tells Jeanne about his upbringing. "My father was a drunk, tough, whore-fucker, bar fighter, supermasculine and he was tough. My mother was very, very poetic and also a drunk. All my memories of when I was a kid was of her being arrested, nude. We lived in this small town, a farming community . . . I'd come home after school. . . . She'd be gone, in jail or something . . . and then I used to have to milk a cow every morning and every night, and I liked that. But I remember one time I was all dressed up to take this girl to a basketball game and my father said, 'You have to milk the cow.' I asked him, 'Would you please milk it for me?' And he said, 'No. Get your ass out there.' I was in a hurry, didn't have time to change my shoes, and I had cow shit all over my shoes. It smelled in the car . . . and I can't remember very many things."

A friend asked him about that particular real-life incident: "Marlon, why didn't you just wipe the cow shit off your shoes? You had time for that."

The reply came in the form of an inquiry: "You've never really hated, have you? When you hate like I do, you have to suffer the pain."

Pain and humiliation were the guiding principles of *The Last Tango in Paris*. Marlon had exposed some of his internal anguish in *The Men*, *Streetcar*, and *Waterfront*. But now he went all the way, referring directly to his upbringing, speaking of his mortality, yoking sex and terror. Paul asks Jeanne to penetrate him anally with her fingers because he wants to "look death right in the face . . . go right up into the ass of death . . . till you find the womb of fear." He talks of his "hap-penis" but shows no sign of joy no matter how overheated the lovemaking. Sometimes the misery is turned inward: "What the hell, I'm no prize," confesses Paul. "I got a prostate as big as an Idaho potato, but I'm still a good stick man. I don't have any friends, and I suppose if I hadn't met you, I'd be ready for a hard chair and a hemorrhoid." At times the masochism turns to sadism, as in a scene that was to become notorious, Paul sodomizes Jeanne with the aid of a stick of butter. Joy is always accompanied by humiliation, and, in the end, Paul's early declaration "We're going to forget everything we know. No names, nothing. Everything outside this place is bullshit" is shown to be false. Obsessed with Jeanne, he seeks her out when she returns to her fiancé. The young woman has had enough of this fixated older man; terrified, she guns him down. Much was made of a last detail, when Paul removes a wad of gum from his mouth and parks it on a banister before his final breath.

Unquestionably, Marlon's was a mature performance, made more so in contrast to Maria's self-indulgent twaddle and Bertolucci's soft-core demand that Paul and Jeanne copulate on camera. Marlon absolutely refused. "If that happens," he pointed out, "our sex organs become the centerpiece of the film." Yet for all the provocative scenes and inventive staging, *Last Tango* had an adolescent soul. In *Tea and Sympathy,* an instructor's wife comments on the self-annihilating term papers of pubescent boys: "So intense! These kids would die for love or almost anything else. . . . Failure; death! Dishonor; death! Lose their girls; death!" The latest Bertolucci film was marked by the same sort of overheated narcissism.

No matter; death, as well as sex, has always sold well, and buzz about the film began long before its October 1972 release. Invited to a private screening, one academic interpreted *Last Tango* as a secular confessional, with Marlon as sinner and penitent. Another observed that the director, hypnotized by the paintings of Francis Bacon, had lit the interiors with sharp red and yellow contrasts, and made Brando into one of those agonized, half-eviscerated Baconian martyrs, "who show on their faces all that is happening in their guts." A third felt that the difference in the lovers' ages showed the cruelty of the clock, very much in the style of Malcolm de Chazal, the French aphorist: "She gave herself, he took her; the third party was time, who made cuckolds of them both." Paul can brutalize Jeanne, he maintained, but she has a longer stay on earth. Which is why, as victim turned victimizer, she predicts that in ten years he'll be in a wheelchair. In a delphic Hemingway style, Marlon commented, "This is a true film. I'll add that it is humane and poetic. In our daily life almost everything is squalid, scandalous or odious. Things which are too true always give us a sense of annoyance, of nausea, and this film is true." Ingmar Bergman had a unique interpretation. To the Swedish director, *Last Tango* was a closeted story of two homosexuals. "If you think about it in those terms, the film becomes very, very interesting. Except for her breasts, that girl, Maria Schneider, is just like a young boy. There is much hatred of women in this film, but if you see it as being about a man who loves a boy, you can understand it." He added that the filmmakers would have been "very courageous if they had made it with a boy. As it is now, it makes no sense as a film." Schneider may have edged closer to the truth when she said simply, "Bertolucci was in love with Marlon Brando, and that's what the movie was about. We were acting out Bernardo's sex problems, in effect trying to transfer them to the film." What the hell, the actress reminded listeners, she was bisexual; she had slept with twenty women and fifty men and damn well knew what she was saying.

5

The squalid, the scandalous, and the odious were waiting to happen off-camera as well. In the latter stages of filming *Last Tango,* Marlon learned that while Anna Kashfi had further descended into a haze of pills and alcohol, Christian's litany of behavioral problems ranged from substance abuse, to attacking classmates, to setting fire to a dorm at his private school in California. And now he had vanished. Anna claimed to know nothing about the youth's disappearance. In fact she knew everything. Afraid that Marlon would try to gain custody of Christian, she had arranged to have the boy spirited out of the States and into Mexico.

Marlon hired a private detective who scoured Baja California, paying informers, flying over the region in a helicopter in search of an encampment. He spotted a tent, landed, enlisted some local police, and raided the place. Five men were at the site, unarmed and apprehensive. They objected loudly to this invasion of privacy, but the *federales* were in no mood to indulge them, and one of the five soon gave the plot away, nodding at the tent. The cops kicked aside a pile of dirty clothing and found Christian, trembling with fever. Aware that cooperation was the only way they could escape long prison sentences, Christian's "guardians" confessed that Anna had promised them $10,000 to kidnap her son, taking him out of his father's reach.

Another court battle began when Christian was taken back to California. The press followed it day by day, announcing in the end that Marlon had been granted sole custody for the next year. Guilty, angry, almost as confused as the thirteen-year-old, he took his son to France, then to Tetiaroa, where his latest family had been holed up all these years. Under a benign tropical sun, Christian played with his little half-siblings Cheyenne and Teihotu, and got pampered by his stepmother Tarita. Marlon was keen to have his oldest boy on the island; in his opinion American teenagers were "the most conformist of people, anything but radical. You've got to learn the right words, dress the right way." When he was satisfied that Christian was zigzagging back to normal, he hied him to Sun Valley, Idaho, in a further attempt "to maintain the kid's health and straighten him out." As the straightening process got under way, Marlon's attention was distracted by the intrusions he hoped to avoid. Advance word on *The Godfather* was euphoric. Newspapers and networks sought face time with the man who had played the title role. Marlon bided his time, waiting for the reviews. Within a week the film was on its way to legendary status.

In subsequent years, numerous historians claimed that *The Godfather* met with unanimous raves. That was far from the case. *National Review* critic John Simon, notoriously hard to please, said that the film was disfigured by its "basic dishonesty." It showed the Mafia "mostly in extremes of heroic violence or sweet family life. Even the scenes of intimidation are grand and spectacular. Missing is the banality of evil, the cheap, ugly racketeering that is the mainstay of organized crime." The acting, he went on, was predominantly good, with the exception of Marlon Brando, who displayed "a weak, gray voice, a poor ear for accents, and an unrivaled capacity for hamming things up by sheer underacting—in particular by unconscionably drawn-out pauses. Only when the character is near death does Brando's wheezing performance lumber into sense."

In *The New Republic*, Stanley Kauffmann complained, "They have put pudding in Brando's cheeks and dirtied his teeth, he speaks hoarsely and moves stiffly, and these combined mechanics are hailed as great acting. Like star, like film, the keynote is inflation. *The Godfather* was made from a big bestseller, a lot of money was spent on it, and it runs over three hours. Therefore, it's important."

Vogue called the movie an "overblown, pretentious, slow and ultimately tedious quasi-epic. The gangsters have their *Greatest Story Ever Told*, but minus [director] George Stevens."

In *New York* magazine, Judith Crist held *The Godfather* to be "dangerous." The function of the film was "to show us that Hitler is a grand sort of family man, gentle with children, daring and ruthless with enemies, implacable in the matter of honor and so loyal to the ties of blood that even a brother-in-law, to a sister's sorrow, must go (juicily garroted) if he happens to have betrayed a son of the house." Still, she added drily, "you can't say the trash doesn't get first-class treatment."

The naysayers were drowned out by their colleagues and overwhelmed by public opinion. *Variety*'s rave was strictly business: "With several million hardcover and paperback books acting as trailers, Paramount's film version of Mario Puzo's sprawling gangland novel, *The Godfather,* has a large pre-sold audience. This will bolster the potential for the film which has an outstanding performance by Al Pacino and a strong characterization by Marlon Brando in the title role." *Time* praised *The Godfather* as "that rarity, a mass entertainment that is also great movie art"; *Newsweek* zeroed in on Marlon: In the 1950s "he was hailed as the greatest actor of his generation. Now the king has come to reclaim his throne." Pauline Kael set up a reclamation project in *The New Yorker*: "Is Brando marvelous? Yes he is, but then he often is; he was marvelous a few years ago in *Reflections in a Golden Eye,* and he's shockingly effective as a working-class sadist in *The Nightcomers,* though the film itself isn't worth seeing." No one has aged better on camera than Marlon Brando, she went on; "he gradually takes Don Vito to the close of this life, when he moves into the sunshine world, a sleepy monster, near to innocence again. The character is all echoes and shadings, and no noise; his strength is in that armor of quiet." And in an unprecedented piece entitled BRAVO, BRANDO'S *GODFATHER*, *New York Times* critic Vincent Canby not only hailed the star's comeback, but took some of his colleagues to task: "After a very long time, in too many indifferent or half-realized movies, giving performances that were occasionally becalmed but always more interesting than the material, Marlon Brando has finally connected with a character and a film that need not embarrass America's most complex, most idiosyncratic film actor, nor those critics who have wondered, in bossy print, what ever happened to him."

Marlon's champions won the day. For on *The Godfather,* they pointed out, he had done his thing and, after a string of unmitigated disasters, this time his thing had worked big-time. He had created a whole man on the screen, an aging, contradictory patriarch capable of ethical behavior as well as ruthless dispatch, an authority figure who exuded clout but knew when to let the next generation take over, an immigrant who was no stranger to capital crime, but whose dislike of the drug trade made him an anomaly among the other dons. There was another element to the actor's renaissance. The exquisite timing, which for so long had eluded Marlon, had returned. More than his talent, more than Coppola's vision, what made *The Godfather* so profoundly effective was its moment of release. Just as the film showed across the country in late spring and early summer, a pervasive malaise spread across the land. The Vietnam War was at its end game; North Vietnam forces had crossed the DMZ into the south. President Richard Nixon, in desperation, had ordered the mining of Haiphong Harbor. The anti-war movement, once the province of the draftable young and the New Left, was joined by middle-class citizens, fed up with phony, euphoric reports from the battlefield and empty promises of peace. The Club of Rome published its report *The Limits of Growth*, warning that Western civilization could not go on with its profligate, irresponsible ways. Paranoid politics stained the presidential campaign. Up for reelection, Nixon worried aloud about Democrats who wanted to usurp his power in the upcoming election. The President's operatives went into covert action, attempting to spy on the opposition, and were caught red-handed. From the White House, denials of official involvement were issued on an almost weekly basis, but with each press conference the administration's credibility weakened. The plot would unravel to become the scandal of Watergate. As if to lend credence to *The Godfather*, mafioso Joey Gallo was shot to death at Umberto's Clam House in Manhattan's Little Italy. The bullets didn't stop there. Governor George Wallace, a lifelong opponent of integration, was shot by a deranged gunman.

New York City Mayor John Lindsay directed his fire at the United States itself: "The insane attack upon George Wallace is yet another terrible and inevitable example of the violence of our nation. From the needless neglect of our most pressing national needs, we have reaped a harvest of division, despair and death." In a *Times* op-ed column, Tom Wicker sought to blame the action of a potential assassin on "violent western movies, the organized violence of professional football, the endless lines around theaters showing *The Godfather*." Attackers of that film agreed with Wicker; they spoke of its apologia for murder and revenge. Defenders pointed out, as Marlon had done for so long, that

The Godfather offered no such rationale. It was instead a metaphor for the United States, with its heritage of vigilantism and feudal retribution, its massive corporations beyond the reach of the law. The message of the film resided in its opening line, they insisted, spoken not by the Don but by one of his supplicants. "I believe in America," says an entrepreneur. "America has made my fortune. And I raised my daughter in the American fashion." When that daughter was beaten by two men, "I went to the police, like a good American. These two boys were brought to trial. The judge sentenced them to three years in prison—suspended sentence. Suspended sentence! They went free that very day! I stood in the courtroom like a fool. And those two bastards, they smiled at me. Then I said to my wife, for justice, we must go to Don Corleone."

Predictably, the debate served only to lengthen lines around the theaters. A lot of ticket buyers were already pre-sold, as *Variety* suggested, because they were fans of the Puzo novel. Those who hadn't read the book found that the movie could stand by itself, a vigorous tale well told, with an outstanding cast and high-gloss production. In addition, they found the post–World War II period of *The Godfather,* with its uneasy shifts of power, its nouveau riche racketeers and Senate investigations, eerily appropriate to their own time. Less than a month after its release, the film had earned more than four times its original cost of $6.2 million. No Hollywood product had ever risen so rapidly. In the first year of release the film grossed $81 million in North America alone. By the end of the year, the catchphrases of the Don and his family had permanently entered the public vocabulary: "I'm gonna make him an offer he can't refuse"; "Keep your friends close, and your enemies closer"; "Leave the gun, take the cannoli."

As always with Marlon, extravagance ruled. When things went bad—as in the case of lawsuits by ex-wives, the misbehavior of alienated children, financial difficulties, and a litany of cinematic failures—waste and tragedy defined the Brando image. When things went right—as in the lustrous years when his career began, and here in 1972—the superstar was spotlighted with a golden gel. The rise of *The Godfather* in the spring and summer of that year was followed by an epochal screening of *Last Tango* at the New York Film Festival. Attended by every important movie critic in the country, it elicited some of the most febrile responses in the history of cinema.

The national controversy was kicked off by Pauline Kael's review in

The New Yorker. The night of the New York Film Festival presentation, October 14, 1972, she wrote, was comparable to the evening of May 29, 1913, when Stravinsky's *Le Sacre du Printemps* had its premiere. The movie had "the same kind of hypnotic excitement as the *Sacre*" and Bertolucci and Brando had "altered the face of an art form." Semicoherently, she went on: The audience is "watching *Brando* throughout this movie, with all the feedback that that implies, and his willingness to run the full course with a study of the aggression in masculine sexuality and how the physical strength of men lends credence to the insanity that grows out of it gives the film a larger, tragic dignity." As for Schneider, when "she lifts her wedding dress to her waist, smiling coquettishly as she exposes her pubic hair, she's in a great film tradition of irresistibly naughty girls."

Kael was to be criticized not for her opinions but for her reportage. She had seen an earlier version. In her review she mentioned Paul "on all fours barking like a crazy man-dog to scare off a Bible salesman who has come to the flat." No such scene was in the finished movie. It had landed on the cutting-room floor. Bertolucci told the *Times*, "Pauline said, 'You shouldn't have done this to me,' but I never liked that scene. It was meant to be funny, but it was sad, terribly embarrassing somehow. A little too phony. I've never seen a Bible salesman in Paris. That was just a scriptwriter's perversion."

Looking back, Marlon decided that Kael, "unconsciously, gave more to the film than was there." Nevertheless, he went out of his way to call her a talented reviewer with a worthy passion. As well he might. She had helped to restore his depleted bank accounts. For what happened after her rave was a kind of mass hysteria, with Kael's acolytes—irreverently labeled "Paulettes" within the business—amplifying her views in national newspapers. United Artists reproduced her four-thousand-word review verbatim, turning it, in effect, into advertising copy. Next came full-throated cheerleading from the newsmagazines. No one was going to put *them* alongside the unsophisticated Parisians of 1913 who had hooted at *Printemps*. *Newsweek* critic Paul D. Zimmerman assured his readers that *Last Tango* was "a genuine masterpiece of staggering proportions." In a lavishly illustrated cover story entitled SELF-PORTRAIT OF AN ANGEL AND MONSTER—the words Bertolucci used to describe his star—*Time* editor Christopher Porterfield wrote, "For boldness and brutality, the intimate scenes are unprecedented in feature films. Frontal nudity, four-letter words, masturbation, even sodomy—Bertolucci dwells uncompromisingly on them all with a voyeur's eye, a moralist's savagery, an artist's finesse." (Thousands of readers disagreed; cancellations followed, usually with a terse explanation: "Since you have stooped to pimping for B-rated peep-show-type movies, this is my last tango with *Time*." "Minutes after my *Time* came, I threw it into the refuse can, whereupon the rest of the garbage got out and walked away." "Where have all the flowers gone? They have wilted into a stinking pile of compost nurtured by irresponsibility, disrespect, laziness, greed and moral decay exemplified by *Time*'s feature story on *Last Tango*.")

The film's profitability rose in direct proportion to its notoriety. A court in Bologna issued a ban: "Obscene content offensive to public decency . . . catering to the lowest instincts of the libido, dominated by the idea of stirring unchecked appetites . . . permeated by scurrilous language." Copies were impounded and destroyed, Bertolucci's civil rights were revoked for five years, and he received a four-month suspended jail sentence. In England the film was the first to be brought to trial under the Obscene Publications Act (the prosecution was dropped after a judge ruled that *Last Tango* was a movie rather than a publication). In the United States, the Catholic Conference placed *Last Tango* on its list of condemned movies. And in Cincinnati, city elders declared the movie to be obscene and theaters stopped showing it.

Given the wild reception, *Last Tango* couldn't fail to show a profit. This one was immense. By the time the dust settled, Marlon had pocketed some $4 million. At this moment the recovered Laurence Olivier was starring in the trivial mystery *Sleuth* and Richard Burton wasted his time and talent in *Bluebeard* and *The Assassination of Trotsky*. Marcello Mastroianni, as always, was doing honorable, original work in Fellini's *Roma* and the World War II drama *Massacre in Rome*. But these were art-house movies that escaped public attention. Marlon Brando was alone at the top. Of course, because it was Brando his stature could not go unquestioned. There were questions about his performance in the Bertolucci film, for example. Was it in fact an impersonation? Or was Paul just a condensed version of Marlon, spewing forth his contempt for social hypocrisy—and for what he had become since the early days? Richard Schickel made the shrewdest assumption: "In the formal sense, this was not really acting, but it was an astonishing act of self-assertion. For Brando had taken it all—his conceptions and misconceptions of himself, our conceptions and misconceptions about the same subject—and made a role of the mess." Whether *Last Tango* mattered as much to the rest of the world as it did to Kael was irrelevant. The film had not only underwritten Marlon's radical credentials; it had renewed his license as a sexual renegade. The erotic persona—the one that had been so instrumental in his early success—had returned, giving him new life at the age of forty-eight. Audiences now regarded him as an amalgam of the fictional Stanley Kowalski and Johnny Strabler and Terry Malloy *and* the real Marlon Brando. Nothing was sexier than that. He was richer than he had ever been. And as if all this were not sufficient, he was considered a lock for Best Actor at the upcoming Academy Awards ceremony. It would not do for a revolutionary to get himself up in a tuxedo and march up to the stage to accept his statuette. He fretted about that for weeks. And then an idea came to him.

An Intense and Hopeless Despair

1

At long last Marlon felt Christian was ready to go back to school. He saw the boy off, packed up, and headed for Tetiaroa—only to turn back when terrible news arrived. Besides Frannie and Jocelyn, only one person had truly known Marlon from the days he was known as Bud, the wayward kid from Omaha. Frannie was more than a thousand miles away, involved in her own exurban life. Jocelyn, even though she lived in Los Angeles, had finally kicked her habit and now counseled other alcoholics. "She was close to Marlon geographically," confided a friend, "but not spiritually." That left Wally Cox, and suddenly, on February 15, 1973, he was gone, dead of a heart attack at the age of forty-seven. The Walrus had been depressed about his fading career and deteriorating marriage. Rumors of suicide circulated, unconfirmed by the Los Angeles coroner.

The childhood cronies and New York City roommates had not been all that close in the last few years, but neither had they been alienated. Too many factors kept pushing them apart, celebrity on one side and the lack of it on the other, domestic miseries, professional obligations. *Child's Play* would have been a kick, working with Wally again. That went bust, and now it was too late to help the little guy. Grieving openly, Marlon caught a plane to L.A., all the while reconstructing the close friendship as if it had never suffered any lapses. "Here I am trying to save the world with all my noble causes," he lamented, "and I couldn't even save my best—my only—friend." After the cremation ceremony, Marlon, rather than the widow, Pat Cox, took possession of the ashes and kept them on his mantel. Wally "was my brother," Marlon told a reporter. "I talk to him all the time."

At the moment his noble cause was the commitment to an old interest: the plight of the American Indian. Marlon had broken off relations with the Panthers, but he had kept in touch with leaders of the American Indian Movement. In February, AIM and members of the Oglala Sioux poured into Wounded Knee on the Pine Ridge reservation of South Dakota. This was the site of the massacre of some three hundred Lakotan Indians in 1890. The idea was to call national attention to the bleak situation of the tribes. As soon as journalists arrived on the scene, spokesmen reminded them that the American Indians had been lied to since Benjamin Harrison occupied the White House. They had been rounded up and placed in reservations, a euphemism for concentration camps if ever there was one. Today their life expectancy was about two thirds of those of American Caucasians, and their rates of alcoholism and suicide were among the highest in the world. Yet thanks to a cherished Hollywood tradition, Native Americans were still being portrayed as savages in war paint, slayers of unarmed women and children on the Western frontier.

In conversation with two old acquaintances, AIM activists Russell Means and Dennis Banks, Marlon spoke of the disconnect between movie imagery and historical reality. They told him that someone had to make the world care about the American Indian, someone who could elicit attention. Marlon was the one who could do it. Together the men hatched a scheme. Marlon would endorse the organization's slogan: "The Red Giant is on one knee, but he's getting ready to stand up." And he would amplify it in a very public arena—the Academy Awards show. After consideration, Marlon began to get cold feet. He believed in the work of AIM, but any civil rights sermon would require a more authentic voice. Suppose a Native American were to deliver it in his place? Russell and Means had a suggestion. They knew an appropriate Indian woman, Sacheen Littlefeather. The twenty-six-year-old Indian possessed the right credentials. She had been born on a reservation. She had always been concerned for her people. She was very presentable and showed great poise in public situations. She could handle it. Marlon liked what he heard. He flew Littlefeather to L.A., worked out a routine, and arranged to have her attend the televised Academy Award ceremonies as his official representative.

On the night of March 27, 1973, Littlefeather showed up at the Dorothy Chandler Pavilion in Apache regalia, complete with buckskin dress and beads. The show's producer, Howard Koch, spotted Marlon's representative holding a fifteen-page speech in her hand. He attempted to head her off at the pass. Just before the announcement for Best Actor, Koch warned Littlefeather to keep her statement brief. Very brief. In fact, if she went on more than forty-five seconds, he would cut off her microphone and move the cameras elsewhere. When the name of the Best Actor was announced, Littlefeather spoke in a small, intimidated voice. "Marlon Brando has asked me to tell you, in a very long speech which I cannot share with you presently—because of time—but I will be glad to share with the press afterward, that he cannot accept this very generous award. And the reason for this being the treatment of American Indians today by the film industry and on television in movie reruns and also the recent happenings at Wounded Knee. I beg at this time that I have not intruded on this evening and that in the future our hearts and our understanding will meet with love and generosity. Thank you on behalf of Marlon Brando."

Scattered applause greeted her, quickly replaced by jeers. Marlon's Oscar refusal rippled throughout the rest of the evening. When Clint Eastwood announced *The Godfather* as Best Picture, he kept his tongue firmly in his cheek, demanding equal time for "all the cowboys shot in John Ford Westerns over the years." Raquel Welch, presenter of the Best Actress Oscar, said plaintively, "I hope the winner doesn't have a cause." Cohost Michael Caine criticized Marlon for "letting some poor Indian girl take the boos, instead of standing up and doing it himself." Charlton Heston, the other host, felt that in view of the academy's embrace of Marlon after years of coolness between them, what Marlon had done was "childish. The American Indian needs better friends than that." *Variety* considered *l'affaire* Brando an instance of unforgivable "rudeness." It developed, in the days to follow, that Littlefeather's credentials were more concerned with show business than with social causes. Gossip columnists delighted in pointing out that she had been named Miss Vampire in 1970, and that, despite her appearance, she was not a full-blooded Indian. Her mother claimed French, German, and Dutch forebears; it was her father who had ancestors from the White Mountain Apache and Yaqui tribes in Arizona.

That was all fine with Marlon. He had reconnected with Miko, the twelve-year-old he'd sired with Movita, and invited him to watch the awards show along with his half-brother Christian, now almost fifteen, in the comfort of their father's bedroom on Mulholland Drive. The trio enjoyed every minute, including the catcalls and jibes—all three knew the value of bad attention. Indeed, the forbidden speech Marlon wrote for Littlefeather gained worldwide circulation a day after she handed it to a reporter.

> For two hundred years we have said to the Indian people who are fighting for their land, their life, their families and their right to be free, "Lay down your arms, my friends, and then we will remain together. Only if you lay down your arms, my friends, can we then talk of peace and come to an agreement which will be good for you."
>
> When they laid down their arms, we murdered them. We lied to them. We cheated them out of their lands. We starved them. . . .
>
> Perhaps at this moment you are saying to yourself what the hell has all this got to do with the Academy Awards? Why is this young woman standing up here, ruining our evening, invading our lives with things that don't concern us, and that we don't care about?
>
> I think the answer to those unspoken questions is that the motion picture community has been responsible as any for degrading the Indian and making a mockery of his character, describing him as savage, hostile and evil. It's hard enough for children to grow up in this world. When Indian children watch television, and they watch films, and when they see their race depicted as they are in films, their minds become injured in ways we can never know.

Good points all, and backed with a vow: "I would have been here tonight to speak to you directly, but I felt that perhaps I could be of better use if I went to Wounded Knee to help forestall in whatever way I can the establishment of a peace which would be dishonorable as long as the rivers shall run and the grass shall grow."

The speech implied that Marlon would travel to South Dakota to stand alongside the new Indian warriors. He never showed up. The Brando version had it that the Pine Ridge reservation was surrounded by federal marshals, state policemen, deputized rangers, "any whites who wanted to hold a gun." He would add: "All I needed was to go to Wounded Knee and be arrested by them and give them an excuse to say I was part of a plot to make headlines. So I wasn't able to go." But Marlon was not through with AIM. On June 12, 1973, he appeared on *The Dick Cavett Show* along with representatives of the Cheyenne, Paiute, and Lummi tribes to reinforce their plea for fair and equitable treatment. And later in the year Marlon announced that he would oversee a feature about the siege at Wounded Knee. This would be Marlon Brando's "conclusive salute," his "retirement film." Abby Mann, scenarist of *Judgment at Nuremberg*, would write the script; Gillo Pontecorvo would handle the direction. Granted, Marlon informed the press, the Brando-Pontecorvo clash had been Homeric in the days of *Queimada*. But a mutual respect shone through even then, and in the actor's view no other talent could bring as much fervor and commitment to the AIM cause. Intrigued by Marlon's phone call, Pontecorvo came to Pine Ridge, where he met a group of glowering Sioux. The director beat a hasty retreat to Italy. "I thought they were going to scalp me," he said. In Marlon's words, "They scared the shit out of him. Indians are strange folks until you understand them." Martin Scorsese, fresh from *Mean Streets*, replaced Pontecorvo. He, too, was uncomfortable with the project. There were more discussions, meetings, wrangles over the script, negotiations about casting. They always ended in promises to film *Wounded Knee*. All along, Marlon stood bail for many Indians in trouble with the law, and attended trials when the AIM leaders were hauled before the court. But somehow the movie got stuck in development limbo, always a year away from going before the cameras.

So *Wounded Knee* would not be Marlon's last film after all. Three years after *Last Tango* he decided to work on an Arthur Penn movie costarring his Mulholland Drive neighbor Jack Nicholson. Penn was excited by the prospect of working with Brando again; they hadn't done anything together since *The Chase* nine years before. Nicholson couldn't wait to begin. Marlon was the indifferent one; he was interested only in the guaranteed $1.5 million salary plus a percentage of the gross. Recent visits to Tetiaroa had reignited his interest in developing the island as a green resort and biological laboratory. As far as he was concerned, *The Missouri Breaks* was just "Bucks and Company."

2

In theory, Marlon's twenty-eighth film would be his third straight winner. The scenario was by the Montana-based author Thomas McGuane, whose novels *The Sporting Club* and *The Bushwhacked Piano* had been praised as "Faulknerian." Jack Nicholson had been nominated four times for an Oscar in the Best Actor category. Penn, a top director since *Bonnie and Clyde* in 1967, had earned new laurels for his revisionist Western *Little Big Man*. In the cast were three fine character actors: Harry Dean Stanton, Frederic Forrest, and Randy Quaid.

As usual in the film business, things were not as they seemed. McGuane had a prior commitment; he was out of the country and thus unavailable for script changes. Some of these alterations were needed to fill holes in the plot, and Robert Towne, who had tweaked the *Godfather* script, obligingly made them. Others had to be put in to accommodate Marlon's eccentricities. His character, Robert E. Lee Clayton, a man defined by McGuane as a "border-ruffian-turned-contract-killer," was unstable at best. Marlon made him into a cross-dressing psychopath. Absent for the first half hour of the movie, Clayton enters on horseback, dangling upside down, caparisoned in white buckskin, Littlefeather-style. He speaks in an Irish accent for no apparent reason. Over the next hour, also for no apparent reason, Clayton assumes the intonation of a British upper-class twit and an elderly frontier woman, complete with granny dress and matching bonnet. Penn, who believed in letting actors do their thing, indulged Marlon all the way. Sometimes the lack of discipline paid off—in a bathtub scene, with Clayton sloshing around like a voluptuous whale, the ad-libbing is very funny. On other occasions, though, Marlon's high-camp performance threw his costar. "Jack would get frustrated by some of the stuff that Marlon was doing," Penn confided. "Every once in a while, it would catch him unawares."

It caught the others unawares, too, and the director's blithe comment was a synonym for disaster: "If you want a simple, clear, coherent narrative, *Missouri Breaks* ain't it." Penn intended to make an anti-Western, a companion piece to *Little Big Man*, with its genocidal attacks on Indians and a sociopathic General George Armstrong Custer. There were a few instances where Penn realized his objective. The unspoiled Missouri background gradually turns to an outreach of Hell, animated by vengeance and littered with corpses. John Williams's dark, challenging score underlines the violence of the place and period. But for the most part, *The Missouri Breaks* is out of control and looks it.

Reviewers were extremely unkind. John Simon coiled and struck. As Clayton, Marlon was "utterly lamentable . . . even more slatternly and self-indulgent than his bloated physique." Vincent Canby criticized his favorite for having no "apparent connection to the movie that surrounds him. Brando grabs our attention but does nothing with it." This was kindness itself compared with British notices. *The Observer* called Marlon's performance "one of the most extravagant displays of *grande-damerie* since Sarah Bernhardt," and *The Sun* complained, "Marlon Brando at fifty-two has the sloppy belly of a sixty-two-year-old, the white hair of a seventy-two-year-old, and the total lack of discipline of a precocious twelve-year-old."

What eluded the critics was Marlon's continuing vulnerability and his willingness to show it to the world. When he was young, slim, and handsome, distress was written on his face and in his performances. He made no attempt to hide his troubled psyche, or his lack of defenses; indeed, they were what made the early films so exciting to audiences and reviewers. Now, more disturbed than ever, weighed down by responsibilities, succumbing to heartache and the thousand natural shocks that flesh—particularly his flesh—was heir to, he still allowed viewers to see the whole Brando, a man at risk, a vastly overweight, compulsive figure for whom meals had become what strong drink had been to his parents. Because he no longer had the attractive qualities of youth, he made reviewers and sometimes audiences uncomfortable. But it was the same man with the same extraordinary aptitude for inhabiting a character, just older and heavier. Even though his late work was met with disapproval, a reexamination shows that often, in the middle of the most pedestrian scene, there would be a sudden, luminous occurrence, a flash of the old Marlon that showed how capable he remained. However difficult he was with directors—ever the father figures in his life—he became generous to the actors he respected, happy to dispense advice, but only when asked. According to his lights in the 1970s, if the reviewers or the public didn't understand, that was their loss, not his.

When work was done he shifted his attention to the one area of life untainted by egos, contracts, and capitalism—Tetiaroa. At night, when all was serene, he lost himself in the ether. As a ham radio operator known only as Martin Brandeaux, licenses KE6PZH and FO5GJ, he chatted with other amateur radio operators, altering his voice, kidding around, slipping free of his movie-star identity. The irony was, to keep the island pristine he would need money. Marlon knew of only one way to fund his dreams: acting in films. Any films, as long as the studios would meet his salary requirements.

In the late spring of 1975 he signed to appear as Jor-El, father of the Man of Steel in *Superman*. The producers felt that Brando was still a magic name even though advance word on *The Missouri Breaks* was negative, and offered a highly agreeable $3 million. Six months later Marlon signed another contract, for even more money—$3.5 million— to play the part of Kurtz in Francis Ford Coppola's *Apocalypse Now*, said to be an epic retelling of Joseph Conrad's *Heart of Darkness*, set during the Vietnam War.

With promised riches coming his way, Marlon settled down on the island. At his side were his third wife, Tarita, and the children she had been raising more or less alone, seven-year-old Cheyenne and fourteen-year-old Teihotu. The environmental movement was then in full swing, echoing UN Secretary General U Thant's official proclamation of 1970: "May there only be peaceful and cheerful Earth Days to come for our beautiful Spaceship Earth as it continues to spin and circle in frigid space with its warm and fragile cargo of animate life." The frailty of the planet was the subject of endless discussions and demonstrations. The Clean Air Act was now in force, along with laws to protect drinking water, the oceans and the wilderness.

Marlon interpreted these activities as a sign that he was again on the cutting edge of a new social awareness. About time, too. His efforts at turning Tetiaroa into a commercial Eden had gone awry. Twenty-one thatched-roof huts had been constructed on his orders, and with his help. Three bars and a dining room were included in the scheme, along with a staff of forty. Violent storms and tsunamis had finished that. And then there were the guests: "middle-aged ladies from Peoria telling me, 'Mr. Brando, we loved you as Napoleon'— Napoleon for Christ's sake—and asking for my autographs while their husbands shove me against the wall to pose with the little lady." A bad idea, he acknowledged, "and it was badly managed." But it didn't have to be this time. He had more money now, and could envision Tetiaroa reborn. It would be like Tahiti at the time of the H.M.S. *Bounty,* a sunshine oasis of breadfruit and coconuts, plentiful fish, protected wildlife, and respectful tourists. At his invitation, new consultants came and went, discussing nonpolluting power sources for the hotel, ecological improvements, fresh water sources.

Months later it became apparent that Tetiaroa and its owner were in a catch-22. If no energy-consuming amenities were available—flush toilets, electric lights, sports and entertainment facilities—visitors would be few and far between. Yet if these were put in place, the island would no longer be a paradise. It would be a Polynesian Vegas. Was the problem going to be insoluble after all? Then why had he bought the place? "I don't want to sit on an island like a meditative Buddha," he kept saying, but there seemed to be no other life left open to him if he stayed in the region. Fretting about it, he took off for Hollywood to work on his next movie.

Superman carried doom wherever he flew. Everyone said so. Jerry Siegel and Joe Shuster, the men who created the comic-book hero, were shortchanged of their royalties and lived in total obscurity while others grew rich off their invention. The men who played the role had met unhappy ends. Kirk Alyn, the Man of Steel in two 1940s serials, found few parts afterward and abandoned show business. George Reeves, star of the 1951 feature *Superman and the Mole-Men* and of a *Superman* television series later in the decade, also had trouble finding parts. He was found mortally wounded on June 14, 1959, a Luger nearby. The death was ruled a suicide. In April 1963 John F. Kennedy's staff approved a Superman story promoting the president's physical-fitness program. It was canceled after the president was assassinated in November.

Perhaps Marlon should have paid attention to the warnings, but he had his own authentic crises and couldn't be bothered with someone else's superstitions. Besides, the money was worth any risk. His contract specified a salary of $3.7 million, plus 11 percent of the domestic grosses and 5 percent of the foreign. Under the direction of Richard Donner, a TV director before breaking through in 1976 with *The Omen,* a wide-screen antichrist melodrama, Marlon did more than behave himself. As Superman's father, he gave his lines a biblical resonance. "Live as one of them, Kal-El," he intoned to the Spawn of Steel, "to discover where your strength and your power are needed. And always hold in your heart the pride of your special heritage. They can be a great people, Kal-El—they wish to be. They only lack the light to show the way. For this reason above all, their capacity for good, I have sent them you—my only son."

For what was essentially a special-effects feature, the film boasted some unusual assets. John Williams wrote a powerful score. A picture is only as good as its villain, and in the part of Lex Luthor, Gene Hackman made a memorable and amusing heavy. Ned Beatty, Jackie Cooper, Glenn Ford, Maria Schell, and Terence Stamp gave their parts a resonance missing in Mario Puzo's script, even after some slick alterations by Tom Mankiewicz. But *Superman*'s main strength came from performances by the paternal Marlon and the unripe Christopher Reeve (whose tragic fall from a show horse would later be cited as an instance of the Superman curse). Reeve's untroubled all-American good looks combined with a hint of other-worldliness. Brando, checking in at some three hundred pounds and outfitted with a white wig and green costume with enough yardage to make a pup tent, had the timbre and demeanor of a mythic deity.

Superman rose to the top one week after its opening. When the final tallies were in, the movie had grossed more than $300 million in the United States and more than $166 million in foreign markets. "I made about fourteen million dollars for less than three weeks' work," Marlon crowed. "When Alexander and Ilya Salkind, the producers, asked if they could use footage from the picture in a sequel, *Superman II,* I asked for my usual percentage, but they refused, and so did I." It didn't matter; he had participated in enough claptrap. Now he could concentrate all his energies on one important television show and one film of moral significance.

The TV program was *Roots: The Next Generations,* inspired by Alex Haley's bestselling novel of African American history and genealogy. Marlon had no interest in playing another heroic type. He delighted in impersonating the American neo-Nazi George Lincoln Rockwell, a plausible, cold-eyed fascist who would be assassinated by a onetime follower. Marlon received $25,000 for his work—the smallest fee he had collected in years. He also collected something else: his first and only Emmy.

3

In 1977, the anguish of the Vietnam War was still fresh in everyone's mind. Four presidents had been unable to stop the progress of Communist forces, despite heavy bombing under Lyndon Johnson and the illegal invasion of neutral Cambodia under Richard Nixon. Only two years before, the South Vietnamese position had collapsed, proving the CIA and American army intelligence wrong. They had predicted that South Vietnam would hold, and that its capital, Saigon, would remain safe from North Vietnamese forces. The collapse of South Vietnam began in March 1975; on April 21, an angry, weeping President Thieu resigned during an accusatory ninety-minute speech to the people of South Vietnam: "The United States has not respected its promises. It is inhumane. It is untrustworthy. It is irresponsible." Aided by the CIA, he was swiftly taken out of the country and exiled to Taiwan. A week later, President Gerald Ford ordered Operation Frequent Wind, a complete evacuation of American civilians and military personnel. With the main airport under heavy rocket and artillery fire, refugees had to be taken out by helicopter—the largest such airlift in history. Saigon fell on April 30, completing the American reversal. It was a costly and humiliating defeat: Fifty-eight thousand soldiers died in Vietnam and another three hundred and four thousand were casualties. The antiwar movement had triumphed, and all the windy assurances of the generals and the White House were swept into the dustbin of history. The words of the late Martin Luther King, Jr., were quoted everywhere: "One of the greatest casualties of the war is the Great Society . . . shot down on the battlefield of Vietnam."

The statement jibed with Marlon's enduring beliefs: "We could honestly believe that a people ten thousand miles from our shore were our dangerous enemies—so dangerous, in fact, that we had to lie that an American ship had been attacked in the Gulf of Tonkin by the North Vietnamese. It took ten or twelve years of a horrific war and tens of thousands of squandered lives to change this perception—even though I sometimes hear people insist that we made a mistake by withdrawing from Vietnam when we did because we did so without 'honor.' " So it was that Brando considered his work in *Apocalypse Now* to be more than a role, albeit a highly profitable one; it was "a duty" to appear as an imperialist American colonel in the movie. "I'm nearing the end of the line," he told a *Time* reporter. "I figure I've got about two shells left in the chamber." One shell was Francis's Vietnam movie. The other? "A picture I want to do about the American Indian."

Apocalypse Now began well, with scenarist John Milius and director Francis Ford Coppola updating *Heart of Darkness*. The British colonialists of nineteenth-century Africa became American soldiers in the swamps of Southeast Asia. The central character, Kurtz, was changed from a Belgian ivory trader gone savage to a U.S. army colonel gone mad.

Coppola knew that Orson Welles once contemplated an adaptation of *Heart of Darkness* and that other important filmmakers had also been attracted to the book. Their plans had fallen by the wayside long ago, and now the still-young filmmaker, with *The Godfather* and *The Godfather: Part II* to his credit, was about to have his way with the story. With high reputation and a generous budget, he cut a deal with Ferdinand Marcos, president of the Philippines, to film in the wild and to use the nation's military helicopters.

And then the discord began. *Apocalypse*'s narrator, Captain Willard, was to be played by Harvey Keitel. Coppola didn't like what he saw, fired the actor after two weeks on location, and replaced him with Martin Sheen. The script, which had never possessed a "through line," following logically from beginning to end, was frequently ignored. Actors, many of them drunk or stoned, started to wing it. Monsoon rains ruined the expensive sets. Sheen suffered a near-fatal heart attack. During a local insurgency Marcos took back his choppers. At the eleventh hour Marlon entered to play Walter E. Kurtz, the crackpot warrior who had crossed into Cambodia with a group of loyal mercenaries.

Brando's appearance shocked everyone. Cinematographer Vittorio Storaro was very familiar with Marlon; he had shot *Last Tango*. "It was not the image of Paul that I saw," he remembered, "but in his place a very nice, pale, gentle, middle-aged man—fat yet fragile—dressed in a canopy of light blue, with this thick cane." Coppola immediately realized that he couldn't have Marlon portray the character of Kurtz as written, "a kind of Green Beret turtle in uniform, because where would you get that uniform to fit him?" The director resolved to shoot his star from the waist up, then use a six-foot, six-inch double in distant shots to create the illusion that the colonel was massive rather than overweight.

Coppola thought Kurtz should be played exactly as Conrad had conceived him. Marlon demurred—that person would be out of place in a contemporary picture. The two men analyzed the part day after day, trying to determine what sort of individual the colonel was, how he was driven around the bend, what made him tick. "Marlon talked and talked and talked and talked and talked," said Coppola. "We did that for five days, and I realized suddenly Marlon only had a deal for three weeks and what he was doing, he was getting out of working."

Coppola determined to put his foot down. But on the fifth day, he remarked, "I come in and I'm astonished. He's cut off all his hair, which is the image of Kurtz from the book." So Brando was going to revert to the original conception after all. " 'But you told me that it wouldn't work, you said you read the book and it would never work.' And he says, 'Well, I didn't read the book,' and I said, 'But you told me you did,' and he says, 'Well, I lied.' "

Ill prepared, unrehearsed, Marlon then proceeded through pure intuition to create Conrad's fanatical recluse. The cinematography helped: A scene in *Last Tango* had used a tight close-up, with Storaro throwing his own shadow across Paul's face. Marlon remembered it well, and requested the same sort of lighting. "So in *Apocalypse*," Storaro said, "it's me in front of the camera, creating the black shadow so that bits of him can emerge, like truth emerging from matter." Marlon disliked the pages handed to him on the set and ad-libbed almost all of his speeches. Some were barely coherent. Others seemed Conradian in the best sense of the word—incantatory, mysterious, threatening. Face-to-face with Willard, the man sent to "terminate him with extreme prejudice," Kurtz is unafraid; to him, doom is as familiar as the night:

KURTZ: You have a right to kill me. You have a right to do that. But you have no right to judge me. It's impossible for words to describe what is necessary to those who do not know what horror means. Horror. Horror has a face, and you must make a friend of horror. Horror and moral terror are your friends. If they are not then they are enemies to be feared.

The colonel goes on to describe one such horror.

> We left the camp after we had inoculated the children for polio, and this old man came running after us and he was crying. . . . We went back there and they had come and hacked off every inoculated arm. They were in a pile. A pile of little arms. And I remember . . . I—I—I cried. I wept like some grandmother. I wanted to tear my teeth out. I didn't know what I wanted to do. . . . And then I realized—like I was shot—like I was shot with a diamond—a diamond bullet right through my forehead. And I thought: My God, the genius of that. The genius. The will to do that. Perfect, genuine, complete, crystalline, pure. And then I realized that they were stronger than we. . . . These were men, trained cadres. These men who fought with their hearts, who had families, who had children, who were filled with love—but they had the strength—the strength to do that. If I had ten divisions of those men our troubles here would be over very quickly. You have to have men who are moral—and at the same time who are able to utilize their primordial instincts to kill without feeling, without passion, without judgment. Without judgment. Because it's judgment that defeats us.

What had begun as extempore maundering had turned into a central truth. In the book, the last day of the colonel is recalled. He "discoursed. A voice! A voice! It rang deep to the very last. It survived his strength to hide in the magnificent folds of eloquence the barren darkness of his heart. . . . I saw on that ivory face the expression of somber pride, of ruthless power, of craven terror—of an intense and hopeless despair." Brando and Kurtz had become indistinguishable.

The day Marlon finished his last scenes he went to Manila to prepare for the voyage home. A messenger arrived with a disconcerting request. Francis wanted to use the last words spoken by Kurtz in the novel: "The horror! The horror!" and he needed his star for one more close-up. It would take no more than an hour. Replied Marlon, "Well, first of all, it's never an hour, you know that. And secondly, you'll have to pay for that day—seventy thousand dollars." He explained, "I'm in the Marlon Brando business, I sell Marlon Brando. Would you go to the president of General Motors and ask him for a seventy-thousand-dollar favor?"

Marlon's demand was met. He returned for the close-up and on

October 9, 1977, departed for Hong Kong, expecting to see a rough cut in a few months' time. By late summer of 1979, months after the triumph of *Superman, Apocalypse* was still in the process of looping—adding sound and dialogue at the Goldwyn studio in Hollywood. Coppola preferred to stay home during these sessions, delivering his instructions via intercom. With only a voice to argue with, Marlon needled the director. "What am I doing now?" he asked one morning, holding his middle finger in the air. Replied Francis, "Well, eventually we won't need actors. All we'll need is a file of Marlon Brando in a computer, and we won't need to go on location—we can just sit here and do anything we like with your image and your voice!" He was more accurate than he knew, but Marlon took it all in good spirits. For by then he had accumulated another $3 million.

Marlon told reporters that the reaction to *Apocalypse* meant nothing to him, but he was just handing them a line. He read every review—the pans as well as the raves. In the Chicago *Sun-Times* Roger Ebert called *Apocalypse* a "good and important film—a masterpiece, I believe." The ending, "with Brando's fuzzy, brooding monologues and the final violence, feels more satisfactory than any conventional ending possibly could." *Los Angeles Times* critic Charles Champlin added, "As a noble use of the medium and as a tireless expression of a national anguish, it towers over everything that has been attempted by an American filmmaker in a very long time." On the other hand, Frank Rich, writing in *Time*, excoriated the movie as "emotionally obtuse and intellectually empty. It is not so much an epic account of the grueling war as an incongruous, extravagant monument to artistic self-defeat." Vincent Canby used his column in *The New York Times* to extol with faint damns, calling *Apocalypse* a "stunning work," before categorizing it as "an adventure yarn with delusions of grandeur" and a "profoundly anticlimactic intellectual muddle," and pointing out that Marlon Brando had "no role to act." Tennessee Williams capped the chorus of nays by suggesting that Marlon had been paid by the pound.

Some of the negatives were brought on by Coppola himself. Referring to the tribulations in the Philippines, he said that his film was "not about Vietnam, it *was* Vietnam." That statement was not calculated to win the approval of veterans, who knew the difference between ego contests and a shooting war. Furthermore, a heavy air of pretension hung over the Kurtz sequences. The director insisted on using literary references like Sir James George Frazer's *The Golden Bough* to emphasize the legend of the man-god who must be killed when his powers lapse. Coppola not only placed the volume in Kurtz's quarters, but showed the book's dust jacket, even though anyone who ever visited a rain forest, let along a jungle, would know that such an item would have rotted away in a fortnight. As for Marlon's recital of T. S. Eliot ("We are the hollow men/We are the stuffed men/Leaning together/Headpiece filled with straw"), that was strictly term-paper stuff, as out of place as horn-rimmed glasses on a ritual mask.

Through *Apocalypse*'s up-and-down reception, no words came from Brando about the studio, the director, the cast. Not until *Life* magazine attacked him for his girth and avarice did he decide to fight back. Even then he felt that Coppola should do the complaining. Marlon drafted a letter in Francis's voice, claiming, "Far from demanding more than his usual fee, Marlon voluntarily cut his then customary cash fee by half (to one half of the amount [*Life* editors] report) in order to help with my budget problems." Peter Cowie, author of *The Apocalypse Now Book*, dryly reports, "Coppola appears to have ignored the appeal."

Worse was in store, this time in clothbound form. Late in 1979 Marlon's first wife, writing under the name Anna Kashfi Brando, published *Brando for Breakfast*. The book described her ex-husband's behavior before, during, and after their unhappy marriage, ending with a list of pejoratives. She considered Marlon "a dilettante of social justice" and "a jaded but still sophomoric recluse." One of Marlon's friends advised him to follow G. K. Chesteron's counsel: "Silence is the unbearable repartee," and for once the accused made no attempt to defend himself. Anna's book didn't sell well, and he took some consolation in that. But what afforded him greater pleasure was an opportunity to get back in the game. Having already played a Nazi twice, he went into full wrongo mode for *The Formula*. The fee: $3 million.

Mass demonstrations had recently wracked Iran, disrupting oil exports and ultimately forcing the Shah into exile. The new hard-line Islamic regime resumed shipments, but at a lower volume. The price of gasoline soared, resulting in what newspapers called "the panic at the pump." At the time, it was widely believed that the fuel shortages were caused as much by the oil companies as by political disruptions in the Middle East. Steve Shagan's suspenseful novel took full advantage of the situation: A detective uncovers a long-lost formula devised by the Nazis. It shows how to make gasoline from cheap synthetic products. Put to use, it would eliminate dependence on fossil fuel and make

oil companies as obsolete as the running board. One of those companies learns about the formula and attempts to destroy it, along with
anyone who gets in the way.

With George C. Scott as the sleuth and Marlon Brando as a malicious
oil baron, expectations were high. These were the only actors to have
turned down their Oscars; both were explosive mavericks who liked to
smash traditions and unnerve authority figures. But neither man
seemed involved in *The Formula*. Under John Avildsen's rather grace-
less direction, Scott was no more than an assembly-line protagonist. As
the heavy in every sense of the word, Marlon disregarded the script in a
new way. It was no longer necessary to paste his speeches on furniture
or cameras. He wore a hearing aid as part of his costume, and an assistant whispered the lines to him. Too many of those were cartoonish
("We're not in the oil business; we're in the oil *shortage* business"); all
the CEO lacked was the label GREED on the back of his suit jacket.

Marlon had bad feelings about this picture, and about all else.
Everything seemed stained by melancholia. One afternoon scenarist
Stewart Stern received an odd phone call from Brando, a man he considered a friend, but not an intimate. "He said, 'I don't know why I feel
the grief I feel.' I said, 'What is it?' And he said, 'Jimmy Durante. So
much sweetness. The funeral is tonight, do you want to go?' " When
they arrived at the ceremony, someone got word to the comedian's
widow. The two men were seated behind the family. "Marlon said,
'This is very unusual because I don't even know him.' He just wanted to
go quietly and pay tribute."

Reviews of *The Formula* did nothing to alleviate his despondency.
The picture opened in late 1980 and was universally slammed. Marlon's work had been edited down to three long interludes, leading critics to wonder if *anyone* was worth $1 million per scene. A Los Angeles
group nominated him for a Golden Raspberry award for his performance, and *Variety* scoffed at him for being "grotesquely fat and
ridiculous."

4

Jack Nicholson called it Bad Boy Hill; the tourists who came to gawk
knew it as Mulholland Drive, the former stomping ground of Errol

Flynn, and current locale of such wayward stars as Warren Beatty, Marlon Brando, and Nicholson himself. Thirteen years younger than Marlon, Nicholson had been an admirer of *The Men* and every Brando film to follow. When he moved to Mulholland he went out of his way to emulate Marlon and to cultivate his friendship. Marlon responded, and over the years watched Jack go from obscure character actor to leading man with more Academy Award nominations than even Laurence Olivier. Soon it was Marlon imitating Jack, acquiring a condominium at Bora-Bora right next to his fellow actor, making them neighbors in the South Seas as well as in Beverly Hills. Once more there was talk of new plans for Tetiaroa—a school for blind children, a hotel, an institute for oceanographers—and for finally making that film about the American Indian. Marlon mentioned a television project he had brought to ABC, entitled *The First American.* During an interview with Lawrence Grobel for *Playboy* magazine, Marlon went into detail about the plethora of ideas and the dearth of financing.

GROBEL: How are you researching it?

BRANDO: We've been on the road, listening to ancient and modern horror stories, looking at old sites, running down the facts of history, remembrances of old people, going to places where there were battles. In one massacre they cut off women's vulvas and wore them as hat bands.

GROBEL: How are you going to show that on television?

BRANDO: You can't. But there are other stories, of Indians getting arrested and assassinated in jail, then calling it suicide.

GROBEL: How long will each show be?

BRANDO: An hour and a half. Hopefully, there's gonna be thirteen or fourteen made. We shouldn't have to go around, hat in hand, scratching and tapping on doors, climbing over transoms, to get money to do a historical survey of the American Indian and how we reduced him to rubble. Jesus Christ!

But they did have to go around grubbing for backers, and thus far very few had turned up. Money was an issue just then, in part because the news from the West Coast was so depressing. Michael Cimino, director of *The Deer Hunter,* the only movie besides *Apocalypse Now* to effectively dramatize the Vietnam War, had just directed a debacle worse than *Mutiny on the Bounty. Heaven's Gate*, originally budgeted at $11 million, came in at $40 million and was the biggest box-office disaster in the history of United Artists. The wrecked studio was sold to MGM. Industry-wide, wary executives closed ranks. The era of the "high-concept" feature had already begun, with carefully assembled blockbusters like *Jaws* reaping enormous profits. From here on, such comic book epics as *Star Wars* would lead the way. Filmmakers, no matter how swollen their reputations, would have to come up with safe, lucrative ideas if they wanted to work. Odds against such projects as *The First American* grew longer by the month.

As usual when he was thwarted, Marlon turned his attention back to the island. Through lawyers he made a will. In the event of his death, most of the atoll would go to Christian, Cheyenne, Teihotu, and Brando's third wife, Tarita. The child he had with Movita went unmentioned. Christian would need some refuge; his life was in free fall. Early in 1981, at the age of twenty-three, he married Mary McKenna, a cosmetician. They lived with Marlon for a few months before going out on their own. A year later they separated; Christian had begun a new descent into drugs and alcohol. Marlon invited him to move in, and once again attempted to provide the support he had been denied by his own father. He paid Christian's debts, bought him a car, sent him to his own therapist, underwrote medical and dental bills. The young man hadn't graduated high school and his skills were few. Marlon helped to set him up as a tree surgeon, and came up with a new idea. Since he, too, was a high school dropout, father and son would get their correspondence-school diplomas at the same time, studying math, social science, history, and English together. Somehow, neither of them could work up the patience to study for the tests. The plan died of inanition.

During the same period Marlon tried to get another project going. The actor who had lately played powerful evildoers wanted to impersonate another. He had seen firsthand what drugs could do to youth: Christian's life was marred by them, and Bryan Englund, the son of George Englund (director of *The Ugly American*), had recently died of a drug overdose. Convinced that the CIA was suborned by drug lords, he thought to make an exposé in film form. Titling the project *Jericho*, he attempted to bang out a script with various scenarists. The last of the scenarists was a man as eccentric as Brando himself. Donald Cammell entered the scene with a backstory. He and Marlon had been introduced to each other back in the 1950s, when both were in Paris.

Originally the two men had gotten along. Then Cammell began seeing China Kong, the fourteen-year-old daughter of one of Marlon's girlfriends, Anita Kong. Marlon found out about it, and broke all relations with a man he condemned as a child molester. Not until Donald married China did the two begin speaking again. Cammell had since become a director of cult films, and Marlon thought he would make an ideal collaborator on *Jericho,* and indeed on other works including a novel, *Fan-Tan,* an adventure set in the South Seas.

The man who had directed Mick Jagger, lodestar of the Rolling Stones, in *Performance,* saw an opportunity to reinvent an icon. There were other greatly talented actors, Cammell believed, but Marlon was "the one chosen to be deified. Much as Elvis was chosen. Part of the icon role is way beyond acting, and comes from being dangerously attractive in a psychosexual way." In the end neither the film nor the novel came to fruition. Not without reason, Cammell blamed Marlon. The actor kept delaying, turning out unusable pages and then becoming unavailable for consultation because he had winged off to Tahiti. By the end of 1988 Cammell was more than ready to give up on *Jericho* and *Fan-Tan.* Marlon refused to pull the plug. He seemed to be jogging in place, unable to go forward or back, when a new opportunity came his way—and this time he made a positive move.

A Dry White Season was based on André Brink's 1979 antiapartheid novel. The thirty-one-year-old black director, Euzhan Palcy, was anxious to have Brando in the small, vital role of Ian McKenzie, an eccentric, righteous barrister. But when they met, she felt compelled to warn Marlon that his customary fee was beyond the scope of this low-budget independent movie. In a rare, quixotic gesture, the man who was in the Marlon Brando business suddenly offered his services gratis. His Screen Actors Guild minimum of $4,000 would be donated to the antiapartheid cause.

Released in 1989, Palcy's tragedy of South African racism was treated with great respect. In the *National Review* John Simon could not avoid carping, but went out of his way to praise "the presence of Brando, aptly pronounced [Orson] Wellesian in both flamboyance and girth, and, despite a somewhat hokey British accent and the signature slow pacing, easily the best thing in the film." *Variety* singled out a line in the script, "Justice and law could be described as distant cousins—not on speaking terms," and pointed out, "Those words are spoken by Ian McKenzie (Marlon Brando), rising with a world-weary magnificence to the role of a prominent human rights attorney whose idealism has been battered into resignation. Sarcasm is his only tactic, the moral high ground his only refuge as McKenzie proves Captain Stolz (Jürgen Prochnow) a murderer, but loses his case before a judge who makes no effort to hide his disgraceful bias." The role won Marlon another Academy Award nomination, this time for Best Supporting Actor. As expected, he stayed away from the Oscar ceremonies. Rather than recognizing a job well done, he said, the statuettes were "part of the sickness in America, that you have to think in terms of who wins, who loses, who's good, who's bad, who's best, who's worst . . . I don't like to think that way. Everybody has their own value in different ways, and I don't like to think who's the best at this. I mean, what's the point of it?"

The protests went on as voluble as ever, but there was no more talk of a final film. Marlon considered *The Freshman,* a whimsical *Godfather* send-up costarring a green Matthew Broderick. For reassurance he asked the director, Andrew Bergman, to come to Tahiti. "It was just surreal," Bergman was to tell a reporter from *Interview.* "For four days we never discussed the movie. We discussed the Holocaust, music, everything but." Ultimately Brando said, "Well, you know, I've been thinking about it. I can only do it if I think of it as some version of the Don." Bergman had an inspiration: "You'll be the guy the Don was based on. You'll be the real guy." Replied Marlon, "That works for me." And the deal was done.

The first day of shooting was complete bedlam. Part of the movie was shot on location, and when reporters heard that Marlon Brando was working in Greenwich Village they flooded Little Italy to cover the story. Marlon looked ready to explode. Glancing around anxiously, said Bergman, "I asked, 'How are you going to get out of here without being photographed?' And he went into the trunk of his car—which was no easy task—and this guy drove him out." Bergman was awed by offscreen Brando as well as the onscreen one: "He loved De Niro when De Niro was fat in *Raging Bull.* He said, 'Just the way he moved . . .' And he kind of leaned over and picked up a chair with his arm, like a fat man would. He became the fat version of Jake La Motta in that instant. In the seventeenth century he would have been burned as a witch." Filming should have been a pleasure from then on, but, as always, Marlon lived by the motto Why have it simple when you can have it complicated? He had taken up with his young maid Maria Ruiz, and in May 1989 she gave birth to their daughter, Ninna Priscilla. As if there were not enough parental responsibilities on his roster, aside from the continuing problems with Christian, there was more trouble brewing. One night in Tahiti Cheyenne borrowed Teihotu's car, flooring the gas pedal. Whether she was driving under the influence of drugs, as police suspected, or merely reckless, she ran off the road. The accident was horrific. Marlon arranged to have his daughter flown to Los Angeles, where she underwent operations for massive injuries to her face and head. He left the *Freshman* set, now in Toronto, and returned shaken and abstracted. Bergman covered for him. Laurence Olivier had recently died after long battles with both cancer and a muscle disorder, and the writer/director told reporters that Brando now had no rivals, and that "he contributes continually to the movie, and he will make you laugh." That Marlon did, but at considerable cost. Disoriented and miserable, he denigrated *The Freshman* just before it opened in 1990. "I'm retiring. . . . I wish I hadn't finished with a stinker." Recalled Bergman, "He didn't realize he was hurting everybody in the movie. I think he'd had a really good time and it went against everything he'd taught himself to believe. Somehow he had to foul his nest. He was an unhappy person and a tortured soul. He paid for that gift many times over." Bergman reminded Marlon of what was at stake and got through to him. Contritely, the star went public with a revised view of *The Freshman:* "There is no substitute for laughter in this frightened and endlessly twisting world." They were empty words. For Marlon's personal world was about to become more frightening, and more twisted, than any filmmaker could possibly have imagined. This time neither laughter nor money would set things right.

1990—2004

Messenger of Misery

1

The torment was reduced to eight words: "The messenger of misery has visited my house." Marlon first used that phrase on the night of May 16, 1990, in a frenzied telephone message to the activist lawyer William Kunstler, whom he had known since the days of the civil rights marches. It was to be repeated when Los Angeles reporters gathered at his front door the next morning. A man had been shot to death in the Brando house only hours before. The victim was twenty-eight-year-old Dag Drollet, scion of a prominent Tahitian family. The killer was thirty-two-year-old Christian Brando.

Cheyenne and Dag had been staying with Marlon. That night she and her half brother ate at the Musso & Frank Grill, and as Christian downed glass after glass of malt liquor, she related a tale of woe. Her boyfriend had beaten her in Tahiti. The other day he attacked her right here in the Brando house. She was afraid to be in the same bedroom with him. When Cheyenne and Christian returned from the grill, she went to bed alone. Fortified by alcohol, Christian went to his own room, then prowled the halls looking for Dag. He found him in the den, watching television. Christian aimed a .45-caliber pistol at the houseguest and demanded, "Are you slapping around my sister?" According to the shooter's account, he was about to leave, arm out-stretched in a threatening manner, when the gun accidentally went off. A single slug hit Dag in the head. The confrontation had taken place in seconds, and when it was done the shooter bent over the body in shock. "I just sat there and watched the life go out of this guy." Marlon heard the report of the gun, dashed to the den, and tried mouth-to-mouth resuscitation. He was too late.

Christian wanted to flee the crime scene; Marlon spoke forcefully but calmly, talking the young man down from his drunken hysteria, convincing him to stay, speak to the police, tell them that it was misfortune, not murder. The advice was sound; there was nowhere for Christian to run. He would surely have been captured within twenty-four hours, looking all the worse for having fled. By the time the police arrived, he had worked out a plausible account. As blood samples were taken, he told patrolman Steve Cunningham, "I shot him, man. But not on purpose. We were both in a fit of rage. Please believe me, man. I wouldn't do it in my father's house." Los Angeles police detective Steve Osti was next to interview Christian. The perpetrator, still manic, with a blood alcohol content almost twice the legal limit for a drunken-driving charge, ran off at the mouth. "I did it because he hurt my sister. He was laying on the couch. He was fighting with my sister. I said, 'You leave my sister alone.' We were both in a rage. The fucking gun went off." That testimony would have been damning enough, but Christian added, "Man, death is too good for the guy."

Perhaps the saddest part of all was that Dag was a physically imposing but gentle man. Cheyenne had invented the tale of abuse. Her entire life had been a shuttle between illusion and fact, drugs and sobriety. She adored her father for his glamour and generosity; she despised him because she had no identity except as the daughter of Marlon Brando. Pursuing a modeling career, she boasted, "I am the most beautiful girl in Polynesia, the most intelligent and also the richest because of my father"; she had no self-confidence at all. She said she was strong enough to go it alone; eight months pregnant, she lived in fear that Dag was about to leave her. Aware of his daughter's ever-precarious state of mind, Marlon had finally persuaded Cheyenne and Dag to leave Tahiti, stay at his house, take it easy, let somebody else do the cooking and make the bed until the baby arrived. In *Christian Brando: A Hollywood Family Tragedy,* Mark Gribben reports that by the time Dag accepted the offer, he was rapidly losing patience with his girlfriend's bipolar moods. The words of his father haunted him: "Stop this life with Cheyenne because she's not balanced. You will have great difficulties—perhaps suicide, perhaps she can kill you or you can die, both of you, because of her." The Brandos and the Drollets had been acquainted for years, and Marlon tried to reach them by phone to break the news as gently as possible. The tabloid television show *Hard Copy* got there first. Jacques Drollet blurted, "Oh, my God! He was a good boy, but that's all over now." As the details of the killing came in, Dag's father had more to say. The young man "never beat Cheyenne.

Perhaps on one or two occasions when Cheyenne was in a rage, she was scratching him, hitting him, throwing things at Dag, perhaps he gave her one or two slaps, but he never beat her and nothing at all since she was pregnant, never."

After Cheyenne testified in a hostile manner to the police ("It's murder, in case you don't know it") she was given sedatives around the clock. Meantime, with each hour things worsened for Christian. A police search of his room turned up a large cache of firearms. Possession of illegal automatic weapons was added to the charge of murder in the second degree. Medical evidence revealed that Dag had been shot in the back of his head, not the forehead, as Christian had said. The den in which the violence had taken place showed no signs of a struggle; Dag had died with a bag of pipe tobacco in one hand and a TV remote in the other. An outraged judge set bail at $10 million. Even with all the money Marlon had earned recently, that sum was beyond his means. As the bad news accumulated, Marlon made two moves. On the advice of Kunstler, he hired Robert Shapiro, a high-profile defense lawyer who had represented the porn star Linda Lovelace on an obscenity charge, film producer Robert Evans on a drug charge, and the flamboyant attorney F. Lee Bailey on a drunk driving charge. Marlon also arranged to have Cheyenne taken back to Tahiti, where she was hospitalized upon arrival. Several weeks later the baby was born and immediately placed in postnatal detox. Bereft and angry, the child's mother got hold of a bottle of sleeping pills and downed them. She was discovered before the narcotic could take full effect. Intensive therapy began, and for a while Cheyenne responded, quieting down and accepting her maternal responsibilities.

After a preliminary hearing Christian's bail was reduced to $2 million. But there were all sorts of other financial obligations, for legal fees and medical bills. Marlon knew he would have to go back to work, and that part of his work would involve exposure to the press. He took a deep breath and faced reporters after the bail hearing. "I have a hide this thick," he told them, stretching his thumb and forefinger as far as they would go. "But when it comes to my son and my children, you're talking to someone with a different impulse." He was still rotund, although his face had harrowed with the pressure of events, and there was a bone-weariness to his conversation, some of it quite odd. He told the journalists that the room where Dag had been shot was now a candle-lit shrine to the deceased. Someone asked if anything could have been done to prevent the tragedy. Marlon replied with his own question: "Where is a feather dropped by a seagull on the heads of two thousand persons going to land? There are too many unknowns."

Robert Shapiro earned his costly fee. He discovered that Christian had not been read his Miranda rights. The tape-recorded statements of the accused were ruled inadmissible. Shapiro also saw to it Cheyenne would not be extradited from Tahiti, persuading the court that cross-examination would further injure an already fragile psyche. With Cheyenne testifying in person, asserted prosecutor Steven Barshop, "this is a murder—at least a tryable murder." Without her presence, he complained, "we cannot legally prove malice and without being able to prove malice, this case is a provable manslaughter." With the charge reduced, Shapiro pressed for a shorter sentence, citing a probation officer who spoke of Christian's drug-induced brain damage and his lack of self-esteem. The prosecutors insisted on the maximum of sixteen years for the crime. The defense countered by calling Marlon to the stand. While Shapiro led him through the peaks and valleys of Brando's marriage to Christian's mother, Anna Kashfi, who was not in the courtroom, Marlon mentioned her temper, instability, and attractiveness. "She was probably the most beautiful woman I've ever known, but she came close to being as negative a person as I have met in my life." Still, he shouldered much of the blame: "I led a wasted life. I chased a lot of women. Perhaps I failed as a father. The tendency is always to blame the other person. There were things I could have done differently." Then he used the same words he had placed in his own father's mouth when he dreamed about Marlon senior shortly after the old man's death: "I did the best I could."

He sobbed during some parts of his testimony, and raged at other moments: "This is the *Marlon* Brando case. If Christian were black, Mexican, or poor, he wouldn't be in this courtroom. Everyone wants a piece of the pie." At the end he lowered his voice, and tears welled in his eyes again. Overtaken by contrition, he returned the withering stares of Dag Drollet's family. Speaking in idiomatic French he addressed them: "*Je ne peux pas continuer voir la haine dans vos yeux. Je suis désolé avec mon coeur entier.*" (I cannot keep looking at the hate in your eyes. I mourn with my whole heart.) The next day Christian also apologized to the Drollets and told the judge, Robert Thomas, he was prepared for the consequences of his deed. Thomas struck a bargain between the prosecution's insistence on the full sentence and

Shapiro's plea for lenience. To the Drollets' distress, on March 1, 1991, Christian pleaded guilty to voluntary manslaughter and received a ten-year prison term at the California Men's Colony in San Luis Obispo. With time off for good behavior, plus the nine months he had already served, he would be eligible for release in as little as four years. In a strange way, he had entered the track to salvation. It was Cheyenne who was the irretrievably lost child. The messenger of misery was not finished with the Brando household.

2

On June 2, 1991, Miko's wife, Jiselle Honore Brando, thirty-four, was driving on a freeway south of downtown Los Angeles when a drunken driver smashed his vehicle into hers. Death was instantaneous. Miko had been acting as bodyguard for Michael Jackson in the heyday of the singer's career, and for a brief interlude the grieving widower received more press attention than his father. Such a condition could not last, and very soon Marlon's name surfaced in the entertainment pages again.

To pay his outstanding debts he would play the part of Tomás de Torquemada, the Grand Inquisitor, in *Christopher Columbus: The Discovery*. Columbus was not looked upon kindly by the American Indian Movement and Marlon objected to making the mariner a hero instead of an exploiter of Native Americans. He was unprepared for the backlash. As Indian spokesmen argued for an Indigenous People's Day to replace Columbus Day, the Order of the Sons of Italy, a group unfriendly to the *Godfather* films, offered evidence in favor of their hero. Columbus had no slaves of his own, nor did he bring any from Africa to the Western Hemisphere. He did not consider the Indians he met to be inferior; in his journals he expresses admiration for members of the Taíno tribe, whom he considers handsome, generous, and intelligent. Moreover, the New World was not the disease-free Eden described by twentieth-century Indians. Tests on exhumed bones indicated that native populations suffered from venereal infection, tuberculosis, arthritis, and dental trouble. The average life expectancy was about forty.

Marlon stopped struggling and did his film work without any further ado. There would be no awards for *Columbus*. *Variety* was one of the few publications to have a kind word: "Brando makes a grand Grand Inquisitor. . . . Drawing upon an actual intersection of historical fact and dramatic symbolism, pic also highlights Spain's expulsion of the Jews, a boatload of whom sail into exile the very same day that the *Niña, Pinta* and *Santa María* leave port. Brando's slyly insincere blessing to both expeditions is a telling moment." Opposing this minority view, *The Washington Post* amused itself at the actor's expense: "When Marlon Brando makes his entrance in the bloated epic *Christopher Columbus: The Discovery*, we know how Ahab must have felt when he first laid eyes on Moby Dick." Swathed in clerical robes that "wardrobe doubtless made from the mainsail, Brando plays the Spanish Grand Inquisitor Tomás de Torquemada, but he would have been better cast as the *Niña*. Brando is that wooden." *The New York Times* made the same points more benignly: "This Torquemada could have dropped in from a lost Jerry Lewis movie. He doesn't look quite real. Though he is strangely familiar, it's not easy to recognize him. Then you have it: the nearly round, evilly smiling face is that of the man in the moon."

Movie offers dried up. So did the cash flow. Marlon had been approached many times to write his autobiography; he had always refused. It was not (or not only) a matter of playing hard to get. He disliked the idea of extreme self-revelation; *Last Tango* was as far as he was willing to go. But debts continued to accumulate for child support, lawyers' bills, divorce settlements, upkeep of the island, and taxes, and the need for money became so acute it swept all other considerations aside. He had already been the subject of numerous books and articles. There was Carlo Fiore's *Bud, the Brando I Knew;* Anna Kashfi's *Brando for Breakfast;* Charles Higham's *Brando: The Unauthorized Biography;* Bob Thomas's *Brando: Portrait of the Rebel as an Artist,* and many others. Marlon resented them all. The speculations kept coming anyway; everyone seemed to have a theory about the real Marlon. One of the brightest of the speculators was Molly Haskell. Her post-*Godfather* consideration of Brando's art and attitude in *The Village Voice* remained the most acute of all.

On his social activism: "If we occasionally wish Brando would get off his minority-group hobbyhorse, we may have to recognize the other side of the coin: that this compulsion to do something is one of the sources of his fascination as an actor, the ambition of Terry Malloy and Johnny to be something more. He may, like Zapata, be the ultimate contradiction—a man 'of the people' who towers above them, a man in constant tension with his own myth."

On his screen presence: "He is intensely physical, strong, sensual, and yet there is a stillness, the hesitation of a troubled soul. He watches like nobody else watches, and behind the glare is a mind that knows more than it will ever, can ever utter."

On his central quality: Brando's "essence is contradiction, conflicts that can never come to rest in resolution, and he will therefore frustrate and disappoint all those who travel society's single track. His coarse language and brute force are not the impulses of a boor, but the masque of a poet, the cry of rage against the imprisoning niceties of civilization."

Richard Schickel also tried his hand at biography; *Brando: A Life in Our Times* was the most discreet of the genre, tracking its subject with dignity and perception: "Whatever Brando has done or not done, no actor in his life and his work has more consistently kept us in touch with the erratic—that which is unpredictable and dangerous in ourselves and in the world." This was not nearly good enough for Camille Paglia, then establishing her credentials as pop intellectual. "My idol, Keith Richards, virtuoso rhythm guitarist of the Rolling Stones, named his son Marlon. Why? You would never know from Schickel's book. Marlon Brando, the wild, sexy rebel, all mute, surly bad attitude, prefigured rock and roll, the great art form of my Sixties generation."

For Marlon, it was all a waste, writers pressing their noses against the window, squinting at a stranger they pretended to know. It was time for him to take the stand. His friend and onetime director George Englund had contacts in the New York book world, and soon every prominent publisher went out to Los Angeles to present his case. "It was kind of a paradox," said Sir Harold Evans, then president of Random House. "He would audition for a part, but we were the ones auditioning for the part of publisher. Which meant being interrogated by him." Over the course of Evans's audition, "We debated everything from anthropomorphism to drilling in Alaska to the native rights of the Sioux Indians. His range was absolutely vast." Brando learned that his English visitor lived with Navajo Indians when he first came to America in the 1950s. That sealed the deal. Evans put Marlon together with Robert Lindsey, who had helped Ronald Reagan with his presidential memoirs. Marlon was cooperative—up to a point, refusing to mention, let alone discuss, his wives or his children. As celebrity and collaborator talked, another Brando book was known to be in the works. Hyperion had signed Peter Manso, biographer of Norman Mailer, to write the unauthorized life of Marlon Brando from birth to the present time. Manso had been at it for several years, speaking to numerous friends and acquaintances from school days, and digging up material relating to Dodie's alcoholism, Marlon senior's brutality, and other family tribulations. The biographer was currently tracking down Marlon's aggrieved lovers, actors from the old days, friends, acquaintances in Omaha, New York, Hollywood—anyone willing to relate memories and anecdotes. With a wary eye on the competition, Hyperion and Random House each implied that theirs would be the definitive Brando book.

The race ended in the fall of 1994, when both volumes reached the stores within a month. Comparisons were inevitable, and many newspapers elected to do a double review, appraising autobiography and biography side by side. Marlon's entry, *Brando: Songs My Mother Taught Me,* had provided him with the one and only chance he would ever have to reach an audience in his own voice. Without makeup, without lines written by another author, he speaks in the first person. The good days of his Huckleberry Finn boyhood are resurrected along with the terrible ones. He recalls in agonizing detail the alcoholism of his parents, the hell of their marriage and what it did to their children, the military-school period, his first days in New York, and then the long up-and-down theatrical and cinematic ventures that established (as well as sullied) his reputation as an actor with outsize gifts and mammoth liabilities. *Songs* has a strangely appealing candor; the man who presents his case in those 468 pages is a complicated, dark, but always charismatic figure. Only later did shrewd readers realize they had been watching yet another Brando performance.

Like all Brando performances, Marlon's autobiography revealed (sometimes unwittingly) the foolishness of a great artist trying to get at the truth of his life. His self-analysis, for example, smacks of too many cognitive-therapy sessions: "Frustrated in my attempts to take care of my mother, I suppose that instead I tried to help Indians, blacks and Jews. I thought love, good intentions and positive action could alter injustice, prejudice, aggression and genocide." He regrets to report that he's "no longer persuaded that any significant change through a course of behavior will make any difference of lasting importance." The only help for suffering mankind is a reordering of its DNA. Marlon's view of patricide also suggests the psychiatrist's couch: "If my father were alive today, I don't know what I would do. After he died, I used to think, 'God, just give him to me alive for eight seconds; that's all I want, just eight seconds because I want to break his jaw. I wanted to smash his face and watch him spit out his teeth. I wanted to kick his balls into his throat. I wanted to rip his ears off and eat them in front of him. I wanted to separate his larynx from his body and shove it into his stomach. But I realized that as long as I felt this way I would never be free until I eradicated these feelings in myself." The statement doesn't jibe with what follows. Since the late Marlon senior is unable to degrade his son anymore, Marlon junior volunteers for the job. Echoing his father's opinion of the performing arts, he calls acting "the least mysterious of crafts." Film work is particularly inflated: "I laugh at people who call moviemaking an 'art' and actors 'artists.' Rembrandt, Beethoven, Shakespeare and Rodin were artists; actors are worker ants in a business and they toil for money. That's why it's always been called 'the movie business.' " Ergo, whatever praise has come his way, Marlon Brando is not an accomplished and revolutionary performer. He never has been; he's the biggest confidence man of them all. "If a studio paid me as much to sweep the floor as it did to act, I'd sweep the floor." *On the Waterfront:* "I was simply embarrassed about myself." *The Godfather:* "When I saw it the first time, it made me sick; all I could see were my mistakes and I hated it." *Apocalypse Now:* "I was good at bullshitting Francis and persuading him to think my way, and he bought it, but what I'd really wanted from the beginning was to find a way to make my part smaller so I wouldn't have to work as hard." *Christopher Columbus:* "I mumbled my way through the part and gave an embarrassingly bad performance. The pay wasn't bad, though: $5 million for five days' work."

Occasionally Marlon drops the cynical pose. He admits that "I have always been lucky with women," but that the good fortune never involved the risk of love. To avoid being hurt, from youth onward he was "like a vaudeville juggler spinning a half-dozen plates at once . . . always keeping several romances going at the same time; that way, if one woman left me there would still be four or five others." Amid the bitter childhood memories are grace notes, recollections of rural life, walking the railroad tracks in the winter, watching locomotives laboring to get going with their wheels sliding and slipping, while in summer he and his friends "sat beside the rails, stuck a penny on the tracks with a wad of gum and waited for a train to flatten it, then made necklaces and belts out of the flattened coins." Near the conclusion are evocations of nights in Tetiaroa. They belong next to Gauguin's memoir: "I've never seen the heavens look so vast as they do from an atoll. The first light is usually a planet, Venus or Mars; then, very slowly, subtle, distant needle pricks appear in space, and as the last glow of the sunset ebbs away and it grows darker, the stars shine more brightly. Finally the sky opens and the Milky Way and other constellations explode in a panoramic umbrella of light that reaches from horizon to horizon."

Manso's doorstop of a book was different. At over a thousand pages, it purported to be a close study of Marlon Brando's accomplishments and distresses. That may have been its original aim, but en route the author clearly came to resent the actor who, in Manso's view, abjectly failed to fulfill his early, middle, and late promise. Interviews with some eight hundred people turned up all sorts of lurid details about Marlon's affairs, many of them asserted by acquaintances who offered no proof. As Brando's waistline expanded, so did the biography, filling chapter upon chapter with details of diets, quarrels with directors, battles with ex-wives, and attempts to deal with his difficult children. No doubt that Marlon had an effect on all of them, and that this effect was mixed. But Manso would not let go of this premise; he speculated that in the Drollet case, Marlon "played a key role in the shooting, not by holding the gun, but by setting the stage and providing the emotional cue that led to the killing." Unable to speak to Marlon himself, Manso tracked down Cheyenne. The young woman was obviously disturbed, and had been for years. She accused her father of sexually abusing her, that she was his "lamb for sacrifice, for his own happiness," that when she saw *The Godfather* she wasn't watching Don Corleone. "It was my father in the flesh. I saw that he had the mentality of the Godfather, of the Mafia—the powerful man able to manipulate people as it pleases him. That's why I think my father has that power, and it reminded me of voodoo. That's why I said, 'He is the demon.' I believe that even today my father keeps a psychological influence over me, which I don't know how to get rid of." In a yoked review of both volumes, Caryn James, a *Times* film critic, made a sadly apt comparison: "Mr. Brando's autobiography is no model of the genre, but it doesn't pretend to be anything more than a quirky memoir. Mr. Manso's book, with its unnecessary bulk and its subtitle, *The Biography,* tries to bully readers into believing it is definitive. It is, instead, wearisome and creepy.

"Three years after the murder, Mr. Manso actually interviewed the emotionally fragile Cheyenne Brando, who railed against her father. There are plenty of disgusting episodes in *Brando: The Biography.* Tracking down an unstable young woman who was living in a psychiatric clinic in Berkeley has to be among the most chilling."

There was no thaw. With few film opportunities left to him, Marlon went into another tailspin, trying to ignore the paparazzi newly aroused by the Manso book, lounging about the house, gaining weight, occasionally visiting his neighbors Michael Jackson and Jack Nicholson, still trying halfheartedly to generate some interest in a documentary about Native American history. The emerging rocker-turned-actor Johnny Depp had been widely praised for his work in *Edward Scissorhands* and *Ed Wood.* He was about to take the title role in *Don Juan DeMarco,* a romantic comedy about a young man, Don R. Marco, who believes he's the legendary seventeenth-century lover. Placed in a mental hospital, he comes under the care of psychiatrist Dr. Jack Mickler, due to retire in ten days. He gives those days to Don—and falls under his spell, as the screen details seductions, duels, and a sojourn in a harem. Mickler comes to see the value in imagination, to appreciate the "healthy sickness" of the young man, and to rekindle romance in his burned-out marriage. "When I read the script," said Depp, "all I kept seeing was Marlon Brando as the psychiatrist. So when they asked me who I thought would be good in the role, I said Marlon Brando. They looked at me like I was insane." The director, Jeremy Leven, thought it was worth a shot. "I said, 'Sure, let's take it to Marlon Brando,' and then we can move on and ask someone who would be serious about taking the role. The next thing I know, I'm sitting in Marlon's living room, and we're making a movie."

It was a happy set in New York City and in Hollywood. Marlon truly seemed to enjoy himself and his colleagues, particularly Depp as Don, and Faye Dunaway as Mrs. Mickler. He pulled no stunts, didn't test his director, didn't fill the days with practical jokes. There was a new seriousness about him, and an unaccustomed ease. With the young actor and the old one in harmony, Marlon seemed in a generous mood, and Warner Bros. publicists dared to hope that he might help to promote what was, after all, a low-budget, if agreeable, fantasy. Events overtook them all. *Don Juan DeMarco* opened on April 7, 1995, to mixed reviews. *Variety* loved it: "The film's greatest asset is its glorious acting, with special accolades to Brando, who here delivers yet another magnificent 'comeback' performance. Despite a huge frame, Brando is extremely light on his feet, playing in an uncharacteristically relaxed, laid-back manner." Roger Ebert hated it: "Brando doesn't so much walk through this movie as coast, in a gassy, self-indulgent performance no one else could have gotten away with." Marlon was used to varied responses, but there is no telling how he felt about these notices. For nine days later, the dirge sounded again: Cheyenne had hanged herself at the Brando home in Tahiti. At the time she was vastly overweight, like the father she had so often denigrated. She was said to be despondent over a court's refusal to allow her custody of her four-year-old, Tuki, her son by Dag Drollet. In fact this was one of many suicide attempts; in his book *My Life as a Radical Lawyer*, William Kunstler wrote about the defense of Christian Brando. He harked back to a dinner at the Brando house, when he asked for a blade to cut his meat. Marlon informed him that there were only butter knives on the premises. "I believe he feared that Cheyenne would use a sharp knife inappropriately."

Jocelyn came by; she did her best to console the grieving father, but he was beyond solace. Marlon issued no statement. His sentiments cannot have differed much from those of Mark Twain, who learned of his own daughter's death from a sudden illness when they were more than a thousand miles apart. Reflecting on the heartbreak, he wrote: "It is one of the mysteries of our nature that a man, all unprepared, can receive a thunder-stroke like that and live." Cheyenne's tragedy was compounded because her funeral could not be attended by her brother, who was still in jail, or by her father, who was too devastated to leave home. Tarita arranged to have Cheyenne buried beside Dag, defying the objections of the Drollets. For Marlon, from this point on, the South Seas lost their power of enchantment, and the panoramic umbrella of light faded to black.

3

Of course not all of Marlon's idiosyncrasies and strange habits could be blamed on his personal tragedies. He had long since become notorious for bizarre behavior—when promoting *Songs My Mother Taught Me* in 1994, for example, he had appeared on *Larry King Live* to give a disjointed, hilarious account of his life, and ended by kissing the host on the lips. But Marlon was obviously a man in pain, and a year after his daughter's suicide he made two ill-advised appearances, one on the large screen, one on the small.

The Island of Dr. Moreau was a remake of the *Island of Lost Souls*, adapted from H. G. Wells's turn-of-the-century novel about a mad scientist who changed animals into men. A 1932 version starred Charles Laughton as Dr. Moreau; in 1977 Burt Lancaster took the role. Both films had an air of serious concern, as if genetic engineering loomed just around the corner. The third attempt was a hammy, camped-up attempt to be frightening and comic at the same time. The screenwriter/director Richard Stanley was fired during the early days, replaced by the veteran John Frankenheimer. His was one of three outsize egos assigned to the movie. The others belonged to Val Kilmer, who played Moreau's oddball assistant, and Marlon, who sported deadwhite makeup and a series of peculiar costumes as if to broadcast the doctor's inner lunacy. Kilmer was going through a divorce at the time; everything seemed to set him off, particularly Frankenheimer's direction. Marlon spoke to Val about the virtues of self-discipline—and then proceeded to do anything he damn pleased. During one break he spotted a metal pail out of camera range, impulsively inverted it, and covered his face. He called it Dr. Moreau's latest invention: a device for keeping cool. "No one was willing to say no to anything," recalled Stanley, "which is why Brando wears an ice bucket on his head in one scene." Marlon masked his grief with a series of similar stunts; they did nothing to improve the picture or lighten his burden. *Island* opened to terrible reviews. The film quarterly *Bright Lights Film Journal* described Brando as "a waddling behemoth who spends most of his time dressing in ornate, flowing caftans and matching do-rags and playing piano duets with a sort of homunculus figure who wears identical outfits." Audiences never see "this ballooned up drag queen do any actual research; with more costume changes than a Lana Turner movie, he's obviously too busy choosing his own gowns." *Island* received six Razzie nominations, including Worst Picture; Brando beat out Kilmer by receiving Worst Supporting Actor.

Marlon had no one to blame but himself. Reviewers could hardly be expected to give him a discount because of a death in the family. Or because, when Christian was paroled in January, the tabloids ran lurid stories about that fatal night at the Brando house. Even so, the impersonation of Dr. Moreau provoked some disproportionately cruel responses, as if the critics got a special kick out of mocking a tormented seventy-two-year-old. None of this kept Marlon from the public. The most notorious of his appearances occurred on Larry King's show on April 5, 1996. During the course of a rambling interview, King brought up the subjects of racism, violence, and immigration. He mentioned the Jews, and his guest ventured an opinion. "Per capita, Jews have contributed more to American culture than any other single group. If it weren't for the Jews, we wouldn't have music, we wouldn't have art, we wouldn't have much theater." Without pausing, Marlon suddenly lurched into a screed about the movies: "Hollywood is run by Jews. It is owned by Jews, and they should have a greater sensitivity about the issue of people who are suffering because they've [been] exploited." He went on: "We have seen the Nigger and the Greaseball. We've seen the Chink. We've seen the slit-eyed dangerous Jap. We have seen the wily Filipino. We've seen everything, but we never saw the Kike because they knew perfectly well that that is where you draw the wagons around."

The next day Jewish organizations furiously responded. Phil Baum, executive director of the American Jewish Congress, said, "Our review of Brando is clear: he should emulate silent movies, because his soundtrack is not worth hearing." Abraham Foxman, national director of the B'nai B'rith's Anti-Defamation League, was more specific. "Mr. Brando should know that what he said is utterly false, extremely offensive and plays into the hands of anti-Semites and bigots. His comments raise the centuries-old canard of Jewish control and conspiracy, and his use of an anti-Semitic epithet is hurtful to Jews everywhere." The Jewish Defense League petitioned (in vain) for the Hollywood Chamber of Commerce to remove Marlon Brando's star from the Hollywood Walk of Fame. Humorist Ben Stein tried to make the affair a tempest in a tea glass: "Hollywood is not really 'run' by anyone (it's far too chaotic for that)." But the damage had been done, and Marlon knew he had bombinated once too often. Rabbi Marvin Hier, dean and founder of the Simon Wiesenthal Center, received a call the following week. Afterward, Hier informed every journalist on his Rolodex that the actor had "expressed his remorse," and that he insisted his comments were not meant to be anti-Semitic. Marlon's defenders got into the act, reminding the ADL and other Jewish groups of his *philo*-Semitism, quoting the passage praising Jews in *Songs My Mother Taught Me:* "Whatever the reasons for their brilliance and success, I was never educated until I was exposed to them. They introduced me to a sense of culture that has lasted me a lifetime." Mollified, the protestors quieted down, freeing the performer for his next indiscretions.

One was called *Free Money,* a "quickie" shot in Canada. Marlon played an inconsequential part in the negligible movie. The other actors—Donald Sutherland, Charlie Sheen, Thomas Haden Church, Mira Sorvino—seemed uncomfortable, and Marlon's portrait of the Swede, a bald, mustachioed prison guard, was cringe-making. Almost all his moves are pratfalls, culminating in a scene where he faints, plunging head-first into a toilet bowl. The plot, a story of revenge against the Swede, failed to work on even the most elemental levels, and when *Free Money* was shopped around to North American theatrical distributors, no one bought it. The film went directly to the video market, where it was mercifully ignored.

The other was entitled *The Brave.* The project was attractive to Marlon because Johnny Depp was to star and direct, and because it dealt with the plight of a Native American. The brave of the title is Raphael (Depp), an alienated, alcoholic Cherokee who lives with his wife and two children in a trailer park. With no skills and no future, Raphael accepts the offer of a mysterious figure, McCarthy (Brando). For $50,000 Raphael will allow the maker of "snuff" films to have him murdered on camera. The filming is to take place one week hence. During those seven days Raphael reexamines his life, connects with his children, falls in love with his wife all over again, and constructs a kind of theme park outside his home for the neighbors to enjoy. *The Brave* was another of those movies undone by its good intentions. McCarthy is too heavily symbolic of the white man's rapacity, Raphael's renaissance is put in by the numbers, and the denouement is brutal and implausible. Shown at the fiftieth Cannes Film Festival, the film was received with a mix of loud boos and polite applause. According to Lisa Schwarzbaum, a critic from *Entertainment Weekly,* Depp's movie "had a nice look to it, it was beautifully lit, had a very moody feeling to it, but was sort of astonishingly not ready to be seen. It was actually kind of embarrassing. He really needed somebody older who wouldn't be afraid to say, 'You know, Johnny, nice idea, but let's sit on this for a while.'" Schwarzbaum added that "with any luck, it will never be released and nobody will ever have to see it, and I mean that for him as well as the audience." That was essentially the case: No American distributor picked up the film, and Marlon's work remained unseen and unappraised, save for *Variety*'s festival reviewer, who found McCarthy "entirely credible," though Brando's "windy philosophizing about death seems an unintended parody of his soliloquies in *Last Tango in Paris*."

For some time Marlon had been experiencing shortness of breath and a dry, hacking cough, but he refused to see a doctor, relying instead on the ministrations of his Filipino housekeeper, Angela Borlaza Magaling, and her sister Vie. Early in 2001 he agreed to play the cameo role of a priest in *Scary Movie 2,* only to drop out in April, when he was felled by pneumonia. Recovery was slow and the symptoms hung on. Marlon's old friend and longtime makeup artist Philip Rhodes grew apprehensive. Evidently the Borlazas had been administering injections, but he was unable to find out just what those syringes contained. Fearful, he called Marlon's sister Jocelyn. "I told her I was afraid something had been done to Marlon. She said, 'Oh, no, I've been talking a lot to Angela, and her sister is an accredited nurse.' " Marlon, convinced that he was on the mend, flew to New York to participate in a tribute to Michael Jackson at Madison Square Garden. He took the opportunity to deliver a lecture. Wearing sunglasses and lounging on a leather recliner, he addressed the full house about conditions in sub-Saharan Africa. "While you're wondering who that old fat fart is sitting there . . . I wanted you to realize that in that minute there were hundreds if not thousands of children hacked to death with a machete, beaten to death by their parents, got typhus and died of a disease." Consulting his wristwatch, he went on, "Hundreds of children have been hacked to death in the minute I've looked at my watch. Hundreds more were beaten. Don't forget that! Think about what I'm saying. It could be you." Restless, the audience greeted him with good-natured boos. He shrugged and got off. There were other items to attend to. He'd been offered another movie.

The Score was a caper that would star three generations of exceptional leading men: Ed Norton, thirty-three, Robert De Niro, fifty-eight, and Marlon Brando, seventy-seven. It would be directed by Frank Oz, who had graduated from moving Muppets around on *Sesame Street* to overseeing such major movies as *Little Shop of Horrors, What About Bob?,* and *Dirty Rotten Scoundrels,* a remake of the

Brando/Niven comedy *Bedtime Story*. Marlon was to play Max, a fey dealer in stolen goods, abetting a middle-aged thief and a young thug in one last heist. Marlon seemed so cheerful and anxious to begin that crew members wondered if he had changed after all these years. He hadn't.

Time reported that "wrangling Brando was anything but simple. When the Method-acting legend showed up to shoot his first scene, he was in full makeup (eye-shadow, rosy cheeks, the works), and his initial performance as the gay Max looked something like Barbara Bush doing her best Truman Capote impression." Oz asked him to "bring it down" and got a sulfurous reaction. Snapped Marlon: "I bet you wish I was a puppet so you could stick your hand up my ass and make me do what you want."

There was no truce in the battle of wills. "It was hell," said Oz. "The first two days with Marlon, I pushed him the wrong way, and as a result I lost him. He hated me, and it was my fault. I was too confrontational, too strong." Relations became so hostile that Marlon refused to come to the set if the director was on hand. Max's central scene was directed by De Niro, with Oz secretly conveying instructions through an assistant director. Long afterward, the director concluded, "All actors are frightened that they won't give you what you want. It was a sad way for me to learn that even Marlon Brando was scared." Perhaps Marlon was nervous, but his fears did not keep him from delivering a deft performance.

New York Times reviewer A. O. Scott offered a perverse view of *The Score:* "There is always a morbid fascination, and a degree of pleasure, to be found in watching first-rate actors trundle through expensive pieces of Hollywood hackwork." Most of the other responses were enthusiastic. In the *Los Angeles Times,* Kenneth Turan called the film a "top-drawer heist movie," taking particular delight in one performance: "The showy, flamboyant Max, given to rakish hats and canes, is not in the role of a lifetime—it's more in the nature of an amusing cameo—but it is still marvelous to see what Marlon Brando does with it." In the *San Francisco Chronicle,* Bob Graham opened his review, "No, that isn't Marlon Brando in a fat suit at the beginning of *The Score.* That's the great man himself. By now, Brando has become as big as his talent." *Rolling Stone* critic Peter Travers added, "Brando—his eyes alive with mischief—is the life of the movie."

Marlon went home to set up as an acting teacher. To cynical producers, this move was strictly venal; remarked one, "I see the Marlon Brando business is still in operation." It was true that the Brando name could attract top-tier actors as well as students, and that he could charge a tidy sum for his intensive two-week seminar. But there was more to it than that. If Marlon was in need of revenue these days, he was also out to pay a nonmonetary debt. An altruistic impulse had threaded through his life from the boyhood days as a rescuer, through the connection with black civil rights activists and Indian demonstrators. It surfaced again in the performing classes. He had been extraordinarily affected by his early teachers, Stella Adler most of all, and he truly wanted to give something back to the generations in his slipstream. He wasn't quite certain how to do it, and enlisted a "faculty" to help him. It included Sean Penn, Jon Voight, Leonardo DiCaprio, Nick Nolte, Edward James Olmos, Robin Williams, Whoopi Goldberg, and Michael Jackson. But most of the instruction was given by Marlon himself, under the rubric "Lying for a Living." Jod Kaftan, a reporter from *Rolling Stone,* was allowed to sit in on some of the classes. Under the headline THE ODDFATHER: MARLON BRANDO IS HARD UP, PISSED OFF AND STRANGER THAN EVER, Kaftan described a typical day. "Seven cameras capture the stars' awestruck faces as they hang on Brando's every word. They have good reason: Brando hardly ever discusses his craft, and for the first time in years he speaks of acting as if it matters." Seated on an overstuffed armchair he advises the paying customers, "Your whole face is a stage," and "Let the drama find you." He does a convincing improvisation on a prop telephone. "When some of the other actors try it, including Penn, DiCaprio and Voight, Brando's boundless talent seems obvious." There are inventive exercises, à la Stella Adler, with black students acting white, and white students acting black ("The white men portray black men as angry, and the black men portray whites as petty and wimpy"). And there are more provocative lectures by Marlon. Then, unforeseen difficulties suddenly arise. The videotape director Tony Kaye shows up dressed as Bin Laden. Voight says he finds "no discernible humor or purpose in the outfit." During an improvised scene between two women, Kaye moves in for a tight close-up. "Cut," he says. "Terrible. Boring." Snaps Marlon, "Let me tell you, what's boring is sticking that camera four inches from their noses and walking around like a police dog."

It is an indication of the storm to come. After shooting for two weeks, Kaye puts together a feature-length documentary called *Lying for a Living,* without clearing it with Brando. The world premiere is canceled when Marlon threatens to sue. Kaye's remark does nothing to solve the dispute: "Marlon Brando should be with the Taliban. I think he'd be very comfortable in that world, with a hundred wives, fourteen thousand children, no music, and no one's allowed to speak." According to a self-described "insider" who spoke to MSNBC, showings of *Lying* had to be canceled. "It's hard to figure out exactly what's going on because Brando has become quite, shall we say, eccentric by this point, and Kaye is a bit of a puzzle himself."

After *Lying,* Marlon once again became more reclusive, rarely venturing out, eating and reading ravenously. Only a few friends were allowed in, principally his business manager, Jo An Corrales, Jack Nicholson, Sean Penn, and producer Mike Medavoy. If he went out for any distance it was to Neverland, Michael Jackson's ranch near Santa Barbara. Brando's son Miko, one of Jackson's bodyguards, said that at the ranch "my father had a twenty-four-hour chef, twenty-four-hour security, twenty-four-hour help, twenty-four-hour kitchen, twenty-four-hour maid service. Just carte blanche. He loved it." There was more to it than unlimited pampering. Jackson had been fighting charges of pedophilia, and Marlon, a loyal friend to those who mattered to him, wanted to show the flag. As evidence of their camaraderie, he appeared in a Jackson video, *You Rock My World,* in which Jackson ventures into the significantly named Waterfront Hotel, owned by a glowering, cigar-chomping Marlon Brando.

In Neverland and out, Marlon declined all interviews. "Once I do one," he insisted, "they all come. It's like sticking your toe in the Amazon thinking that it won't attract piranhas. I'd rather they just portray me as a fat slob and a hoot, and just leave it at that." Every so often filmmakers asked to visit but such proposals were infrequent, and tended to be unattractive—curious people trying to get a glimpse of Goliath in winter. But there were three offers he couldn't refuse.

4

Friends of Ridha Behi, a soft-spoken North African filmmaker, got a script to Marlon. Entitled *Brando and Brando,* it followed a Tunisian who comes to America in search of Marlon Brando. Marlon would play himself, at first resistant, then growing warmer, until, over the course of time, the young man and the old one form a bond. Something about the story appealed to Marlon; he spoke of approaching Johnny Depp or Sean Penn to play the secondary role. Early in 2004 Behi came to Mulholland Drive. He found his host in a state of severe depression: Marlon was sad about the atrocity of 9/11, sad about the Middle East, sad about the war in Iraq. He said if he had it to do all over he would be a scientist, not an actor. "He cried and said that he had lost his life." Behi searched for backers, imploring them, "Please, quickly, I saw this man with oxygen tubes." Meanwhile, Marlon edited the script. He got a little lift out of being busy, and signed on to a couple of other projects that allowed him to stay at home while he worked.

The first was a device for video-gamers called "*The Godfather*: The Game," based on the film. On a morning when Marlon was feeling a little bit better, his housekeeper led a recording crew into the bedroom. The visitors turned out to be new-millennium geeks, full of technical knowledge. And yet with all their new equipment, the lavalier and shotgun mikes, the DAT tape recorder, Marlon saw that they were like all the others. The look was the same, the awe in the eyes, the deferential manner, the tiptoeing around. If they were bothered by his weight, or by the oxygen tank at his side, they didn't show it. He decided to play the icon this one last time, but in a new way for a new medium.

They edged the microphone closer. Philip Campbell, the creative director of Electronic Arts, cued him and he spoke the line. Dissatisfied with his reading, he reached for a tissue, ripped it up, and stuffed it into his cheeks, just as he had done thirty years before. He took a breath and began anew, speaking in the distinctive, cloudy voice of Vito Corleone: "I would like you to go see this man and discover what makes him tick. Then we can make him an offer and see if justice is truly on our side." Marlon relaxed, comfortable in his own identity.

Somewhere else Jimmy Caan and Bobby Duvall were doing their own thing for the *Godfather* game. Jimmy was funny about being a voice-over. "I love it," he said, "because this way my kids can play with me after I die." Francis Ford Coppola was not so enthusiastic. "The game has taken the work we all did on the film, and transformed it into a 'kill or be killed' slaughter session." He worked himself into a fury. "I did not give permission for the game, nor was I asked. Any courtesies I extended, and I did make the invitation to see our archives, were given before I knew that the game was already done. I did not cooperate with its making in any way, nor do I like or approve of what I saw of the result."

You couldn't blame Francis for his passion. That was what made him such a force in the good, crazy days. But Jimmy had a point, too, a personal one. And maybe it was bigger than all the objections: *My kids can play with me after I die.* That was something to think about, to obsess about, really.

How much time was left, how many breaths? Not a lot. Every mouthful of air was a war. Brando couldn't stand the strain of travel anymore, even in the backseat of a limo. The people from Electronic Arts understood. They knew he was anxious to go to work on an interactive video. People thought he was broke. There were stories in the tabloids. A lot they knew; there were plenty of assets. He was doing this recording for other reasons. To keep his piece on the board. To stay in contention. To surprise the Hollywood smart money who were forever marking him as obsolete.

The very word "interactive" appealed to him. "In a game," he told the E.A. people, "it's the audience that's doing the acting." Between takes he spoke about the role, about Don Corleone's need for respect, for family, for not being careless. "Women and children can be careless. Not men." They started talking about the past. He cleared his throat, took another hit of oxygen, and gave them a scrap of Terry Malloy, the "contender" speech. The crew had that look again. The respect and care stayed on their faces for the rest of the session. Then they backed away and left, deferential to a fault. And once more he was alone in his sanctuary. California light dazzled through the big windows, but it never seemed to rid the room of darkness.

A month later another group came in to record his voice. This session was for an animated comedy, *Big Bug Man,* about a candy maker who gets superpowers after being stung by superinsects. The writer/director, Bob Bendetson, tendered the part of a miserly, six-hundred-pound foreman. Marlon, typically, had some odd demands. He would appear in *Bug* only if he could play the short, purse-mouthed Mrs. Sour, owner of the candy company. Naturally Bendetson agreed. Marlon added one more stipulation: Though *Bug* would only use his voice, he insisted on dressing the part. The actor "was gorgeous," exclaimed Bendetson. "I guess it was part of his Method training or something, where you almost embarrass yourself as the character, so that way you're free to be the character."

The dialogue was recorded in Marlon's bedroom, as he sat on a couch, using the oxygen tank when he needed it. Along the way Bendetson encountered the two Marlons. "He didn't want to be treated like an icon. When you dealt with him you had to talk to him like a regular guy—he was very anti-Hollywood. But then the other part of him—he wanted a little gift to be brought. It was Persian caviar, imported cheeses and red wine. He loved it."

Marlon's devotion to calories dropped off in the late spring of 2004, when a precipitous weight loss began. It was an extremely difficult time physically and emotionally. So many had passed: family members, colleagues, enemies. The young—Cheyenne, Dag, Miko's wife, Jiselle—and the not-so-young, like Wally and Stella and Tennessee and his sister Frannie. The rivals: Monty Clift, Jimmy Dean, Burton, Mastroianni. The hostile authors: Truman Capote, Irwin Shaw. The pal turned treacherous, Carlo Fiore—friends don't write books about friends. The critics, sometimes sympathetic, sometimes hostile: Brooks Atkinson, Vincent Canby, Pauline Kael. Mr. sui generis himself, Elia Kazan. Marlon could never make his mind up about Gadge, and neither could anyone else. No wonder half the crowd applauded and the other half sat on their hands when he got his Lifetime Achievement Oscar. So many more were gone: Rod Steiger, Christian Marquand, Marilyn Monroe, Anna Magnani, John Huston, David Niven, Anthony Quinn. How could a survivor be anything but a recluse at the age of eighty? Holden Caulfield was right: "Don't ever tell anybody anything. If you do, you start missing everybody."

He turned his attention back to the script of *Brando and Brando.* It was hot in Los Angeles in July. Outside, the atmosphere was mephitic; indoors the filtered oxygen made little difference, and he struggled for air. Angela and Vie saw him gesturing and finally acknowledged that a real doctor had to come to the rescue. Angela dialed 911 and asked the operator for help. An ambulance arrived; the EMS crew loaded Marlon onto a stretcher and took him to the UCLA Medical Center. The physicians quickly learned the identity of their patient; they did the requisite tests in an attempt at resuscitation. They discovered that Marlon Brando, age eighty, was suffering from obesity, pulmonary fibrosis, diabetes, cardiac failure, and an enlarged liver that indicated the presence of cancer. They summoned his closest relative, Jocelyn Brando, from her home in Santa Monica. She sat at Marlon's bedside and on July 1, 2004, at 6:30 p.m., saw him out. "He just took off," she said. Her brother's passing was "quick, it was easy—just the way he wanted it."

Word immediately went out. It was common knowledge that Marlon had been ailing; even so his demise sent shock waves through the show-business community and beyond. The White House issued a rare statement: "America has lost a great actor of the stage and screen. His award-winning performances in films such as *On the Waterfront* and *The Godfather* demonstrated his outstanding talent and entertained millions across the country. Marlon Brando was one of the 20th century's finest actors and will be missed by his many fans and admirers."

All major newspapers ran lengthy and conflicted obituaries, extolling his finest roles, noting the profound changes he brought to live and film performance—and lamenting the many ways in which he squandered his gifts. The *New York Times*'s lead was typical: "Marlon Brando, the rebellious prodigy who electrified a generation and forever transformed the art of screen acting but whose obstinacy and eccentricity prevented him from fully realizing the promise of his early genius, died on Thursday at a Los Angeles hospital." *USA Today*'s headline was more succinct: BRANDO REMEMBERED AS BRILLIANT, BIZARRE. There were also irresponsible and unfounded reports of Marlon's indigence. Legal bills for Christian Brando's defense were still to be paid, it was said; there were ten surviving children to support and all sorts of household expenses. In Britain *The Independent* reported that Marlon "was by all accounts living in virtual penury. His home was a shabby one-bedroom bungalow in Beverly Hills." And *The Scotsman* told its readers that the star "who was credited with reinventing acting for the screen . . . went from the first man of Hollywood to a highly eccentric and cantankerous recluse forced to live on social security." Another biography, *Brando in Twilight,* by Patricia Ruiz, claimed that Marlon owed banks almost $5 million. "So frightened was he of debt collectors," Ruiz wrote, "that he hid away his Oscar statuette for the 1954 performance in *On the Waterfront.*"

More incidents occurred the following week. Marlon had asked his business manager, Jo An Corrales, to ease his mind: In the event of his death the corpse would be locked from public view. And then, in another of her boss's mercurial gestures, she was fired only a few weeks before he was taken to the hospital. Absent her authority, Marlon's heirs and assigns took over the funeral arrangements, allowing visitors to view the body at a Sherman Oaks funeral home. To have the ultimate private figure exposed in this manner "was appalling," complained Marlon's longtime makeup man Philip Rhodes. "That was the last thing Marlon would have wanted, to be put on display like that." On principle, Rhodes stayed away from the viewing, as did almost all of the Brando cronies. One wish of the deceased did come to pass: In accordance with his instructions, he was cremated. The ashes, along with those of Wally Cox, kept for decades in the Mulholland house, were scattered in Death Valley and Tahiti. During the mourning period a distraught forty-year-old woman named Lisa Warmer suddenly showed up at the front door of the Brando house. "Marlon Brando is my father," she sobbed. "I found out about him six years ago when my mother [actress Cynthia Lynn] told me. He was always too ill to see me, but now I want to be where I belong, with my siblings." Security guards turned her away. In contrast to Warmer's unhappy account, the seventy-seven-year-old Greek actress Irene Papas chose this time to tell a correspondent for the Italian newspaper *Corriere Della Sera* that she and Marlon had enjoyed a long, clandestine love affair. "Perhaps I'm wrong to speak about it," she said, "now that he's not around to contradict me, but I'm confessing it precisely because, as of today, he's in the absolute, far from everybody, belonging to everyone." Papas was hardly alone in her nostalgia for the lost lover. But almost all the others—and there were scores of them—chose to keep their emotions private. One who did not was Angela Borlaza Magaling, who called herself the "majordomo" of the Brando household in Marlon's final years. She sued his executors, claiming to be "the victim of fraud, deceit and a broken oral contract with Marlon, who promised to give her a house." She sought proceeds from the sale of the home, whenever it was bought by a new owner, plus $2 million in punitive damages.

Whatever her other qualifications, Magaling had a much better idea of the Brando fortune than the rumormongers who said that Marlon had died broke. Probate documents filed in Los Angeles court showed that he left an estate valued at over $21 million. Investments alone gave him an annual income of $500,000. Yet the reports were not wrong when they suggested that he had lopsided financial and moral obligations. Marlon's will identified many surviving children. They included Christian, forty-six, by Anna Kashfi; Miko, forty-three, by Movita Castaneda; Teihotu, forty-one, and Rebecca, thirty-eight, by Tarita Teripaia (Cheyenne was the third child by this marriage). Also mentioned were three children he had by Maria Ruiz: Ninna, fifteen; Myles, twelve; and Timothy, ten. In addition there were Maimiti and Raiatua Brando, ages twenty-eight and twenty-three, mother unacknowledged. An instance of Marlon's quixotic kindness and antipathy was also revealed during the reading of the will: In addition to the biological children, he had a daughter by adoption. Petra Brando, thirty-one, was the biological daughter of his onetime assistant Caroline Barrett and James Clavell. The man who had written *Shōgun* and written and produced *The Great Escape* was married, and would not leave his wife to marry Barrett. Marlon stepped in, paying the bills for Petra's education in college and law school, suing Clavell (unsuccessfully), and later setting up Caroline and Petra in London. Petra had flown to his side when news of Cheyenne's suicide came in. The two were very close until, at the time his income began to dry up, he asked mother and child for repayment. It was not forthcoming, and he initiated a lawsuit. The court judgment went against him. Furious, Marlon responded in his last will and testament. Still hurt and bewildered by Cheyenne's suicide in Tahiti nine years before, he also made certain that Tuki, Cheyenne's fourteen-year-old son, would not be considered part of the family. "I intentionally, and with full knowledge of the consequences," read the legal statement, "do not provide in my will or in my living trust for Cheyenne's issue or for Petra Brando, or for any of Petra's issue."

Film historian David Thomson observed that Brando's millions seemed "like enormous wealth, but in truth it doesn't eliminate the possibility that Brando was at the end of his rope." Thomson crunched the numbers. The house was evaluated at $10 million, although repairs and maintenance had been severely neglected. Any new owner had to be prepared to spend seven figures in improvements and restorations. Tetiaroa and the other small islands were probably worth several million, but Marlon had put a lot more than that into their development, only to see it all come to nothing. To the end, his outlay was enormous—taxes, and gifts to activists and their social causes, hangers-on, out-of-luck actors, friends, offspring. The checks in the mailbox, on the other hand, were nowhere near as sizable as they might have been.

On the films that established his reputation—*The Men, Streetcar, Viva Zapata!, Julius Caesar, On the Waterfront*—Marlon had been paid a flat fee. Those classics had made other people rich. When actors began to get large pieces of the profits, he was not enough of a businessman to negotiate profit-making deals. *Mutiny on the Bounty* was the one picture that gave him a chance at real participation—10 percent of the gross. But for good and bad reasons it never made a profit and didn't contribute a cent to his old age. Concluded Thomson, "I do not seek your tears on Brando's behalf—he was too often his own greatest enemy—so much as understanding. The way in which he became so hostile to the picture business and to acting had to do with his savagely mixed feelings about the money. And that's how a movie star sitting on a twenty-million-dollar estate could feel himself tricked, exploited and just scraping together the means of existence."

In Marlon's final years more was written about what he registered on the scales than what he did on the screen. Scrutinizing the newspaper coverage, Peter Bogdanovich remarked that almost every obit showed photographs from the first six films and *The Godfather*, barely acknowledging the other thirty-three movies. "Had his death come twenty-five years earlier," wrote the cineaste, "it felt as though the references about his professional legacy would not have been very different." Marlon's was indeed a front-loaded career, with only a handful of noteworthy features after *Waterfront*. In his wake new and exciting young actors came to attract public attention, different studios were established, and fresh cinematic techniques supplanted the old ones. The public memory is short. Given the examples of so many of Hollywood's leading men, including John Barrymore, Paul Muni, and, for that matter, Montgomery Clift, his reputation was expected to suffer a posthumous decline. That never occurred—though there were many who tried to bring it down. The Brando image continued to glow despite their efforts. Until July 1, 2004, everyone agreed that Marlon was larger than life. Just then, no one understood that he was also larger than death.

The King Who Would Be Man

1

The posthumous slurs began with Tarita Teriipaia's curious little volume, *Marlon, My Love and My Torment*. Now that her husband was safely dead, she described the marriage as a living hell. On the basis of a lone entry in the disturbed Cheyenne's diary, she accused Brando of sexual abuse. Darwin Porter's larger but equally distasteful *Brando Unzipped* concentrated on Marlon's nocturnal prowls. "At Brando's peak," ran the publisher's blurb, the actor's "list of lovers read like a *Who's Who* of the cultural elite": Bob Dylan, Gore Vidal, Leonard Bernstein, Joan Collins, Faye Dunaway, Bianca Jagger, Kim Stanley, Rita Moreno, Shelley Winters, Tyrone Power, Gloria Vanderbilt. Denials by Brando's alleged bedmates were useless. (Vidal had an especially tart disclaimer in his memoir *Palimpsest*.) Having cashed in on the subject's faults and inadequacies, Porter finished with a flow of crocodile tears. "The kids who had flocked to see *The Wild One* in the 1950s had grown up and sired rebellious children of their own. Now, they could even scoff at the idol of their teenage years.

"To his new best friend of the 1990s, Michael Jackson (of all people), Marlon confided, 'My good-bye has been the longest good-bye in the history of show business. My tragedy was I didn't know enough to get off the stage when the play had ended.' "

This was followed by a stage version of *Unzipped* at the Minnesota Fringe Festival. Devoted to the relationship between Marlon and Wally Cox, *Bud 'n' Wally* was set in Marlon's hospital room hours before his death. As Brando lamented the loss of his old pal, Cox's apparition materialized and the two conversed in what a local critic called "tedious whininess."

On the assertive new medium of the Internet, a chorus of denigrators chimed in. *Wall Street Journal* theater critic Terry Teachout disgorged his long-held malice under the headline NON-CONTENDER. The *New York Times* obit, Teachout reminded his readers, claimed that Marlon's " 'erratic career, obstinate eccentricities and recurring tragedies prevented him from fully realizing the promise of his early genius. . . . ' For what it's worth I never cared for Brando, not even in *A Streetcar Named Desire*—I thought he was a self-indulgent, undisciplined ham . . . it strikes me that his admirers, however fervent, ought to squirm at the use of the word 'genius' to describe him."

Richard Schickel's biography, written in Marlon's last years, contrasted two actors. "Paul Newman is almost exactly Brando's age and he is everything Brando is not. He is fit and attractive. He has endured personal tragedy [the suicide of a son] with dignity and courage. He continues to find serious work that engages and challenges him. He has also found causes that elicit his concern, and he is practical-minded and effective on their behalf. He has, as well, found a way to remain present in the world, and at the same time to maintain his privacy. . . . One thinks that perhaps, in his sleepless early morning hours, Brando, too, wishes he were Paul Newman. Wishes, that is to say, that he did not have to waste the gains he considered ill-gotten on a stunned and reclusive search for coherence."

Similarly, at intellectualconservative.com, Nicholas Stix compared Marlon to another performer with a different track record. "In the field of acting, Gene Hackman may not be Brando's equal in raw talent, and certainly hasn't had the sort of scripts sent to him that Brando did. Hackman, the plain-looking, balding, quintessential late-bloomer, who as an acting student flunked out of the Pasadena Playhouse, where he was considered the worst student in its history, got his first role after his thirtieth birthday. And yet, Hackman has had the more brilliant career, fully exploiting his own considerable gifts, and making the most of every role he has played." It was "as if the young Brando had made a deal with the Devil to quickly attain greatness, but Lucifer had now exacted his price, which required that Brando continually disgrace himself and his profession, and become a porcine parody of his formerly handsome self."

The popular Web site listology.com presented a roster of ten over-rated actors. Marlon Brando came in fifth: "His only good role was as Vito Corleone; everything else was self-absorbed, pretentious crap."

On the Left-leaning buzzle.com, Timothy Sexton castigated the director and star of *On the Waterfront*. "Having destroyed several lives with his [HUAC] testimony, Kazan came under attack from certain quarters for his cowardly action. His response was a film that is so highly regarded it verges on the nauseating. (I'm not even going to get into the almost campy melodrama and the hysterical acting. I know it verges on a sacrilege to suggest that Marlon Brando was ever anything but brilliant during the 1950s, but in my opinion you won't see a more affected piece of acting in any other movie released during that decade.)"

On the Right, the Fundamentalist Baptist Information Service used Marlon as an exemplar of sinful profligacy: "Brando had everything this world has to offer, looks, talent, money, fame, and the means to pursue every whim and pleasure, but he squandered his life on rebellion against Almighty God and rejected salvation through Jesus Christ. He 'had it all,' but in reality, he had nothing."

Among the "all" that Marlon had were his worldly possessions. These went up for auction at Christie's New York showroom a year after his death. Examining the goods, British journalist Anthony Haden-Guest found the process cringe-making: "Marlon Brando was so uncomfortable as an icon and so reflexively private a man that rummaging through his things made me feel less a reporter than a voyeur." Among the 320 objects were some knickknacks (Marlon preferred the Yiddish word *chotchkes*) that could be found in any middle-class suburban home: shell chimes, a Japanese paper fan, a wooden Buddha figurine, a black and white ceramic dolphin. Some parts of the sale seemed a violation of privacy: Brando's American Express cards, his driver's license, his Screen Actors Guild membership card, 00003839. Listed in the catalog were a framed photograph of Rita Moreno, nude; doodles idly drawn in pencil; a foosball table; a black Yamaha piano; drums, one bearing a drumhead tensioning device for which he had obtained patent number 6,812,392; letters from family members and colleagues, including one from Karl Malden that obviously meant a great deal to the recipient: "Last night I went to see *A Dry White Season* and I don't care if you are five hundred pounds or fifty pounds. You are a fucking genius."

There were medals won in high school for canoeing, boxing, and dancing, and an award for his work in *Truckline Café,* but no Oscar for his performance in *Waterfront.* Somewhere along the line, Marlon had lost track of the statuette. There were annotated scripts, books underlined and marked up—above a passage in Eric Hoffer's *In Our Time* was the single word "Horseshit!" And there were some surprising videotapes. "Who would have guessed," mused Haden-Guest, "that the brooding and reticent—except when preachy—man would be so in love with comedy? That he would own wodges of Abbot and Costello, Richard Pryor and *The Best of British Comedy*, to say nothing of well over three dozen cassettes of Laurel and Hardy?" All this led a Christie's executive to remark, "It was strange. Just looking around the house, you wouldn't have been able to guess what his career had been."

Marlon's effects were estimated to be worth, in toto, about $1 million. They brought in more than double that amount. One item, an annotated *Godfather* script, was sold for $312,000, the highest price ever for a typed scenario. Proceeds from the auction were divided among the children, all of whom had given permission for the sale. Some outsiders objected, to no avail. Biographer Peter Manso spoke for them when he said the auction bordered "on complete tastelessness and Brando would never, ever have wanted this. I can assure you that Marlon is turning over in his grave to think that someone has his driver's license."

The degradation continued; in the same year, the *Los Angeles Times* ran a story on the sorry state of Tetiaroa. According to Matthew Heller, during Marlon's decline the island came to be "more like a dystopia than a utopia. Brando, a massively flawed product of the Hollywood dream factory, couldn't isolate his fantasy island from the storms of his personal life." Heller quoted George Englund: Cheyenne's suicide "shattered" her father; "he has never been able to stand on the place where it happened." Isolated in Beverly Hills, Marlon left the day-to-day operations to Tarita, who had no administrative or financial experience. "In his absence, the roofs and walls of the hotel bungalows, which should have been replaced every six years, fell apart; garbage, rather than being composted, stacked up where the tourists couldn't see it; and poachers raided the lagoon, depleting the stock of fish . . . and the bills kept coming."

With Marlon gone, Tetiaroa and the other islands were leased to Richard Bailey, a luxury-resort developer. He promised to keep the area an "eco-resort," with thirty villas set back from the beach and invisible from the lagoon. But Bailey, Heller wrote, "could build the world's most environmentally sensitive resort and still wouldn't satisfy the Brando cohorts, including [his former business manager Jo An] Corrales, who claimed, 'they are changing the island forever.' " The friends were particularly unhappy with the exploitative name Bailey gave to his Tetiaroa development: The Brando. Grumbled one of them, Marlon "wanted people to go there for Tetiaroa, not because of some movie actor."

2

While the predators went about their business, popular culture took a very different course. *Fan-Tan*, the long-abandoned potboiler by Marlon and Donald Cammell, had begun as a screenplay, with Marlon improvising the story and acting out the characters. Cammell then fleshed out the adventures of Anatole Doultry, an amiable middle-aged rogue who sails the South Seas in the company of Chinese pirates. After Cammell's suicide in 1996, the idea was abandoned. His widow rescued the manuscript and got it to a British publisher. David Thomson adeptly edited the pages and supplied an ending. The prose was reminiscent of a Fu Manchu novel: "Untruth was a violin on which he played like a Paganini of bunkum," but the plot was rollicking enough to earn some surprisingly good reviews in 2005, among them Joe Queenan's tongue-in-cheek salute in *The New York Times:* "To its credit, *Fan-Tan* never sounds mass-produced or generic; it never has the weary, phoned-in quality of books by Tom Clancy and Stephen King. Instead, it sounds like the boys had a heap of fun cranking out this page turner while throwing back a few hundred martinis. There's a lot to be said for this approach; if you can't write a great novel, at least write a peculiar one and have a few laughs along the way."

All the while, rockers, who had never lost their admiration for Marlon, kept his name on the charts. Back in 1980 an Australian teenager named Russell Crowe had prophetically written and recorded the song "I Want to Be Like Marlon Brando." Later there were numbers like Bruce Springsteen's "It's Hard to Be a Saint in the City":

> *I could walk like Brando right into the sun . . .*

and Jefferson Airplane's "Madeleine Street":

> *I took an Airplane named Desire,*
> *I sat next to Marlon Brando . . .*

and David Bowie's

> *I'm feelin' tragic like I'm Marlon Brando*

Billy Joel's "We Didn't Start the Fire" also cited Marlon, as did Elton John's "Goodbye Marlon Brando," and the Doobie Brothers' "8th Avenue Shuffle" and Neil Young's "Pocahontas":

> *Marlon Brando, Pocahontas and me . . .*

as well as Madonna's "Super Pop":

> *If I was an actor, I'd be Marlon Brando . . .*

Finally came numbers like Robbie Williams's "Advertising Space":

> *I saw you standing at the gates*
> *When Marlon Brando passed away . . .*

In the pop pantheon he had been an amalgam of Stanley Kowalski, Terry Malloy, the Wild One, and the Godfather. With his death in 2004 he became one man—the actor Marlon Brando, first among equals. The Establishment, anxious not to be left in the dust, feverishly began working on its own act of rehabilitation.

3

Budd Schulberg, scenarist of *On the Waterfront*, led the reappraisals. In a memoir for *Vanity Fair* entitled "The King Who Would Be Man," he wrote of Marlon's marital conflicts, of the murder and suicide, of the celebrity who had run from fame, who had quested all his life for privacy and peace of mind, and was suddenly dragged into his worst nightmare, a public scandal that became a tabloid dream. "At times," Schulberg commented, "it seemed to me that some madman was writing Marlon's story and overdoing it." In Los Angeles, shortly after Marlon's death, the author looked up some of Brando's old friends. All of them mentioned one actor: "Have you talked to Harry Dean Stanton yet? In these last years Harry Dean was closer to Marlon than anyone."

Stanton, another "bad boy" resident of Mulholland Drive, was quite forthcoming about his friend. The tall, gaunt character actor, who was something of a searcher himself, spoke of long early-morning conversations the two men had toward the end. Brando "was into poetry, philosophy, and religions. He was curious about everything. We talked about ego from the Buddhist point of view. We talked about Shakespeare. Marlon really knew Shakespeare, and sometimes he would recite whole long monologues from *Macbeth, Twelfth Night.*"

Schulberg visualized the two Hollywood seekers of solace, talking from dusk until the first rays of sun entered the room, Harry Dean cast as the misfit and the ailing Marlon "beginning to look like, and think like Buddha." At one point, said Stanton, Brando caught him off guard. " 'What do you think of me?' he demanded suddenly. And I said, 'What do I think of you? I think you are nothing. NOTHING!' And Marlon began to laugh, and he went on laughing and laughing."

Schulberg imagined Marlon happy. "He had finally achieved his goal. *Peace, peace at last. What I always wanted to be. Nothing.*"

But it could never be as simple as that, not with Brando. At his memorial on the Mulholland hilltop, with some grown children and a few friends who cared deeply for him, his sister Jocelyn had made a final plea: "It's over now. Let him be."

Concluded Schulberg: "It was a kind and gentle thought. But sorry, Jocelyn. And sorry, Marlon. It's not your fault. You were just too damned famous. And too damned good. You can turn down those awards all you want. But, like your worst dreams, they'll keep on coming."

The writer was borne out by events. On the American Film Institute's list of the top fifty stars of the American cinema, Marlon Brando came in fourth, just behind Humphrey Bogart, Cary Grant, and James Stewart.

When the AFI got around to its list of the top one hundred movie quotations, Marlon's *Godfather* line "I'm gonna make him an offer he can't refuse" was second, just behind Clark Gable's *Gone with the Wind* pronouncement "Frankly, my dear, I don't give a damn." Brando also had the third most famous quote—*Waterfront*'s "I coulda been a contender" monologue.

Time named Marlon Brando one of the one hundred most influential people in the twentieth century; *Variety* put him on its list of one hundred icons of the century: "Brando elevated acting to such a degree that scores of acolytes emulated his at-times extreme approach to inhabiting a role, from James Dean's tormented Oedipal thrashing in *East of Eden* to Robert De Niro gaining forty pounds to pummel his way through *Raging Bull.* If Stanislavski's writings became the bible for anyone serious about digging deep for a character's essence, then Brando became the poster boy for the Method." The entry for Brando in the *St. James Encyclopedia of Popular Culture* was no less flattering; it stated that he would remain "unchallenged as the most important actor in modern American Cinema, if not the greatest of all time."

Looking back, Francis Ford Coppola spoke of Marlon's way of working. "He felt that in life you don't know your lines. So why learn your lines and then try to make people feel as if they're coming to you spontaneously? He liked to struggle for the lines because that's a real thinking process." In 2007 the Turner Classic Movie channel examined that process in a three-hour documentary. The life and times of Marlon Brando were traced from Omaha to Broadway to Hollywood, before going on to Tahiti and the poignant finale. Marlon's contemporary Martin Landau remembered the classes with Stella Adler. His fellow student "was theatrical without *being* theatrical. It came out of an honesty, but because of its size and scope, it had a style and [Adler] was smart enough to see it." Martin Scorsese underlined Marlon's "understanding of suffering and obsession." Now was the time, said the director, especially for younger people, to go back and see the Brando films "in the order in which they were made. Mainly because, I think, now they're too hip to feel those emotions that were exploding on the screen with him. It's about being human." The actors who came of age under Marlon's influence, among them Johnny Depp, Frederic Forrest, John Turturro, Dennis Hopper, and Jane Fonda, delivered awed tributes. Bernardo Bertolucci and Arthur Penn added their own accolades. Several major figures in Marlon's life were missing from the screen; Jocelyn, who had died at the age of eighty-six in 2005; Coppola, who preferred not to participate; and Jack Nicholson, who had written about his late friend and obviously felt that nothing more need be said.

"Marlon Brando is one of the great men of the twentieth and twenty-first centuries," Nicholson wrote in *Rolling Stone,* "and we lesser mortals are obligated to cut through the shit and proclaim it.

This man has been my idol all of my professional life, and I don't think I'm alone in that. The impact of movies is enormous, and his impact in the movies was bigger than anyone else's—ever. . . .

"I think Marlon knew he was the greatest. I don't think he dwelled on it, nor did he ever say as much to me. But, come on, there was a reason people expected so much from him right to the end. That's why people always expected him to be working. And believe me, there were times when he told me he wanted to work and couldn't. It disturbs me that toward the end, all some people could speak about was his weight."

In those hortatory lines, Nicholson encapsulated all that was right and wrong about the film industry—and about too many people on its periphery. Half a century before, that industry had enthusiastically introduced Marlon Brando to the world, and found good work for him to do. As soon as he displayed a temperament as unprecedented as his talent, though, the executives gave up on him. If Marlon had done something romantic and picturesque to himself—smashed a sports car, perhaps, or overdosed on heroin—that they could have dealt with. But his continual challenges to producers, directors, actors, and scenarists were outside their frame of reference. When he began the long period of regression, the withdrawal, the hiding in layers of adipose tissue, they repeated Tennessee Williams's callous line about Marlon Brando being paid by the pound, and wrote him off. They were not alone. A large percentage of the paparazzi worldwide amused themselves by invading his property and then chiding him for being a hermit, marking him down for the sin of avarice and then hustling their photos to newspapers in hopes of a big return, dilating on every rumor of his sexual exploits and then wagging a finger at his wanton behavior. They repeatedly, and sometimes sadistically, examined his litany of personal flaws and dramatic family sorrows, rarely mentioning the contributions he had made to American cinema. At the time of his death, they were still at it. Dismayed, Diane Keaton commented, "The one thing that has been disturbing to me in the tone in some of the obituaries is that even in death they were never satisfied with him. It was never enough."

In the short Penguin Lives book *Brando,* Patricia Bosworth reports that late in life Marlon "confided to a friend that he had spent a lifetime trying to be less crazy." In that admission lies the key to all that came before. If there was a "Rosebud" in Brando's life it was the mental illness that had dogged him for decades, probably from early childhood.

So many of the actions he took were not those of a rational man, and the wonder, in the end, is not that he made so few essential films but that he made so many. He knew as much; the only book he published in his lifetime, *Brando: Songs My Mother Taught Me*, was dedicated to his sisters, his children, and his psychiatrist. Concluded Marlon, "Thanks to Dr. Harrington, my own efforts, and the simple passage of time, I can finally be the child I never had a chance to be." In the competition with his great rival Montgomery Clift, he seems to have won the self-destruction contest; Clift's may not have been the longest suicide in Hollywood after all. Occasions of sanity and sanctity were not unfamiliar to Marlon, but he found them very late in life: meditating in solitude; reading philosophy; speaking to strangers on ham radio; lying out on the sand under the stars; attempting, however inexpertly, to speak up for those who had done wrong, or who had been wronged. He had spent a lot of time in both camps.

Even in death, Marlon could not stay out of the tabloids. Christian Brando got into more trouble when actor Robert Blake was accused of murdering his wife, Bonnie Lee Bakley. Blake in turn accused Christian, who had been romantically involved with Bonnie, and who Blake believed was the father of her year-old daughter. DNA tests proved otherwise: Blake was the father. Moreover, police determined that Christian's alibi was sound—he happened to be out of state on the night of the shooting. When Blake was acquitted, Christian's name receded from the headlines, only to surface one more time at his death in January 2008. He had died, said one of his friends, "from too much living."

Marlon's name never did leave the newspapers for long. Frequently it was in the show-business pages, and once in the real estate section, when Jack Nicholson bought Marlon's house for $5 million. The place, he remarked sadly, was "derelict," and "getting the mold out would be difficult. It is more than likely that we'll take the house down."

Marlon's estate has long since been evaluated, fought over, and dispersed. But he left two bequests that lie beyond the reach of his heirs and assigns. The first is to the public. Five of his early films are indisputable classics of black-and-white cinema: *The Men*, *A Streetcar Named Desire*, *Viva Zapata!*, *Julius Caesar*, and *On the Waterfront*. *The Wild One* has made its own place in popular culture. Between those astonishing features and *The Godfather* there is widely (and incorrectly) supposed to be a desert with only a handful of oases. Marlon took a lot of significant roles between his debut as Ken Wilcheck in 1950 and the Vito Corleone of 1972. Sky Masterson, Major Gruver, Snakeskin Xavier, Rio, Fletcher Christian, Robert Crain, Major Weldon Penderton, Sir William Walker, and Peter Quint are memorable figures that no one else could have played with such convincing passion. Post-*Godfather* came such indelible personae as Paul of *Last Tango*, Robert E. Lee Clayton of *The Missouri Breaks*, Colonel Walter E. Kurtz of *Apocalypse Now*, and Ian McKenzie of *A Dry White Season*. These creations have aged well, even if the motion pictures themselves show the erosions of time.

The second bequest is to the acting community. John Saxon recalls the first time he saw Brando. The Oscars had recently been given out for *Waterfront*, and Marlon was a bit wary as he parked near Schwab's drugstore on Sunset Boulevard, a famous hangout for show folk. He had reason to smile a minute later. The thirty-year-old "emerged from his car," says Saxon, "and I remember an actor saying, 'Marlon, you did it for us!' These were not the Tyrone Power kind of good-looking people. 'You did it for us' meant you gave us an opportunity to be somebody. It was a break in the system."

As things turned out it was more than a break; it was a complete severance. The opportunity to be "somebody," in Saxon's phrase, mirrored Terry Malloy's famous protest in *On the Waterfront:* "I coulda had class . . . I coulda been *somebody.*" By taking chances, by jumping without a net in film after film for more than fifty years, Marlon Brando rewrote the conventions of screen acting. In the process he helped to make somebodies out of performers who, in previous times, would have settled for character parts—if they worked at all. There can be no doubt of James Caan's observation, made after his hero had passed away: "Anyone of my generation who says he hasn't 'done Brando' is lying."

Will Marlon retain his iconic status in the years to come? The collective memory is short, and in the epoch of the twenty-four-hour news cycle, the iPod, YouTube, TiVo, and video games, there are more distractions than ever before. Yet, in a crowning irony, there are also unprecedented devices for information retrieval. Today the Brando oeuvre can be fetched by hitting a few computer keys. Skeptics who think the man's impact is exaggerated can find the truth easily enough. All they have to do is compare the leading male performances before his debut with those afterward. Once observed, these astonishing performances cannot be unseen. The Bud who blossomed into a superstar, the champion who called himself a bum, the artist who denied his art, remains a dominant presence in contemporary cinema. Another generation has taken over from Caan's, and its members are still "doing Brando." The generations that follow are likely to be doing him for the rest of this century—and beyond.

Appendix

Broadway Credits

I Remember Mama, Music Box Theatre, 1944
Truckline Café, Belasco Theatre, 1946
Candida, Cort Theatre, 1946
A Flag Is Born, Alvin Theatre, 1947
A Streetcar Named Desire, Ethel Barrymore Theatre, 1947

Film Credits

1950 *The Men*
1951 *A Streetcar Named Desire*
1952 *Viva Zapata!*
1953 *Julius Caesar; The Wild One*
1954 *On the Waterfront; Desirée*
1955 *Guys and Dolls*
1956 *The Teahouse of the August Moon*
1957 *Sayonara*
1958 *The Young Lions*
1959 *The Fugitive Kind*
1961 *One-Eyed Jacks* (actor-director)
1962 *Mutiny on the Bounty*
1963 *The Ugly American*
1964 *Bedtime Story*
1965 *Morituri*
1966 *The Chase; The Appaloosa*
1967 *A Countess from Hong Kong; Reflections in a Golden Eye*
1968 *Candy; The Night of the Following Day*
1969 *Burn! (Queimada)*
1970 *King: A Filmed Record . . . Montgomery to Memphis* (documentary)
1972 *The Nightcomers; The Godfather; Last Tango in Paris*
1976 *The Missouri Breaks*
1978 *Superman; Raoni* (documentary, narrator)
1979 *Apocalypse Now; Roots: The Next Generations* (TV)
1980 *The Formula*
1981 *The Rebels* (biographical documentary)
1989 *A Dry White Season*
1990 *The Freshman*

1991 *Hearts of Darkness: A Filmmaker's Apocalypse* (documentary)

1992 *Christopher Columbus: The Discovery*

1995 *Don Juan DeMarco*

1996 *The Island of Dr. Moreau*

1997 *The Brave*

1998 *Free Money*

2001 *The Score*

2004 "*The Godfather:* The Game" (video game, voice-over); *Big Bug Man* (animated film, voice-over)

2006 *Superman Returns* (posthumous appearance from archival footage)

2007 *Brando* (television biographical documentary on Turner Classic Movies)

Acknowledgments

Marlon Brando died in 2004 at the age of eighty. His contemporaries from the Midwest and New York City are few in number. Those who remain tend to have minor, conflicting, or faulty memories of the young Marlon.

But there are exceptions, and no one is more exceptional a memoirist than Elaine Stritch, one of the most gifted and versatile actresses in Broadway history. Despite a heavy schedule and precarious health, Ms. Stritch spent many hours with me reminiscing about her acting apprenticeship at the New School for Social Research, and about her classmate Marlon Brando. Her brilliant showpiece *At Liberty* includes recollections of Brando, but these conversations went far beyond anything she had put on the record.

Ellen Adler, Stella Adler's daughter, knew the actor from his first days in New York and remained a friend until his final days in California. She was also kind enough to share her memories in lively and intelligent detail. Lance Morrow introduced me to Leila Hadley Luce, whose memories of Marlon on Broadway and on the New York party circuit were entertaining and invaluable. Lisa Reitman-Dobi offered sharp editorial commentary and was kind enough to bring Diane Ladd into the picture. The actress was a close friend of Jocelyn and Marlon Brando. Marlon evidently regarded Diane as a colleague rather than a romantic interest; they had both lost children and he became, in her words, "a kind of soul mate." Ms. Ladd was extremely helpful about the actor's later years. Others who knew Marlon through the decades, and who were willing to share their reminiscences with me, included Josh Greenfeld, Daniel Melnick, Paul Maslansky, and the late Brad Darrach, Elia Kazan, Eliot Asinov, and Alan Schneider.

Considering Brando's life, his friend and fellow actor Maureen Stapleton once told an interviewer, "Marlon, oh, man, you want to talk about pain?" As this book demonstrates, the anguish that showed in so many of his performances was earned, not imitated. To trace its roots and branches, I consulted several psychiatrists and therapists who specialize in the emotional difficulties of those in the performing arts. Dr. John Rodman referred me to Dr. Gary Lefer, who was remarkably insightful and jargon-free; Dr. Charlotte Doyle of Sarah Lawrence College added worthy information, as did psychotherapists Antoinette Lynn and Sybil Baran. Other doctors gave their points of view about Marlon's afflictions, but were unwilling to be quoted by name.

My colleagues at *City Journal* were unfailingly helpful and kind, especially Myron Magnet and his successor, Brian Anderson, and their aide, Benjamin Plotinsky. John Leo and Harry Stein proved to be more than allies; they were astute advisers.

Jess Korman offered many discerning and heartening words, as did my fellow Centurion Hugh Nissenson. I am also grateful to my former *Time* colleagues Gerald Clarke, Paul Gray, Christopher Porterfield, Roger Rosenblatt, and R. Z. Sheppard for their sound historical and literary counsel. Andrew Ettinger, a student of Brando's social activism, pointed the way to troves of material that might otherwise have escaped my attention.

Again, as in the case of so many of my previous books, the Rivertowns group provided stalwart support. Among the most valuable were Will Shortz, the great editor of the *New York Times* crosswords; Amy Hsu; my fellow cofounder, Steve Zeitlin, director of City Lore; Rob Bernstein; Fred Gordon; Bob Mankoff; John Ng; Robert Roberts, the most skilled table-tennis player I have ever encountered; Guizhong Xu, Peter Wolf; and all the other pongers who kept me in shape for this journey.

As always, Peter Gethers made what seemed to be impossible requirements; as always, they turned out to be not only possible but mandatory. And Claudia Herr was encouraging every step of the ramp. Villette Harris was once again the invaluable and tireless researcher for both references and pictures; Kathy Robbins, agent, adviser, and friend, lightened the burden with wisdom and humor, and the librarians at the Lincoln Center and Forty-second Street libraries were helpful beyond measure.

In first place, though listed last, is my family. Once again a glass of gratitude and love is lifted to May, Lili, Ethan, Andy, Daniela, and Lea and Aly, who will want to rent black-and-white movies someday.

Bibliography

Biographies and Background

Adler, Jacob. *A Life on the Stage,* translated with a commentary by Lulla Rosenfeld, Applause, 2001.

Adler, Stella. *The Art of Acting,* compiled and edited by Howard Kissel, Applause, 2000.

Alpert, Hollis. *Marlon Brando and the Ghost of Stanley Kowalski,* Hearst, 1961.

Biskind, Peter. The Godfather *Companion,* HarperPerennial, 1990.

Bly, Nellie. *Marlon Brando: Larger Than Life,* Pinnacle, 1994.

Boller, Paul F., Jr., and Ronald L. Davis. *Hollywood Anecdotes,* Morrow, 1987.

Bond, Rudy. *I Rode A Streetcar Named Desire,* Birch Brook Press, 2000.

Bosworth, Patricia. *Marlon Brando,* Viking, 2001.

———. *Montgomery Clift: A Biography,* Limelight Editions, 2001.

Bragg, Melvyn. *Richard Burton: A Life,* Little, Brown, 1988.

Braithwaite, Bruce. *The Films of Marlon Brando,* Confucian Press, 1982.

Brando, Anna Kashfi, and E. P. Stein. *Brando for Breakfast,* Crown, 1979.

Brando, Marlon. Last Will and Testament, filed with the Los Angeles Superior Court, July 2, 2004.

———. *Listing of Personal Property for Auction,* Christie's, June 30, 2005.

———. and Donald Cammell. *Fan-Tan,* edited and with an Afterword by David Thomson, Knopf, 2005.

———, with Robert Lindsey. *Brando: Songs My Mother Taught Me,* Random House, 1994.

Capote, Truman. *A Capote Reader,* Random House, 1987.

Carey, Gary. *Marlon Brando: The Only Contender,* St. Martin's Press, 1985.

Clurman, Harold. *The Fervent Years: The Group Theatre & the 30's,* Da Capo, 1983.

———. *The Collected Works,* Applause, 1994.

Comery, Douglas. *The Hollywood Studio System,* St. Martin's Press, 1986.

Conrad, Joseph. *Heart of Darkness,* Signet, 1950.

Coppola, Eleanor. *Notes on the Making of* Apocalypse Now, Limelight Editions, 2004.

Cowie, Peter. *The* Apocalypse Now *Book,* Da Capo, 2001.

Dewey, Donald. *Marcello Mastroianni,* Birch Lane Press, 1993.

Dick, Bernard F. *Engulfed: The Death of Paramount Pictures and the Birth of Corporate Hollywood,* University Press of Kentucky, 2001.

Downing, David. *Marlon Brando,* Stein and Day, 1984.

Fiore, Carlo. *Bud: The Brando I Knew,* Delacorte, 1974.

French, Philip. *The Movie Moguls,* Regnery, 1969.

Friedel, Robert O. *Borderline Personality Disorder Demystified,* Avalon, 2004.

Englund, George. *Marlon Brando: The Way It's Never Been Done Before,* Harper, 2005.

Gabler, Neal. *An Empire of Their Own: How the Jews Invented Hollywood,* Anchor, 1989.

———. *Life: The Movie: How Entertainment Conquered Reality,* Vintage, 2000.

Garfield, David. *A Player's Place: The Story of the Actors Studio,* Macmillan, 1980.

Gifford, Barry. *Brando Rides Alone: A Reconsideration of the Film One-Eyed Jacks,* North Atlantic Books, 2004.

Gill, Brendan. *Tallulah,* Holt, Rinehart & Winston, 1972.

Goldman, William. *Adventures in the Screen Trade: A Personal View of Hollywood and Screenwriting,* Warner Books, 1983.

———. *Which Lie Did I Tell?: More Adventures in the Screen Trade,* Vintage, 2000.

———. *The Big Picture: Who Killed Hollywood and Other Essays,* Applause, 2002.

Grobel, Lawrence. *Conversations with Brando,* Cooper Square Press, 1991.

———. *The Art of the Interview: Lessons from a Master of the Craft,* Three Rivers Press, 2004.

Hecht, Ben. *A Child of the Century,* Simon & Schuster, 1954.

———. *Perfidy,* Milah Press, 1999.

Higham, Charles. *Brando: The Unauthorized Biography,* New American Library, 1987.

———. *Merchant of Dreams: Louis B. Mayer, M.G.M. and the Secret Hollywood,* Laurel, 1994.

Hofstadter, Richard. *Anti-intellectualism in American Life,* Knopf, 1964.

Horne, Gerald. *Class Struggle in Hollywood 1930–1950: Moguls, Mobsters, Stars, Reds & Trade Unionists,* University of Texas Press, 2001.

Jordan, Rene. *Marlon Brando,* Galahad Books, 1974.

Kael, Pauline. *For Keeps,* Plume, 1996.

Kanfer, Stefan. *A Journal of the Plague Years: A Devastating Account of the Era of the Blacklist,* Atheneum, 1974.

———. *Stardust Lost: The Triumph, Tragedy, and Mishugas of the Yiddish Theater in America,* Knopf, 2006.

Kazan, Elia. *A Life,* Da Capo, 1997.

Koppes, Clayton R., and Gregory D. Black. *Hollywood Goes to War: How Politics, Profits and Propaganda Shaped World War II Movies,* University of California Press, 1987.

Lawrence, Jerome. *Actor: The Life and Times of Paul Muni,* Samuel French, 1974.

Levy, Emmanuel. *Oscar Fever: The History and Politics of the Academy Awards,* Continuum, 2001.

Lewis, Robert. *Slings and Arrows: Theater in My Life,* Applause, 1996.

Lingeman, Richard. *Don't You Know There's a War On?: The American Home Front, 1941–1945,* Thunder's Mouth, 2003.

Litwak, Mark. *Reel Power: The Struggle for Influence and Success in the New Hollywood,* Morrow, 1986.

McCann, Graham. *Rebel Males: Clift, Brando and Dean,* Rutgers University Press, 1993.

Manso, Peter. *Brando: The Biography,* Hyperion, 1994.

Miller, Arthur. *Time Bends: A Life,* Penguin, 1995.

Mordden, Ethan. *The Hollywood Studios: Their Unique Styles During the Golden Age of Movies,* Fireside, 1989.

———. *Medium Cool: The Movies of the 1960s,* Knopf, 1990.

Morella, Joe, and Edward Z. Epstein. *Brando: The Unauthorized Biography,* Crown, 1973.

Mulano, Rebecca and Sam. *Donald Cammell: A Life on the Wild Side,* FAB Press, 2006.

Nachman, Gerald. *Raised on Radio,* University of California Press, 1998.

Nickens, Christopher. *Brando: A Biography in Photographs,* Dolphin, 1987.

Offen, Ron. *Brando,* Regnery, 1973.

Parrish, James Robert. *The Hollywood Book of Death,* McGraw-Hill, 2002.

Porter, Darwin. *Brando Unzipped,* Blood Moon Productions, 2006.

Powell, Elfreda. *Marlon Brando,* Parragon Publishing, 1998.

Puzo, Mario. *The Godfather Papers and Other Confessions,* Fawcett Crest, 1973.

Quirke, Anita. *Choking on Marlon Brando,* Overlook, 2007.

Raphael, Phyllis. *Off the King's Road: Lost and Found in London,* Other Press, 2007.

Redfield, William. *Letters from an Actor,* Limelight Editions, 1967.

Reynolds, Jonathan. *Geniuses,* Samuel French, 1983.

Rosenfeld, Lulla. *Bright Star of Exile: Jacob Adler and the Yiddish Theater,* Thomas Y. Crowell, 1977.

Ross, Lillian, and Helen Ross. *The Player: A Profile of an Art,* Limelight Editions, 1984.

Russo, William, and Jan Merlin. *Troubles in a Golden Eye: Starring Taylor & Brando with John Huston,* Xlibris, 2005.

Ryan, Paul. *Marlon Brando,* Carroll & Graf, 1994.

Schatz, Thomas. *The Genius of the System: Hollywood Filmmaking in the Studio Era,* Pantheon, 1988.

Schickel, Richard. *Brando,* Thunder's Mouth, 1999.

———. *Intimate Strangers: The Culture of Celebrity in America,* Ivan R. Dee, 2000.

———. *Elia Kazan: A Biography,* HarperCollins, 2005.

Schirmer, Lothar. *Marlon Brando: Portraits and Film Stills 1946–1995,* Stewart, Tabori & Chang, 1996.

Sherwood, Robert. *Reunion in Vienna,* Kessinger Publishing, 2006.

Shipman, David. *Marlon Brando,* Warner, 1990.

Sievers, W. David. *Freud on Broadway: A History of Psychoanalysis and the American Drama,* Hermitage House, 1955.

Simon, John. *Reverse Angle: A Decade of American Films,* Clarkson N. Potter, 1982.

Sperling, Cass Warner, and Cork Millner, with Jack Warner, Jr. *Hollywood Be Thy Name: The Warner Brothers Story,* University Press of Kentucky, 1998.

Spoto, Donald. *Rebel: The Life and Legend of James Dean,* Cooper Square Press, 2000.

Staggs, Sam. *When Blanche Met Brando: The Scandalous Story of "A Streetcar Named Desire,"* St. Martin's Press, 2005.

Strasberg, Lee. *A Dream of Passion: The Development of the Method,* Plume, 1988.

Taraborelli, J. Randy. *Michael Jackson: The Magic and the Madness,* Ballantine Books, 1991.

Teriipaia, Tarita. *Marlon, My Love and My Torment,* XO Editions, 2005.

Thomas, Bob. *Brando: Portrait of the Rebel as an Artist,* W. H. Allen, 1973.

Thomas, Tony. *The Films of Marlon Brando,* Citadel, 1973.

Thompson, David. *Last Tango in Paris,* British Film Institute, 1998.

Thomson, David. *Marlon Brando,* DK Publishing, 2003.

Updike, John. *Essays and Criticism,* Knopf, 1999.

Van Druten, John. *I Remember Mama,* Dramatists Play Service, 1972.

Vergin, Roger C. *Brando: With His Guard Down,* Cabot Riley Press, 2001.

Vineberg, Steve. *Method Actors: Three Generations of an American Acting Style,* Schirmer, 1991.

Wallace and Davis. *Marlon Brando,* Vidas De Cine, Edimat Libros, 1998.

Williams, Tennessee. *A Streetcar Named Desire,* Best American Plays, Third Series, Crown, 1952.

———. *Memoirs,* Anchor Press, 1983.

Willingham, Calder. *End as a Man,* Donald I. Fine, 1986.

Woititz, Janet Geringer. *Struggle for Intimacy:* Adult Children of Alcoholics Series, Health Communications, 1990.

Zierold, Norman. *The Moguls: The Power Princes of Hollywood's Golden Age,* Avon, 1969.

Zuckerman, Ira. *The* Godfather *Journal,* Manor Books, 1972.

Some Important Magazine Articles

Bodeen, DeWitt. "Marlon Brando," *Films in Review,* December 1980.

Brodkey, Harold. "Translating Brando," *The New Yorker,* October 24, 1994.

Bush, Lyall. "Doing Brando," *Film Comment,* January–February 1996.

Goldstein, Richard. "A Streetcar Named Meshuge," *The Village Voice,* April 23, 1996.

Haden-Guest, Anthony. "Behind the Scenes," *The Observer* (London), May 1, 2005.

Haskell, Molly. Series on Marlon Brando in *The Village Voice,* June 14–August 30, 1973.

Houseman, John. "Filming Julius Caesar," *Films in Review,* April 1953.

Janos, Leo. "The Private World of Marlon Brando," *Time,* May 24, 1976.

Life. Apocalypse Now, June 1979 cover story.

McVay, Douglas. "The Brando Mutiny," *Films and Filming,* December 1962.

Malden, Karl. "The Two Faces of Brando," *Films and Filming,* March 1958.

Peary, Gerald. "The Wild One," *American Film,* June 1986.

Porterfield, Christopher. *Last Tango* cover story in *Time,* January 22, 1973.

Sarris, Andrew. "A Tribute to Marlon Brando," *Film Comment,* May–June 1974.

Schickel, Richard. "Celebrity," *Film Comment,* January–February 1985.

Schulberg, Budd. "The King Who Would Be Man," *Vanity Fair,* March 2005.

Watters, Jim. *Desirée* cover story in *Life,* October 11, 1954.

N.B.: In addition to the lengthy newspaper obituaries available on the net, the Internet Movie Database (www.imdb.com) lists more than a hundred invaluable pieces and pictorial layouts from newspapers and magazines worldwide, ranging from *The New York Times* and *The Washington Post* to *The Sydney Morning Herald,* the London *Daily Telegraph,* and *The Honolulu Advertiser.*

Index

Permissions Acknowledgments

Grateful acknowledgment is made to the following for permission to reprint previously published material:

Hal Leonard Corporation and Holliday Publishing: Excerpt from "Sentimental Journey," words and music by Bud Green, Les Brown and Ben Homer, copyright © 1944 (Renewed) by Morley Music Co. and Holliday Publishing. All rights reserved. Reprinted by permission of Hal Leonard Corporation and Holliday Publishing, administered by Songwriters Guild of America.

Molly Haskell: Excerpts from Molly Haskell's series on Marlon Brando from *The Village Voice,* June 14–August 30, 1973. Reprinted by permission of Molly Haskell.

Henry Holt and Company, LLC: Excerpt from "A Semi-Revolution" from *The Poetry of Robert Frost,* edited by Edward Connery Lathem, copyright © 1969 by Henry Holt and Company. Copyright © 1942 by Robert Frost, copyright © 1970 by Lesley Frost Ballantine. Reprinted by permission of Henry Holt and Company, LLC.

Miriam Altshuler Literary Agency: Excerpt from "The King Who Would Be Man" by Budd Schulberg (*Vanity Fair,* March 2005), copyright © 2005 by Budd Schulberg. Reprinted by permission of Miriam Altshuler Literary Agency, on behalf of Budd Schulberg.

Random House, Inc.: Excerpts from *Songs My Mother Taught Me* by Marlon Brando and Robert Lindsey, copyright © 1994 by Marlon Brando. Reprinted by permission of Random House, Inc.

Photographic Credits

1. Marlon Brando, age 8: Getty Images
2. Brando and sisters, age 13: The Kobal Collection
3. Brando and sisters: The Kobal Collection
4. Brando as Stanley Kowalski with Jessica Tandy as Blanche DuBois: Time & Life Pictures/Getty Images
5. Brando rehearsing for *The Men:* Time & Life Pictures/Getty Images
6. Brando as Mark Antony: MGM/The Kobal Collection
7. Brando in *The Wild One:* Columbia/The Kobal Collection
8. Brando and Montgomery Clift: Columbia/The Kobal Collection
9. Brando with Elia Kazan: Columbia/The Kobal Collection
10. Brando in *On the Waterfront:* Time & Life Pictures/Getty Images
11. Brando and cat: Getty Images
12. Brando and Marilyn Monroe: The Kobal Collection
13. Brando in *The Teahouse of the August Moon:* MGM/The Kobal Collection
14. Brando with first wife Anna Kashfi: The Kobal Collection
15. Brando in *The Young Lions:* 20th Century–Fox/The Kobal Collection
16. Brando with Anna Magnani in *The Fugitive Kind:* United Artists/The Kobal Collection
17. Brando in *One-Eyed Jacks:* Paramount/The Kobal Collection
18. Brando with second wife Movita Castaneda: Getty Images
19. Brando with third wife Tarita Teriipaia: Getty Images
20. Brando at a civil rights rally in Washington, D.C.: Getty Images
21. Brando with Charlie Chaplin: Time & Life Pictures/Getty Images
22. Brando in *Burn! (Queimada):* United Artists/The Kobal Collection
23. Brando and cat on the set of *The Godfather:* Paramount/The Kobal Collection
24. Brando as Vito Corleone: Paramount/The Kobal Collection
25. Brando with Maria Schneider in *Last Tango in Paris:* Prod Europee Asso/Prod Artistes Assoc/The Kobal Collection
26. Brando with Jack Nicholson in *The Missouri Breaks:* United Artists/The Kobal Collection
27. Brando and George C. Scott in *The Formula:* MGM/The Kobal Collection

Photo research by Villette Harris